4. Mechanics

Grammar

Gaa	Incorrect use of adjective or adverb
Gant	Incorrect antecedent
Gdp	Dangling participle
Gpr	Incorrect pronoun reference
Gsf	Sentence fragment
Gsi	Split infinitive
Gs/v	Subject/verb agreement
Gts	Tense shift
Nu	Incorrect use of number

Punctuation

Pua	$\lor$	Apostrophe
Puc	$\land$	Comma
Pucl	:	Colon
Pud	—	Dash
Puel	⊙	End of line punctuation—period
Puel	?	End of line punctuation —question mark
Puh	=	Hyphen
Puq	$\lor\lor$	Quotation marks
Pusi	;	Semicolon
Sp		Spelling error
Ty		Typing error
WD		Word-division error

5. Writing Techniques

WAV	Use active voice
WEU	Avoid euphemisms
WIA	Inaccurate word
WPC	Lacks parallel construction
WRD	Writing is redundant
WSCt	Check sentence construction
WTS	Needs better transition
WW	Poor choice of word
3W	Wrong word

Business Communication

Business Communication

LaJuana Williams Lee, McNeese State University
Sallye Starks Benoit, Nicholls State University
Wilma Collins Moore, McNeese State University
Celeste Stanfield Powers

Rand McNally College Publishing Company
Chicago

Sponsoring Editor: Edward Jaffe
Project Editor: Stella Jenks
Design: Hayward Blake & Co.

80 81 82 10 9 8 7 6 5 4 3 2 1

Preface

Experienced business executives tell us that often their most significant problems at work are caused by miscommunication. The role of this book is to make students aware of the communication process and its practical implications for their everyday business lives. *Business Communication* is the result of many years of experience in teaching, consulting, and research related to business management and business education. In addition, a market-research study, provided by the publisher, was used to ensure that the content would satisfy the needs of present and future business people.

Approach

A traditional, instructional approach is used to explain the principles, functions, techniques, and format of business communications, as well as grammar, punctuation, and word usage. Research has indicated that many college students still have difficulty with grammar, punctuation, and choice of words. These skills are explained in Chapters 6 and 7, and this knowledge is applied in a practical way to business-letter writing in Chapter 8.

Basic philosophical, psychological, and communication principles are discussed in the early chapters of the book. In addition to skill development, the human-relations requirements of business communication are emphasized throughout the book. The use of a positive tone and empathy in business writing are stressed as important human-relations techniques.

Organization and Format

Each chapter begins with a listing of the major topics to be discussed. Since a practical step-by-step approach is taken throughout the book, marginal notes have been used to reinforce textual concepts.

The book is written in a conversational manner. The "you-attitude" and the important role that communication plays in improving human relations in a business setting are emphasized.

Depending on the information presented in the chapter, Questions for Discussion, Exercises, or practical Business Situations are provided at the end of each chapter for review of the concepts discussed. Instructors may use some or all of the problems given to reinforce classroom lectures and discussion.

Illustrations

Illustrations play a unique role in this book. Approximately thirty drawings and photographs are used to reinforce the communication techniques and procedures described. The illustrations are used as supplemental devices to augment the textual discussion. Many of the illustrations appear in the early chapters where such visuals are especially appropriate.

Other Special Features

The book includes cultural and subcultural approaches to communication (Chapter 2) and the ethical and legal aspects of oral and written messages (Chapter 15). All facets of dictation techniques are thoroughly discussed (Chapter 14), and the future of both oral and written communications is considered (Chapter 16).

The appendixes provide a large volume of reference material to supplement the information presented in the text. Important appendixes cover abbreviations, use of numbers, word division, guides for addressing envelopes and preparing mailable letters, information on word processing, and telecommunication equipment.

A complete glossary of business communication terms makes the appendixes even more useful to the student. Associated terms are cross-referenced after many of the definitions in the glossary. Furthermore, a complete bibliography is provided for the use of students or teachers who wish to do additional research on a particular topic mentioned in the book.

Instructor's Manual

A valuable resource for the teacher is the Instructor's Manual. The Manual provides, on a chapter-by-chapter basis, the behavioral objectives for the students. Answers and guidelines are presented for all of the Questions for Discussion, Exercises, and Business Situations in the text. The Manual also contains a number of objective questions (true-false) that the instructor may use for evaluating student understanding of the text information.

Acknowledgments

We acknowledge the help and assistance we have received from a number of people in preparing this book for publication.

First, we thank the following people for their suggestions for improvements in the book: Margaret Barnwell, Brevard Community College, Melbourne Campus, Florida; Roger Ellis, Emporia State University, Kansas; Eugene Gentzel, Pensacola Junior College, Florida; Dale Hanson, Southwestern Oklahoma University; Barbara Jewell, Ft. Steilacom Community College, Washington; Marie La Caze, University of Southwestern Louisiana; Mary Ann Losi, Mercer County College, New Jersey; and Pauline Rice, Western Carolina University, North Carolina.

We appreciate the help and support we have received from our husbands, Richard H. Lee, Jr., Patrick J. Benoit, Roy "Toddy" Moore, and David A. Powers. We extend sincere gratitude to Charles Carwile, Elizabeth P. Davis, Virginia K. Durrett, Douglas Goings, Deanna Mayes, Susan H. Reed, Ann Robinson, Frances A. Summers, and the many others who have helped to make this book a reality.

As an outstanding editor, Edward Jaffe's interest, ideas, and imagination inspired us to write this book. Through her diligent efforts, enthusiasm, and experience, Stella Jenks supplied excellent editorial expertise in the completion of this text for everyone interested in *Business Communication*.

LaJuana Williams Lee
Sallye Starks Benoit
Wilma Collins Moore
Celeste Stanfield Powers

Contents

Part Five   Your Role in Employment

Part Six   Your Role in Oral Communication

Part One   Your Role in the Communication Process

Chapter 1   Concepts of Communication

Overview

Why Study Business Communication?

Foundations of Communication

Theories of Communication

The Communication Process and Its Model

Obstacles to Communication

Semantics

Societal Demands

Listening Skills

Noise or Distraction

Bias

Mental Attitude

Experiences

Interest

Appearance

Personality

"... knowledge is power, ... knowledge is safety, and ... knowledge is happiness." —Thomas Jefferson

Communication means many things to many people. What specifically does the word or concept *communication* mean to you? Which forms of communication are most important?

Communication encompasses a wide array of activities. Any way to attract attention is a way to communicate. You can communicate through pictures and visual signs, through facial expressions or gestures, through mathematical and scientific signs, through touch, through the arts, and through spoken and written words.

Human beings have communicated from the beginning of time. Very early in the time line of human development, signs and symbols were added to vocal communication and gestures. The origins of writing are not known. Many historians attribute the invention of writing to the priests in early societies. There was a need to record the secrets of healing and the magic rituals in order to pass them on. Writing also provided a way to send messages to others in distant places without revealing any secrets to the messenger. There are other explanations, but the conclusion is obvious. Writing was needed because someone wished to communicate with another who was not there to receive the message in person.

Writing was a skill possessed by a very few.

Writing was once taught only to wise men and priests. This skill was used to preserve the lore and laws of the tribe. Knowledge of writing created a social role applicable to both religion and government. The writing process was laborious and time consuming. Books were copied by hand on parchment with a quill. To put the amount of labor that went into the production of the first books into proper prospective, how long would it take to copy this textbook in longhand?

In the Middle Ages and before, writing was such a chore that few people had ever seen a book, and even fewer people owned one. Only the very wealthy had access to books. In the world of the ancients, ownership of a library could guarantee a place in history.

One of the greatest events in the history of the Western world was the invention of printing using movable type by Johann Gutenberg around 1438. From this time on, many copies of new or existing books could be made as easily as one copy. The written word had come into its own, and the old saying "the pen is mightier than the sword" took on new meaning.

With the invention of printing, knowledge became the property of everyone, not just the prize of the few. People had a way to express their ideas. Printing provided a rapid and easy way to communicate. Francis Bacon, the English philosopher and statesman (1561–1626), said "knowledge itself is power" and "writing maketh the exact man." He could hardly have envisioned the extent of the changes predicted by these statements. Armed with knowledge and the power of the written word, the common people began to question the right of being governed without consent. This questioning led to new ideas of representative government.

When Christopher Sholes developed the first practical typewriter, little did he realize the advances that would be made in technology. Today we have typewriters that allow the material to be changed after it is typed, systems machines that produce 1,100 words per minute through an ink-jet spraying process, machines that reproduce many copies in a matter of seconds, and equipment that can move information at electronic speed from one office to another over ordinary telephone lines.

Civilization has progressed from the grunt and groan, sign and symbol eras to our highly technical society in which almost instantaneous written communication is possible through machines. You, living in the second half of the twentieth century, have many sources open to you in the field of communications that were never before available. Today's communication problems are often the result of an oversupply of means and sources.

Technology is advancing very rapidly.

Overview

Developments in the field of communications during the last two decades have been so phenomenal and literature in this field has been so prolific that experts have had difficulty keeping abreast. Books about communication range from the simple do-it-yourself book to the highly sophisticated and technical theoretical book. *Business Communication* is a practical approach planned for the student who is interested in the business world. It is designed to help refine your written and oral communication skills. This book gives you practical information and helps you solve everyday business and personal communication problems.

What is business communication? To answer this question, think of the two words together: *business* and *communication.* Business, as defined by the *American Heritage Dictionary,* is "(1) the occupation, work, or trade in which a person is engaged; (2) commercial, industrial, or professional dealings; the buying and selling of commodities or services; (3) any commercial establishment, such as a store or factory; (4) volume or amount of commercial trade; (5) commercial policy or practice." Associating these definitions of business with the word *communication* will produce, for the purposes of this text, a working definition for the term *business communication:* the transmitting of information in connection with an occupation or the conduct of commerce.

The ability to communicate effectively is not something inherited; it is a skill that is learned and improved with study and practice. The greatest menace in our society today is not the neutron bomb but *miscommunication.* Miscommunication is the failure of the receiver of the message to understand exactly what the sender intended to convey. To understand this, listen to your friends or read the newspaper. Whether writing or speaking, how many times have you been misunderstood during the past week because of miscommunication?

Why Study Business Communication?

Why are you taking a course in business communication? Whatever the reason you enrolled in this course, take a look at some of the benefits you can reap. One of the psychological guides to learning is that people learn most quickly and lastingly whatever has meaning for them.

Communication is an essential part of your everyday existence, both in your business and personal life. Some type of communication is occurring almost every minute of your day. You communicate at home, at school, at social functions, in church, and in business. This communication is with relatives, with friends, with acquaintances, with people you do not like, and even with yourself. If you cannot communicate, what will happen? You can answer this by saying that a great deal of what makes life livable or interesting will be lost.

Does communication occur almost every minute of the day? You can react by saying, "Every minute? Oh, I don't think so. Nothing happens when I'm asleep." The next night while you are asleep, the smoke detector goes off. What is this alarm doing? Is something communicating with you while you are asleep?

Communicating effectively can improve many aspects of your life.

The person in the next apartment invites you to "do the town" this weekend. However, you do not have the time or money to accept. You know that she is a very sensitive person, and, if you are not careful, you can destroy a budding relationship. Can you possibly refuse the invitation without losing a friend?

Various surveys and studies, conducted by both business and educational institutions, have reinforced the initial belief that the individuals who can successfully communicate have many doors open to them that are closed to those who are less skilled in this art. Robert R. Aurner, a management consultant and author, stated, "The objective record will show that the individual who can write well has a significant 'promotable' edge over the one who cannot."[1] Management is always looking for the bright person who can communicate effectively on all levels of the organization and in society.

For example, your immediate supervisor asks you to compile a report justifying a new procedure. Top management has recognized the inefficiency of dictating on a one-to-one basis. The office manager believes that you can develop a more efficient procedure and present the report at the next meeting of department heads. You are not aware that you are being considered for a promotion. But you do know that you have been asked to plan the new procedure and write the report. And you know that the report will be presented to top management to assist them in making a decision. With your written report, can you sell management on the project and on your ability? People who have learned to communicate effectively find this type of assignment a challenge.

Effective communicators know how to convey their ideas as well as to listen and be receptive to the ideas of others. These abilities help to maintain an atmosphere that enables everyone to be more productive. Whether your goals are personal or business, achieving them is your key to success.

Foundations of Communication

Compare the study of effective communication to the building of a house. A house will fall if it has no foundation; a foundation is necessary to acquire communication skills. A clear understanding of communication theory is part of the foundation for your communication skill. The frame of a house is built on its foundation; the frame of communications consists of the process and the model.

Success and effective communication go together.

Shared ideas bring more profits.

Understanding the why of communication increases your how-to ability.

[1] "Communications Impact: Power Source for Decision Makers," *Journal of Business Communication*, 5, No. 2 (Winter 1967), p. 29.

When a house is built, most of the building time is spent on the inside. So it is with this practical approach to effective communication; the inside work of communication is found in the later chapters. The first two chapters are a prerequisite for the balance of the book. To comprehend more fully *how* to communicate, you must first understand *why,* the theoretical part of communication.

Theories of Communication

Since World War II, literature and research in the field of communication have veritably exploded and now provide a wealth of information. Seldom has the explosion of knowledge included scholars from so many diverse fields. The various disciplines such as social psychology, information technology, linguistics, sociology, and psychology have contributed to the vast array of data. Laboratory research and the findings of communications practitioners have also added their dimensions to knowledge. As was so aptly stated, "Few phenomena of human life are of greater concern to more of our number than communication."[2]

During the 1960s communication theory broadened its scope and range. For the purposes of this book, however, two theories are important in your mastering the skill of communicating effectively: the *mathematical theory* and the *behavioral theory.*

Mathematical Theory

Computers can do anything! Certainly you have heard this exclamation, and you may believe what you hear. In this age of electronic hardware, you can easily believe that computers can solve all the world's problems. You may find it difficult to believe that the same hardware that solves so many important problems creates almost as many problems as it solves. You have heard of the million-dollar check written by mistake by the computer. The computer age is built on a communication theory that adds to the general knowledge of a very complex process.

Samuel F. B. Morse developed a code for each letter in the alphabet to use with the telegraph. He was probably the first person to use a mathematical concept in communication. His code used only two symbols, dots and dashes. This dot-and-dash code was the forerunner of the binary code used in the basic information elements of the computer, such as punched cards, tapes, etc.

The first math concept.

[2]Lee Thayer, ed., *Communication Theory and Research Proceedings of the First International Symposium* (Springfield, Ill.: Charles C Thomas, 1967), p. v.

In 1948 Claude E. Shannon, a mathematician at Bell Telephone Laboratories, developed a theory of information. His basic idea was that information transmitted over a channel could be measured by counting how many different alternative messages could be sent. In establishing a method of measuring information, Shannon was able to transmit the desired signals in a very efficient manner. But his interest was only in the technical or engineering aspects of communication, "How accurately are my symbols of communication being transmitted?"[3]

Messages are predictable.

Shannon theorized that normal messages were very predictable. They contained well-known patterns of sounds, notes, or colors that were not just random sequences. When communicators or engineers familiarized themselves with all possible patterns in the messages, duplications could be omitted. Then, only the part of the message that was different would be transmitted. This theory applied to speech, music, pictures, and anything else that could be transmitted. In looking at a written message, you can readily see that the consonants are the most unpredictable part. Hence, conso-

Consonants are transmitted.

nants are the parts of the message that would be transmitted.

A brief practice session will enable you to understand this. Write the following two quotations, omitting the vowels.

Communication is the heart of the business world. —E. P. Davis

Goodwill is the one and only asset that competition cannot undersell or destroy. —Marshall Field.

Ask two or three friends to decode your message. Time them. Is the decoding process second nature? Most people are able to decode without much effort; it is something we do automatically. We are conditioned to recognize the predictable. Because of Shannon's work, today's communication channels are much more efficiently used. And, in an era that relies more than most of us realize on the accurate transmission of data, such knowledge is invaluable.

After studying Shannon's work, Warren Weaver visualized a blending of the engineering and the human applications of communication. The combined efforts of the two men produced a

A model was devised to simplify the explanation of communication.

model (Figure 1–1) that permitted a better understanding of human communication. Weaver coded the brain of the sender as the originator of the idea or the information source, the voice box as the transmitter, the vocal sound as the signal, the ear of the listener as the receiver, and the brain of the listener as the destination. Noise source, which is represented by the solid box on the lower side of the model, is part of Shannon's original concept and

[3]Claude E. Shannon and Warren Weaver, *The Mathematical Theory of* *Communication* (Urbana, Ill.: University of Illinois Press, 1949), p. 96.

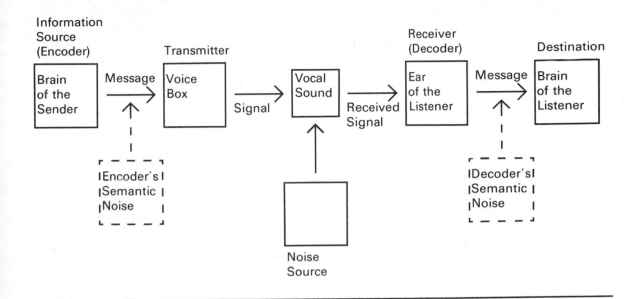

Information
Source
(Encoder)   Transmitter

| Brain of the Sender | → Message → | Voice Box | → Signal → | Vocal Sound |

Receiver
(Decoder)   Destination

| Ear of the Listener | → Message → | Brain of the Listener |

Received Signal

┌ ─ ─ ─ ┐
│Encoder's│
│Semantic │
│Noise   │
└ ─ ─ ─ ┘

┌ ─ ─ ─ ┐
│Decoder's│
│Semantic │
│Noise   │
└ ─ ─ ─ ┘

Noise
Source

indicates that messages sent can be distorted by noise that might be present in the channel. To distinguish from semantic noise, "noise source" was later changed to "engineering noise."[4]

Weaver added to Shannon's original model the dimension of semantic noise, which is the unplanned misrepresentation of words by the encoder and/or the decoder.[5] With this addition he promoted the idea that the message sent was not always the message received. Other connections could be made between the Shannon-Weaver model and human communication, but the parallel has been established.

Behavioral Theory
Similarities exist between the mathematical theory and the behavioral theory; the same communication model can be used to study both (Figure 1–1). The basic difference between the two theories is that the mathematical theory deals with machines, while the behavioral theory deals with people. As stated before, the physical scientists are concerned with the accuracy of transmitting symbols from one piece of equipment to another. The behaviorist is concerned with what people think and feel on an intrapersonal and interpersonal basis. The problem in human theory is to connect the two minds that wish to communicate. Many times this is accom-

[4]Ibid., p. 99.
[5]Ibid., p. 116.

Figure 1–1
Shannon's model of a communication system is designated by the solid boxes and the captions above and in the middle of the model. Weaver's additions are the broken-line boxes and the labels within the boxes.

Source: C. E. Shannon and W. Weaver, *The Mathematical Theory of Communication* (Urbana: University of Illinois Press, 1949), p. 98.
© 1949 by the Board of Trustees of the University of Illinois.

plished by a very inadequate procedure—the use of words.

During the past twenty years, researchers in the behavioral sciences have contributed a vast amount of information to the field of communication. Dr. Jurgen Ruesch, a psychiatrist, is one of the pioneers. He developed a theory of human communication that deals with a social situation in which the behavior of the people involved is organized around a common task that implies the existence of rules, of status assignment, and of role differentiation.[6]

The social situation.   Social situations carry a number of official labels: institutionalized situations, as going to church; recreational situations, as playing tennis; occupational situations, as going to work. In the life of a typical college student, a social situation would be "I have to go to the Student Union." This identification of a situation helps people put the event in its proper perspective and also helps to identify appropriate behavior. If a person can recognize the situation and set limits on what can be expected, it is possible for this person to relate the situation to the identification of status and roles.[7]

Status.   Status and roles are very closely related. The primary difference is in the way in which these two identifications are assigned. Status is assigned by others; roles are action patterns learned by individuals in the course of their development. The term *status* refers to the position of an individual in society. When the terms *president, mayor,* and *senator* are used, we refer to a position in society. In communicating with the president of the company or the file clerk, our approach would be slightly different. Would you speak or write differently to the president of the United States and to the instructor of your communication class? Is there a difference in status? Does this affect the communication process?[8]

Roles.   Roles are relationships among individuals that often imply certain social behavior. Terms such as *wife, daughter, brother,* and *tax collector* describe roles. As Dr. Ruesch stated, "There is no wife without a husband, no daughter without a mother or father, and no tax collector without a taxpayer."[9]

Roles and status can be identified in many ways. Uniforms, titles, automobiles, office size, and types of desks are just a few of the clues used to recognize these positions. Daily we find ourselves in

The social situation dictates human behavior.

Identifying a social situation helps you select the desired behavior.

Status is assigned to you by others.

Roles are assigned by relationships.

[6]"Synopsis of the Theory of Human Communication," *Psychiatry,* 16 (August 1953), p. 221.
[7]Ibid., p. 223.

[8]Jurgen Ruesch and Gregory Bateson, *Communication, The Social Matrix of Psychiatry* (New York: Norton, 1951), p. 29.
[9]Ibid., p. 30.

places where roles and status are the keys to the interpretation of messages. What is your reaction when questioned by a judge? By a campus security officer? Both are officers of the law. A real-estate agent responds one way to a client selling a house and another way to the prospective buyer of a house. The role and the status of the people involved in the situation often influence how the message is interpreted.

Rules. In our everyday lives, each social situation is governed by rules—written or unwritten, verbal or nonverbal. We must all know our status and role to abide by the "rules of the game." Rules usually set a limit; therefore, they often restrict the action of the people involved. Rules can be ancient or newly formed. The participants in the social or business situation understand that the rules must be followed. Failure to observe the rules generally invokes a penalty. We have rules for courts of law, church ceremonies, football games, and office procedures. Everyone knows what can happen if the rules are not followed. People learn as they become involved in a society or an environment what the rules are and how to live and work with them. If people cannot adapt to the situational rules, they find existence in that situation very difficult.

> You must know the rules of the situation before you can play the game.

The person who understands the social situation with its accompanying status, roles, and rules will be able to make fast adjustments and will communicate effectively in most circumstances.

> *Important!* Read this paragraph again.

Networks. According to Ruesch, we also communicate by using various networks.[10] The first is the intrapersonal network that operates within the individual. The intrapersonal network is concerned with your feelings and your thinking. The second is the interpersonal network. This network links you and one or more persons.

A third, larger, and more complex network is the group network. Because of the nature of a group and the involvement of many people, effective communication is not always achieved in the group network.

The last and most complex of all the communication networks is the cultural network. In this network there is no origin or destination of the message. The cultural network has a deep effect on us because, as individuals, we feel powerless to change these cultural factors. This network also has a strong influence on the interpretation of the communications received.

The importance of communication theory cannot be overempha-

[10]"Psychiatry and the Challenge of Communication," *Psychiatry,* 17 (February 1954), p. 13.

You can communicate more effectively if you understand the networks that exist.

sized. To accomplish business and personal objectives, you must recognize the various networks that exist and how they affect you every day. The better we understand behavioral theory, the more effective we will be in dealing with ourselves and others.

The Communication Process and Its Model

The communication process is influenced by the relationship of the sender, the message, and the receiver. Communication is very complicated and involves all of your senses, experiences, and feelings. Theorists (experts) in this field have made the study of this process easier by isolating each factor. *Models* are a way of simplifying the study, and a combination of models and examples can further clarify an explanation of the process. Usually when the whole is broken into parts, the process becomes easier to understand.

Understand the parts.

What actually takes place when you send a message? Table 1–1 dissects the steps in sending a message.

All communication, large or small, worthy or unworthy, begins with an idea. When an idea is born, the decision must be made

Table 1—1
Steps in Sending a Message

1. Idea	I think I need some new tennis socks.
2. Encoding (organizing information about the idea into a message)	I will order some tennis socks today by letter.
3. Message	Please send me one dozen pairs of tennis socks.
4. Transmission (the channel)	A letter is typed and mailed. The letter is received.
5. Decoding (interpretation of the message)	This person ordered one dozen pairs of tennis socks. No color is given; guess I'll send white.
6. Feedback (response from the person receiving the message)	One dozen pairs of white tennis socks were shipped today.
7. Idea (and the cycle begins again)	I forgot to say that I wanted red socks.

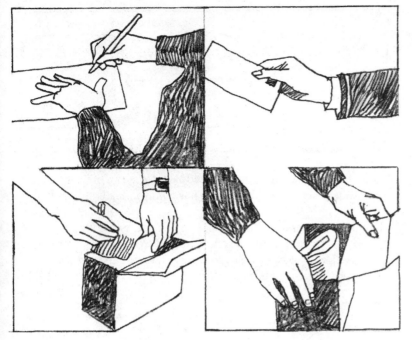

An idea is organized into a message. The message is transmitted to the receiver. The receiver interprets the message and acts on it. Finally, the sender gets feedback from the message.

whether the idea is to be communicated. You, the sender, make the decision to communicate. What will the message be? What symbols will be used? All these questions must be answered. The decisions will be based on the knowledge and experience of the sender.

The first decision is how to transmit the message—will it be conveyed vocally or in writing. Maybe just a sign or a symbol will be all that is necessary to communicate the message. In the case of the tennis socks, a letter is the channel. You prepare the letter and drop it in the mailbox.

You have communicated with someone else. The letter carrier has delivered your letter. The receiver has your message. The communication is now out of the mind of the sender and into the mind of the receiver. The receiver works with the message or (as the experts would say) decodes the communication. Interpretation is now taking place. Did the receiver assimilate the message that was in the mind of the sender? Did miscommunication occur?

The sender does not know whether the message sent was the message received until the final step in the process is completed. The receiver of the message transmits an answer (feedback). The answer can be a hand gesture, a simple "yes," or even a thirty-page report. In this example the feedback was shipping the order. Whatever form the feedback takes does not matter; what is important is how effectively the message is decoded. Feedback is used to evalu-

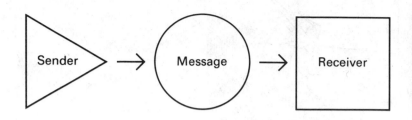

ate the decoding. Evaluating the feedback from the message in the
illustration, can you say the sender has communicated effectively?
No!

From the example and the dialogue just presented, you have
some idea how communication is achieved. A study of several other
models will help to provide a more complete understanding.

Aristotle's model of communication is shown in Figure 1—2. This

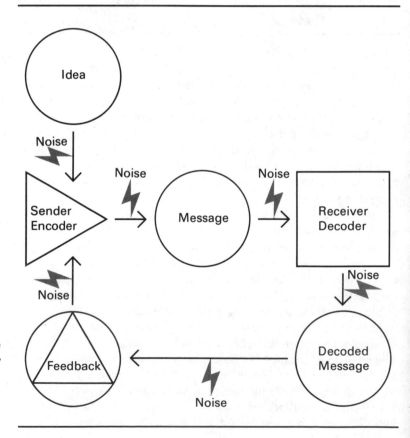

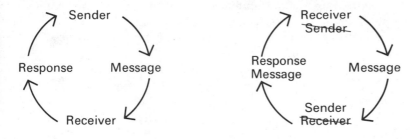

Figure 1—4
The loop or closed-circle model.

model represents the sender-message-receiver concept. As far back
as 350 B.C., the receiver was recognized as an integral part of the
communication process. The basic idea down through the ages has
been, and still is, that communication cannot take place unless
someone receives the message.

The simple model shown in Figure 1–2 is refined, and noise and
feedback are added to provide communication students with a
more realistic model, as shown in Figure 1–3. Today's communicators realize that noise (language noise as well as physical noise) can
have an immense effect on the messages we send and the ones we
receive.

Noise affects the communication process.

An interesting concept in communication models is shown by a
loop or closed circuit. Often you may not have feedback; the receiver may respond internally. When this is the case, the action
stops with "response"(Figure 1–4). If feedback does occur, the dia-
gram on the right in the figure illustrates what happens. The sender
becomes the receiver, and the receiver becomes the sender. The
roles reverse.

Communication models are used to help us understand how the
communication process works. Remember these are just models,
and you as a communicator must be aware that there may be internal and external factors causing miscommunication.

Obstacles to Communication

When we transmit a message, internal and external *obstacles* may
affect the encoding and decoding of the message. The message received may be so strongly influenced by these obstacles that the
original idea is destroyed. Shall we use prevention or cure? The
effective encoder understands that the message can be in danger
and that a communication breakdown is possible. If you, as a

Encoding and decoding can be
affected by obstacles.

student of communication, can recognize these obstacles, you will be better prepared to counteract or prevent many of the breakdowns that might interfere with the message.

All message-sending and -receiving activities are influenced by two basic principles:

1. All messages are based on certain arbitrary agreements.

2. No message is valid except within the setting in which it is sent and received.

There are myriad examples to illustrate both of these principles. You may wish to draw from your own experience and add to these examples.

In most Western countries an up-and-down motion of the head means "yes" and a back-and-forth motion of the head means "no." In certain African countries the same signals have opposite meanings.

All spoken-language messages are also merely agreed-upon arbitrary signals. These signals can seldom be transferred from one language to another. In English stress is a carrier of meaning in the spoken language. Read the following sentences aloud, stressing the italicized word each time.

1. *I* am going to town.

2. I *am* going to town.

3. I am going to *town*.

Do the three sentences have the same meaning? The same oral effect cannot be achieved in French. Stressing words is an agreed-upon arbitrary signal in English; a signal, incidentally, that can vary somewhat with the particular English dialect being spoken.

"Mayday!" What does this message mean? Received over a shortwave radio from a ship at sea, it is a signal of distress. Spoken by a young person working with a group making flower garlands, it designates the celebration of a spring festival.

"She made a little bow." What does this message mean? What is the setting? A gift-wrapping counter? A stage? What is the pronunciation of the word *bow?*

Semantics

Semantics is the science of word meanings or, in this instance, the way we use words. Words have meaning in the mind of the user. The word *cloud* will produce one thought-picture for Sharon and a completely different one for Greg. Sharon's thoughts could be of a bright, blue sky with light, wispy clouds moving overhead. Greg might be thinking of a black, threatening sky with heavy-hanging clouds.

You might choose a word to express an idea but find that it conveys an entirely different meaning from the one you intended. Any dictionary shows that most words have more than one meaning. How many meanings does the word *ring* have? What is the meaning you most often connect with *take?* Find these two words in the dictionary and record the number of meanings for each. If asked for a definition of *ring,* which one would you give?

Raymond Lesikar, in *Report Writing for Business,* stated that the 500 most commonly used English words have a total of 14,000 dictionary definitions—an average of 28 meanings per word. Confronted with this information, we can readily understand why miscommunication can occur.

Another obstacle to recognize in the use of language is that different words have varying shades of meaning and this can obscure the message. For example:

1. Michael is a janitor.

2. Michael is the maintenance engineer.

Or:

1. Do you have any inexpensive jeans?

2. Do you have any cheap jeans?

What are your thoughts when you hear these words: *skinny, thin, slim, slender?* Do these words mean the same thing to you or is there a shade of difference in their meaning?

Many times in an effort to impress, we will search for a word not usually included in the average person's vocabulary. There are two dangers inherent in this type of word choice. First, we, ourselves, may not be as knowledgeable as we should be concerning the shades of meaning or the accepted pronunciation of the unfamiliar word. Second, if our purpose is communication, the receiver of our message may gather no information at all. Or, through misunderstanding, the receiver may infer an incorrect meaning and take a different course of action from the one we originally intended. Generally, the simplest language is the most effective.

Something else to remember is that words with values attached to them are much harder to understand than words with concrete meaning. Your classmates will understand when you use words like *jeans, purse, comb,* and *bike.* But, if you inject the word *morals* or *honesty* into a message, will the receiver have the same values you have? Consequently, will your word convey the intended message?

Semantics can create many obstacles in communication, but the alert communicator can learn to recognize and cope with these barriers.

Societal Demands

Because of the avalanche of information and the communication of this information through different channels, such as television, radio, newspapers, etc., society has found it necessary to become selective. Do you hear or see everything presented to you? Usually, consciously or unconsciously, you make a decision as to what you will receive. Because you as a receiver decide what you will hear and see, you as a communicator must be aware that the messages you are sending, by whatever method you choose, may or may not be received.

Listening Skills

What do you do most of your day, speak or listen? Stop and think about this. Most of us spend approximately 60 percent of our time listening. Many of us speak at the rate of approximately 140 words per minute, but we can absorb roughly 500 words a minute. No wonder our minds wander, and we think of other things as someone speaks to us.

Pay attention!

Listening is a skill that requires effort. You must learn to listen actively and concentrate on the message that is being delivered. You must learn to listen for the ideas the speaker is communicating. The development of this skill will help you receive the messages being sent.

Noise or Distraction

You will find it most difficult to concentrate on what someone is saying to you with forty typewriters operating in the background. Noise not only interferes with communication, but it also diminishes efficiency and makes concentrating exceedingly difficult.

Noise makes a difference.

Any outside influence that affects our senses—visual, auditory, olfactory, etc.—can have an adverse effect on the reception of a message.

Bias

Do you have any biases? Most of us do whether we want to admit we have them or not. How do your beliefs or biases affect communications? When a subject arises that you do not like, have you ever

Are your biases obvious?

"tuned the speaker out"? For instance, if the Viet Nam war is brought up, what is your reaction?

Your prejudices or biases may be conscious or unconscious. Whichever is the case, you will be swayed by them, and the messages you receive will be influenced accordingly.

This barrier is perhaps the most difficult to overcome. Education is the answer, but it can be a lengthy and unrewarding process. Perhaps a better way to handle bias is to show people how they can benefit from a given situation. An attitude can change immediately when someone realizes that there is a reward at "the end of the rainbow" if the bias can be overcome.

Active listening requires effort and concentration on the message. Ellis Herwig/Stock, Boston, Inc.

Mental Attitude

Your emotions have a decided impact on how a message is sent or received. If you are extremely angry with a person, your anger will be transmitted to the receiver. When you have an emotional reaction to a happening, you may find it difficult (or maybe next to impossible) to communicate anything but the strong emotion you feel—hate, fear, love, etc. If you are emotionally involved in a situation, calm yourself before you communicate something you might regret later.

Your attitude can affect your encoding and decoding processes.

By the same token, strong emotion can be used to your advantage. If you are extremely excited about some vital project, such as a sales promotion or a new office, your enthusiasm may persuade others to positive action.

Experiences

You are a product of your experiences.

Because you have a different background than Elizabeth Taylor, you might react differently to a given situation. Your grandfather is sixty and you are twenty; do you have the same ideas about life? Your experiences, your culture, your age, your interests will have an impact on what you see and hear. No two people receive exactly the same message. The message you receive is based on what you, as an individual, are.

Interest

Interest is vital to effective communication.

Have you ever found yourself turning someone off because you are not interested in the message that person is conveying? Or if you are on the sending end, not saying anything? Interest in a subject will certainly make a difference in the amount of communication taking place.

Most people can be interested in a given topic if they can see a personal connection or relate to it personally. Humans are very self-centered; if they are involved in some way, interest can be generated.

Appearance

Often people must be interested in what they see before they can hear.

If you are the speaker at a $100-a-plate dinner, you would be dressed for the occasion. If you are sending a letter of application, your letter would be perfect. In both of these cases you have a message to deliver, and you want the receivers to give you their undivided attention. Appearance can have a decided effect on the receiver of a message. If you want a message to be received as it was sent, remember that appearance will certainly have an influence on reception.

Personality

"I wish Skip would do something about his personality; he is just obnoxious. I dislike being around him!" We have all said or, at least, thought this about someone we know. What is happening to the messages Skip sends? Are the messages being sent the messages that are received? In most cases, the answer is "no."

Any idea transmitted by a person who has a serious defect in personality has a chance of being miscommunicated. If miscommunication occurs frequently with the messages you send, maybe you should take an objective look at yourself and see if something in your personality needs changing.

Certainly other obstacles exist that may hinder effective communication. Can you remember something that has kept you from sending or receiving a message? No list could be complete, but the obstacles set forth for you in this chapter will enable you to understand better what can and does happen to your communication. (Some of the obstacles we have touched on in this chapter will be discussed in more detail in other chapters.) Now that you are aware that breakdowns can and do occur, hopefully you will be able to understand them better and take corrective measures that will guard against miscommunication.

If you are often misunderstood, examine yourself.

Questions for Discussion

1. In your opinion, why has the study of communication grown so explosively during the past decade?

2. Write your personal definition of business communication.

3. How can the study of the history of communication help you solve your communication problems?

4. Discuss the two theories of communication presented in Chapter 1. (Write approximately 200 words.)

5. How can the understanding of these two theories help you achieve effectiveness in communicating?

6. Name the men responsible for these two theories.

7. What is the basis of the mathematical theory?

8. What is the major concern of the physical scientists?

9. What is the major concern of the behavioral scientists?

10. According to Jurgen Ruesch, identifying a social situation is important. How can this identification help you communicate more effectively?

11. What is the major difference between the communication model depicted in Figure 1—2 and the model illustrated in Figure 1—3? How does this difference relate to effective communication?

12. List several communication obstacles.

13. How have societal demands contributed to miscommunication?

14. What can you, as an effective communicator, do to eliminate bias as an obstacle to communication?

15. Which two obstacles would be most difficult for you to overcome? Explain why, and how you might overcome them.

Exercises

1. Compose five test questions for Chapter 1. Test these questions on three or more of your classmates. Did miscommunication occur? If so, correct the question(s) to avoid this.

2. Write a two-page report on your most memorable experience with miscommunication.

3. Browse through business periodicals and record the number of references to effective communication or the necessity for effective communication. Your instructor will suggest the names of various periodicals.

4. Use the information you obtained in exercise 3 to write a two-page report on the necessity for studying business communication.

5. Describe an obstacle not discussed in this chapter that might cause you to miscommunicate.

6. Draw your version of a realistic communication model.

Chapter 2 Forms of Communication

The Problem

**Perception: Access to
  Communication**

**Signs and Symbols:
  Content of
  Communication**
Signs
Symbols

Nonverbal Communication
Facial Expressions
Gestures
Handshakes
Posture and Appearance

**International Cultural
  Influences**
Smiles and Frowns
Eye Contact

**National Cultural
  Influences**

Summary

"Words realize nothing, verify nothing to you, unless you have suffered in your person the thing which the words try to describe." — Mark Twain

The Problem

Have you ever found yourself in a conversation in which the communication process became so mixed up that the only messages that got through were those of frustration? That peppery bigot Archie Bunker provides you with such a scene:

> (Edith heaves a sigh)
>
> Archie: What was that for?
> Edith: What, Archie?
> Archie: What was that for?
> Edith: No, I didn't mean "what?" meaning "what did you say, Archie?" I meant "what?" meaning "what was what for?"
> Archie: What other "what" was there? The sigh, Edith. You heaved a sigh.
> Edith: Did I sigh?
> Archie: Yes, you sighed. . . . And you heaved it right over here, it's like eatin' in a wind tunnel.[1]

At least this is a scene you can leave before the infamous Bunker anger breaks loose. However, you may be faced with many instances that are not so easily dismissed. This popular slogan found in offices states the problem in a different way:

I know that you believe you understand what you think I said, but, I am not sure you realize that what you heard is not what I mean.

Whether you find yourself as angry as Archie when trying to sort out the forms of communication, or just confused by a language maze, hope exists for more effective communication. This chapter examines how communication stimuli are received and the

[1]Eugene Boe, comp., *The Wit and Wisdom of Archie Bunker* (New York: Popular Library, 1972), p. 21. Written by Don Nicholl. © Copyright (1971). Tandem Productions, Inc. All Rights Reserved.

forms available for communicating. Perception as the access to communication, signs and symbols as the content of communication, nonverbal forms of communication such as kinesics and gestures, and both international and national cultural variations will be discussed.

Perception: Access to Communication

Perception may be defined as the act or ability of understanding or knowing by means of stimuli received by the senses and conveyed to the brain, either consciously or unconsciously.

You are constantly bombarded by stimuli that are registered by the senses. Archie reacted to Edith's sigh. Your eyes work hard to convey the words in this book to your brain. Even when you are asleep, the nerves in your body are transmitting signals to your brain. To the extent that you have consciously or unconsciously become aware of anything, communication has occurred.

Since man has a neural transmission rate of 30,000 cycles per second,[2] it is impossible to be conscious of all the messages received by the five senses: vision, smell, touch, taste, and hearing. Subliminal advertising on television in the 1950s and 1960s was controversial because of the ethics of communicating messages to viewers without their conscious knowledge. This technique flashed messages that were so brief in duration that the viewer was not aware of them consciously, but they were received by the brain. Consequently, a viewer might desire a particular product without making a conscious choice.

Your mind selects the particular stimulus or combination of stimuli to which you respond in conscious communication. This selection process, perception, is learned and begins at birth. As an infant, you employed sounds, gestures, and other forms of behavior on a random basis in a natural, reflexive way in an attempt to communicate your needs. When you were wet or hungry, you cried. When you were sleepy, you yawned. When you were content and happy, you smiled.

Between the ages of one and two, you began to imitate the actions of others to make your needs known because you perceived that these actions communicated needs and attitudes more efficiently. You stamped your foot when you were angry. You nodded your head when you were offered a cookie. You reached out your hand when you wanted a toy.

To live is to perceive.

Perception is highly selective.

Perceptual skills are learned.

[2] Alvin Toffler, *Future Shock* (New York: Bantam Books, 1971), p. 350.

26

Gradually, you learned that certain combinations of sounds (words) were more effective in making your needs known to others. Your skill in behavioral communication increased as you consciously and unconsciously learned what verbal signals were most easily understood by others. By the time you began school, you had learned that words and language had a great advantage over non-verbal behavior by itself, and you entered a new stage in your growth, the development and refinement of intellectual or cognitive perception.

With your growth, the raw sensations of smelling, seeing, touching, tasting, and hearing became more ordered and processed for thinking operations and word power. Your meaning of *fun* was not necessarily your friend's meaning. Your perceptual skills were used to find the common and unique meaning of fun and all the other words shared by your cultural group. Awareness and understanding became the filters for screening the stimuli being received by your senses. As you developed, your senses and perceptions became sharper and gave satisfaction and meaning to your interests and hobbies: This tennis racquet doesn't feel right. This guitar chord sounds better. Those colors look good together.

In the business world, the sharpness of sensual perception is needed everywhere. Selecting the right image for a firm is a prerequisite in advertising and becomes critical for maintaining the advertising account. Choosing personnel who make an initial impression consistent with the desired image of a firm is also critical in sales. From the sound of the receptionist's voice to the appearance of the reception room, a possible client is assessing what is important to the firm through sensual perception. From the initial contact with a company through advertising, referral, or sales to the delivery of products or services, perception is shaping attitudes and providing pertinent information about the company and its business transactions. Your ability to perceive—how you gather, process, and interpret information from your environment—is crucial to verbal and nonverbal communication in all areas of life. The importance of perception as an independent field of knowledge and as the starting point of thinking and communicating is expressed by the philosopher Maurice Merleau-Ponty:

> The perceived world is the always presupposed foundation of all rationality, all value and all existence. This thesis does not destroy either rationality or the absolute. It only tries to bring them down to earth.[3]

What do you "sense" in a store window?

[3]"The Primacy of Perception and Its Philosophical Consequences," in *The Primacy of Perception,* ed. and trans. James M. Edie (Evanston, Ill.: Northwestern University Press, 1964), p. 13.

You may find it helpful to think of receiving and sending communications as a three-step process, an *awareness staircase,* in which perception is the first step.

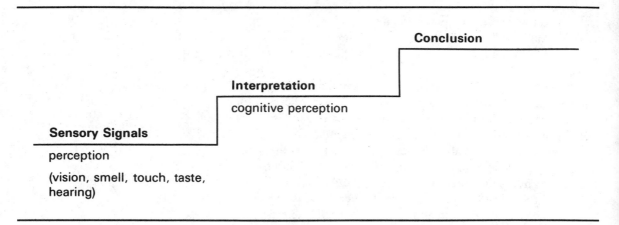

Conclusion

Interpretation
cognitive perception

Sensory Signals
perception
(vision, smell, touch, taste, hearing)

Your skill in communicating begins then with developing an awareness of the sensory signals brought into play in a particular situation. A heightened awareness of raw sensory data provides you with a greater base for the second step in communicating, interpretation. Your perception of the sensory signals is essential in drawing more accurate conclusions about the transaction at hand. Avoid jumping to conclusions too quickly by remembering to use your five senses on the first step to "keep five alive before you arrive!"

Signs and Symbols: Content of Communication

As soon as your senses perceive stimuli, your brain goes to work ordering them into a structure for possible meaning for you. Raw data becomes manageable when your mind organizes, categorizes, and makes the stimuli meaningful. This is the second step, interpretation, on the awareness staircase. This interpretation may be divided into *signs,* or *symbols,* or *some combination of both.* You may think of signs and symbols as something you see, but in the language of communication, they may be seen, heard, felt, smelled, and even tasted. "How absurd!" you think. "Whoever ate a billboard sandwich or felt a stop sign?" However, everything on the list in Table 2–1 can be either a sign or a symbol.

Table 2—1
Sign or Symbol?

Market	Apple pie
Office memo	Bumper stickers
Love letter	Rainbow
Television ad	Carbon copy
Computer printout	Steeple
Raised eyebrow	Hug
A Rachmaninoff piano concerto	· · · —
Merchandising inventory	Anything else you can name or
A touch on the arm	describe!
U.S.A.	

Signs and symbols are critically important in shaping the meaning and knowledge by which life is lived. Distinguishing the difference between a sign and a symbol and understanding their functions in communication are essential because they constitute the content of all communication.

Signs

A sign is anything that indicates the existence of a thing, event, or condition. A sign may be natural or devised for a specific purpose. A sign may also be a selective part of a larger condition or event. In this case, the sign serves as an important feature of the situation and is a natural sign. Natural signs function in the manner shown in Table 2–2.

Signs refer to objects.

Table 2—2
How Natural Signs Function

Subject (perceiver)	Sign (stimulus)	Indicates (refers to)	Object (beyond sign)
You	smell smoke	indicates	fire
You	see dark clouds	indicates	rain
You	see tears	indicates	crying
You	itch	indicates	a bug bite
You	see tire tracks	indicates	a vehicle

The term *common sense* can be described as the ability to recognize these natural signs. Unnatural signs, however, may not be recognized unless their specific intent has been learned in the given situation. For example, the ringing of a bell may indicate a time to do something. But what? The bell could mean:

Turn on a switch.
Turn off a switch.
Take a coffee break.
Come back from a coffee break.

The possibilities of what the bell indicates are nearly endless, unless you have learned in the specific situation what the bell tells you. Mistaking the purpose of a sign is the most common error in communications. Archie was frustrated in finding the reference point in Edith's sign. You had to find out which pronouns went with which verb in the communications slogan at the beginning of this chapter. The sigh, the pronouns, and the verbs functioned as signs.

1. Signs function in place of their correlated objects.

2. Signs stand in a one-to-one relationship to their objects.

3. Signs call attention to the objects to which they relate, not to themselves.

Another characteristic of a sign is that it calls for action when encountered; thus, a sign has a command aspect. The command aspect of several signs is given in Table 2–3.

Table 2—3
Signs Have a Command
Aspect

Sign	Command
Red light	Stop
Comma	Pause
Icy street	Drive carefully
"Past due"	Remit
Invoice	Look for your order

Ignoring the command aspect may or may not have significant consequences for you. But any stimulus that registers on your consciousness as a sign demands attention before the sign can be ignored or dismissed.

1. A sign *indicates* the existence of a thing, event, or condition.

2. A sign *functions* to announce the object in a one-to-one relationship, or draws attention through itself to the object.

3. A sign may be *naturally* related to its object as an important feature of its object.

4. A sign may be *unnaturally* related to its object (devised).

5. A sign's *meaning* is clear, limited, and not as important as its object.

Signs are points of reference upon which you fix the daily routine of living and negotiate your way in communications and life.

Symbols

Remember the list of words that could either be signs or symbols? The first word was *market*. Contrasting the use of *market* as a sign and as a symbol can help you recognize how the use or function of what you perceive determines whether you are confronting a sign or a symbol. For a shopper *market* means where to go to purchase something. This is simple sign functioning. However, to an economics or advertising student, *market* is an entire conceptual system. *Market* can mean the process of manufacturing and distributing goods from designer to producer to retailer to user. The word *market* serves as a symbol for the business student and as a sign for the shopper.

"Symbols are not proxy for their objects, but are *vehicles for the conception of objects.*"[4] A sign is something to act upon. A symbol is an instrument of thought. Unlike a sign, a symbol's value is not determined primarily by how well the symbol refers to the object. Rather, a symbol's value lies in how well the object, idea, or concept is incorporated in the symbol. Without the symbol, there might be a question that the object, idea, or concept exists. In other words, thinking of the object without using the symbol is difficult. Symbols function in the manner shown in Table 2–4.

Table 2—4
How Symbols Function

Subject	Symbol	Conception	Object
You (perceiver)	Market	Product design Manufacture Packaging Selling Shipping Wholesale distribution Retail outlets Advertising	All conceptions possible within the symbol

[4]Susanne K. Langer, *Philosophy in a New Key* (New York: New American Library, 1951), p. 61.

"Hello, my name is Chris Metz."

Proper names serve as the most obvious illustration of symbols. When you meet someone for the first time, your sensual perception seeks concepts by which to give a unique and multileveled identity to the name (symbol) of the person.

A symbol then participates in the thing, event, condition, or experience that is conveyed and functions as the vehicle for the conception of the object. Several characteristics are part of this functioning:

1. A symbol is closely related to its object, elicits a variety of responses, and draws attention to itself.
2. A symbol does not require action.
3. A symbol leads you to conceive its object.
4. A symbol is not as clear in its meaning as a sign.
5. A symbol carries more of the original experience from which it was derived than does a sign.
6. A symbol has creative conceptual possibilities.

Public-relations firms and advertising firms concentrate on creating symbols for their clients rather than just making signs. To a great extent their success depends on how well they persuade the potential customer to imagine using the client's product through their choice of symbols. Television commercials strive to create an atmosphere symbolic of the prospective buyers' desired life-style, their system of values and goals. Political campaigns succeed through the symbolic power of words: *American, law and order, honest, taxes,* etc.

As you remember to "keep five alive before you arrive," attempt to determine if your perceptions are providing information concerning signs (action) or symbols (thinking).

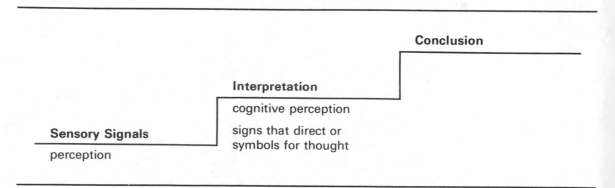

Conclusion

Interpretation

cognitive perception

Sensory Signals

signs that direct or
symbols for thought

perception

Except for the anecdote about Archie, very little has been said about how you personally communicate signs and symbols by your behavior. Keep your perceptual skills in mind as you explore various forms of nonverbal communication.

Nonverbal Communication

You transmit messages, consciously and unconsciously, through your body motions. These motions often have more influence on your listener's perception of your messages than your verbal language does. You can confirm or contradict your spoken words by your appearance, posture, facial expressions, and gestures. Over half of the meanings received by your listener are expressed through body motions. If the majority of all communication is nonverbal (approximately 65 percent), you would do well to investigate "body language."

In the early 1950s, Dr. Ray L. Birdwhistell recognized the need for further research in the field of body motion and meaning. His study of body motion and posture as related to nonverbal communication has been labeled *kinesics*.[5] Although kinesics is a relatively new science, more and more communicators are turning toward body language for an insight into effective communication.

With practice, you will be able to use nonverbal signals, or clues, to interpet more accurately or to reinforce the meaning of someone else's message. As you "keep five alive" to the messages being sent you, be aware that the other person is also detecting your nonverbal clues. Facial expressions, gestures, posture, and voice inflection (both the other person's and yours) are signals. Remember that all of these nonverbal clues are parts of a context. "No motion is a thing in itself. It is always part of a pattern."[6] Archie became angry because he did not know to which pattern of Edith's behavior her sigh referred.

Facial Expressions

Facial expressions can provide your first insight into evaluating the sender's messsage. Your eyes are one of the most expressive parts of your body. Eye contact, or the avoidance of eye contact, can be an important nonverbal signal. You can show trust and agreement or distrust and disagreement with your eyes. Your eyes convey your interest or disinterest in a conversation. Unless you are a very good

Body motions transmit messages that influence your listeners. H. Armstrong Roberts.

---

[5] *Introduction to Kinesics* (Louisville, Ky.: University of Louisville, 1952).

[6] Ibid., p. 10

actor, your communications partner can tell whether your heart is in the conversation or whether you are just putting up with what is being said until you can escape. Normally in this situation, darting eyes mean you are looking for an exit. If your partner is a perceptive salesman, he knows he has lost a sale. A glance can be suggestive; a stare can be threatening. Consider the following situation:

Mr. Procter, a public-relations executive, returns to the office to find Fran, his secretary, speaking with a client, Mary Van Horn. Ms. Van Horn is a very valuable client, but unfortunately she comes in almost daily and stays too long. Fran knows Mr. Procter has a very important meeting and does not have time to visit with Ms. Van Horn.

As Mr. Procter enters the door, Ms. Van Horn's back is toward him, and he does not recognize her. Fran quickly glances at Mr. Procter, then at Ms. Van Horn, then again at Mr. Procter. Mr. Procter catches her signal and makes a silent and hasty exit.

Thus, two glances and a stare (signals) alert Mr. Procter to quick action in order to avoid Ms. Van Horn (at that moment, a symbol to be avoided). Placed on the awareness staircase, the exchange looks like this:

Conclusion

"I can't talk to her now. I'm getting out of here!"
("Thanks, Fran!")

Interpretation

cognitive perception

"What is Fran trying to tell me? It's something she doesn't want this person to know. Yikes! It's Ms. Van Horn.
(Symbol: conceptions of time-consuming client that only fit Ms. Van Horn.)

Sensory Signals

perception

Mr. Procter: two glances and a stare received from Fran.

Remember not to trip on the awareness staircase by jumping to a premature conclusion without considering all the data, thereby jeopardizing yourself and your position. A new employee, unfamiliar with the employer's pattern of nonverbal behavior, could easily be tripped by misinterpreting a signal. An early morning stare from the boss may just mean he or she hasn't had coffee yet.

Your eyes convey interest or disinterest in a conversation. H. Armstrong Roberts.

Conversely, a soft glance at the end of the day may have nothing to do with your efforts on your job. The boss may just be tired.

In a majority of cases, knowledge of the sender, the sender's background, and the business situation can be most helpful in avoiding an unnecessary stumble on the awareness staircase. Consider the signals shown in Table 2–5 and their *possible* interpretations.

Table 2–5
Sensory Signals and Possible Interpretations

Sensory signals	Possible interpretations
Wink	Joke, tease, flirt, intimacy
Raised eyebrow	Doubt, disapproval, surprise
Lowered eyebrow	Anger, concentration, worry
Enlarged pupils	Interest, honesty, innocence
Contracted pupils	Distrust, dislike, annoyance

How do you choose which interpretation is the most accurate? Check all other nonverbal messages and see if they seem to make a consistent pattern. You might take the risk of asking, "Why did you wink at me?" But, then, asking for communication feedback tends to threaten people who are unaware of communication skills. That could tell you something, too, about your partner's knowledge, security, and openness in personal communications.

As you become more adept in interpreting your sensory information, try this card trick, used by magicians, to test your friends.

Have your subject select any card from a regular deck of playing cards. After he or she selects the card, have him or her place the card anywhere in the deck. Shuffle the deck and then show each card one by one. As you turn over each card, watch the pupils of your subject's eyes. When you reach the selected card, the pupils of the eyes will become larger.

The change is slight, but with practice you can determine the correct card by the change in the subject's pupils. Changes in the size of the pupils of the eye are indicators of emotional arousal.[7]

Your eyes may give you away.

Gestures

Hands and eyeglasses, in a sense, are both extensions of the body. Glasses are often used in gesturing, and their use may give you nonverbal signals about your communication partner. Peering over the top of glasses gives the impression of emotional distance, or disagreement. But it might also be that your partner has a visual problem. The same gesture might imply superiority or authority. Handling glasses can also be used to gain time for a response by placing the ends in one's mouth, taking them off, or putting them on.

Glasses are often used in gesturing. Peering over the top of your glasses may imply superiority or disagreement. H. Armstrong Roberts/Free Lance Photographers Guild.

If someone tied your hands behind your back, would you be able to communicate as effectively? Would you be able to allow your eyes, your facial muscles, etc., to convey your feelings of consternation, helplessness, joy, or excitement as clearly as you could if you used your hands? Think about it. Expressing yourself is difficult.

[7] Audrey Haber and Richard P. Runyon, *Fundamentals of Psychology* (Reading, Mass.: Addison-Wesley, 1974), p. 265.

How would you describe a sailboat ride in rough weather without using your hands?

What would cheerleaders, referees, traffic cops, or umpires do without hand gestures? How would you indicate a $500-a-month raise to your spouse without using your hands? Could you show the exhilaration you feel without any gestures?

Historically, gestures have been employed politically, as well as culturally. Gestures change with time and culture. Anyone old enough to remember World War II would recognize the "V-for-victory" sign used by Winston Churchill. When expressed in Morse code ($\cdots-$) or by the four opening notes of Beethoven's Fifth Symphony, "V" became a powerful symbol. This symbol gave strength to the war efforts of all the English-speaking world. In the 1960s, the same gesture symbolized peace to an entire generation of young Americans.

This is an example of two concepts embodied in the same symbol with two conclusions: your grandmother interpreting the "V" as a victory sign, and your seeing the same gesture and interpreting it as a peace sign. You will also recall the raised arm salute of the Germans under Hitler and the clenched fist expressing black power as gestures conveying a message by nonverbal means.

Gestures are used most often when necessity demands omission of words or when a gesture will help emphasize the word. In war or hunting, gestures are used frequently. Marcel Marceau, a master of pantomime, can hold an audience's attention for a long time with-

Gestures add power to expression.

Words alone aren't enough.

Television has placed added pressure on candidates running for political office. Their gestures must match their words. Tommy Noonan/Uniphoto.

out uttering a word. Speakers are more likely to get their point across to the audience if they employ gestures to emphasize the spoken word. Consider speakers who stand rigidly at the podium, moving neither one way nor the other. They stare either at the ceiling or at a vacant seat. Does this lack of movement also mean a lack of communication? Of course, they are communicating. However, do their messages carry as much weight as those of speakers who make gestures work for them? Which kind of speaker would hold your attention?

Think about the political campaigns. Some candidates are adept in using gestures to emphasize and describe attitudes and feelings. Television has placed added pressure on candidates running for public office. Too often, however, their gestures contradict their spoken words. What do the common gestures listed in Table 2–6 imply?

Table 2—6
Implications of Common Gestures

Gesture	Implication
Two fingers raised	Peace, or symbol for victory
Thumbs up	Agreement
Thumbs down	Displeasure
Thumb pointed	Hitchhiker's plea
Clenched fist	Anger
Tapping on desk	Nervousness, or disinterest
Palms up	Plea, or sympathy
Hand extended	Greeting
Shrug	Misunderstanding
Yawn	Bored

Hand gestures can be used
1. to describe
2. to emphasize
3. to separate
4. to enumerate
5. to locate.

These meanings may not seem obvious to you, but see if you recognize some of the following gestures. You may have used all these gestures and not realized how much of a message your body language was communicating.

Imagine a typical Thursday afternoon before the general staff meeting of the employees at LJL Memorial Hospital in the conference room. Dr. Long and Dr. Short, two young interns on the staff, are discussing the new secretary in Medical Records. Dr. Long proceeds to draw a 36-24-36 outline with his hands. Dr. Short immediately responds with a nod. Dr. Long employed one of the most familiar descriptive gestures used by men in American society.

Meanwhile, Sue Green and Beverly Lane walk in discussing the new logo for the hospital stationery. Sue closes her hands in the shape of a small oval to emphasize the size and shape of the logo to be used in the advertising campaign. Beverly's eyes light up with recognition of the symbol. Sue's gesture of emphasis replaced many words that would have been necessary to communicate the same message to Beverly.

As time passes, the room fills. James Reed, the hospital administrator, calls the meeting to order and informs the group that today the members are going to work in small groups according to special interests. He points to the far left side of the room to indicate where he wants the doctors to sit and to the right side of the room for nurses. The administrative group receive their signal when he points to the middle of the room. His gestures of separation save the group time and frustration.

In the small administrative group, Susan Trimm begins to explain the plans for the new wing for the hospital. First, she draws a rectangle with her hands; then, she extends the rectangle by additions to each side. She adds a second story, a second rectangle, with additions to each side. Then she adds another story, another rectangle, to the one she just gestured. Susan then shows how the drive would circle in front of the wing. Finally she adds trees and shrubs. She did all of this by gestures to indicate the complete picture. Further, she pointed to the model of the new wing to show where the new addition is to be located. Susan's rectangles and pointing gestures enumerated or added to the picture. Her pointing to the new wing indicated the location of the addition.

Although you may not be able to place yourself in a hospital setting, recall how often you point to indicate where something is located.

Handshakes

The handshake was originally a symbol of peace, indicating that the other person held no weapon. Today, however, the handshake can reveal much about the personality of a person. Do you remember the last time you received a damp, limp hand? Your impression of that person probably was one of weakness, a lack of initiative, or disinterest. You were probably turned off to some extent. How about the time your ring became imprinted on your next finger because of the pressure of the handshake while meeting someone you wanted to impress? Maybe you were suppressing the desire to scream in pain while you smiled despite your discomfort. A handshake that leaves you wondering whether all fingers are still intact frequently gives the impression of an individual who is overbearing and aggressive.

Men shake hands from the time they are children. However, women tend to shake hands infrequently. Today's woman executive, therefore, is often in a quandary about how to shake a man's hand. Sometimes she is considered as aggressive if her handshake is too firm. There is a happy medium between a limp handshake and a painful one that is appropriate for both sexes.

Women usually remain in the same place after hand contact. Men tend to step back after the handshake because they don't feel comfortable at this close range. American men are culturally influenced to avoid closeness, and this reaction is encouraged through the education process.

Posture and Appearance

What does your posture and appearance reveal about *your* personality? A first impression is usually a lasting one. Emotions and feelings are conveyed by the way in which you stand and dress.

Your posture can portray eagerness, enthusiasm, alertness, boredom, even disgust. Every pose and body attitude, in effect, has a potential meaning all its own. Standing tall and erect, yet relaxed, indicates confidence. Determination can be displayed by squaring your shoulders. An extremely rigid stance, however, often indicates nervousness.

Your attitudes and feelings toward others may be revealed by the way in which you sit in a chair. Leaning forward in the chair can show interest or agreement. Simply moving closer to a person says in body language that you approve or like that person. On the other hand, when you disagree with someone, you are likely to move away from that person. You tend to move away or steer clear of things or people you dislike or unpleasant situations.

Appearance and clothing tend to symbolize different social classes because of their high visibility. A person's clothing provides a quick clue to the cultural class of the wearer. Your clothing can be a clue to your occupational status as you tend to adopt the same basic attire as the group to which you belong.

Proximity is revealing.

International Cultural Influences

No discussion of the various forms of communication would be complete without consideration of cultures and subcultures. A culture may be defined as

that which distinguishes one society from all others. It comprehends the activities and values passed on from one generation to another and governs the way people act and the things they do. Although based on the past, it is not static, but constantly evolving. Culture not only facilitates the achievement of personal goals, it assists in determining what those goals should be. Looked at in the aggregate, it is the way of life followed by a society.[8]

You belong to an altruistic, materialistic, and affluent culture—the American culture. One symbol for this culture is the flag. This flag represents the common beliefs shared by the culture: free enterprise, democracy, and freedom of religion. You live under a legal system that respects individual rights. The common beliefs shared by our culture separate it from dictatorial or socialistic cultures.

Cultures shape our symbols.

The language spoken by most business people in our culture is English. English is one of the few languages making no distinction between the formal and familiar forms of address. Many American business people have inadvertently insulted their clients in other countries by using a familiar form of address in a situation where a formal form would be more appropriate. Although you are fortunate that English is spoken in many countries, differences in idioms create barriers to communication. Don't expect someone unfamiliar with your culture to understand expressions such as "cool it" or "right on!"

Cultural protocol communicates.

If you were invited to a party in Latin America, you would need to be aware of the difference in cultural concepts of time. An invitation to a party might state that the time of arrival is 7 P.M. However, unless the invitation indicated "American time," don't plan to arrive until 8:30 or 9:00.

In Japan exposing the sole of your foot is considered extremely rude. If you are in the habit of sitting with your legs crossed, you will have to risk insulting your Japanese friends. However, customs do change with time. A few years ago the lower a Japanese bowed, as a greeting, the more respect he showed. Today Japanese bow very slightly. The slightest bow is sufficient to acknowledge respect. Bowing too deeply may be misinterpreted by an American or European.

[8] Joe Kent Kirby, *Consumer Behavior* (New York: Donnelley Publishing, 1975), p. 561.

Smiles and Frowns

Smiles have different meanings in different cultures. Southerners tend to smile more quickly and more often than do Northerners. This in no way implies that Southerners are more sincere and friendly than their northern neighbors. Smiling in certain situations is learned and passed on according to the culture in which you are reared. In many oriental cultures, to bare one's teeth in a smile is considered rude.

Whether you are comparing smiles or any gesture, if you travel from the United States to other countries, you will discover wide differences in expressions. A frown, which Americans associate with disapproval or dislike, may carry a completely different connotation in another country. In this country smiles generate warmth and invite conversation. If the corners of your mouth turn upward, your receiver assumes you are pleased. You are off to a good start in presenting your point of view.

Eye Contact

Avoid jumping to conclusions in evaluating nonverbal expressions because sometimes your perceptions, your interpretations, and your conclusions do not agree. For example, eye contact patterns vary from culture to culture. In Latin America or Mexico, for an adolescent to look directly into the eyes of an adult is a sign of disrespect. In North America, just the opposite is true. Americans are taught from an early age to look directly at the speaker. Reluctance to look at the speaker implies sneakiness, distrust, or disinterest. Consider the following case where eye avoidance is associated with guilt:

Looks can be deceiving.

Juan, 18 years old and a Latin American, has been working for Ed Brown for two weeks. This is his first job in America. Mr. Brown calls Juan into his office to ask him about some merchandise that is missing from his department. Juan, when confronted, does not meet his employer's eyes. Mr. Brown interprets this to mean that Juan is avoiding the truth. Juan looks away because he feels chastised and wants to show his respect for his employer. Juan loses his job.

This is an example of Mr. Brown jumping to a conclusion because of a disagreement between the sensory and interpretation steps. Mr. Brown's ignorance of cultural differences caused him to trip on the awareness staircase and draw the wrong conclusions. Had Juan looked Mr. Brown directly in the eyes and said that he did not know anything about the missing merchandise, he probably would not have lost his job. Therefore, your sender's background must definitely be considered in interpreting his or her message.

National Cultural Influences

As if there is not enough difference between cultures, the United States, with its wide variety of ethnic groups, has problems with subcultures. Subcultures are segments of the main culture that are characterized by their own customs, traditions, values, beliefs, and attitudes. Differences in age, religion, national origin, income, race, and geographical location create subcultures.

Individuals in different social classes often use different language patterns. Studies have shown that social class can be recognized by the speaker's choice of words, sentence structure, and ability to convey exact shades of meaning. More credibility is associated with the communications of individuals with a higher status than those of lower status. People in the lower social classes tend to mispronounce more words and use more slang and trite phrases than those in higher social classes. Upper-class people use 20 percent fewer words than do lower-class people in expressing the same thoughts.[9]

Learning the culture in which one is reared is called *socialization* or *enculturation.* Learning a new culture or subculture is *acculturation.*[10] If you move to a different part of the country or to another country, you become acculturated to the language patterns and the signs and symbols of the new area. The same is true if you move significantly up or down the social ladder. People who often preface their remarks or opinions by saying "everybody knows that . . . " have not become acculturated. You would be wise to restrict your communication with them to a more parochial or encultured level if you wish to avoid conflict. Bigots are the epitome of rigid enculturation.

These, of course, are only a few of the differences in cultures. As American firms move more and more rapidly into foreign markets, your need for knowledge of cultural differences increases. Modern technology and transportation have made visits to different cultures possible, either through travel or mass communication.

[9]Clifton Fadiman, "Is There an Upper-Class American Language?" *Holiday,* 20, No. 4 (October 1956), p. 8, as cited in *Consumer Behavior,* by James F. Engel, David T. Kollat, and Roger D. Blackwell, 2nd ed. (Hinsdale, Ill.: Dryden Press, 1973), p. 148.
[10]Engel et al., p. 73.

Summary

As Alvin Toffler points out in *Future Shock,* the contemporary environment is changing at a pace outstripping man's capacity to perceive, to organize signs and symbols, and maintain rationality. Even though people have a neural transmission rate of 30,000 cycles per second to help them perceive, they can't keep up with a computer. Today's technological age is changing the signs and symbols you depend upon much faster than you can assimilate and order them. "In short, the more rapidly changing and novel the environment, the more information the individual needs to process in order to make effective, rational decisions."[11]

Of equal importance is the recognition that there is a difference in the way individuals interpret signs and an even greater difference in the way they interpret symbols.

As the pace of civilization increases and the demand for acculturated skills grows, communications will continue to become more complex. Your effectiveness is dependent on your increased ability to perceive, interpret, and visualize the many possibilities in any given context. Dependence on verbal communication alone is insufficient to this task. Greater tolerance of cultural differences in nonverbal signs and symbols is demanded in today's business world. Your own gestures often reveal more than your words.

Conscious use of the awareness staircase can greatly assist you in becoming more adept in communication. The exercises at the end of this chapter will give you a chance to try out these skills. Remember to "keep five alive before you arrive," to gather all possible information; then, carefully consider your partner's background before drawing your conclusions. Good luck at better communication!

[11]Toffler, p. 351.

Exercises

Perception

1. In a conversation with a friend, list as many sensory stimuli as you can in fifteen seconds. After listing them, evaluate which ones caught your attention the most. Why? Which ones did you choose to ignore? Why? Which ones assisted in the communication?

2. Choose any small business reception room. Record as many sensory stimuli as you can perceive in ten seconds. Mentally sort this data for interpretation. Draw conclusions about the atmosphere you perceive. Be aware of any emotional reactions that shape your judgment. Analyze what factors seem most important to you. Assuming you were in the reception room for a business transaction, how did your perceptions influence your first words to the person you met?

3. Observe any two people in conversation. Describe the differences in behavior between the speaker and listener. How engrossed was the listener in the conversation?

Signs and Symbols

1. Choose any billboard advertisement that leaves you unmoved. Does the ad represent a sign or a symbol to you? Now choose a billboard that serves as a symbol for you. Explain the visual content of the billboards and how they functioned as a sign or a symbol to you.

2. Contrast two brief television commercials in terms of their attractiveness for you. Note what perceptual skills came into play and what concepts they attempted to convey.

3. With a partner, attempt to describe a well-known product without using its proper name. Can you do this? Can your partner recognize it without your using the name?

Nonverbal Communication

1. What nonverbal messages do you transmit when you are: (a) happy, (b) sad, (c) confused, (d) angry, (e) frustrated, (f) impatient? List your habitual (a) facial expressions, (b) voice inflections, (c) posture and gestures. What conclusions can be drawn by others from your habitual behavior?

2. Watch someone talking on the telephone. How many nonverbal messages cannot be heard by the listener?

3. Watch two people shaking hands. What inferences can you draw about how they feel about themselves?

4. The next time a salesperson approaches you, pay attention to the behavioral patterns that influence your trust or distrust of his or her words and manner.

5. With a good friend of the opposite sex, take five minutes to give as many interpretations as possible using only the words: ''I love you.'' Reinforce, contradict, and emphasize your meaning with facial expressions, gestures, and voice inflections.

Cultural Variations

1. In five minutes list as many idioms, slang words, jargon, and expletives you or someone else uses as you can. What would be left for a person from another country who has only learned ''school'' English if all these words and expressions were removed from your conversation?

2. If possible, visit a shop or business managed by a person of foreign extraction. What differences did you notice in communication, especially words and gestures?

**Part Two Your Role in Using the
Principles and Psychology
of Business Communication**

Chapter 3 Principles and Practices of Effective Communication

Basic Techniques of Communication

Unity
Coherence
Emphasis

Seven Signposts for Successful Communication

Clarity—Avoid Misunderstanding
Completeness—Leave Nothing Undone
Conciseness—Make Every Word Count
Correctness—Clear Your Reader's Path
Concreteness—Detail and Define Your Communication
Consideration—Use the "You-Attitude"
Courtesy—Use a Pleasant, Positive Tone

Summary of the Basic Steps in Effective Communication

"With words, we govern men." — Benjamin Disraeli

One of the vital doors to promotion to the executive suite is the ability to compose effective correspondence and to communicate effectively. When you can express your thoughts, feelings, ideas, and attitudes clearly, you hold one of the keys to top management.

Basic Techniques of Communication

In order to compose effective communications, study the correspondence written in your business situation and try to follow the procedures of your company. However, whenever you can, if you can, improve on these policies because, as you know, many business communications violate the basic principles of effective writing—unity, coherence, and emphasis. Your good judgment, intelligence, and basic communication skills, developed through your experience and education, will ensure the more effective communications you need as you climb your career ladder.

Use the basic techniques of unity, coherence, and emphasis when you communicate!

Unity

Unity means that each sentence, paragraph, or message expresses one main idea. Each word you choose should be sincere, concrete, and meaningful to your receiver and should contribute to unity.

Unify sentences, paragraphs, and messages.

An effective communicator realizes that *written communication* is actually no more than *oral conversation polished*. You polish your communication in order to ensure accuracy in grammar and form as well as to avoid being offensive to your reader.

Talk words—words that your readers understand according to their educational and experience level—are the most efficient communications media. Choose these words for clarity, completeness, conciseness, courtesy, and coherence.

To unify each sentence, choose each word carefully. Each sentence should convey one main idea. Modifying statements may be added if they are subordinate to the principal idea and help to achieve unity. Therefore, include all the words that are necessary to understand and to relate to the main idea. *Say enough,* but *just enough!*

As you unify sentences, you will work toward paragraph and message understanding. Avoid grammatical errors such as incomplete sentences, long and involved sentences, improper connectors, and omission of important information. Then your sentences and paragraphs may be joined correctly through coherence to build a unified message—an efficient communication.

Coherence

Coherence, as unity, begins with words, sentences, and paragraphs. Coherence may be achieved by the effective joining of your thoughts, as expressed in your words, sentences, and paragraphs, into your whole message. To ensure coherence, use devices that help your reader travel smoothly from one idea to the next. For example, you might write: "The Pittsburgh-Acme Manufacturing Company uses ordinary credit procedures. These procedures enable our retailers to buy goods they need now and to pay for them later." The word *procedures* is repeated to ensure coherence. Repeating *procedures* has made the meaning more understandable.

Linking words and phrases are helpful in tying sentences and paragraphs together for effective messages. For example, you may write: "The Fair Company has a popular credit plan. Furthermore, the Fair Company gives a choice of credit terms to make the payment easier for you, the customer." *Furthermore* is a linking word helping your reader to understand the message.

Words like *morever, however, nevertheless, as soon as, for example.* or *similarly,* chosen for a smooth transition as you tie the various parts of your message together, can be overused. Usually, such words, used with effective modifiers, parallel construction, and appropriate pronouns, will help to provide communications that are instantly clear and coherent to your reader. Then your unified, coherent message may be given *power* through the use of a third technique—*emphasis.*

Coherence links or ties your message together.

Emphasis

To add to unity and coherence, a third technique is necessary—*emphasis*. Emphasis gives power through effective word order, use of climactic words or sentences, selection of comparisons or contrasts, and variation between simple sentence structure and subordination to achieve effective communication.

Emphasis gives you power!

Effective use of word order places the most important parts of your communication at the beginning or ending of sentences, paragraphs, or messages. If you were able to choose the order of your contestant in the beauty competition, you would probably pick the first or the last position. The hosts of the pageant subconsciously emphasize the *first* beauty from Alabama. And, similarly, they emphasize the *last* contestant from Wyoming. In a parade, the first and last places seem to gain more attention—even if through unconscious emphasis. These same factors support the idea that the beginning and ending sentences are the most important parts of your message to achieve the emphasis necessary in your communications.

If your reader scans your message, the first and last sentences may be the only ones read carefully; the other sentences may be reviewed briefly. Therefore, to emphasize a portion of your message and have your reader perceive this part as extremely important, use the most desirable word or sentence order when you write. The most important things are positioned *first* or *last!*

As an executive you may use comparison and contrast, subordination, shorter sentences, or even mechanical devices such as underlining or capitalization for emphasis. You provide a message that gets attention. However, neither word or position emphasis alone nor the use of sentence length or mechanical devices will substitute for the tone, content, and appearance of your message.

The use of correct punctuation, good grammar, excellent structure, and effective fundamentals will help you achieve good communication as you climb your managerial ladder. These will be discussed in more detail in Part Three.

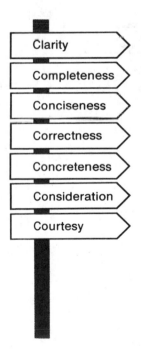

Clarity

Completeness

Conciseness

Correctness

Concreteness

Consideration

Courtesy

Seven Signposts for Successful Communication

The seven signposts for successful communication are clarity, completeness, conciseness, correctness, concreteness, courtesy, and consideration. Because they all begin with the letter "C," they are easy to remember.

Use the signposts for effective communication!

To begin using them, choose one of these signposts and concentrate on this one principle. Then, add to your power by including and focusing on the other "C's of communication," just as you add daily to your skills and ability in completing office assignments or administrative duties.

You may visualize these seven signposts as scales—weight scales, diet scales, ornamental scales, justice scales, pharmaceutical scales—as instruments or guides to measurement. When measuring, you use a certain amount of each ingredient. In communicating, similarly you need a balance of each of the seven principles. Too much of one principle or too little of another can impair your effective communication. Therefore, balance the scales of communication as accurately as possible to provide correspondence that will convey your and your company's effective image.

Blending these elements of effective communication may make you feel like a juggler with seven bowling pins in the air at one time. As you know, conciseness, completeness, and even courtesy may conflict with each other. If you can influence people and maneuver appointments, you can learn to manage and follow the seven signposts of communication effectively.

Clarity—Avoid Misunderstanding

The signpost of clarity makes your meaning easy to understand. Clear writing is the outgrowth of organized planning—you cannot be *misunderstood*. Write to avoid misunderstanding!

Some examples of ambiguity are:

"Drive by our store when shopping."

Should your customer *drive on by* or *visit* your store?

"For four years, I have worked in the Registrar's Office at McNeese State University for Dr. Linda Hohnstein, whom I am sending you as a reference."

Is the applicant sending *Dr. Hohnstein* or *her name* as a reference for employment?

"When replying, include your statement for $77.78."

Does the company want only the statement for $77.78 or both the *statement* and *your check?* Should the company ask for a *remittance and the statement?*

Occasionally someone says, "I know, but I just can't explain." Often they may not be thoroughly familiar with the information.

Almost every communicator has trouble expressing ideas clearly without misunderstanding sometimes. But the more clearly you can express your ideas, the more valuable you are in business.

Write so you cannot be misunderstood.

Talk words can help. These talk words are easily understood by the person to whom you are writing. When you are writing to an accounting firm, choose precise, technical terms that will convey your meaning to an accountant. However, if you must use a technical accounting term in writing to someone with less knowledge of the field, choose the word skillfully and tactfully without "talking down" to your reader. Talk words help a communicator convey messages that can be understood easily and correctly.

Do you remember your first-grade reader? Many times, this primary text contains pages and pages of only one picture and one word. However, these talk words are as meaningful to the first grader today as they were to you. Do you remember Dick and Jane, Nancy and Bob, or Puff and Muff? You remember these characters now because the writer of the text used *your* talk words.

In fact, you may remember your first-grade reader more easily than some of the texts you have studied recently. This illustrates the importance of clear writing through using the vocabulary your reader understands. As you know, however, talk words for the engineer are extremely different from talk words for the elementary student.

The following guidelines will help you achieve clear writing and effective communication.

1. *Write the way you talk.* Good *written* communication is actually good *spoken* conversation, *polished!* Conversational terms will help you to achieve good writing. These conversational terms, however, must be used in sentences that are complete and grammatically correct.

2. *Avoid unnecessary words.* Nothing weakens business writing as much as extra words such as *each and every* or *repeat again.* These are doublets or redundancies—using two words when one would do as well—both are examples of stereotyped expressions.

3. *Put action into the verbs used.* By using active verbs, needless words may be cut out. For example, *hurried* is better than *came quickly,* or *shouted* is better than *repeated loudly.* Your communication will not only be clearer but will also save needless words.

4. *Keep your sentences short.* For clarity and easy reading, sentences should vary in structure and length. On the average, business sentences should be reasonably short, generally containing less than fifteen words.

5. *Make use of variety.* Different arrangements of words and sentences are necessary. However, the meaning must be clear so you cannot be misunderstood when you are varying your sentences.

6. *Use the simple rather than the complex.* Many complex terms are unnecessary if an easier, simpler way of saying something is available. Complex sentences are unnecessary except to provide for the variety that is necessary for more interesting reading.

7. *Relate your words to your reader's experience whenever possible.* Phrases that pinpoint the exact nature of the subject you are discussing help to prevent misunderstanding by your reader.

8. *Develop your vocabulary.* A preference for short words and talk words does not limit your vocabulary. Shorter words and talk words are useful in business; however, intelligence and vocabulary size are closely linked. Longer, unusual words may be necessary to *think* with so you may successfully *write,* using the shorter talk words necessary for effective communication on your reader's level of experience.

9. *Write to* express *not to* impress. For clarity, present your ideas simply and directly. As an effective communicator, you know that long words, sentences, and paragraphs do not necessarily show greater intelligence. Winston Churchill noted: "Usually big people use little words; little people use big words" as they express their meaning simply and concisely.

Intelligent communicators remember that "the more you know, the more you owe to others." Therefore, when you are communicating, light your reader's path and generate writing power through clarity. Usually, the simpler your language and the clearer your words, the greater will be the impact of what you say. Your job is to express ideas so the receiver of your message cannot misunderstand you. By expressing your thoughts in a direct, natural way, employing familiar words and phrases, explaining technical words if necessary, and using a conversational tone, your communications will not be misunderstood.

Completeness—Leave Nothing Undone

To achieve the second signpost of completeness, select the points of your message carefully. Planning will help you decide what should be included and what can be omitted.

Incompleteness multiplies errors and cost. Your communication should leave nothing undone that might require additional correspondence.

An incomplete letter is a wasted and expensive communication; at least one other piece of correspondence must be written to obtain what is missing. The first written communication costs money; the second written communication usually consumes the profit; the third written communication often destroys goodwill. Communication costs are constantly rising. No company or organization can afford these extra communication costs for long.

Did you include everything necessary?

To achieve completeness, outline before you write. The chief enemy of completeness is *carelessness*. An untrained writer might try to communicate without planning. However, as a trained communicator, always outline on paper or in your mind the thoughts you intend to include.

You may need to list the main points you should make. Then, under these ideas, enumerate the steps that will support these ideas. As you gain experience as a correspondent, you probably will shorten this outlining procedure. However, no good writer will attempt to communicate without having some plan—either written or mental. As a Dartnell Corporation publication said: "Spouting details without an outline is like expecting bricks to take their place in a wall as they tumble from the back end of a truck."

When answering letters, reply to the writers' questions and discuss all matters they mention. Similarly, when you are making an inquiry, ask all the questions to which you need answers. Make replying easy by listing your questions and giving necessary back-

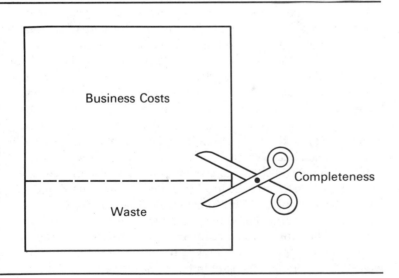

Completeness cuts waste from business costs.

ground information that will help the reader of your letter understand and answer your communication.

Incomplete orders are so prevalent that mail-order companies have to budget for them. For example, these companies often find that information such as the width of shoes is not given on the order blank. To help prevent such omissions, most mail-order companies put a checklist on the order blank itself, as well as one on the envelope used, to remind the person ordering to check all details for clarity and completeness.

Answering these questions will help to ensure inclusion of all necessary information in your order.

1. Did you give your name and complete address?
2. Did you give the complete catalog number?
3. Did you give the size and color?
4. Did you give a description of the article?
5. Did you add shipping charges?
6. Did you enclose your remittance or indicate how payment would be made?

Even when such questions are asked, many orders are still incomplete. As an effective communicator, you should be especially careful that you give all the information needed when writing a purchase order, filling in an order blank, or ordering by telephone. Similarly, you try to help the person who is ordering from you to remember to send the information you need. Your job to ensure completeness is a two-fold one as a writer and as a receiver of communications. As an effective communicator, you can help solve the problem by asking yourself: "Did I provide an answer to the questions *who, what, when, where,* and *why?*"

As long as people are people, they will forget to include many obvious things. You might add your personal examples to this one. The letter read: "Please send me five reams of your colored mimeograph paper." The writer meant: "Please send me five reams of pink mimeograph paper, size $8\frac{1}{2} \times 11$ inches." The person ordering needed the paper immediately. However, another letter had to be written, and time was lost because of incompleteness. The customer's order was delayed, and the company made no profit because of the cost of writing for additional information. Both parties were inconvenienced by the transaction, and profits were lost.

Incompleteness occurs not only in orders but also in actions. For example, a message may begin: "Enclosed are several samples of our application forms." The forms may not be sent. In fact, often enclosures are not included in communications that are sent or received. Therefore, as a communicator, check outgoing mail carefully to be sure that everything you promised is included. Similarly, your incoming mail should be checked to ensure that all enclosures indicated are received. If an enclosure is missing, note this fact immediately and take steps to obtain the missing information.

If all communicators check each outgoing message for completeness, management costs will be cut. Industry and management demands that efficient communicators *leave nothing undone!*

Conciseness—Make Every Word Count

Conciseness requires that every word in a communication is necessary. Words cost money! However, never sacrifice completeness or clarity for *brevity. Brevity* is not necessarily *conciseness!*

How long should your communication be? Abraham Lincoln was once asked, "How long should a man's legs be?" He answered, "A man's legs should be just long enough to reach to the ground."

This same reasoning applies to the length of your communication. Three sentences could be too long if you have been redundant. Conversely, three pages could be concise if every word is necessary to ensure complete understanding of your message.

Many times, clarity and brevity do go hand in hand. A balance between clarity, completeness, and conciseness ensures that you say everything necessary and no more and that your message cannot be misunderstood.

Make every word in your communication count. Be brief but clear. H. Armstrong Roberts.

Table 3—1
Express Your Message
Concisely

Wordy Expressions	Concise Expressions
I am in receipt of your letter of December 3 in which you inquire concerning the cost of paper for the XYZ copy machine.	Thank you for your letter of December 3 concerning the price of copy paper.
Hoping that we can be of maximum service to you at all times, we beg to remain,	Please call us when you need help.
We are extremely grateful for your exceptional cooperation and we want to take this special opportunity to tell you how much we appreciate your order of December 3.	Thank you for your order.

Table 3—2
Use Clear, Concise Statements

Wordy Statement	Concise Statement
In the month of July	In July
Sometime in the early part of the coming month	In early August
In the city of San Francisco	In San Francisco
In the near future	Soon
In the event that	If
The general consensus of opinion of most of the people on the committee is	The committee's opinion is
For the period of a month	For a month; for June
Owing to the fact that	Because
Terminate the illumination	Turn out the light
In the state of Texas	In Texas

For example, a wordy letter is often difficult to understand because the message lacks clarity. A long letter consumes extra time for both the writer and the reader. Time is money, and money is profit in business. Therefore, your clear, complete letter must also be concise. The wordy and stereotyped expressions shown in Table 3–1 should be avoided.

However, your communication should not be so brief that the message seems curt, incomplete, insincere, or unclear. Strike a happy medium! Conciseness can be overdone by being too brief or curt, thus destroying valuable goodwill.

Further illustrations of conciseness combined with clarity, completeness, and courtesy are given in Table 3–2. You should differentiate between the state of Washington and Washington, D.C. Similarly, distinguish between the city of Lake Charles, Louisiana, and Lake Charles as a body of water.

Removing needless words and stereotyped phrases will achieve conciseness. Avoid redundancies—using two words when one is sufficient—to save your reader's time. Cross out words that do not ensure clarity, completeness, or correctness. Compare the redun-

Is every word in your communication necessary?

Table 3–3
Avoid Redundant Expressions

Redundant	Correct
Basic fundamentals	Fundamentals or basic
Consensus of opinion	Consensus or opinion
Absolutely necessary	Necessary
Actual truth	Truth
Refer back	Refer
Red color	Red
True facts	Facts

Table 3–4
Doublets Express the Same Idea

Doublets	Concise Revisions
each and every	each or every
full and complete	full or complete
first and foremost	first or foremost
rules and regulations	rules or regulations
fair and just	fair or just
plain and simple	plain or simple
right and proper	right or proper
round trip and return	round trip

dant expressions in the left column of Table 3–3 with the shorter, more desirable versions in the right column of the table.

As an efficient communicator, you should avoid the use of two words when only one is necessary. For economy and conciseness, also avoid doublets. Similar to redundancies, doublets are two words that express almost exactly the same idea, joined by *and* (Table 3–4).

The Gettysburg Address is a masterpiece of simplicity and conciseness—a message containing only 270 words. Of these, 195 words contain one syllable; 43 words have two syllables. When the Gettysburg Address is typed on a sheet of paper, less than three-fourths of the page is used. This masterpiece, however, says all that is needed—*concisely,* but *completely* and *clearly.* Every word in the Gettysburg Address counts!

Avoid stock phrases, stereotyped expressions, overworked words, doublets, and redundancies. Take out unnecessary words, by saying enough, but just enough! Then, as an effective business communicator, you can achieve conciseness, which, with clarity and completeness, will help you follow the signposts to successful communication.

Correctness—Clear Your Reader's Path

Are your messages correct in appearance and facts?

You add force, direct your reader's attention to your message, and help cut management costs through correctness. Correctness in its dual role applies to both *form* and *content.*

One part of correctness is the appearance of the communication. It may provide the first impression of your company—good or bad. You are primarily responsible for this part of the message whether you are the administrative assistant or the executive. Appearance does count; your communication may be the only contact your reader has with you and your organization. Check to see that your letters look as if they were framed on the page with even left, right, and bottom margins. Are they free from strikeovers, misspelled words, and errors? Also, your communication must be correct in form, grammatical construction, and punctuation. Check to be sure you have provided correctness in both form and appearance.

The second factor of correctness includes accuracy of content. Accuracy of content is vital; no errors must occur. Avoid transpositions—$41.14 is quite different from $14.14. Check numbers carefully, whether you are dealing with 400 or 4,000 items—or just one. All of your figures must be correct to avoid a disastrous error.

An almost-disastrous error occurred in the central office of a county school district. In this case, a bid was accepted for shades

Four score and seven years ago our fathers brought forth upon this continent, a new nation, conceived in Liberty, and dedicated to the proposition that all men are created equal.

Now we are engaged in a great civil war, testing whether that nation, or any nation so conceived, and so dedicated, can long endure. We are met on a great battle-field of that war. We have come to dedicate a portion of that field, as a final resting place for those who here gave their lives, that that nation might live. It is altogether fitting and proper that we should do this.

But, in a larger sense, we can not dedicate— we can not consecrate— we can not hallow— this ground. The brave men, living and dead, who struggled here, have consecrated it, far above our poor power to add or detract. The world will little note, nor long remember, what we say here, but it can never forget what they did here. It is for us, the living, rather, to be dedicated here to the unfinished work which they who fought here, have, thus far, so nobly advanced. It is rather for us to be here dedicated to the great task remaining before us— that from these honored dead we take increased devotion to that cause for which they here gave the last full measure of devotion— that we here highly resolve that these dead shall not have died in vain— that this nation, under God, shall have a new birth of freedom— and that, government of the people, by the people, for the people, shall not perish from the earth.

The Gettysburg Address. Illinois State Historical Society.

for every window in every classroom in the county. The shades arrived on time for installation before the beginning of the school year in September. However, much to the distress of all concerned, the person who typed the order had transposed the length and the width. Since the shades were a special order, they could not be returned. Great expense and inconvenience resulted from an avoidable and extremely serious error. The typist made an error; the administrative assistant should have caught the error; the top executive, who signed the order, was actually responsible for releasing the incorrect information. All persons involved were at fault because none of them checked carefully to be sure the order was accurate.

A spelling error could be embarrassing—even hilarious! For example, in an industrial company, one temporary secretary ordered a *wench* for the executive instead of the *winch* requested. Although the executive who signed the letter was responsible for approving it with his signature, the secretary never quite recovered from this error. All the executives wanted to place a similar order through this secretary.

You as the communicator must earn the MLT degree. This is not an honorary degree; no college or university can confer it on you. You must earn it for yourself! The MLT degree is the "Master of Little Things." As an administrator you must be a checker; in fact, even a double-checker. Although you will employ the most capable persons you can find to help you, you will need the MLT degree to double-check for accuracy in form, in content, and in all details to ensure correctness.

Can your business communication pass this correctness test?

1. Your statements must be in harmony with your company's policy.

2. Your correspondence should be free from grammatical, spelling, capitalization, and punctuation errors.

3. You have checked all figures, facts, and details when preparing your communication.

4. You will then double-check all the names, addresses, and figures in your finished message against the original source.

5. You will proofread your communication closely and carefully for clarity and accuracy of facts, figures, spelling, punctuation, grammar, and details.

After you have followed these five steps, proofread carefully *again* for content in the context of your communication, even though an administrative assistant may be responsible for this.

If you do make a mistake, correct your error quickly, because the success of your firm depends on the accuracy of your communication. Report any serious error immediately. According to the Western Electric Company: "English mistakes cost more than engineering mistakes!"

Furthermore, correctness is a form of good manners and courtesy. A well-placed, attractive, accurate communication shows that you and your organization care about your message and the receiver. Correctness is definitely related to completeness and clarity. A message that is not complete cannot be correct.

Again, try to follow the signposts! Errors in correctness may amuse or irritate the reader. Your reader laughs at you and your organization when the errors are amusing. You lose dignity and influence. On the other hand, errors that irritate your reader create more communication problems than they solve.

Although others make mistakes, they still notice yours. Therefore, check all the facts and details to achieve correctness. Prevent stumbling blocks and provide easy reading for effective communication.

Concreteness–Detail and Define Your Communication

Concreteness makes words, phrases, and sentences easy to understand because the ideas are vividly and specifically expressed. The details are sharp and definite. Concreteness utilizes word pictures; not only do these sharp, vivid words convey your message clearly to the mind of your reader, but they also contribute to completeness and conciseness.

Refer to a "long communication" as a "seven-page report." Define an "extremely fast typist" as a "90-word-per-minute typist." A knife is razor-keen instead of sharp. In every instance, use concrete details to make your message more concise and clear.

Similarly, select a specific word rather than a general word. When you write about a good book, your reader does not get a clear, concrete picture. How is the book good? Instead of using *good,* an effective communication describes a book as "a thrilling, historical novel," "an inspiring biography," "a well-organized travelogue," or "a thought-provoking commentary." These specific adjectives give word pictures to your reader. Avoid using a second, unnecessary word, such as *very good.* By adding *very,* your expression is no longer concise or concrete.

You may find concreteness one of the hardest communication principles to achieve. Some people seem to have this ability to pick specific words; others do not. If you are fortunate to have "picture power" through words, use this skill. If not, you can still appeal to your reader's senses of smell, sight, hearing, taste, and feeling through the use of concrete words and phrases. Try to develop the art of "hitting the nail on the head" with your choice of words.

Details in your communication present a definite message.

Consideration—Use the "You-Attitude"

Consideration

Follow the people-oriented sign-post of consideration.

You must think of your reader *first* for consideration—the people-oriented communication principle. Consider your reader by making *what you say* have value to him or her. Put your reader in the center of your message. Any correspondent must learn to listen carefully to the needs of others for effective communication.

You must also be able to "climb into the envelope" as you prepare your communications. This simply means that your correspondence should sound like you while directed to the needs of your reader. Why should you say "I wish to announce" when you can say "you may have noticed"? Why say "it is my opinion" when you can mention "your experience will have shown you"? Why say "I think" when you can say "you will agree"? Before mailing your communication, check for the "you-attitude" of consideration. Put your reader first. Talk your reader's language. Consider your reader's interests. Visualize your reader.

To show consideration, you must be helpful and go the extra mile. The Sioux Indian prayer of consideration, "Great Spirit, help me never to judge another until I have walked two weeks in his moccasins," will help you understand those with whom you communicate. This plus of consideration in your correspondence wins the goodwill of your reader. Even from a materialistic point of view, you know that "to sell Tom Brown what Tom Brown buys, you must see Tom Brown through Tom Brown's eyes."

"To sell Tom Brown what Tom Brown buys, you must see Tom Brown through Tom Brown's eyes." Donald Dietz / Stock Boston, Inc.

Consideration cannot be pretentious. Merely sprinkling "you's" all over your communication will not ensure the "you-attitude." Consideration is the outward evidence of your inward attitude of empathy—the projection of your feelings into someone else's situation. Consideration helps promote goodwill for you and your company. Your final test for consideration might be: "How would I feel if I were receiving this communication?"

Courtesy—Use a Pleasant, Positive Tone

Many of the rules for courtesy are the same as those for consideration, such as thinking of the reader first. Although consideration and courtesy are closely related, courtesy is more situation-oriented; consideration is more people-oriented.

Courtesy is often called the "lubricant that cools the world's friction points." Courtesy is an expression of your inward attitude of consideration. It causes you to use words and actions that express friendliness and goodwill—attitudes that are always positive. Emerson said, "Life is not so short but that there is always time enough for courtesy."

Although "please" and "thank you" will never become trite, courtesy consists of more than just words. Courtesy is an *attitude* you take toward others, as expressed in the language and tone in which you write what you want to convey.

Nothing is gained by writing a discourteous communication. If you are tempted to write a hasty or irate letter, remember that you must communicate for *tomorrow* as well as for *today!* Most persons feel differently tomorrow. Therefore, preserve courtesy and avoid difficulties by never mailing a discourteous communication. Write it if you must—but don't mail it!

Follow the situation-oriented signpost of courtesy.

Do your communications achieve consideration and courtesy?

1. Use positive, pleasant-toned words.
2. Express appreciation in every message.
3. Be friendly, helpful, and tactful.
4. Express goodwill.

As a business person, the Golden Rule is still important: "Do unto others as you would have them do unto you." This primary principle of courtesy is always effective in business communications.

Courtesy in writing, speaking, and in working with people is an important investment in your career. Courtesy contains all of the sound business policies that promote goodwill. Goodwill is good business!

Summary of the Basic Steps in Effective Communication

By using these seven principles, you can compose effective communications that are forceful, courteous, and cost saving. These principles actually complement each other when they are used correctly.

Courtesy and consideration help to ensure that your writing will be received favorably and that you can help your reader. Completeness helps you determine what and how much to put in your writing; clarity makes this meaning easy to grasp. Correctness focuses your reader's attention on your attractive, accurate communication and prevents stumbling blocks in form and content. Conciseness helps you save your reader's time by cutting needless words. Through concreteness, you can paint word pictures that make your communication interesting and informative.

This rhyme may help you check your communication signposts as you use these principles to become more effective in your work.

> If you want to communicate with others,
> You have to be *understood*.
> To help you achieve this goal,
> Do the things you *should*.
> Show your *courtesy* by being
> *Considerate* and *complete;*
> Use *clear* and *concise* statements
> That are always *correct* and *concrete*.

Questions for Discussion

1. Define unity and explain its role in the effective communication message.

2. *Written communication* is actually no more than *oral conversation polished.* How do you polish your communications? Give at least two examples.

3. To ensure unity, you must *say enough,* but *just enough!* Explain how this ensures unity.

4. Define coherence. How is coherence relevant to effective communications? List two or more devices that help to ensure coherence.

5. What are linking words and phrases? Give three examples.

6. What should you avoid when using linking words? What are the advantages and disadvantages of using linking words to ensure coherence?

7. How can you use emphasis to give power in communication? What methods can you use to emphasize a part of your message?

8. Why are the beginning and ending sentences extraordinarily important to achieve the emphasis necessary in your communication?

9. How are the seven "C's of communication" compared to scales? What different types of scales can you use to remember them?

10. How can you as the writer of a communication ensure that your message is complete?

11. Why is an incomplete letter a wasted and expensive communication?

12. Conciseness ensures that every word counts. Explain how conciseness works and give two examples.

13. Why is correctness important to your communications? Explain the dual role of correctness.

14. How may the appearance of your communication give a good or bad first impression of your company?

15. What contribution does concreteness make to an effective communication? Why is concreteness difficult to achieve?

16. What is the relationship between consideration and the "you-attitude"?

17. What is empathy? Give an illustration.

18. Define and explain what makes a communication courteous. Give an example.

19. Explain the relationship between the seven C's as signposts to effective communication and management in general.

Exercises

1. Assume that you are a professor of business communications at a local university. You serve as a consultant to industry, often conducting management seminars or workshops on communications. You have received a request from the executive of a plant that often uses your services. The executive is extremely interested in improving the quality of correspondence in her department. She asks that you write her giving a brief summary of "those seven C's" you mentioned in your recent speech.

As the professor, compose a letter reviewing and summarizing the seven C's of effective business communication. Make it clear but concise. You may offer any additional help to the executive and assume needed information. (To write an introductory and concluding paragraph plus seven other paragraphs about each of the C's would be adequate. But you may want to dress them up a bit. You are a consultant and honorariums can be nice; therefore, you want to grant the executive's request graciously. Maybe you should also offer additional help.)

2. Find at least twenty violations of the seven "C's of communication" in the following letter. Check carefully for wordy expressions, stock phrases, redundancies, doublets, and inaccuracies.

Rewrite the letter using the seven "C's of communication."

Miss Ruby R. Kenny
209 West Orleans Street
Skokie, IL 60076

Dear Miss Kenny:

In compliance with your request of the 15th inst., we wish to advise you that a copy of our latest catalog is being mailed to you immediately under separate cover. Upon receipt of same you will certainly want to avail yourself of the opportunity to make real savings by placing your order in the near future.

Due to the fact that our stock is manufactured by nearby factories, we take pleasure in advising you that we are able to maintain a complete inventory of rugs at all times. We also beg to state in this connection that our Mr. Taylor will be happy to talk with you with reference to your requirements, irregardless of the number and kind of rugs you are planning to purchase at the present time.

May we take the liberty of inviting you to visit our new and modern showroom at your earliest convenience? Upon investigation you will find that we are in a position to help you in regards to your floor-covering problems.

Please be assured that we look forward to the privilege of serving you. The writer also wishes to state that you will find our service different than that of other floor-covering concerns.

Hoping to hear from you soon, we remain,
Yours truly,

3. Rewrite the following paragraph of a thank-you note especially improving the *clarity* and *correctness*.

We commend your cooperative spirit of which your cake was concrete evidence.

4. Rewrite the following paragraph especially using *completeness* and *correctness*.

Please send me the shoes illustrated on page sixty-six of your brochure. The catalogue number is A24H1498. The coler is "Blue Sky." The cost is $29.00. The shipping weight is 1 lb. 4 oz. I need a size 6.

5. Rewrite the following paragraphs being especially aware of *conciseness* and *correctness*.

Sometime in the early part of the coming month, we plan to arrange a meeting of the retailer's convention in the city of Bufalo. In the event that all goes well in the near future, I hope that you can serve on the program committee. However, I do realize that each and every one of us have committments.

May I take this opportunity to thank you for all the past favors rendered. You will be hearing from me in the near future.

6. Rewrite the following paragraphs especially using *clarity* and *correctness*.

Please place our order for thirty-six cases of XYZ soap. Each cases cost $2.00.

Theretore, wear inclosing our check for $74.00 which includes tax and shipping charges.

Thank you in advance for attention to our order.

7. Rewrite the following paragraph improving the *concreteness*.

I read a very good book. This book was interesting. It was a historical novel of the South. I am sure you would enjoy it.

8. Rewrite the following paragraphs using *consideration* and *correctness*.

We wish to announce the opening of our store on 1 Plaza. You may have noticed our advertisement on radio and television.

It is our opinion that we have the best Tire Shap in Milwaukee. Furthermore, we are firmly of the belief that we have the lowest prices.

Therefore, we think each and every one of you should take the opportuntity of visiting us on Sep't. 9th.

9. Rewrite the following paragraphs especially using *courtesy*.

I want you to come by my office in the morning, J'ly 9th. I do not understand your complaint concerning the size, quality of the merchandise you received, especially that of the dress your p'chased.

Evidently, you did not check the measurement guide in our catalogue. However, we will attend to you needs if you insist.

Thank you for your past co-operation and considerate.

Chapter 4 Psychological Aspects of Communication

Perception Skills

Using Your Skills of
   Observation
Using Your Reading Skills
Using Your Writing Skills
Using Your Listening Skills
Using Your Feedback Skills

**Organization and
Interpretation Skills**

Analyzing Your
   Data—Deduction
Synthesizing Your
   Data—Induction
Checking Your Data

Human-Relations Skills

Positive Tone

Goodwill

Ensure Timeliness
Use Empathy

**Social-Business
   Correspondence**

Congratulatory Letters
Appreciation Letters
Welcome Letters
Invitations
Other Goodwill Messages

Summary

"No man is an island." — John Donne

When you follow the signposts of the seven C's of effective communication—clarity, completeness, conciseness, correctness, concreteness, courtesy, and consideration—you will be a more effective communicator. Expanding these principles with effective beginning and ending sentences, timeliness, perception, logical organization, interpretation, human relations, positive tone, and goodwill will produce even more effective communications. The skills through which you can motivate, persuade, and obtain action—perception, organization and interpretation, and application—will help you achieve your goals.

Perception Skills

Perception, the first communication skill, uses all of the sensory processes—hearing, seeing, smelling, tasting, and touching. Actually, your ears, eyes, nose, mouth, and sense of touch provide the information input your mind uses to blend the sensations from outside with the stored memories and responses previously made. Through perception, you make assumptions, evolve attitudes, and establish your beliefs and values. You are unique! Because no other person is really like you, no one perceives things exactly as you do!

Perception is related to the skills of observation and interpretation. Your environment is based on two worlds—*reality,* or the *empirical world,* and *symbolism,* or the *symbolic world.* Your *real* world is defined through observation and experimentation; your *symbolic* world comes from your perception of reality. For example, you observe not only through real things, such as talking, seeing, and touching, but also through symbolic things, such as pictures, maps, graphs, and documents.

Therefore, you send and receive communications through your

Use your skills for perception as you observe, read, listen, and obtain feedback.

senses from both the empirical and symbolic worlds. Your brain creates a view of what reality is and influences your ability to communicate. For example, you tend to observe the stimuli that you are trained or conditioned to notice. This observation, as a part of perception, must be selective. Your senses are bombarded with an innumerable amount of sights, sounds, and smells from the empirical world as well as the symbolic world—signboards, television, and spoken and written language. The human brain, therefore, must filter out many of these stimuli. However, as an expert communicator, you are careful not to misinterpret stimuli or to interpret them improperly through the selective perception you develop.

When you examine your memories, like most people, you may find that you recall positive, satisfying events more vividly than negative, unpleasant ones. Many advantages do result from selective remembering of pleasant happenings and forgetting other situations as a defense device. For example, in the working environment, you become psychologically unaware of part of the real world when you screen out background noises, conversations, or visual stimuli not directly related to your immediate task. You perceive the stimuli that help to satisfy your needs; you ignore the disturbing influences that occur when you work with others.

However, you generally react to stimuli that may be dangerous to you in your environment. In these cases, perception must be especially keen.

In summary, you will probably learn to observe and mentally record stimuli that you think will satisfy your needs and ignore those that are disturbing or nonessential. As you become more expert in the field of observation, you should watch the events that persist carefully and increase your skills.

Using Your Skills of Observation

A successful communicator is an expert noticer. However, the world you see is not necessarily the real world. Your experiences and observations influence the way you react to situations. For example, if your experience in your first job interview was traumatic, you may fear later ones.

A football referee may make a decision on a touchdown pass to which many people in the stands react ecstatically favorably. You may feel disapproval. You simply observe the situation differently. Similarly, whether you are warm or chilly depends not only on the thermostat in the office but also on your personal feelings. A situation or position that seems superior to you may appear inferior to others, depending on observation and experience.

You select stimuli from the empirical and the symbolic worlds.

Satisfying events are remembered more effectively than unpleasant ones.

Use selective screening to communicate effectively.

Are you an expert noticer?

Your experiences and observations influence your reactions.

Regardless of the real world, you observe through the *symbolic world.* Selective observation is necessary because giving attention to all stimuli at one time is impossible. Only a small portion of the stimuli to which you are exposed reaches your level of awareness.

Unconsciously, you react in the symbolic world to signs such as the traffic signs shown. Selective screening helps you to respond positively to those that are important to you and to ignore those that do not concern you.

You use perception when you read printing. Unfamiliar symbols among the black marks on white paper may affect your total observation process. You hear unfamiliar or familiar speech sounds. You are aware of sensations inside yourself such as pain, strong emotion, discomfort, or happiness. All of these affect and are part of your perception process or observation.

For example, what do you see when you look at Figure 4–1? You may focus on the white space and see a vase; you may focus on the black area and see two profiles. Actually, if someone tells you that you should see two objects in the picture, you may be disturbed by your lack of observational ability if you see only one. As a communicator, this example serves to show how people perceive things differently.

Another example of selective observation is illustrated in Figure 4–2. What do you see? How old is the woman? This picture is intentionally ambiguous. You may see an ugly old woman with a long, crooked nose or a reasonably attractive profile of a young girl whose hair is covered by a scarf. You may even see something else.

As an expert observer, you will *see* both figures if you *know* you are looking for both. However, if you can see only one when you are looking at two, you may experience tension or discomfort because you think you are missing something others can see. You want to close this gap in your observation to improve your perception.

Figure 4–1
What do you see?

People perceive sensations from outside themselves.

Use external and internal cues to communicate more effectively.

Your primary goal is to realize that people do see things differently. Physical senses enable you and others to perceive sensations from outside themselves—an important facet of the communication process.

It is important to you to consider how observation affects the behavior of other people. Constantly search for the external and internal cues or signals that will help you to communicate more effectively. Welcome opportunities that can help you see things as others do. For example, you may visualize the writer of your letter if you *read* the communication carefully. You need to analyze and improve all of your skills of perception including observation, reading, and listening to become a more effective communicator. Dean Rusk, former secretary of state, commented: "If you think you are confused, take heart. You are only in touch with reality."

Using Your Reading Skills

Do you read for ease, speed, and comprehension?

Just as two skills are involved in observation—empirical and symbolic—your skills in reading have two aspects: your ability to read quickly with comprehension, and your ability to write carefully and to consider the difficulty of reading your message. Both are important to you as you work toward achieving your goal of correct, concrete, complete, and clear communications that *cannot be misunderstood.*

You realize the importance of the ability to read well; you probably are efficient in this skill. However, you may need to increase your reading rate and comprehension. Most persons can read textbook materials at 225 words per minute with a reasonable amount of comprehension. However, more efficient reading habits will allow you to read 300 or more words per minute and to understand business messages effectively.

You as a business communicator may find yourself involved in a mass of paperwork; therefore, your ability to read quickly and meaningfully—understanding both the obvious and hidden messages—is vital. If you want to become a more rapid reader or one who comprehends more quickly, you might consider a developmental—or speed—reading course to improve your abilities. Such a course would train you to read quickly and easily and to comprehend the between-the-lines messages you receive each day.

Even if you are an excellent reader, you can improve your technique and increase your reading and comprehension skills. Learn to scan the material while understanding what you are reading. Reduce eye fixation—the stopping points of eye movement in read-

Figure 4—2
How old is the woman?

74

ing—by trying deliberately to focus your eyes a minimum of three times a line: near the beginning, at the middle, and near the end of the line. Avoid moving your lips when you read silently because pronouncing or whispering the words slows your reading rate and makes your reading inefficient.

As you read your business communications, try to find the gist or purpose of the message. Furthermore, check for both implied and stated meanings as well as any responses you are expecting.

Using Your Writing Skills

Through careful choice of words, control of the length of your sentences, and the effective arrangement of your communication on the page, you can make your message more readable. Business people need to be able to scan and understand correspondence immediately. Generally correspondence should be written at a lower level than your readers understand. They will give you credit for considering the time element involved and the necessity for putting ideas into words that are quickly and easily understood.

Sentences averaging approximately twelve to seventeen words in length are preferred. Some authorities think fifteen-word sentences are more effective. Of course, you cannot limit the length of all your sentences to fifteen words, nor would you want to. A variety of sentence lengths, using some short sentences and a few long ones, is most desirable. Short sentences are emphatic, but they can make a letter choppy and may not clearly convey your message. Long sentences may be effective; however, too many of them may lose your reader's interest and decrease understanding.

Sentences in business letters are relatively short.

To ensure that your reader can understand your communication with reasonable ease, you may want to determine the readability of your writing. Several formulas for measuring reading difficulty are available. All of them use average sentence length and size of words (number of syllables) to determine reading level. Edgar Dale and Jeanne S. Chall of the Bureau of Educational Research at Ohio State University developed a fairly simple readability formula based on Dale's list of 3,000 common words.[1] Because their formula is based on the word list, writers do not use it very often. Rudolf Flesch developed another formula for readability, as well as a measure of human interest in writing.[2]

Check various formulas for readability.

[1] "A Formula for Predicting Readability," *Educational Research Bulletin,* 21 (January 1948), pp. 11–20.

[2] *The Art of Readable Writing* (New York: Harper & Bros., 1949).

Gunning Fog Index

Robert Gunning developed a readability formula that is easy to apply, the Gunning Fog Index.[3] By applying his Index, you can estimate the grade level for which your writing would be most appropriate. Most business letters should be written for a reading level between the eighth and the eleventh grades.

Determining the Fog Index has three simple steps:

1. In a sample of at least 100 words (or use several samples of 100 words or more), count the number of words and the number of sentences. Count independent clauses as separate sentences even though they are separated by a comma or semicolon. Count all words regardless of length—both *a* and *communication* are counted as one word. Hyphenated words are counted as one word. Groups of numbers, regardless of length, are counted as one word—both *2* and *200,000* are counted as one word. Divide the total number of words by the number of sentences to get the average sentence length.

2. Count the number of difficult words, those containing three syllables or more, in the selected sample or samples. Do not count as difficult those that (a) are proper names, (b) are combinations of short easy words like *whatever* and *bookkeeper,* and (c) are verb forms made three syllables by adding *-ed* or *-es* like *dictated* or *expresses.* Divide the difficult words by the total number of words in the selection and multiply by 100 to get the percentage of difficult words.

3. Add the average sentence length and the percentage of difficult words, and multiply this total by 0.4. This gives you the Fog Index.

The Fog Index corresponds to the school grade level of the writing; that is, the Index will show that the sample is written at the seventh-grade level, tenth-grade level, or fifteenth-grade level (junior in college).

For practice, apply the formula to the following quotation (difficult words are shown in italics):

You are learning the tasks of the office at a time when changes are taking place in the way office work is performed. Persons who have studied *developments* in the office ever since the *introduction* of the *typewriter* in the 1870s believe that the office of 1990 will be very *different* from most offices of today. Some even predict, for instance, that record handling will be *completely electronic,* that *correspondence* will be read from TV-display *terminals,* and that *communications* among *executives* in *different compa-*

---

[3] *The Technique of Clear Writing,* 2nd ed., revised and updated (New York: McGraw-Hill, 1968), pp. 38—39, and used with the permission of Mr. Gunning, the copyright owner.

nies will require no paper! These *predictions* may be a little far-fetched, but *advancements* in *technology* are *continually* changing office *procedures* and *activities.* You should be prepared to accept new ways of doing office jobs after you find *employment.*[4]

1. The passage has 122 words in 6 sentences; average sentence length: 122/6 equals 20.3 words.
2. The number of difficult words per hundred: 19/122 times 100 equals 15.6 percent of difficult words.
3. Add 20.3 and 15.6 to get 35.9. Multiply 35.9 by 0.4 equals the Fog Index (reading grade level) of 14.36.

Therefore, this quotation is written at the upper college-sopho-more grade level.

Use the formula for the Gunning Fog Index to review your communications to see if you are close to your correspondent's reading level and to see if you are using the talk words of your reader.

The Fog Index has been reevaluated by Gunning several times. After much use and observation, he has made no modification in the Index.[5]

Readability Rater

Another readability rater used to determine the appropriate grade level of written material has been developed by The Perfection Form Company based on data developed by Edward Fry of the Rutgers University Reading Center in New Jersey. Fry's data was published in 1968.[6]

The Readability Rater (Figure 4–3) is used by randomly selecting three (or more) 100-word passages from the written material. Count numbers, proper names, and initializations as words. Determine the average number of sentences per hundred words to the nearest tenth. Determine the average number of syllables in the 100-word passage. Count one syllable for each symbol in a group of numbers or letters—*1980* is four syllables; *AMS* is three syllables. Slide the rule to the position where the average number of sentences and the average number of syllables meet. The arrow will indicate the grade level of the material based on factorial components of word and sentence length.

This Readability Rater points out the differences between readability and difficulty. The instructions note that generally *long words* in *long sentences* create a higher degree of difficulty for the reader.

[4]William R. Pasewark and Mary Ellen Oliverio, *Clerical Office Procedures,* 6th ed. (Cincinnati: South-Western, 1978), p. 3.
[5]"The Fog Index After Twenty Years," *Journal of Business Communication,* 6, No. 2 (Winter 1968), pp. 3—13.
[6]"A Readability Formula that Saves Time," *Journal of Reading,* 11 (April 1968), pp. 513—516, 575—578.

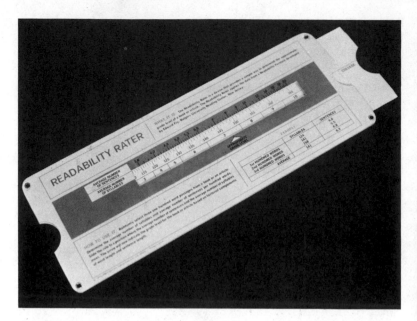

Figure 4—3
The Readability Rater developed by Edward Fry.
Used by permission of The Perfection Form Company, Logan, IA 51546, © 1974.

Short words in *short sentences* are easier to read. The Rater also points out that difficulty may not be related to either word or sentence length. For example, writing in short words and sentences may be difficult if a complex interrelationship of ideas is to be expressed.

Words used in symbolic ways may increase the degree of difficulty. Therefore, the Readability Rater and all similar devices are not sensitive to all problems, but only to the quantitative measure of word and sentence length. In fact, readability indexes can be deceptive by indicating that *easy* communication is really *difficult* because of the complexity of the ideas expressed. Therefore, any index must be used with careful judgment.

Furthermore, you should consider your reader. The technical language you will use with an electronic engineer might be easy reading for this person. However, this same technical information sent to the user of a television set might be extremely difficult reading, regardless of the readability rating. Almost any readability index will be a reasonably reliable tool in determining the reading level from a narrow set of data when combined with all these other variables. You can develop standards that should enable you to determine the level on which you are writing.

Write to express, not impress.

In other words, you write to *express* not to *impress*. You as the communicator have the responsibility of being sure that your reader understands. Use the talk words of your reader. Remember that these talk words vary from individual to individual. Consider your reader's intellectual and experience levels.

Paragraph Length

Usually, paragraphs are relatively short in business letters. In contrast to other writing, a one-sentence opening paragraph is permissible in a business letter. In fact, the opening paragraph is usually four or less typewritten lines.

The other paragraphs should be divided at logical points—the places where changes in thoughts occur. If your paragraph is more than eight or nine typewritten lines, try to break it into two paragraphs. Also, try to vary the paragraphs so they will not all be the same length.

For easier readability, you may also end with a short paragraph. Your opening and ending sentences are the most important positions for emphasis in your business communication.

Variety in sentence length increases readability.

Arrangement

By carefully arranging your letter on the page, you can make reading easier. Allow for ample white space around your typewritten material by double-spacing between paragraphs, double-spacing before and after any numbered or listed material, and leaving at least a one-inch margin on all sides.

People will appreciate your writing for understanding; they will not think they are undereducated when you write at a lower level. Concise, correct, concrete, and complete writing, using short sentences and words, saves time and money and ensures no misunderstanding.

When you improve your reading skills so your work becomes easier and you increase your skills in writing by using readability indexes, you will become a more efficient communicator. You will vary your writing, keep your tone positive, and empathize to meet the major needs of your written communication—effective conversation polished.

Write to express ideas.

Using Your Listening Skills

As a communicator, you need to be an expert listener as well as an effective observer, reader, and writer. You may listen through your correspondence as well as through your ears. Through effective listening, you learn more about the people with whom you communicate, about their values and their jobs as well as their relationships and attitudes toward you and your company.

Because your thought processes move faster than the speed of speech and much faster than the speed of reading written communications, most people have difficulty in listening—both written and oral. As a communicator, you can use the time lag to concentrate on what is being said or written. Listen for ideas; summarize what is being said or written to you; consider the thoughts behind the words; anticipate what may follow. Concentrate carefully on what your communicator is saying. Then you can better express your attitudes or answers through written or oral communication.

Listening makes up more than half of daily communication. Listening is only effective if this channel is efficiently used. Listening involves more than just *hearing sounds* or *reading words.* Unless the mental state of your communication partner is changed in some way by your ability, active involvement in the communication process does not exist. Similarly, unless you are able to listen to your partner through her or his words—oral or written—you will be unable to respond as an effective communicator.

Actually, good listeners are rare! Excellent listeners block out all distractions and focus ears, eyes, and mind on the sounds or printed words being received. In other words, as a communicator, you not only identify mentally with the sounds and words, but you also receive them effectively.

What are your barriers or deterrents to effective listening? Are they physical, psychological, or emotional? Are they caused by your attitude or preconceived notions about the situation? The following suggestions will help you become a more effective listener and communicator in business.

1. You are aware that listening is an attitude that shows genuine interest in other people.

2. You put aside, as much as possible, your preconceived biases or attitudes toward any matter before forming an opinion.

3. You really are a good listener. Often a person develops the habit of appearing to be a good listener in order to give others assurance.

4. You avoid becoming uninterested in a subject that you consider dull. While the speaker or correspondent may be tedious, subjects themselves are not uninteresting. Separate the subject from a boring approach.

5. You avoid distractions and becoming sidetracked. Concentrate, anticipate, and summarize to understand the motives and purposes of the speaker or writer.

6. You refrain from spending your time composing rebuttals; you listen carefully for ideas.

7. You react unemotionally to words or phrases you do not prefer.

8. You avoid *shaping* what you are hearing—listening only to the part of the message with which you agree.

9. You avoid deciding that a message is irrelevant to your needs.

Are you listening or are you just waiting for your chance to speak?—R. W. Sims

Misunderstanding is caused by listening barriers.

Listen helpfully in oral or written communication.

Instead, you find the connection between your communicator's message and your interest.

10. You avoid note-taking as a crutch. Unless you can take short-hand rapidly, you will fall behind. You can think more quickly than a speaker can talk, but you cannot write everything a speaker says. says.

11. You listen carefully, instead, and jot down the main points and purposes of the communication.

12. You stay alert while listening, especially during important conferences or interviews. Listening causes fatigue and consumes energy. Avoid divided interest that tires you.

Decide on what you are listening for in your communicator's oral or written message. The following checklist may help you analyze the message.

Use your checklist to analyze your communicator's oral or written message.

1. Why is the person communicating with you?

2. What is your communicator's purpose?

3. What does this person expect you to understand?

4. How can you weigh the details the communicator is presenting?

5. How prejudiced or biased is your communicator?

6. How opinionated or self-interested is your communicator?

7. What sincere interest does your communicator have in relating this message to you?

As you know, you cannot analyze a message merely by checking the qualifications of a correspondent. You must also check your feelings toward the contents of the communication carefully. To check your feelings, you might ask yourself the following questions:

Check your feelings about the message.

1. Do you understand the language of the message?

2. Does the message contain material you already know, share, or can discuss?

3. Can you read between the lines and know what subjects or ideas the language symbols stand for as used by the correspondent?

4. Does the message have merit even though you feel differently about the point of view expressed?

5. Are you really absorbing the content of the message? Are you really listening to the facts, details, and opinions?

Like most people, you as a business communicator usually find listening to persons you admire talk about subjects that interest you relatively easy. You also enjoy listening to ideas in which you believe. Conversely, distractions, attitudes, ego-involvement, and lack of interest are barriers to listening skills. Oral or written listening ability requires concentration on new information as well as on familiar topics. Good listening can be a developed skill even regarding messages that do not interest, involve, or concern you or complex subjects about which you know or understand little.

You may find that you listen more thoughtfully to one person who speaks or writes than you do to another. Why do you respect what this person implies or says? Your perceptive powers and your evaluation of the person affect your willingness to listen, to accept, and to retain information. These impressions come from a combination of clues—verbal or written—even voice or body language or behavior. Consequently, creditability—your judgment of the character and knowledge of your communicator—sets the stage for the listening you do.

Empathy, putting yourself in the other person's shoes, also helps you as you listen to the verbal and nonverbal messages sent by your receivers. Empathic listening allows you to sense how your communicator wishes to be heard. This type of listening helps to keep the channels of communication open between you and the other person. Remember that person may also be asking you to hear what she or he is *not* saying.

Nevertheless, listening is a responsibility that requires significant discipline, both mental and physical. You must participate willingly and actively; you must listen well, consider the message, extract the meaning, and decide on the appropriate action. As a good listener, you are more than a passive bystander waiting for something to happen. You are poised and ready to be involved as well as to provide effective verbal or written feedback.

Your goal is to use your listening skills, whether oral or written, to improve your communications through observation, reading, and perception. If you listen carefully, learning will be easier. You learn to communicate with your receiver by listening to the thoughts or actions expressed or implied. After listening, use feedback to complete your communication process. Emerson has said: "A friend is a person with whom I may be sincere. Before him I may think aloud."

Check your listening skills.

Using Your Feedback Skills

Observing, reading, writing, and listening are all parts of the perception process. However, the feedback you receive as you try to meet your goals makes you feel inadequate or secure. Your perception influences the way you receive feedback. For example, if you feel a threat to your self-image, you may put on a false front to guard against revealing what you really think and feel. You may not respond honestly.

However, feedback is an especially important communication tool. You obtain verbal or written feedback from your peers, subordinates, or superiors as you observe, read, write, and listen carefully. Feedback establishes the understanding necessary for perception between you and your communicators.

Feedback is easier to detect when you are talking to someone. In this case, you can observe the person's reactions as you listen and respond, give and receive opinions. Through oral feedback, you can vary your responses according to those of the persons with whom you are communicating and keep the communication channels open.

Written feedback is more difficult to evaluate. For example, you cannot see the reaction of the person who opens your letter; you are unaware of the situation under which your communication is received. You are unsure how your reader is perceiving your message; you are uncertain what is being read into your message. However, through your perception and your ability to create a climate for positive feedback, you can attempt to use a positive and reinforcing tone in writing a communication that you would like to receive.

Again, use empathy to see the other person's point of view and respond sensitively in your communication. Find common bonds of interest and recognize the relationship between you and your reader.

Empathy reduces negative feedback.

Listen to the written communications you receive. Be sure you check the communications for understanding before replying. Answer completely, following the principles of effective communication. Give your reader the chance to make interpretations, choices, and decisions from your communication.

Ideally, the feedback you receive will always be positive. However, as an efficient communicator, you should use negative feedback to help you achieve your goals. For example, your correspondent may imply that you are stupid or lack intelligence. These implications may make you angry; but, as an expert noticer and master of perception, you must keep the communication channels open in order to minimize hard feelings and to promote goodwill.

Negative feedback may help you reach your goal.

You may improve interpersonal feedback—a delicate and complex activity. Your relationship with others grows stronger as you learn to receive and integrate positive feedback into your communications.

Interpersonal communication simulates images in the minds of others.

To obtain positive feedback, train your senses to observe accurately. Accurate observation helps you overcome external and internal barriers erected by the people with whom you work. Then you are ready to accept feedback honestly *before* you ask others for criticism or evaluation.

As a communicator, you realize that some of the feedback you receive will be of little assistance. However, most feedback will help you learn more about your abilities and the effects of your communications. You need feedback to train your senses to observe. Feedback assists you in increasing your reading level and writing more readably. Feedback allows you to overcome communication barriers and to prepare yourself to accept an honest evaluation of what you are doing.

Your most important perception tool is feedback—the response to communication messages. If there is no response, there is no message. Feedback permits you to understand how effectively you are communicating. It enables you to check your writing for content, understanding, empathy, integrity, and clarity. Then you can communicate for tomorrow as well as for today through your effective observation skills.

Organization and Interpretation Skills

You integrate your skills of observation, reading, writing, listening, and feedback with all the sensations you have stored from your previous education and experience. Now you select, analyze, identify, and synthesize the information you have gained through perception.

When you organize this information for interpretation, you should consider that perception and interpretation vary greatly from person to person. Therefore, the information requires careful organization so your interpretation will be meaningful and accurate. Fallacies, errors in reasoning, or improper use of logic can greatly modify or even destroy the effectiveness of the information you have collected through your skills of perception.

Before you write your correspondence, observe and organize the information carefully. Information may be organized through *analysis* or *deduction* and through *synthesis* or *induction*. Both processes—analysis and synthesis—are helpful skills in organizing and interpreting information.

Organize your information carefully.

Analyzing Your Data—Deduction

When you analyze the information you have, you break down your material into the smallest units. You identify the parts. Analysis helps you decide what facts you should include to support your explicit statements.

In analysis, you use the process of deduction. For example, through your perception skills, you know that the ABC Branch of your company is not making profits comparable to those of the FGH, STU, or XYZ Branches. You verify that this statement is correct. Using the deductive process, you make a general statement, then support it with specific details. Using a deductive approach, your communication could begin something like this:

Use careful analysis for deduction.

Dear ABC Branch:

Your branch office must make an intensive effort to increase productivity because during the fiscal year 1979–80, your net profits were less than those of our other branch offices. For example, FGH Branch showed a net profit of $220,000; STU Branch, $210,000; and XYZ Branch, $190,000. Your profit was only $170,000.

If your analysis shows that your conclusion cannot be supported and is largely based on ideas and feeling, rather than on facts, it will be unacceptable.

Synthesizing Your Data—Induction

To synthesize your data, you use the same ideas and facts and combine them into an effective communication that conveys the same message to the ABC Branch. But the arrangement is different.

Induction organizes the items or facts beginning with particular examples that lead to the generalization. When you synthesize, you gather many pieces of data or information and draw your conclusion. You arrange the information to begin with the specific details, then make the generalization. Using an inductive approach, your letter could begin something like this:

Dear ABC Branch:

During the fiscal year 1979—80, the following net profits were reported by our branch offices: ABC Branch had $170,000; FGH Branch, $220,000; STU Branch, $210,000; and XYZ Branch, $190,000. Therefore, I conclude that the ABC Branch needs to make an intense effort to work for additional productivity.

Checking Your Data

Whether you use the inductive or synthesizing process or the deductive or analyzing process, check your data once more before you begin organizing or interpreting. Here are some specific checking techniques:

1. Use more than one of your senses to evaluate the information you have gathered.

2. Review the information and your conclusion from the point of view of other people who might be involved.

3. Compare your conclusion with the conclusion other people might reach. Does the information support your conclusion?

4. Empathize. Put yourself into the position of the person to whom you will communicate the information and your conclusion. What information would you like to have?

5. Ask questions of all persons involved with the information and your conclusion. Listen, read, and observe their answers carefully.

6. Review and clarify any feedback you receive from the preceding techniques.

When you have done this, apply the information you have to your communication through perception, organization, and interpretation.

Human-Relations Skills

Human relations are closely allied with cooperation and courtesy. Your reader is a person of individual dignity and worth. Effective human relations ensures that your message will be understandable and acceptable—one you would appreciate receiving.

The *six* most important words: "I admit I made the mistake."
The *five* most important words: "You did a good job."
The *four* most important words: "What is your opinion?"
The *three* most important words: "If you please."
The *two* most important words: "Thank you."
The *one* most important word: "We."
The *least* important word: "I."[7]

Words can help you as you strive toward effective human relations in communication. They can portray tenderness or harshness. They can be torturous, thought-provoking, demanding, meaningful, confusing, or fresh and positive. Language is an essential asset of culture; only mankind uses words. Your skillful word choice will help you achieve effective human relations.

Words are an essential part of our culture.

Positive Tone

Positive tone, combined with effective human relations, helps to keep your reader's goodwill when you are replying to a request. Saying "yes" is an *art.* Saying "no," while maintaining goodwill, is a *skill.* Strangely enough, some writers are not able to say "yes" graciously and courteously. These communicators make their readers feel obligated, guilty, or even unintelligent for making a request that is granted.

Saying ''yes'' is an art; saying ''no'' is a skill.

Other people, however, can say "no" in such a way that the reader will not have negative feelings. In writing, you can easily be positive in tone when you are responding favorably or saying "yes" to a request. By avoiding negative words, you can usually keep a positive tone even though you must decline or answer "no" to a request.

For a positive tone, avoid words like *complaints.* Today, we seldom hear of a complaint department. Adjustment, customer-relations, and customer-service departments are names now being used to identify those who handle customer dissatisfaction.

Similarly, avoid phrases like "don't hesitate to call" when you can say "please call." If your customer or correspondent is in error, and you plan to adjust the complaint favorably, disregard the mistake or complaint. Instead, indicate positive action by statements such as "as soon as we hear from you concerning the width of the shoes, we shall ship your order to you immediately." Your reader, without a direct statement, will know that the size was omitted!

[7] Anonymous.

Most people prefer words such as *advantage, agree, beauty, opportunity, truth, understanding, success, cooperation,* and *generosity.* Conversely, people usually dislike words such as *disadvantage, disagree, ugly, uncertainty, untruth, misunderstanding, defeat, refusal,* and *selfishness.* Therefore, through your choice of words, you can make the tone of your letter an effective part of your business communication to build goodwill.

Choose your words carefully for effective human relations.

Basic rules that may help you as a communicator to achieve the correct tone are:

1. Answer your communicator immediately; use timeliness as your goal.

2. Use the "you-attitude"; focus the reader's attention on favorable points.

3. Use empathy; write the kind of letter you would like to receive.

4. Use talk words. Use the same natural language you would use when speaking to your reader. Use technical words when writing to the engineer; use simpler words when writing to the consumer. Be yourself as you meet your reader's needs.

5. Make your communication sound like a personal message even though you are writing a form letter to thousands of people. Write to the person, not to the list.

6. Use a positive tone; eliminate all negative elements. Make your communication sound like *good news* by telling your reader what you *can* do.

These principles of effective human relations and positive tone keep your reader's goodwill. Again, goodwill is more difficult to maintain when you decline a request than when you grant one. A reader who is disappointed by a negative answer is doubly sensitive to the tone of your letter. Therefore, avoid any trace of curtness or negative implications that might produce illwill for you or your firm.

''Against company policy'' is not always an effective reason for refusal.

In answering a refusal letter, avoid statements like "surely you must know better." Also, avoid using company policy as a reason for refusal. Statements such as "this is against company policy" sometimes sound phony and offer little explanation to your reader.

Apologizing for every "no" decision may convey the feeling that you or your company is being unfair. Therefore, avoid repeating statements such as "we are extremely sorry to tell you." Substitute positive words for negative words like *we can* for *cannot, we are able* for *unable,* or *we can do this for you* for *impossible.* Use effective human relations when saying "no" by saying "yes" to something else.

Consider the sign blocking the sidewalk at a construction site that states: "Please let us share this sidewalk with you. The inconvenience is temporary; the progress will be permanent." Another illustration of positive tone is found comparing the signs in front of two stores that make keys. The sign on one reads, "keys made while you *wait*." The other sign reads, "keys made while you *watch*." These two stores, separated by only a few blocks, are miles apart in conveying a positive tone.

The tone of your communication may be compared to the flavor of coffee. You know that the right flavor makes a cup of coffee good—even great! However, you probably cannot really explain or describe the flavor of coffee. To define or describe appropriate tone for a letter is just as complicated!

Yet, you know that readers are more cooperative when letters are courteous, friendly, helpful, and honest. You also know that you resent a communication with a negative tone, but you are glad to receive another message with a positive tone. The tone of your letter must be "brewed in" just as the flavor of coffee is.

To "brew in" good letter tone, include a little bit of the company, a little bit of yourself, and a *great deal* of courtesy and consideration in communicating with your readers. Then, you will realize and recognize the goodwill that you and your company achieve through a positive tone, timeliness, empathy, and the "you-attitude."

"Brew in" positive tone.

Goodwill

Goodwill is good business—good business for your organization or outside your company. Effective human relations and positive tone help you achieve goodwill.

Goodwill is good business!

Goodwill in business extends beyond kind feelings and harmonious relationships. For example, goodwill may be an experience, a commodity, a personal asset, a professional asset, an intangible asset, a psychological asset, and an empathic attitude—that of "othering" yourself. In other words, goodwill creates a successful business relationship between you and the receiver of your message.

Goodwill as an experience includes your observation and participation in efforts to work with other people. Goodwill as a commodity is the confidence and loyalty given for satisfaction with the personnel and products of the firms with which you deal.

Goodwill as a commodity extends to the feeling of those who deal with you. In fact, according to a famous court decision: "Goodwill is a decision of the customer to return to the place where he has been well served." In your writing, you as the communicator must ensure this decision through your written message that should be effective in language and tone, in what you say, and in the manner you portray yourself to your reader.

Goodwill is a personal feeling that portrays you as someone possessing empathy and good human relations. Your professional attitude ensures goodwill through your ethical and interested feelings toward your readers or customers.

On a balance sheet, goodwill is listed as an intangible asset. Although intangible, goodwill is real because this quality affects you personally and professionally as you meet your goals of an effective communicator.

Furthermore, goodwill has psychological and ethical aspects that affect human behavior. The psychological aspects of goodwill involve people's reactions in behavioral situations. The ethical aspects of goodwill encompass the ways in which people should act in certain situations.

You as an effective communicator need to be ethical concerning the necessity or obligation to fulfill your personal goals, to advance your career, and to add to the prosperity of your company. Self-preservation will usually be your first goal.

If you can achieve fulfillment and communicate the psychological idea that you are willing and able to help others, you will convey goodwill effectively. Avoid becoming a "pseudo goodwiller," a person who is well intentioned, who talks about what can be done but rarely provides the assistance that is promised. As a psychological and ethical user, goodwill is a blending of ideas and emotions communicated through effective human relations by appropriate words and a positive tone.

Ensure Timeliness

Communicate on time for good-will.

When you are courteous and considerate of your reader, you time your communications so they are originated or received within certain time limits. Timely communications project empathy and ensure the "you-attitude" that shows your reader that you are interested in the communication. Let others be late. Your communications should be written as soon as possible while the facts are fresh in your mind—especially if you are originating the communication.

Incoming communications to be most effective should be answered the same day. All communications should be answered within two days, either through positive action or an interim acknowledgement. If you are unable to answer fully the questions of the letter writer, compose an interim communication—a "meanwhile message"—that acknowledges the correspondence. This communication will tell the writer when to expect positive action or specific information. Goodwill, sales, customers, and clients are often lost because of slowness in acknowledging communications.

Use Empathy

Just as you practice timeliness to ensure the effectiveness of your correspondence, you are empathic, you relate your feelings to those of the people with whom you communicate. You enter the world of others in order to understand their needs. Empathy—the ability to see from the other person's point of view—helps to reduce defensive feedback and to ensure the "you-attitude" and considerate actions.

Empathy relates to the "you-attitude" of consideration.

To have this "you-attitude," you must live it, you must believe it, and you must feel it. The "you-attitude" is real and comes from inner feelings. Empathy and the "you-attitude" help you to concentrate less on your own personal goals and more on those of others.

In the spirit of empathy, build your letters and memos around your reader's point of view, not your own. The use of the words *you* and *your* instead of *I, me, our,* or *we* will assist you in this respect. However, these words are only helpful. These special goodwill qualities are based on your ability to identify yourself emotionally and intellectually with other persons and their emotions.

Repeating the Sioux Indian prayer: "Never judge another until you have walked two weeks in his mocassins." Put yourself in the other person's shoes before you write a communication. Write the kind of letter you would like to receive.

Social-Business Correspondence

Many communications have the promotion of goodwill as their chief function. Sometimes, they are classified as social-business correspondence. Although the chief purpose of these communications may be goodwill, they are often used as low-powered promotional or sales devices.

Congratulatory letters, thank-you notes, and condolence messages are a few communications that could be classified as social-business correspondence. Welcome messages, invitations, announcements, and a host of others also fall in this category of goodwill messages that necessitate written or spoken responses immediately.

Use every opportunity to send special goodwill messages.

As an alert executive, you recognize that your organization and you will profit from your using these special goodwill opportunities. For example, if you notice a picture or an article in a newspaper, magazine, or other publication that would interest someone you know, you should certainly write a goodwill message. You can merely attach the picture or article to your letterhead with a personal note.

Not using opportunities to express goodwill can injure the sensitive, personal feelings of people with whom you work and your customers or clients. Similarly, goodwill messages can inspire mutual respect and consideration even in competitors.

These special goodwill messages require the same prompt action and timeliness as other communications. Positive tone and the use of the "you-attitude" will also help you to achieve effective human relations in writing goodwill letters.

Here are a few examples of some of the types of goodwill letters you may need to write. These letters and others are discussed further and illustrated in Chapter 8. Remember, goodwill is good business!

Congratulatory Letters

Congratulatory messages are often combinations of personal and business goodwill.

To help obtain and maintain goodwill, you express congratulations when someone receives an award, a promotion, or some other honor. These messages are also appreciated by the person who wins an election, receives an appointment, or celebrates an anniversary, a wedding, or the birth of a child. You may feel these occasions are more social in nature. However, written communications at these times are actually combined expressions of personal and business goodwill.

When you write or compose these messages, strive for naturalness, enthusiasm, and sincerity. Avoid reducing the recipient's pleasure by suggesting or implying that you are using a happy occasion as an entering wedge for a business contact or an invitation. In other words, your letter of congratulations should stand alone and be written only to commend the person for a successful achievement.

The following is an example of a congratulatory letter:

Dear Mr. Barbour:

In yesterday's evening paper, I read that your fund campaign for the Kappa Sigma fraternity house has exceeded the goal! Your hard work in planning and working with the fund-raising drive has made possible a splendid forward effort for the Kappa Sigma fraternity in Lake Charles. Especially inspiring to us is the fact that you are the *oldest*—while yet *youngest*—member of Kappa Sigma in the United States.

I join with other members of the university and the community in congratulating you on your job well done as leader in the fund drive and as the young-at-heart member of your great organization.

Enclosed is the picture that was in last night's paper. I know you will cherish these remembrances. We have enjoyed seeing you and your wife work for the many causes in which you believe. Sincerely,

This type of social-business letter is important to you and your organization in establishing goodwill.

Appreciation Letters

Letters of appreciation—sometimes more *business* and oftentimes more *social* in nature—are goodwill messages. Many letters of appreciation are routine and are sent regularly by you and your office. Whether you are writing a specific thank-you note or a form letter from your organization, you should express appreciation sincerely, simply, and concisely.

Appreciation letters help to promote business and social goodwill.

Welcome Letters

Greeting a new employee of your organization or company is a good opportunity to establish friendly and profitable associations. You show your goodwill by communicating your pleasure on the person's affiliation.

The recipient of your welcome note is generally grateful for your hospitality and friendship when you help to eliminate his or her first feelings of loneliness. As an executive, you will want to be sure you assist the new employees in your firm. You might want to write a letter similar to this one to welcome a new employee.

Welcome letters build personal and professional goodwill.

Dear Miss Jackson

We are happy to know you, happy to have you with us, and welcome you to our organization! All of us at the XYZ Manufacturing Company greet you.

Our company's success depends upon you and your co-workers. Many of our policies are explained in the enclosed pamphlet.

Should you have additional questions, ask us so we may keep you informed.

You have our confidence in your ability, Miss Jackson, and our pledge of cooperation in exchange for your help, your efforts, and your loyalty. We are very happy that you have chosen to be with us.

Sincerely

Jim Jordan
Personnel Manager

Welcome messages can create goodwill and provide a low-pressure sales promotion to a newcomer to your community. However, your message of greeting is primary; otherwise, your letter may sound insincere. This is an example of a welcome message including a secondary sales promotion.

Dear Mr. Sherman:
Welcome to Springfield! We are happy to have you here. While you are getting settled, you may find the enclosed map of our city helpful. If you have a particular question, just telephone our office: 323-7072. We may be able to supply the information you need.

Also enclosed is a courtesy card from our store. We will be happy to give you a 20 percent discount on your first purchase — just in time for the spring sales. But most of all, we want to say welcome to you and your family.

Sincerely,

Henry Thomas
Sales Manager

These two forms of welcome messages open doors for new persons in the community who may use your firm for business purposes and for new employees who are beginning a different career or life-style. Welcome letters build personal, professional, and business goodwill. Goodwill is good business!

Invitations

Both executives and administrative assistants should understand matters of etiquette such as extending and answering invitations. You should study them and know how to handle all invitations — formal and informal — correctly.

A cordial invitation is a social-business message.

Extending An Invitation
When you extend a formal invitation, you will want to make sure you follow the rules of etiquette concerning formal invitations.

Printed or engraved cards are often used for these messages. Formal invitations are generally worded:

Mr. and Mrs. Thomas Ryan
request the pleasure of
Miss Toni Waters'
company at dinner in honor of
their silver anniversary
on Friday, the seventh of June,
at seven o'clock
Pelican Club

Be sure to include all the necessary details in your invitation. Your job is easier because most formal invitations follow a similar style, although the trend is toward simplification.

In many cases, informal invitations are handwritten.[8] However, there is a trend toward typing social-business and informal invitations to business associates. These invitations differ in length with the information that needs to be included and the circumstances that prompt the invitation. Sometimes, informal invitations contain only one or two sentences. The plan that follows may help you ensure that all necessary information is included.

1. Picture your invitation. Include who, why, when, where, and what.
2. Give any desirable explanatory information.
3. Request a favorable action and acceptance.
4. Add any other appropriate statement.
5. Ask for a reply.

Asking for a reply is vital. Informal invitations may include R.S.V.P. (which asks that guests respond whether or not they plan to accept the invitation). The number of guests who will attend is especially important and determines the amount of food, drink, or space that must be provided. In issuing formal invitations, too, you also need to know how many people to expect.

Another trend in invitations is to use the expression "Regrets only." When you use this, you consider all those who do not respond to your invitation as acceptances. Sometimes, "regrets only" is more risky than R.S.V.P. To ensure goodwill, you are careful to respond promptly to an invitation. The recipient who does not plan to accept the invitation and forgets to respond to the "regrets only" request will be embarrassed, and the person who extends the invitation may be disturbed by the violation of the rules of etiquette.

[8] The U.S. Postal Service no longer accepts envelopes smaller than $3\frac{1}{2} \times 5$ inches in size.

When you accept an invitation, you express goodwill by your promptness and courtesy. Acceptances of formal invitations should be handwritten in the same style and person as the invitation. The following illustrates a formal acceptance:

Accept an invitation in the same person and style in which it was extended.

> *Miss Toni Waters*
> *accepts with pleasure*
> *Mr. and Mrs. Ryan's*
> *kind invitation for dinner*
> *on Friday, the seventh of June,*
> *at seven o'clock.*

Typewritten replies may be made if the invitations are less formal or are typewritten. The plan that follows may be useful in accepting informal invitations.

1. State your acceptance of the invitation first.
2. Repeat your understanding of the invitation by stating the exact date, time, and place.
3. Add any other appropriate or courteous comments.
4. Close with an expression of appreciation.

When you are answering an informal invitation, use the tone, style, and person in which the invitation was issued just as you did in accepting the formal invitation. The following serves as an example of an informal acceptance:

We are happy to accept your invitation for dinner next Friday evening, September 28, 7:00, at the Western Country Club. We are looking forward to being with you. Discussing the coming events of the Ballet Society will be most interesting.

Thank you for inviting us to dinner.

Sincerely,

Declining an Invitation

If you cannot accept an invitation, decline promptly and courteously. Just as in accepting an invitation, you will decline a formal one in the same style and person in which the invitation was extended. A handwritten note of regret is illustrated. The reason in the third line of this example may be omitted.

Miss Toni Waters
regrets exceedingly that,
because of a previous engagement,
she is unable to accept
Mr. and Mrs. Ryan's
kind invitation for dinner,
on Friday,
the seventh of June.

The following typewritten letter effectively declines an invitation:

Dear Ms. Sassoon:

Thank you for inviting me to the dinner held by the National Secretaries Association, International, on December 12, at 7:30, at the Hilton Hotel to install the officers. I wish it were possible for me to attend. However, a special committee meeting has been called to which I have been invited by Dr. Thomas S. Bryan, president of Colorado State University. The date and time of this special meeting conflict with the NSA installation dinner.

Please accept my appreciation for the invitation. I hope that you will call upon me again as I always enjoy being with you.

Sincerely,

As an executive you know all R.S.V.P. invitations must be answered whether or not they are accepted. These special messages involve personal feelings.

All R.S.V.P. messages must be answered.

Other Goodwill Messages

Numerous other correspondence is included in goodwill and human-relations messages. These personal-business letters written on an appropriate occasion can make your job more rewarding for you and everyone else. You may express condolences or show appreciation for a favor, a gift, or a special service. Other personal-business correspondence may involve congratulations on an anniversary, the birth of a new baby, or a birthday. Some of these other goodwill messages will be discussed in Chapter 8.

The main thing to remember is that business letters become personal, and personal letters become business when they are exchanged between you and your business friends, whether or not the letters pertain to business transactions.

Summary

When you as a communicator use the principles of clarity, completeness, conciseness, correctness, concreteness, consideration, and courtesy, a positive tone, sound human relations, and goodwill, your messages will be more effective. Before you begin to write, perceive your message through your skills of observation, reading, listening, and feedback. Organize and interpret this information applying the facts, then compose the various types of business communications that will aid you in becoming an effective business communicator through successful use of well-chosen words.

Questions for Discussion

1. Define and discuss the use of perception, organization, interpretation, and application in communications.

2. List and explain the steps in perception. Include observation, reading, writing, listening, and feedback skills. How can you use these skills as you become an effective communicator?

3. What are the two worlds of perception? Compare reality and symbolism.

4. How is observation important in the communication process? Give examples of observational fallacies.

5. Define selective observation. How does an effective communicator use or misuse selective observation? Give examples.

6. Define and explain the skills or aspects of reading and writing for effective communication. How can each be misused?

7. What is readability? Why is it important in business communications?

8. What are the three steps in determining the Gunning Fog Index for readability? How is this index useful to business writers?

9. Name and describe at least one other readability index. Show how this index can help you as a business executive.

10. List five barriers or deterrents to effective listening, including physical, psychological, and emotional barriers. How can each one be overcome?

11. How can you use the difference in a person's speaking and listening rate to your advantage in communication? Explain in detail.

12. List four poor listening skills. Which ones particularly apply to you?

13. Define feedback. Show how effective feedback can be used as a communication tool.

14. Differentiate between verbal and nonverbal feedback.

15. Show how the skills of observation, reading, listening, and feedback relate to the organization and interpretation of your communication.

16. Explain analysis as a deductive process in composing your communication. Give an example of the deductive process.

17. Show the use of synthesis as an inductive process in developing your communication. Give an example of the inductive process.

18. List at least four steps you should take in checking your information before organizing and interpreting your data.

19. Is human relations important in effective communications? Why?

20. Explain the art of saying ''yes'' in effective human relations. Explain the skill of saying ''no.''

21. List at least four rules that may help you achieve a positive tone.

22. Discuss in detail the purposes of goodwill as good business. List the various psychological, ethical, and business aspects of goodwill that affect human behavior.

23. How do timeliness, empathy, and the ''you-attitude'' affect goodwill?

24. List three occasions when special goodwill messages will promote friendship as well as business.

25. Explain how congratulatory letters help develop goodwill. What are the primary aspects of these messages?

26. Show how an appreciative letter may establish goodwill. Give two examples of when these letters could be used.

27. Why are the various welcome letters goodwill ambassadors? How can they be used for low-keyed sales promotions?

28. Differentiate between formal and informal invitations. Show how each type should be extended and answered.

Exercises

1. Using the seven signposts in the previous chapter, write several paragraphs about one of your experiences in the business world either as an employee or as a consumer.

2. List the names of the members of your class whom you knew at the beginning of the semester or quarter. Add the names of those persons you have met since the first class period. Since your skills in observation and perception are involved in this activity, make an effort to learn all names by the last class period.

3. Design an illustration that can be interpreted two ways, depending on a person's sense of perception and / or observation.

4. Choose a cartoon you find difficult to understand or one that can be interpreted in several ways. Redesign or recaption this cartoon.

5. Find an article in a business magazine. Choose several paragraphs, each approximately 100—125 words. Use the Gunning Fog Index to determine the difficulty of the reading matter or the readability level. Submit your findings and a copy of the paragraphs to your instructor.

6. Choose several paragraphs that you have written (exercise 1 would be acceptable). Use the Gunning Fog Index to determine the readability level.

7. Write a series of ten job-related instructions that might be given to a new employee. For example, our working hours are nine o'clock to five o'clock. Choose a partner who will play the role of the new employee. Read your instructions clearly and slowly to your partner. Question your partner about the directions you gave. Rewrite them if they were not clear. Then, reverse roles.

8. Read a business letter you have received. List the gist or main purpose of the message and any secondary purposes. Write an analysis of your reading habits. What did you do best? What could you improve? Concentrate on listening for written feedback.

9. Write a paragraph about the effective use of feedback in communication. Develop this paragraph through the deductive approach.

10. Write a paragraph about the importance of perception in communication. Develop this paragraph inductively.

11. Write a short letter accepting a request to attend a meeting of Phi Chi Theta. Use human relations to express the art of saying ''yes.''

12. Write a short letter refusing a request to attend a business conference of Delta Sigma Pi. Use positive tone to demonstrate your skill in saying ''no.''

13. Choose a paragraph in a business letter that you find difficult to understand. Use talk words to rewrite it.

14. Write a message accepting a formal invitation to the Accounting Society's Spring Banquet to be held Friday, February 1, 19— at 8:00 P.M.

15. Write a letter of thanks, of congratulation, or of appreciation. If possible, use a real situation so you can actually mail your letter.

Part Three   Your Role in Shaping
Business Communications

Chapter 5   Formats of Communications

"Letters which are warmly sealed are often but coldly opened."
— Richter

The Importance of Appearance

Perhaps the most important form of communication in your future
in the business world is the written message. The written message
can be quite influential in forming the image you wish to present of
yourself and your business. Both the words used and the medium
by which a message is conveyed are important. The receiver of your
communication is consciously or unconsciously affected by neatness, letter style, and even the color, shape, size, and quality of
paper that you use. Your reader quickly sorts out all this information that your letter communicates and makes a value judgment
about its appropriateness for conveying your message.

    If your letter contains a vast amount of data, as a sales contract
might, your reader has preconceived ideas of appropriate forms and
words that he or she expects you to use. Messages of this sort are
not expected to involve the emotions.

    If you are advertising a product, your reader expects her or his
emotions to be involved. In this case, your message can be quite
creative in its content and packaging in order to stimulate interest.
Of course, an appropriate format and letterhead are essential. The
letterheads for a construction company and for a ladies boutique
are designed to convey different images.

    This chapter will guide you in selecting stationery and formats
appropriate for the various kinds of messages you will be sending.
By following these suggestions, your messages will be warmly received.

Messages are symbols.

Paper

Your stationery should be selected to reflect the quality of your business. You will want to use bond paper with 20 to 25 percent rag content in a sixteen or twenty pound weight for letter-writing purposes. The paper should contain a *watermark,* a translucent marking showing the brand name or trade number of the company that produced the paper. To type on the right side of the paper, place it in the typewriter so you can read the watermark. Corrections can be made easier on corrasable or erasable bond, which has been treated with a coating that prevents the typewriter impression from being permanent when first typed. However, the typing smudges more easily than on an untreated bond.

If you are preparing rough drafts or forms, sulphite paper is less expensive. Because it will not be mailed, a lower-quality paper can be used. Always consider the purpose of your message, and select the proper stationery for the occasion. Second sheets should be the same quality and color as the letterhead. However, because letterheads are more expensive than plain bond paper, use letterheads only for the first page. Copies for your files should either be made on a copy machine or on a lighter-weight paper, such as onionskin.

Color

Although white paper is used most frequently in the office, color can be most attractive and effective in some instances. Soft, light colors can add to the appearance of your message if used appropriately. For example, a garden center or nursery might use a light green for effect. Bold, bright colors are seldom used as they distract from the message. Sales letters, however, are an exception as better results have been realized when colored paper was used. The color itself can capture the reader's attention. Care should be taken when deciding upon a color. When in doubt, use white paper, which is always in good taste. Envelopes should match the paper in quality and color.

Different colors of paper are used most frequently for brief, informal messages or interoffice forms. Figure 5–1 illustrates one style of preprinted form for a short message. When used for interoffice forms, different colors make distribution throughout an office easier. For example, the yellow copy could be sent to the purchasing department, the blue copy to the accounting department, and the buff copy retained for your files.

Figure 5—1
A preprinted, short-message form. The second copy (yellow) is kept by the initiator, the third copy (pink) is used for the reply.

© by Day-Timers and used with their permission.

Size

Most companies use 8½ by 11 inch paper for their letters, memorandums, and reports. Some executives prefer the Monarch size, 7¼ by 10½ inches, for personal use. A major disadvantage of this size is that the original or file copy can be misplaced in the files. Another disadvantage is that special envelopes need to be purchased for the Monarch-sized stationery. All branches of the U.S. government use 8 by 10½ inch paper.

Letters

Some companies have handbooks or guides to follow in planning the arrangement of business letters, memorandums, reports, and forms. However, you will usually decide on the arrangement and organization of your correspondence. You may have the responsibility of selecting a letter style for your company. These styles are illustrated in Figures 5–5, 5–6, and 5–7 in this chapter.

Standard Letter Parts

Seven standard parts of a business letter are required for the modified block style and the block style. The AMS simplified form omits the salutation and the complimentary close.

Letterhead or Heading

Every letter mailed from a company should be written on the company letterhead. The letterhead identifies the company name, address, telephone number, and a cable address, if needed. The type of letterhead used depends on the nature of the business. A conservative organization, such as a bank, would probably use clear lettering and simple, sleek lines in its letterhead (Figure 5–2). An adver-

Figure 5–2
The First National Bank of Chicago's letterhead shows the name of the executive initiating the letter; second sheets are printed. The envelope also carries the logo.

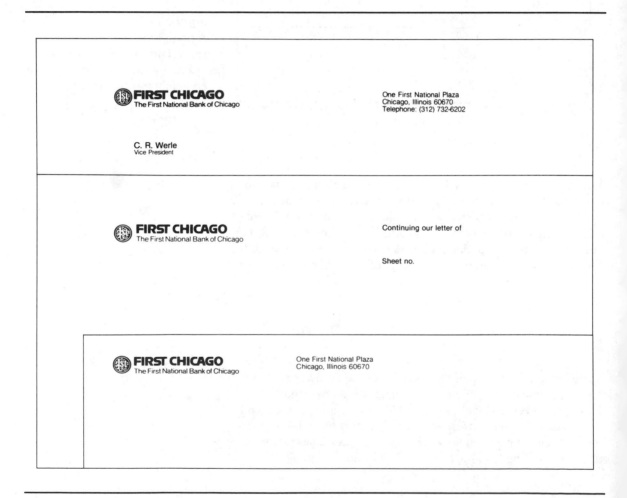

tising agency or fine dress shop might exhibit its creativity with bold colors, larger type, and an unusual design (Figure 5–3). The letterhead or heading should generally not exceed two and a half inches as a deeper letterhead distracts from the message (Figure 5–4).

The letterhead may contain the company logo (trademark) or design. Product pictures can also be used in the letterhead. Many times the names of executives and locations of branch offices are included as part of the letterhead. These names and locations help the reader identify the closest branch and the correct executive to whom correspondence may be sent.

When you type personal letters, use bond paper without a letterhead. Your return address is typed at the top of the page to enable the recipient to reply if necessary. However, do *not* type your name in this heading because it appears in the signature line.

Your letterhead is a symbol of your company.

Figure 5–3
Lord & Taylor uses Monarch-sized paper and puts their return address on the back of the envelope.

835 NORTH MICHIGAN AVENUE, CHICAGO, ILL. 60611

835 NORTH MICHIGAN AVENUE, CHICAGO, ILL. 60611

You should not depend on the return address on your envelope as the envelope could be discarded or become separated from the letter.

Always date your letters.

The current date should be typed on every letter. Use the date the letter was dictated rather than the date it was transcribed if the letter is not transcribed the same day. The date is generally typed in conventional form, February 2, 1982, without abbreviations. In military correspondence and in some foreign countries, the date precedes the month, 12 September 1981 (no commas are used in this style).

Inside Address

The second standard part of a business letter is the inside address. This contains the name of the person to whom the letter is being sent and the complete address with the proper ZIP Code. No one likes his or her name misspelled so be certain you have double-checked the correct spelling. Include an appropriate courtesy title before the name of the addressee (Dr., Mrs., Mr., Ms., Miss). If you know it, use the official position of the person to whom you are writing. The company position can be put in one of three places:

Figure 5—4
This office supply company repeats their name on their envelope in the same style as they use on their letterhead.

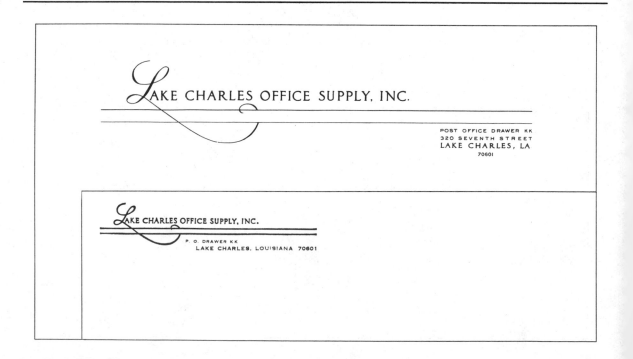

directly after the name, on a separate line, or before the name of the company.

Mr. Eric Smythe, Vice President
ANO Company
1214 Lake Road
Sacramento, CA 95812

Mr. Eric Smythe
Vice President
ANO Company
1214 Lake Road
Sacramento, CA 95812

Mr. Eric Smythe
Vice President, ANO Company
1214 Lake Road
Sacramento, CA 95812

In this example, the best placement would be with the position and company name on separate lines to better balance the inside address. Each line begins at the left margin. If possible, use a maximum of four lines.

Salutation
The salutation is your formal greeting and is typed a double space below the inside address beginning at the left margin. Although the conventional salutation is *Dear* plus the title and name, some organizations are using only the title and name.

Dear Mr. Goings   Mr. Goings

Dear Mrs. Parks   Mrs. Parks

Some business letters could sound hypocritical with *Dear* in the salutation if they are not written in a friendly spirit. Where the letter is not of a friendly nature, the best style to use might be the AMS simplified where the salutation and complimentary close are omitted.

If you have only the company name, not the name of an individual, you may use the salutation *Gentlemen.* This greeting is still acceptable even though some of the "gentlemen" are probably ladies.

Body
Following the salutation comes the heart of your letter, the body or message. It generally starts two spaces below the salutation. Single-spacing should be used, even with short letters. The date line can be

adjusted depending on the length of the letter. The date line may be placed between the twelfth and twentieth line from the top of the page to adjust the body of the letter for better balance. Paragraphs are separated by a double space.

Complimentary Close
Probably the most acceptable closing, which is typed a double space below the body, is *Sincerely.* Other frequently used closings are *Cordially* or *Sincerely yours.* Only the first word in the complimentary close is capitalized. *Yours truly* is rarely used now. Avoid trite wording such as *I remain* or *Your faithful servant.* These closings are antiquated.

Signature Line
Your name should be typed four spaces below the complimentary close to allow your signature to be written in ink above the typed line. The typed line ensures proper spelling of your name. Signing your name indicates that you have read the correspondence and are assuming the responsibility for your letter. If someone else signs your name in your absence, the initials of the person signing or the entire name should be included. You generally do not use a title in your signature line unless you are a woman and wish to let the reader know your marital status. Some women object to the courtesy title Ms. However, unless the woman indicates to the reader that she prefers to be addressed as *Miss* or *Mrs.,* the term *Ms.* is generally used. The title is usually not enclosed in parentheses. Below the signature line, it is customary to show your company position.

Kendall Masters
President

David A. Brown
Treasurer

Mrs. Frances Summers
Vice President

Miss Heather Powers
Secretary to the President

Reference Notation
The typist's initials should be typed two spaces below the signature line. Either capital or lower-case letters may be used. The dictator's

initials, or the entire name, may also be included in the notation especially when the letter is signed by another person.

cs   DAB/cs   dab/cs

DABotzong/cs   DAB:cs   dab:cs

If someone other than the person whose name appears in the signature line dictates the letter, the initials of the dictator should appear in the reference line. In that case, the dictator's initials might be in all capital letters with the typist's initials in lower-case letters.

Sincerely

James Reed

James Reed
President

VKD/cs

Special Notations

As special letter parts are often necessary, you will want to become familiar with when to use them and how to correctly place them in the letter.

Mailing Notations
Instructions for the post office, such as "Special Delivery," may be typed between the date and the inside address.

Attention Line
If you are unable to obtain the name of a specific person in a company or are not sure whether the person is still employed there, use an attention line. Attention lines direct letters to particular departments or people in charge of specific divisions. For example, if you are uncertain who the purchasing agent of a company is, address the message to the company and use an attention line.

ABN Company
Attention: Purchasing Agent
2345 Bentwood Road
Houston, TX 77020

Your letter will be routed to the proper person, and your order will receive prompt attention. Note that the attention line appears a single space below the company name.

Subject Line

Identification of the subject of the message is helpful for both the recipient and the person in charge of filing the correspondence. However, if you are writing a letter in which you must deny a request or give a negative response, avoid using a subject line unless you can state it in a neutral way. For example, if you must deny a request for a pay increase, the subject line could be: "Your request for pay increase." The psychology of beginning a letter in a pleasant manner may be destroyed if the subject line is negative.

When used, the subject appears two spaces below the salutation and two spaces before the body. This line may be centered, begun at the left margin, or indented the same number of spaces as the paragraphs. If you are using the block style or AMS style, begin the subject line at the left margin.

Company Name

The name of the company may also be included in the signature lines. Type the company name, generally in all caps, two spaces below the complimentary close. You rarely need to prove the legality of a letter, but the use of the company name indicates that you are acting as an agent for your organization.

The company name can be used when the letter is short and using the name would better balance the letter.

Sincerely	Cordially yours,
LBMS CORPORATION	BROWN-GOODWILL, INC.
Bennett Reed	*Suzanne Dark*
Bennett Reed	(Mrs.) Suzanne Dark
President	Assistant Buyer

Enclosure Notations

If something is enclosed in a letter, the notation should be typed two spaces below the typist's reference initials and even with the left margin. If you have more than one enclosure, the number of enclosures should be indicated. This notation helps to guard against omitting any enclosures when preparing the letter for mailing.

cs	wm	sj
Enclosure	Enclosures 3	3 enclosures

Copy Notations

You may send copies of your communication to more than one person. Indicate the names of those receiving a copy of your message. This notation appears two spaces below the enclosure notation or two spaces below the reference initials if there is no enclosure. The letters *cc* or *c* may precede the first name. Note that a courtesy title is generally included in the name.

cc Mr. Bill Moore   c: Ms. Phyllis Eason
  Mr. Tom Savoy

Because you keep a copy of every communication you write for your files, no notation is necessary to indicate a file copy. Only use the notation when copies are sent to other people in addition to the person to whom the letter is addressed.

If you do not wish the recipient to know you are sending another person a copy, type *bcc* or *bc* to indicate *blind copy* only on the copy and your file copy. To do this easily, place an index card over the original copy in the proper place for the notation, and type on the card. The notation will not appear on your original letter but will be on the copies.

bcc: Mr. B. J. Kemmerly
    Miss Elizabeth Masters

Many offices use copying machines to make file copies. If your office does not have such a machine, make carbon copies on onion-skin paper.

Postscripts

You might be indicating poor organization if you ended every letter with an afterthought, but postscripts are often used for emphasis. Reminders or personal notes may be added after the body of the letter is completed. The position of the sentence or paragraph indicates an addition. The letters *P.S.* may or may not be used.

cs
Hurry! The coupon is good from June 1 to July 1 only.

cs
P.S. Don't forget our luncheon date after the conference!

Layout

The placement of your letter on the page is extremely important. Your reader notices the layout first. The first impression will be a favorable one if your letter is well balanced on the page. The let-

What are blind copies?

terhead determines the top margin, but the left, right, and bottom margins should be approximately equal to balance your message.

In some offices, standard margins are used to save time. However, the layout is more attractive when side margins are varied according to the length of the letter. Side margins should be at least one inch and not more than two inches. Some companies place the date two spaces below the letterhead and vary the space between the date and inside address. Most companies type the date between the twelfth and the twentieth line from the top of the page and leave three blank lines between the date and inside address.

If your letter is too long to fit attractively on one page, use two or

---

LBMS CORPORATION
305 Contour Drive
East Lansing, MI 48805

517-403-8731

Current Date

SPECIAL DELIVERY

Mr. Mark E. Stanfield
ABC Corporation
2020 Hodges
Lansing, MI 48901

Dear Mr. Stanfield:

    Subject: Modified Block Style Letters

    This is an example of a letter typed in modified block style. Begin the date and closing lines at the center of the page. Paragraphs are indented five spaces in this example, but the paragraphs need not be indented.

    This letter contains all of the seven standard parts of a business letter: a letterhead showing the name and address of the company and the current date, the inside address, the salutation, the body of the letter, the complimentary close, the signature line, and the reference initials of the typist.

    Mixed punctuation is used; a colon follows the salutation, and a comma follows the complimentary close. Notice that the reference initials are typed in small letters against the left margin. The notation for "Special Delivery" falls between the date and the inside address. The subject line appears two lines below the salutation and before the body of the letter.

    The modified block style letter is attractive and is used in most businesses today.

          Sincerely,

          LBMS CORPORATION

          Don Robinson
          Don Robinson
          President

cs

Figure 5—5
A letter typed in modified block style with mixed punctuation.

more pages. The second and subsequent pages should contain a heading placed one inch from the top of the page.

| Mr. Karl Jones | 2 | Current date |

Mr. Karl Jones
Page 2
Current date

The body of the letter starts three lines below this heading. The last page should contain at least two lines of the body of the letter.

In determining where to start the letter on the letterhead page, remember you have to allow for the inside address, using the company name in the signature lines, enclosure notations, copy notations, and postscripts.

Three popular layouts of letters are in common usage and will be illustrated in this chapter: modified block style, block style, and AMS simplified style.

Modified Block Style

Probably the most widely used of the three styles, the modified block style (Figure 5–5) requires slightly more time to set up. Most businesses continue to use the modified block style letter because it is aesthetically pleasing and balanced. Table 5–1 provides a basic guide for positioning the date line and varying the margins to produce an attractive letter format.

The date is begun at the center of the page as are the complimentary close and signature lines. Paragraphs may start at the left margin or be indented, usually five spaces. Punctuation may be either *mixed* (a colon after the salutation and a comma after the complimentary close) or *open* (no punctuation after either the salutation or complimentary close).

Table 5—1
Letter Placement Guide

5-stroke words in letter body	Side margins	Date (lines from top of page)
up to 100	2 inches	20
101-300	1 $\frac{1}{2}$ inches	18—12*
Over 300	1 inch	12
Over 350	1 inch	12 as two-page letter

*Date line is moved up two line spaces for each additional 50 words.

```
                    ULTRA TRANSPORTATION
                       155 East Parkway
                      Clayton, SD 57092
                                                        605-457-9822

         Current Date


         Mr. David A. Powers
         Tri-State Business College
         2020 North Common Street
         Chicago, IL 60609

         Mr. Powers

         Subject:  Block Style Letter

         If efficiency is a major concern in your organization, the block style
         letter will be a favorite for your secretaries.  All lines begin at
         the left margin.

         Open punctuation is used in this letter.  The colon after the
         salutation and the comma after the complimentary close are omitted.
         If you desire, mixed punctuation can be used.  A subject line has been
         used (typed two spaces below the salutation) to identify the contents
         of the letter.  The subject line aids the reader and helps in filing.

         The position of the date line and the width of the margins vary according
         to the length of the letter.  After the date is typed, space four
         times to begin the inside address.  Two spaces follow the body before
         the complimentary close.  Space four times before the signature line
         to allow room for the signature.  The reference initials of the typist
         appear two spaces below the signature line.

         Sincerely

         Celeste B. Stanfield

         Celeste B. Stanfield
         Personnel Director

         tb
```

Figure 5—6

A letter typed in block style with open punctuation.

Block Style

The block style letter has one major advantage over the modified block style in that all lines begin at the left margin (Figure 5–6). Some executives feel that the format is off balance, but the time saved may compensate for the difference. The style is easy for the typist, and the letters have a uniform look.

The position of the date line and the width of the margins vary with the length of the letter. Table 5–1 may also be used as a guide for this style letter. Either mixed or open punctuation may be used. Special notations, such as a subject line, are spaced the same as in the modified block style.

AMS Simplified Style

The AMS simplified style letter uses an extreme block form with open punctuation (Figure 5–7). In order to save time, the Administrative Management Society recommends the omission of the salutation and the complimentary close. A subject line is always used, typed in capital letters, three lines below the inside address. The word *subject* is not used. The body of the letter is started three lines below the subject line. The signature line is also typed in all capital letters at least four lines below the body of the letter.

Most companies that do not use this style feel that recipients of letters written in this style are bothered because it is unfamiliar to them.

WEAVER LOOMS
1526 Cramton Road
Huntley, NE 68946

402-932-7011

Current Date

Mr. Joe Inabnett
Inabnett Enterprises
6162 Main Street
Omaha, NE 68132

AMS SIMPLIFIED STYLE LETTER

This letter is an example of an efficient way to prepare correspondence. The Administrative Management Society has recommended this style of letter to save time. The following steps are followed to set up an AMS simplified letter.

Begin all lines at the left margin.

Omit the salutation and the complimentary close.

Use a subject line typed in all capital letters with three spaces before and after the subject line. The word Subject is not used.

Type the writer's name in all capital letters at least four spaces below the body of the letter.

Place the reference initials two spaces below the writer's name in lower-case letters.

Copy notations and other special notations are typed in their usual position at the left margin. Costs can be lowered and the typist's time saved by using this letter style. With the increased costs of correspondence, the AMS simplified letter may well be used by most companies in the future.

Courtney Robinson

COURTNEY ROBINSON, PERSONNEL MANAGER

db

Figure 5—7
A letter typed in AMS simplified style.

```
1237 Rue Crozat
Baton Rouge, LA 70810
June 20, 1980


Ms. Patricia Nunnery
Ray Jones Travel Agency
2040 Lake Street
Baton Rouge, LA 70808

Dear Ms. Nunnery

Mexico was fabulous!  The food was terrific, the weather was hot but
not humid, and the people were helpful and friendly.  When we arrived,
the agency representative met us at the airport and promptly took us
and our baggage directly to the hotel.

The only problem we had was our time.  Mazatlun is a city with more
places to see than four days would allow.  After discussing
possibilities with the representative, we did almost everything we
wanted to do and always had a car from the agency waiting for us.

Your suggestion for a stay in Mazatlun was terrific.  In December we
have a week's vacation.  Where do your think we should go this time?
Please send brochures for several cities with pleasant weather and, of
course, a seashore.  Thanks for your help with our Mexico trip.

Sincerely


Jayne Allen
```

Figure 5—8
A personal letter typed in block style with open punctuation.

Use plain bond for personal letters.

Personal Business Letters

Occasions will arise when you need to write personal business letters. If the correspondence does not apply to your work, use plain bond paper without a letterhead. For example, you may wish to type a letter applying for another position. Using company stationery would create a poor first impression. Inquiries about personal business should also be typed on plain paper (Figure 5–8).

Your address should be typed at the top of the page directly above the date. The current date is typed in the same position as used for a letter on a letterhead, between the twelfth and twentieth line from the top of the paper. All other parts of the letter are spaced the same as in a business letter. If someone else types your letter, it is appropriate to use a reference notation two spaces below the name.

Interoffice Memorandums

In many business firms today, the use of internal communications rivals the use of external communications in quantity. The business memorandum (memo) is typically the format used most often for internal communication. The memo can flow vertically or horizontally within an organization. Because communication by memo is an integral part of almost all segments of management, business firms expect all managers to communicate effectively and efficiently with memos within an organization.[1]

Company forms that have a printed heading are usually available for memorandums. A printed heading allows the typist to set up the information quickly. If your company does not have these forms, your secretary can create one (Figure 5–9). The memorandum heading should begin on the seventh line from the top of the page and contain the following information:

    TO:
   FROM:
    DATE:
SUBJECT:

Margins are usually one inch on both sides, regardless of the length of the memorandum. Paragraphs are generally not indented. If the memorandum is extremely short (one paragraph), it may be double-spaced. When the memorandum is single-spaced, use an extra line between paragraphs, as in the body of a letter.

If several people are to receive the same memorandum, list the names alphabetically or in order of importance. Names should be alphabetized if all are on the same level. Subject lines help in identifying, routing, scanning, and filing memorandums.

The body of the memorandum, like the body of the letter, is the most important part and should be as carefully written as a letter to a client or customer.

[1] Jo Ann Hennington, "Memorandums—An Effective Communication Tool for Management," *ABCA Bulletin,* 31, No. 3 (September 1978), p. 10.

```
                TO:  Sandra C. Brown

              FROM:  Jennifer L. Swenson

              DATE:  August 14, 1980

           SUBJECT:  Standardization of Letter Styles

           On July 30, James Lyle and I met to discuss the different styles of letters
           used by the secretaries in our company.  LBMP has never had an established
           policy regarding letter styles, and we believe that standardization would
           simplify the question of style for our secretaries.

           The block style with open punctuation should meet our needs.  The uniformity
           is appealing, and the secretaries should find the setup easy to follow.  Please
           use the attached example for a stencil to be distributed throughout the
           company.

           cs

           Attachment

           cc  David Crowe
               Virginia Pierson
```

Figure 5—9

An interoffice memorandum typed with standard one-inch margins.

. . . Most memorandums are generally informal typewritten messages of things to be remembered, as in future action, and make great use of listings and itemizations, or are directives going down the chain of command and requests coming up the chain of command.[2]

The typist's reference initials are placed two spaces below the body. The dictator should either initial or sign the memorandum. As the interoffice memorandum contains no signature line, the dictator's signature or initials would appropriately be placed in the heading. Attachments and copy notations are positioned exactly as in a letter, although titles are not generally used.

[2]Ibid., p. 12.

Envelopes

No company can exist for long without mail service. Because the volume of mail handled by the U.S. Postal Service is so great, and continues to grow, you should know the recommended way to address your envelopes to speed their processing. All addresses should contain complete delivery information. The major elements of a good address in the order in which they should appear on the envelope are:

1. The name of the person or company to whom the message is to be delivered.
2. The street number and street name, including the unit number of any multiunit building; the post office box number; or the rural or star route and box number.
3. The city name, state abbreviation, and ZIP Code number.

The ZIP Code (Zone Improvement Plan) has been in use since 1964. Each post office is assigned a five-number designation that permits efficient sorting of mail for that post office without extensive training and rehandling. The *National ZIP Code Directory* gives the proper ZIP Code for all post offices according to street addresses. This Directory is available at nominal cost from the U.S. Postal Service, and every office should have at least one copy.

Addressing Envelopes for Automated Equipment

Envelopes, cards, and other first-class mail prepared for processing by the latest automated equipment can be handled more quickly and accurately. Typewritten envelopes properly prepared for the Optical Character Recognition (OCR) equipment can be sorted at a rate of 42,000 per hour. Handwritten addresses or typewritten addresses that are not prepared for the OCR equipment are processed by the Letter Sorting Machine (LSM), which handles approximately 3,600 pieces of mail per hour. The time advantage for properly prepared envelopes is obvious.[3]

For fast mail service, follow postal guidelines.

The Postal Service recommends these basic guidelines in addressing envelopes for efficient processing by the OCR equipment:

1. Capitalize everything in the address.
2. Eliminate all punctuation.
3. Use the standard two-letter state abbreviations.

[3] Judy F. West and Daniel R. Boyd, "Mail Processing Updated," *The Secretary,* February 1978, p. 16.

Table 5—2

Two-Letter State, District, and Territory Abbreviations

Alaska	AK	Montana	MT
Alabama	AL	Nebraska	NE
Arizona	AZ	Nevada	NV
Arkansas	AR	New Hampshire	NH
California	CA	New Jersey	NJ
Canal Zone	CZ	New Mexico	NM
Colorado	CO	New York	NY
Connecticut	CT	North Carolina	NC
Delaware	DE	North Dakota	ND
District of Columbia	DC	Ohio	OH
Florida	FL	Oklahoma	OK
Georgia	GA	Oregon	OR
Guam	GU	Pennsylvania	PA
Hawaii	HI	Puerto Rico	PR
Idaho	ID	Rhode Island	RI
Illinois	IL	South Carolina	SC
Indiana	IN	South Dakota	SD
Iowa	IA	Tennessee	TN
Kansas	KS	Texas	TX
Kentucky	KY	Utah	UT
Louisiana	LA	Vermont	VT
Maine	ME	Virginia	VA
Maryland	MD	Virgin Islands	VI
Massachusetts	MA	Washington	WA
Michigan	MI	West Virginia	WV
Minnesota	MN	Wisconsin	WI
Mississippi	MS	Wyoming	WY
Missouri	MO		

4. Abbreviate only those items listed in the "Address Abbreviations" section of the *National ZIP Code Directory*.[4]

Envelope addresses should be single-spaced regardless of the number of lines in the address. The OCR equipment can read up to a four-line address. Everything should be typed in capital letters. No punctuation should be used. City names that contain more than thirteen letters and spaces may be abbreviated according to the list in the *National ZIP Code Directory* (pages xiv–xvi). The state should be designated by the standard two-letter abbreviation (see Table 5–2). A maximum of twenty-two letters and spaces should be

[4] Ibid.

used for the last line, with one space between the city and state, and one space between the state and ZIP Code.

No printing should appear to the left, right, or below the address. The address should begin at least one inch from the left edge of the envelope and end at least one inch from the right edge. The last line, containing the city, state, and ZIP Code should be more than one-half inch from the bottom of the envelope.

Special information lines on the envelope should also be in all capital letters. On-arrival directions, such as *hold for arrival, please forward, confidential,* or *personal,* should be indented at least three

Figure 5—10
Recommended placement of address elements on large and small business envelopes. Use large envelopes for letters over one page or containing enclosures. Use small envelopes for one-page letters.

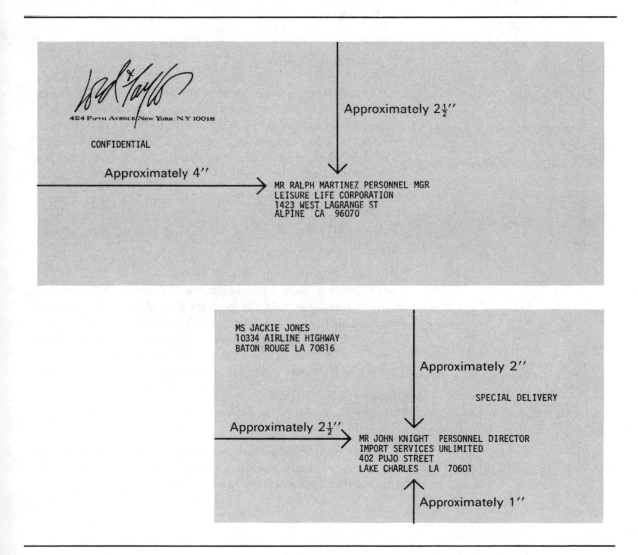

spaces from the left edge of the envelope and placed three spaces below the bottom of the return address. Special mail instructions, such as *special delivery* or *certified mail,* should be typed below the stamp or meter imprint, at least three spaces above the first line of the address. If an attention line is used, it should be the second line of the address. Figure 5–10 shows the proper position of all elements on the envelope.

Additional information and examples of various good address formats are shown in Appendix E of this book. Your Postmaster or Consumer Service Representative can give you postal service publications that provide more information about addressing practices to expedite your mail.

International Mail

Some foreign countries use a system similar to the U.S. ZIP Codes. Canadian postal codes contain six letters and numbers in two groups of three each. When you address an envelope to Canada, show the city name and province and the full postal code number on one line. The country name should appear alone on the last line and be underlined.

MR ROBERT LAYTON
508 MANSFIELD AV
OTTAWA ONT K2A 2S9
CANADA

Mexico uses postal zones only in Mexico City.

Mail sent overseas has certain limits and restrictions. Envelopes for overseas mail should be marked for airmail service in the upper left corner, just below the return address, with *Par Avion* in blue. The post office has gummed labels for this purpose. In addressing an envelope for overseas mail, include the postal delivery zone number and the name of the country.

MISS HEIDI SCHROEDER
450 HAMBURG 68 (LOKSTEDT)
BERLIN 84 WEST GERMANY

The U.S. Postal Service has a publication available giving regulations and detailed information on postage rates, services, prohibitions, and restrictions on mail to other countries.

Envelope Size

The U.S. Postal Service no longer accepts envelopes smaller than 3½ by 5 inches in size. First-class mail weighing one ounce or less and third-class mail weighing two ounces or less can be sent in odd-shaped or oversize envelopes (larger than 6⅛ by 11½ inches) only by paying a surcharge. (Mail weighing more than the minimum is not subject to the surcharge for the larger envelopes.)

Some companies, for economic reasons, use a standard size (No. 10) envelope for all correspondence. Many follow the practice of using smaller (No. 6¾ or No. 6¼) envelopes for one-page letters without enclosures and larger (No. 10) envelopes for one-page letters with enclosures or for letters of two or more pages. Letters are folded differently for each envelope size.

Folding Letters for Small Envelopes

When using small envelopes (No. 6¾ or No. 6¼), fold the bottom of the letter up to one-half to one-fourth inch from the top. Fold the right side about two-thirds of the paper width to the left. Fold the left side to about one-half inch from the right fold. Insert the last

Figure 5–11
How to fold letters for small business envelopes.

Folding a letter for a small envelope

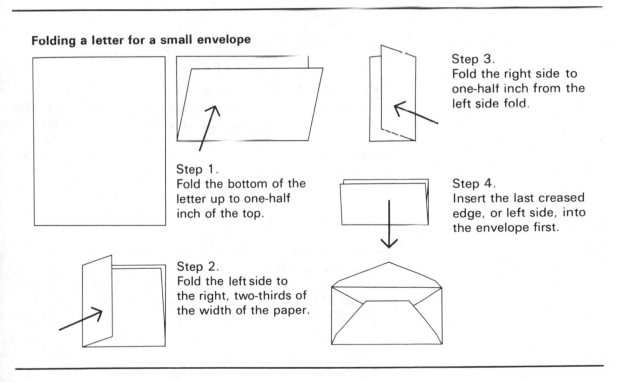

Step 1.
Fold the bottom of the letter up to one-half inch of the top.

Step 2.
Fold the left side to the right, two-thirds of the width of the paper.

Step 3.
Fold the right side to one-half inch from the left side fold.

Step 4.
Insert the last creased edge, or left side, into the envelope first.

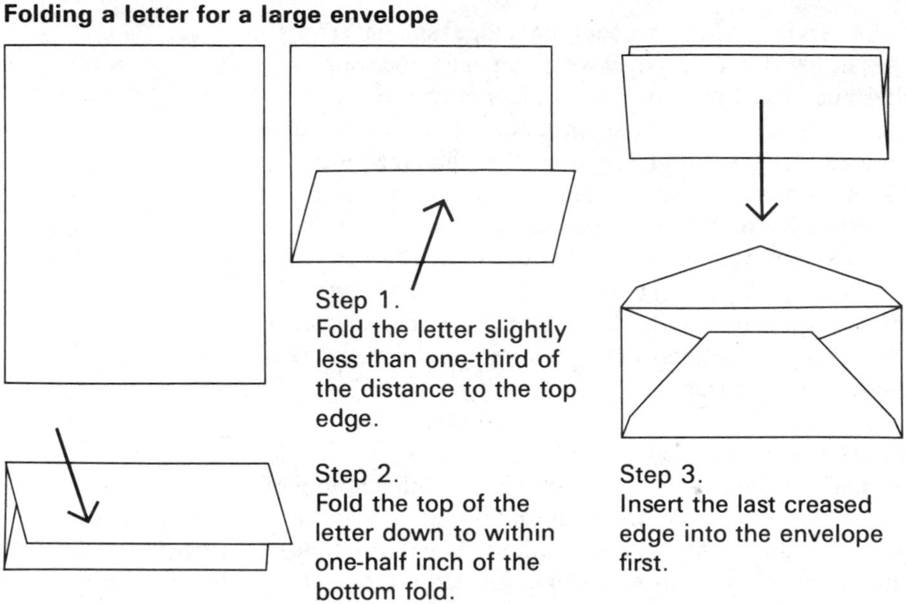

Folding a letter for a large envelope

Step 1.
Fold the letter slightly less than one-third of the distance to the top edge.

Step 2.
Fold the top of the letter down to within one-half inch of the bottom fold.

Step 3.
Insert the last creased edge into the envelope first.

Figure 5–12
How to fold letters for large business envelopes.

creased edge, on the left side of the letter, into the envelope first (Figure 5–11).

Folding Letters for Large Envelopes
When using the larger or standard envelope (No. 10), fold the letter from the bottom to slightly less than one-third of the distance to the top of the letterhead. Fold the top of the letter down to within one-half inch of the bottom fold. Insert the last creased edge, at the top of the letter, into the envelope first (Figure 5–12).

Memorandum Envelopes

Letters and memorandums sent through company mail need not contain complete addresses. All that is necessary for the address is the person's name, title, department, and location. The words *company mail* and, perhaps, the use of a different colored envelope will help distinguish interoffice communications from other correspondence. Interoffice mail sent from branch to branch is generally consolidated into a single package.

```
                            MR JAMES R WHITE
COMPANY MAIL                ACCOUNTING DEPARTMENT
                            COLTON BRANCH
```

Summary

Concern for correct formats reflects care in your work. Attractive letters, memorandums, and other communications are important in the business world. Planning is required to ensure attractive layout. The reader of your letter forms an image of you and your company as soon as he or she sees your letter. Make sure your reader's first impression is a favorable one by following the suggestions given in this chapter.

Questions for Discussion

1. Imagine that you are beginning a new company, and you are to select new stationery for it. What are two qualities to look for in making your selection?

2. "The responsibility for correctness in form lies with the typist." Is this statement true? What responsibilities does the executive have for correct form?

3. What important parts must be included in a letter and why?

4. What are some differences in the format of a letter and an interoffice memorandum? What are some similarities?

5. What is "mixed punctuation"?

6. What is the traditional style of letter format? Why does it continue to be used?

7. List at least two reasons for using a postscript.

8. What information should appear at the top of the second and succeeding pages of letters? Why is this information necessary?

9. What is the proper courtesy title for a woman when you do not know her marital status?

Exercises

1. Select five letterheads from actual businesses. Analyze each letterhead and determine whether it depicts the image the business wished to portray. Can you suggest any improvements?

2. Design a letterhead for a company you would like to work for, or improve one of those you collected for exercise 1.

3. Collect business or sales letters or any other forms of communication. Which appeal to you and which do not? What are your reasons?

Chapter 6 Parts of the Communication Puzzle

Introduction

Word Selection
Expand Your Vocabulary
Know Your Communication
   Partners
Use Correctly Spelled Words
Avoid Overused, Outdated
   Expressions

Sentence Structure
The Simple Sentence
The Complex Sentence
The Compound Sentence
Active and Passive Voice

Paragraph Structure
Deductive Organization
Inductive Organization
Organization for Emphasis

Message Structure

Summary

"The power of words is immense. A well-chosen word has often sufficed to stop a flying army, to change defeat into victory, and to save an empire." — Emile De Girardin

Introduction

Each communication is a unique puzzle. The pieces are the same but are put together in varying ways to achieve the objective of the message and to satisfy the needs of the individuals who write the message as well as the needs of those who receive the message.

Use your message objective to guide your writing.

Words must be selected carefully to ensure clear meaning and tactful expression. Then, these words must be joined to form correctly constructed, interesting sentences; and the sentences, organized into paragraph units that tell a clear, complete story when arranged in a logical sequence.

One of the hardest tasks of the communicator is to get something on paper—to actually begin writing. Follow these steps to solve this problem.

1. *Outline the message to be written,* including a brief statement about the important points that need to be discussed in the communication.

Begin your message with an outline.

2. *Write topic sentences* for the paragraphs to be written.

3. *Develop each topic sentence* into a *paragraph.*

4. *Proofread the rough draft,* consulting the dictionary for preferred spellings of words about which you are uncertain and inserting punctuation where needed. The rough draft should also be checked to see that all of the points in the outline appear in the message.

5. *Revise the rough draft* so the paragraphs are arranged in a logical order, repetition and redundancies are eliminated, correct grammatical construction is used, and the communication satisfies the reasons for writing and for reading the message.

Your communication is effective when word selection, sentence structure, and paragraph arrangement and sequence work together to achieve the overall objective of the message.

Word Selection

The average modern English dictionary contains approximately 600,000 words, quite a contrast to the 50,000-word English dictionary compiled by Samuel Johnson in 1755. The maximum number of English words known by any one person is approximately 100,000, according to Graham Berry in his article "The Lore of Language."[1]

Most English words have several different meanings. For instance, some of the definitions for the noun *note* in *Webster's New Collegiate Dictionary* (8th ed.) are: "a written symbol used to indicate duration and pitch of a tone by its shape and position on the staff; a memorandum; a condensed or informal record; a printed comment or reference set apart from the text; a written promise to pay a debt; a piece of paper money; a short informal letter; a sheet of notepaper; distinction;" etc. Then, when you throw into this "verbal stew" the unlimited interpretations placed on words by the chief users of words, people, you have an age-old communication problem.

How do you say what you want to say? The answer to this question is to say it with words, words that *you* understand and that you are reasonably sure the *receiver* of your message will understand. These five procedures will help to ensure effective word selection:

1. Use every available opportunity to expand your vocabulary and your understanding of words.

2. Use every available opportunity to learn something about the people with whom you communicate.

3. Match your knowledge of words with that of the receiver of your message.

4. Spell words correctly using preferred, conventional spellings.

5. Avoid overused, outdated expressions.

Expand Your Vocabulary

Reading and listening are the two best methods you can use to expand your vocabulary. The more you read, the more words you are exposed to; but exposure alone will not enlarge your vocabulary. The more people you talk and listen to, the more words you are exposed to; but again exposure is not enough. Well-read, socially oriented persons[2] will develop a better understanding of an

---

[1] Berry, *Modern Maturity*, February-March 1978, p. 63.

[2] Socially oriented persons are persons interested in people, like to be with, talk to, and listen to them.

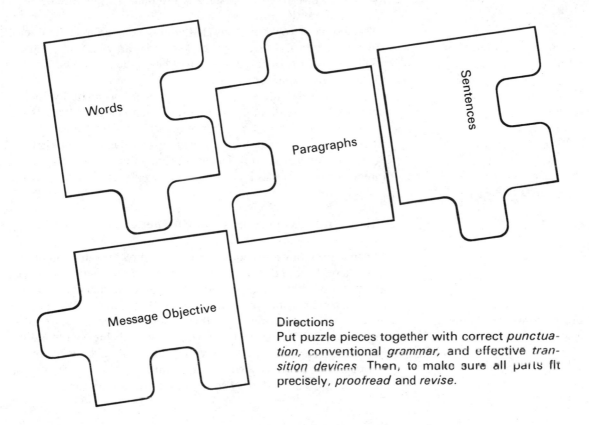

Directions

Put puzzle pieces together with correct *punctuation*, conventional *grammar*, and effective *transition devices*. Then, to make sure all parts fit precisely, *proofread* and *revise*.

increasing number of words only if they possess intellectual curiosity.[3] Intellectual curiosity motivates the communicator to consult a dictionary or to ask questions in order to satisfy a need to know and to understand spoken and written words.

Suppose a typewriter sales representative comes to your office to talk to you about buying a new typewriter. The sales representative recommends an electric typewriter with dual pitch, interchangeable typing elements, a nineteen-inch carriage, a paper injector, a card holder, a cartridge-ribbon mechanism, and a palm tabulator. Your intellectual curiosity should motivate you to find out, by asking questions or by reading the typewriter manuals, what each of these terms means. Once you satisfy your curiosity, you will probably add

[3] Intellectual curiosity is a strong mental need to understand what is heard and read.

Figure 6—1
The communication puzzle.

five or six words to your vocabulary and make a more intelligent decision about the purchase.

Expand your vocabulary by challenging yourself to learn at least one new word each day. At the end of one year, your vocabulary will be 365 words richer; and you will be on the road to becoming a more effective communicator.

A person learns under three circumstances—accidentally, incidentally, and intentionally. The most efficient learning takes place when it is intentional. A number of books and word games designed to increase your vocabulary are presently on the market. Some of them are listed in Table 6–1. Expand your vocabulary intentionally as well as incidentally and accidentally.

Learn at least one new word each day.

Expand your vocabulary intentionally.

Know Your Communication Partners

The interpretations placed on words are a direct result of an individual's background, culture, environment, education, experience, and age. To ensure success in your communication efforts and to avoid costly miscommunication, you need to gather information about your communication partners, those who receive your messages, whether oral or written. Listen for verbal clues to the individual's background when talking with a person. Read between the lines when you receive a written communication so you can properly interpret the words used by your communication partner.

Gather information about communication partners.

Table 6–1
Build Your Vocabulary

Theodore M. Bernstein. *Bernstein's Reverse Dictionary.* New York: Quadrangle / New York Times Book Co., 1975.

Marion Lamb. *Word Studies.* 6th ed. Cincinnati: South-Western, 1971.

Maxwell W. Nurnberg. *Fun With Words.* Englewood Cliffs, N.J.: Prentice-Hall, 1970.

Maxwell W. Nurnberg and Morris Rosenblum. *All About Words.* Englewood Cliffs, N.J.: Prentice-Hall, 1966.

———. *How to Build a Better Vocabulary.* New York: Popular Library, 1977.

Devern J. Perry and J. E. Silverthorn. *College Vocabulary Building.* Cincinnati: South-Western, 1977.

Kathleen Rafferty, ed. *Dell Crossword Puzzles.* New York: Dell Pub. Co., published monthly.

Scrabble, the word game put out by Selchow and Righter Co.

Vocabulary, accents in oral communication, idioms and slang words, grammar, speaking effectiveness, and writing techniques reveal much about the communicator's personality, life-style, experience, background, and age. Analyze the letters you receive, talk to communication partners on the phone, ask other company personnel—salesmen in other areas and personnel in your office, or in branch offices—about communication partners. If you keep records of the personal and business characteristics of these communication partners, the time spent will be well rewarded. The rewards are better public relations, increased dollar sales, and self-satisfaction.

As an example, suppose you work for a business-forms company and receive the letter in Figure 6-2 from a prospective customer

---

ATLANTIC OILFIELD SUPPLY COMPANY
P.O. Box 1066
Lake Charles, Louisiana 70883

(318) 529-6265

November 13, 19--

Collins Business Forms, Inc.
651 Morgan Road
Beaumont, Texas 77709

Dear Sirs:

I process forms every day and am going bananas trying to get the people who work for my company to give me forms I can read. The biggest gripe I have is that the copy we keep for our records is always the third copy in a form set, the copy that is the lightest and hardest to read.

Someone told me at the basketball game the other night that your company makes a carbonless form and that they can even read the fourth copy on their forms. Please send me some info about your carbon forms and your carbonless forms. I would like to know prices, kinds of paper used, delivery time, and methods used to indicate distribution of forms.

Thanks.

Yours truly,

Patrick O'Shonnassey

Patrick O'Shonnassey

wm

Figure 6—2
What does this letter reveal about the writer?

asking you for some information about carbon interleaved and carbonless forms. As you read the letter, answer the following questions:

1. Is the writer young, middle-aged, or older?
2. Is the writer a man or a woman?
3. Does the writer have a high-school education? A college education?
4. What type of business does the writer represent?
5. How much knowledge of business forms does the writer possess?
6. Do the writer's words reveal anything about his background?

From Mr. O'Shonnassey's letter, you can conclude that he is probably in his late twenties or early thirties because he uses the expressions *going bananas* and *some info*, typical of those under thirty-five. His choice of salutation may indicate that he has been out of school several years or that the company he represents is

Table 6—2
Dictionaries

Clarence L. Barnhart, Sol Steinmetz, and Robert K. Barnhart, eds. *The Barnhart Dictionary of New English Since 1963.* Bronxville, N. Y.: Barnhart / Harper & Row, 1973.

The Concise Heritage Dictionary. Boston: Houghton Mifflin, 1976.

Philip B. Gove, ed. *Webster's Third New International Dictionary.* (Unabridged) Springfield, Mass.: G. & C. Merriam Co., 1966.

David B. Guralnik et al., eds. *Webster's New World Dictionary of the American Language.* 2nd college ed. Cleveland: Collins & World Pub. Co., 1976.

Virginia Haines and Catharine Ryan. *Dictionary for Secretaries.* Los Angeles: Parker & Son, 1971.

Eric Louis Kohler. *A Dictionary for Accountants.* 5th ed. Englewood Cliffs, N.J.: Prentice-Hall, 1975.

Norman D. Moore. *Dictionary of Business, Finance, and Investment.* Dayton, Ohio: Investor's Systems, 1975.

William Morris, ed. *The American Heritage Dictionary of the English Language.* New York: American Heritage Pub. Co., 1969.

Jack C. Plano and Milton Greenberg. *The American Political Dictionary.* 4th ed. New York: Dryden Press / Holt, Rinehart & Winston, 1976.

Charles J. Sippi and Charles P. Sippi. *Computer Dictionary and Handbook.* 2nd ed. Indianapolis, Ind.: Howard W. Sams & Co., 1972.

Webster's New Collegiate Dictionary. 8th ed. Springfield, Mass.: G. & C. Merriam Co., 1975.

conservative. The salutation preferred now, when the inside address is the name of a company, is *Gentlemen, Ladies,* or *Ladies and Gentlemen,* depending on the company.

His writing shows a good background in grammar and punctuation and a knowledge of conventional letter style. However, starting a business letter with *I* should generally be avoided. Also remember that to thank the recipient of the letter before the information is received is not appropriate. Most progressive businesses prefer *Sincerely yours* or *Yours very truly* for the complimentary close.

From the letterhead, you know that Mr. O'Shonnassey represents an oilfield supply company. Because he mentions both carbonless and carbon forms, you know that he has considerable knowledge of office forms and their requirements. He seems to be a thorough, down-to-earth person who is genuinely interested in doing his job well.

By analyzing Mr. O'Shonnassey's letter, you know quite a bit about him that will help you to communicate with him more effectively—to use words he will find interesting and easy to understand.

Use Correctly Spelled Words

A good dictionary with letter tabs for easy reference is the writer's best friend. Table 6–2 lists some widely used, popular dictionaries you may want to consider for your personal library.

Consult the dictionary while reading or writing to make sure you are using correct words and spelling them properly. Remember, the dictionary is an inanimate object and helps you only if you open its cover and use it. Table 6–3 lists some words that are often confused. Every communicator should know how to use each word, when to use each word, and how to spell each word correctly.

> Use a dictionary to clarify confusing words.

This is by no means a complete list of all of the confusing words in the English language. You must take the initiative and learn intentionally. Compile your own glossary of words that confuse you and keep this glossary nearby when you write.

To compile your glossary, write down any words that confuse you when you read. Then, when you can, look up the correct spelling and definitions for these words. Put the words and definitions on 3 x 5 inch index cards so you can keep them in alphabetical order, and place the cards in a box. Use alphabetical dividers so you can locate words easily and quickly when needed.

> Compile a glossary of confusing words.

A misspelled word in a business message can be either a typographical error or a "writer-ignorance" error. The receiver of your written communication may assume either of those two reasons for misspelled words. You hope the reader does not assume that writer-

> Avoid typographical and "writer-ignorance" errors.

Table 6—3
Words Often Confused

accept, except	good, well
access, excess	guarantee, guaranty
adverse, averse	hour, our
advice, advise	imply, infer
aesthetic, ascetic	its, it's
affect, effect	later, latter
agenda, addenda	lay, lie
aid, aide	lend, loan
all together, altogether	like, as
amount, number	loose, lose
appraise, apprise	ones, one's
ascent, assent	past, passed
assistance, assistants	personal, personnel
bad, badly	petal, pedal, peddle
balance, remainder	precedence, precedents
between, among	principal, principle
can, may	rational, rationale
canvas, canvass	right, rite, write
casual, causal	role, roll
capitol, capital	sell, sale
command, commend	set, sit
compliment, complement	site, cite, sight
continuous, continual	slow, slowly
credible, creditable	stationary, stationery
device, devise	statue, statute
disillusion, dissolution	there, their, they're
disinterested, uninterested	to, too
elicit, illicit	wages, salary
eminent, imminent	want, won't
envelop, envelope	waver, waiver
every one, everyone	who's, whose
farther, further	your, you're
fewer, less	

ignorance is the cause. But regardless of the cause, spelling errors are still *errors*.

Could the reader assume that if you are so careless with your business messages, you may also be that careless with your business? This possibility is one important reason why you must take the time to spell correctly.

Business procedures change daily and become more and more sophisticated to meet the needs of the nation's consumers of goods

Help your reader maintain confidence in your business.

acknowledgment, acknowl-
edgement
cannot, can not
catalog, catalogue
catsup, ketchup
cigarette, cigaret
curricula, curriculums
formulas, formulae
judgment, judgement
kerosine, kerosene

labor, labour
memorandums, memoranda
percent, per cent
postpaid, post-paid
rancor, rancour
sulfurous, sulphurous
syrup, sirup
template, templet
traveler, traveller

and services. Competition among product manufacturers and service personnel is often based on this constant updating. Everyone wants the most modern, up-to-date goods or services available. In fact, an almost unbelievable emphasis is placed on the modernity of everything offered for sale in the American economy.

As a business communicator, if you wish to convey an up-to-date, modern image of your company, you should use current, preferred spellings for words. The reader of your communications may just assume that outdated, unconventional spellings for words reflect an outdated, unconventional business. Use a recent edition of your favorite dictionary to check on the *preferred* spellings. Add the preferred spelling for the words in Table 6–4 to your glossary card index and let your communication partners know that you are up to date.

Use current, preferred spellings for words.

Avoid Overused, Outdated Expressions

Any word or group of words that is repeated over and over again tends to lose meaning and fails in its purpose for being included in the business message. Outdated expressions, likewise, have no place in business communications because they might relay a kind of unwritten message to your communication partner that your company is a little behind the times. And who in today's society wants to do business with an out-of-date company? Modernity is the watchword for every viable business. You need to be aware of the detrimental effects of overused, outdated expressions and avoid their use. Some of those most often found in business letters are shown in Table 6–5.

Table 6—5
Overused and Outdated
Expressions

Dear Sir	at your earliest possible
Dear Madam	convenience
enclosed you will find	we just received your letter and
please find enclosed	thank you for your interest
begging your favor	due to the fact that
in the amount of	With best personal regards
in the near future	With kindest regards, I remain
do not hesitate to	Yours truly

Select words that lead to mutual understanding.

Select your words carefully. Be sure to use words that produce mutual understanding between your communication partner and you. Use preferred, conventional spelling; and avoid overused, outdated expressions.

Sentence Structure

Use only complete sentences.

To communicate clearly, completely, and concisely, you must use only complete sentences in your business message. Complete sentences have at least one subject and one verb and can stand alone. Sentences are classified as simple, complex, or compound and may be written in either the active or passive voice.

The Simple Sentence

The *simple sentence* contains one subject, one predicate, and only one idea. This idea may be expressed in the form of a question, a command, or a statement. Because only one concept is expressed, the simple sentence is an especially effective tool for communicating clearly and concisely. If your objective is to emphasize one idea, use a simple sentence.

Use a simple sentence to emphasize an idea.

1. You should send your order by December 1.

You is the only subject, and *should send* is the only verb. The statement is complete because the active verb *should send* has an object of the action, *order*. This sentence expresses the one thought that the order should be sent by December 1.

2. Your request for a vacation the last two weeks of January has been approved.

The only subject is *request,* and the only verb is *has been approved.* The verb is passive and needs no object. The single thought expressed is that you may have your vacation the last two weeks in January.

The Complex Sentence

The *complex sentence* contains an independent clause and a dependent clause. A clause is a group of words that contains a subject and a verb and may be either independent (complete) or dependent (subordinate). An independent clause can stand alone as a simple sentence. A dependent or subordinate clause is incomplete without further explanation and must be accompanied by an independent clause. The meaning of the subordinate clause depends on the content of the independent clause. The most important idea should be placed in the independent clause.

Use a complex sentence to qualify, compare, or contrast statements.

If you go to the store (dependent clause), please buy a loaf of bread (independent clause).

The dependent clause contains a subject, *you,* and a verb, *go.* But if you put a period or some other punctuation after the dependent clause (after *store*), you have an incomplete sentence because the thought is not complete. The meaning of *if you go to the store* depends on the information in the independent clause that follows, *please buy a loaf of bread.* The independent clause could stand alone, but the person making this statement communicates her wishes that the communication partner buy the bread only if he is going to the store.

The independent clause contains the main idea but is qualified or changed by the content of the subordinate clause. In this case, a simple sentence would not be nearly as effective as the complex sentence. Complex sentences should be used when you want to qualify, to contrast, or to compare statements.

The Compound Sentence

The *compound sentence* contains two complete sentences joined by either a coordinating conjunction or a semicolon. The principal coordinating conjunctions are *and, but, for, nor, or, either,* and *neither.* The complete sentences may be simple, complex, or both.

1. If George brings the report to you, start typing the final draft (complex sentence); but if Tom calls and says George will be late, start transcribing the letters I dictated to you this morning (complex sentence).

2. You and Mary are doing a good job (simple sentence), and I am sure Mr. Veillon will see that you both receive promotions (complex sentence).

3. Continue assembling the report for the staff meeting (simple sentence); but if the letter comes from Mr. Brown, please gather the information he requests (complex sentence).

Compound sentences should be used when the two ideas expressed are of equal importance. The coordinating conjunction also indicates that a close relationship exists between the ideas expressed in the compound sentence. If the ideas are unrelated, the sentence should be revised.

Carrie looked for a job all day Tuesday, but she likes to play tennis.

Revised, the compound sentence is composed of closely related ideas:

Carrie looked for a job all day Tuesday. She usually plays tennis on Tuesdays, but her partner was not able to play.

Use a compound sentence to show close relationship between two ideas of equal importance.

If a compound sentence contains more than two independent clauses connected by different coordinating conjunctions, it becomes a run-on sentence. Run-on sentences confuse the reader and are poor communication tools.

The typewriter salesman brought a Technique electric typewriter for me to use (independent clause), and I tried it out for about a week (independent clause), but it was not satisfactory (independent clause).

This run-on sentence is connected by *and* and *but*. Revised into a compound sentence and a simple sentence, it becomes much easier to understand:

The typewriter salesman brought a Technique typewriter for me to use (simple sentence). I tried it out for about a week, but it was not satisfactory (compound sentence).

Active and Passive Voice

Sentences may be written in either active or passive voice. In active voice, the subject *performs* some action. In passive voice, the subject *receives* some action. Plan to write most sentences in the active voice.

1. Mr. Jones gave me a raise.

Mr. Jones performed an action.

2. If you will call me tomorrow, I will write the report.

The subjects perform an action in both the independent and dependent clauses.

3. My salary has been increased.

The subject receives the action of the verb.

4. If you will call my supervisor tomorrow, I will be given the opportunity to write the report.

The subject in the independent clause receives the action of the verb.

If you wish to emphasize an idea, use the active voice. The active voice permits the reader to visualize and understand your idea. To subordinate or to minimize an idea, use the passive voice. Pleasant, important ideas are best expressed in active sentences; unpleasant or less important ideas are best expressed in passive sentences.

For variety, efficient communicators incorporate into their business messages some simple sentences, some complex sentences, and some compound sentences. To achieve clarity, efficient communicators use mostly simple sentences; to show comparison, complex sentences; and to show a close, equal relationship of ideas, they use compound sentences.

Use the active voice to emphasize an idea.

Use the passive voice to minimize an idea.

Use variety in sentence structure.

Paragraph Structure

A paragraph is a group of sentences that explains, describes, or supports the topic of the paragraph. Each paragraph contains a topic sentence that may be either the first or the last sentence in the paragraph. If the topic sentence begins the paragraph, it tells the reader *what will be discussed.* If the topic sentence ends the paragraph, it summarizes *what was discussed* or *what conclusions are drawn* from the information presented in the paragraph.

Place your topic sentence either at the beginning or the end of the paragraph.

Topic sentence. _____

_____

_____

_____

_____. Topic sentence.

Deductive Organization

A paragraph is written in deductive order when the topic sentence begins the paragraph. All other sentences in the paragraph explain, support, or describe the idea expressed in the first sentence.

Secretaries, in general, are not interested in joining labor unions. In the past thirty years the percentage of office employees who have joined unions has increased from 2 percent to 42 percent, but less than 1 percent are classified as secretaries. Secretaries say that good pay, excellent working conditions, adequate fringe benefits, and job mobility deter unionization within their ranks.

The first sentence (in italics) is the topic sentence. It expresses the basic idea to be discussed. The rest of the paragraph supports the validity of the topic sentence.

Inductive Organization

A paragraph is written in inductive order when the topic sentence ends the paragraph. All previous sentences in the paragraph supply reasons, explanations, and descriptions of the idea expressed in the topic sentence.

In the past thirty years the percentage of office employees who have joined unions has increased from 2 percent to 42 percent, but less than 1 percent are classified as secretaries. Secretaries say that good pay, excellent working conditions, adequate fringe benefits, and job mobility deter unionization within their ranks. *Secretaries, in general, are not interested in joining labor unions.*

The last sentence (in italics) is the topic sentence, the reason for writing the paragraph. All previous sentences supply supportive information and reasons why the reader should consider the topic sentence to be a true and logical statement.

Organization for Emphasis

A paragraph may contain a topic sentence at the beginning and at the end. If you want to emphasize your point, construct a paragraph with a good introductory sentence and a good closing statement, both containing the topic of the paragraph.

Members of the secretarial profession appear to be almost totally uninterested in membership in labor unions. In the past thirty years the percentage of office employees who have joined unions has increased from 2 percent to 42 percent, but less than 1 percent are classified as secretaries. Secretaries say that good pay, excellent working conditions, adequate fringe benefits, and job mobility deter unionization within their ranks. *Secretaries, in general, are not interested in joining labor unions.*

For emphasis, a paragraph may contain one sentence. One-sentence paragraphs should be the exception rather than the rule, however, since emphasis is usually achieved only by doing something different, something out of the ordinary.

Members of the secretarial profession appear to be almost totally uninterested in membership in labor unions.

In the past thirty years the percentage of office employees who have joined unions has increased from . . . . Secretaries, in general, are not interested in joining labor unions.

The criteria for correctly written paragraphs are:

1. Each paragraph has a topic sentence at the beginning, at the end, or at both the beginning and the end.

2. Every sentence in the paragraph is related to the topic sentence.

3. Every sentence in the paragraph is a complete sentence.

Message Structure

Organizing the message is a critical stage of communication. You now begin to put the parts of the puzzle together, the objective being to relay a message to your communication partner. Planning is a must at this point. As you organize your message, use the following checklist:

1. What is the purpose of the communication?

2. What key points must be discussed?

Place topic sentences at both the beginning and at the end of a paragraph.

Use a one-sentence paragraph for emphasis.

Structure your message to satisfy the message objective.

3. In what order should these points be discussed (deductive or inductive)?

4. Is the message clear, concise, and accurate?

Business communications, both written and oral, constitute a major part of all business activity and all business expense. Writing letters, writing reports, filling out forms, talking on the telephone, instructing subordinates, and informing superiors are some of the ways business people communicate. They communicate to create goodwill, to conduct business activities efficiently and effectively, and to improve employee work habits and working relationships. Postage, equipment, supplies, and especially labor compose the major portion of business communication expenses. These factors point to the reason business communications should be valid, important, and, above all, clear to both you and your communication partner.

The important prerequisite for all communications is determining the purpose of the communication. This purpose must be of equal importance to you and to your communication partner. When you consider, prior to writing, both your purpose and your reader's purpose, you can more easily include in your list of important points to discuss everything you *need to say* as well as everything you *would want to know* if you were in your communication partner's place.

For example, you are asked to prepare a sales message for the Technique correcting typewriter. Table 6–6 shows an outline of the steps you could have used to develop this message.

Whether you present information in a message in inductive or deductive order depends on the purpose of your message. If you wish to emphasize a point, present the idea both at the beginning and at the end of your communication. If you are going to convey good news, write deductively. If you are going to convey bad news or if you are trying to persuade someone to do something, write inductively.

A deductive message presents the key idea or purpose in the first paragraph. An inductive message presents the key idea or purpose in the last paragraph. The order in which you present key ideas is an important decision and should be given careful consideration. More information about this phase of communicating is presented in Chapter 8.

Table 6—6
Outline for the Development of
a Sales Message

A. Purpose of the communication
1. Purpose for communicator: sales promotion of the Technique correcting typewriter
2. Purpose for communication partner: to secure information about the electric Technique correcting typewriter
B. Key points to be discussed
1. Carriage length
2. Type fonts
3. Cost
4. Warranty
5. Availability of service
6. Size of the machine
7. Ribbons needed
8. Colors of machines
9. Availability of trial period
10. How customers can acquire machines
C. Organization of key points
1. Introduction (interesting anecdote, catchy phrase, or an astounding statement)
2. Machine parts
a. Carriage length, platens interchangeable
b. Type fonts, elements
3. Size of machine
4. Colors available
5. Ribbons needed
6. Factory warranty period
7. Office-machines company warranty
8. Service (local and factory)
9. Trial period
10. Purchasing details
11. Delivery date
12. Cost
D. Development of topic sentences for each point to be discussed
E. Development of paragraphs based on topic sentences
F. Proofreading and revising to achieve a clear, concise, accurate message

Summary

The words have been carefully selected and arranged to form clear, complete sentences. The sentences have been arranged in a logical order within paragraphs to achieve the purpose of your message. But your task is not complete. Punctuation, correct grammar, and a smooth transition from idea to idea must be used effectively to complete the communication puzzle.

"All words are pegs to hang ideas on," Henry Ward Beecher said.

Exercises

1. Write a paragraph presenting your ideas in inductive order.

2. Write a paragraph presenting your ideas in deductive order.

3. Read the first paragraph in the section in this chapter titled ''Expand Your Vocabulary.'' Is the paragraph written in inductive or in deductive order? What is the topic sentence?

4. Look at Figure 8—2. Determine the topic sentence outline that Mark Collins used to write that letter.

5. Look at Figure 8—4. Is this letter written in inductive or deductive order? Why is this order used?

6. Analyze the third paragraph in the letter in Figure 8—6. Is the paragraph written in inductive or in deductive order? Why is it written in this order?

7. Rewrite the following paragraph so the topic sentence appears either at the beginning or at the end of the paragraph.

Check your desk calendar each day for notes about work that must be done. Establish priorities by analyzing each task to determine its relative importance. For maximum production efficiency, you must plan and organize your work each day. Make a list of telephone calls you need to make, and plan to make these calls at optimum time periods. Acquire files you will need in order to prepare your business communications—both oral and written.

In each of the following sentences, select from the confusing words in parentheses the word that best fits the meaning needed in the sentence.

8. I (accept, except) your invitation to dinner.

9. Bring me a cup of coffee (to, too).

10. I, (to, too), am interested in the negotiations.

11. The (effect, affect) of the new grading system is questionable.

12. I hope that my new procedure will (effect, affect) a change in the need for additional funds for supplies in the office.

13. The lack of light (effected, affected) my ability to see the figures on the report.

14. Mr. Thompson placed me in charge of all office (personal, personnel) while he was away.

15. Carrington's department store is having a gigantic (sell, sale).

16. Mrs. Phelps is trying to (sell, sale) her house.

17. I am a very good swimmer, and I know that I (can, may) swim five laps across the pool.

18. (Can, May) I have the day off tomorrow; if so, I (can, may) renew my driver's license before the due date.

19. Before next Tuesday, I (want, won't) (everyone, every one) of you to come to my office to look at your term paper.

20. Her (wage, salary) is $9,500 a year which surprised (everyone, every one).

21. His (wage, salary) is $14.50 per hour.

22. Drive (slow, slowly) when you are in a school zone.

23. The dog got (it's, its) paw caught in the swinging door.

24. Roger Slauter asked me for some (advise, advice) about setting up the report for the Executive Committee.

25. I told him that he should ask Joan to (advise, advice) him.

26. Quite a large (amount, number) of employees were absent from work today.

27. Give me the (remainder, balance) of the paper clips.

28. I was surprised at the small (remainder, balance) in my bank account.

29. My boss asked me to (canvas, canvass) the office to determine how many of the office workers were going to attend the meeting.

30. The (canvas, canvass) on my deck chair is wearing out.

31. My supervisor (sighted, cited) some well-known authors in the business world.

32. The vacant lot across the street from my house will soon be the (sight, cite, site) of a new drive-in bank.

33. My (sight, cite, site) is getting worse every day.

34. Mr. Harris (compliments, complements) his workers when they do an especially good job.

35. The desk that Mrs. Smith bought for my office (compliments, complements) my other furniture.

36. The balance in your account is (past, passed) due.

37. Yesterday, Carolyn (past, passed) a car on a curve and almost had a wreck.

38. Eric is the man (who's, whose) always late for work.

39. Kevin is the secretary (who's, whose) house burned last year.

40. (Rite, right, write) your address on the card.

41. I asked Mary if she was convinced that she was going the (rite, right, write) way; I thought we were supposed to turn (rite, right, write) at Elm Street.

The following paragraphs contain a number of misspelled words. Rewrite the paragraphs, using your dictionary to correct all of the misspelled words.

42. Last weak, I ran in to a mutal freind of ours at the Conover City National Bank. He was teling me about an inovative loan programy that the bank is startin this month. Acording to him, the economie in hour area is on the upswing; and the Conover Bank has devised a low-interst-loan insentive program to atract new businessesses and to help existing ones.

43. The jist of the magazen artical was the responsibilitie that lending institutions and businesseses excepting credit purchases have to there customers. The author pointed out that when credit purchasurs gets in trouble finantially and can not pay there bills, their creditors or vary much too blame.

44. This morning I recieved you order for 12 dosen fishing rods. Three days ago, I shiped 40 dosen of the same rods to a sportin-goods store in Akron. Champion makes a vary poplar rod that is used bye many fishermen in this area, and Carver's is happy that you or planing to stock you store with this item.

Analyze each of the following sentences to determine whether it is simple, complex, or compound.

45. Tom and I organized a company basketball team.

46. Margaret called Tulsa last week to trace that purchase order, but the Tulsa office could not locate the order.

47. Since Louise Thompson has more seniority than Phillip Langston, I recommend Thompson for the promotion.

48. We should attend the next council meeting, and John should come with us.

49. Dorothy Williams was employed by Zapp, Inc., on October 8, 1968; but she took a year's leave of absence in 1971 to work on an M.B.A. at Sumpter, North Dakota.

50. John Larousseau called you this morning and asked that you call him back as soon as possible.

51. Craig Smith was employed by Zapp, Inc., on January 15, 1968, and has worked continuously since that date.

52. May I take this work home with me tonight?

53. If we should decide to give Knox the promotion, we should call La Mont in and console him in some way.

54. Please go to the meeting with me tomorrow night.

55. Maybe the best way to handle the situation would be to promote Evelyn laterally.

56. Yesterday, I asked my secretary to write a letter to Verco Chemicals and to request that Verco send a representative to our next Community Action Committee meeting.

Analyze each of the following sentences to determine whether it is written in the active or the passive voice.

57. Could I come over to see you around noon?

58. Roy told Mary Lyons that she should apologize.

59. Bring the book to me, please.

60. The book was sent to me about a month ago.

61. The office was redecorated last year.

62. Carrie spoke to the committee members about ethics and legality in business communications.

63. Ten days ago I was given a promotion to assistant office manager.

64. Max called the service representative to repair his typewriter.

65. The typewriter was repaired by an expert technician.

66. Wanda was suspicious when she saw that the door was ajar.

Chapter 7 Completion of the Communication Puzzle

Introduction

Punctuation
Eight Guidelines for Comma
  Usage
Four Guidelines for Semicolon
  Usage
Two Guidelines for Parenthesis
  Usage
Three Guidelines for
  Apostrophe Usage

Grammar Essentials
Subject-Verb Agreement
Verb Tense
Noun and Pronoun Case and
  Person
Pronoun Reference
Dangling Modifiers
Parallel Construction

Transition Methods
Parenthetical Words
Repetition
Introductory and Summary
  Statements

Proofreading and Revising

Summary

"Beautiful forms and compositions are not made by chance, nor can they ever, in any material, be made at small expense. A composition for cheapness and not excellence of workmanship is the most frequent and certain cause of the rapid decay and entire destruction of arts and manufactures." — Josiah Wedgwood

Introduction

Putting the pieces of your communication puzzle together requires a knowledge of punctuation and grammar rules, transition methods, and proofreading and revising techniques. This chapter covers not only the rules to be followed, but also the reasons for each of the suggested procedures and techniques.

Punctuation

To ensure readability and mutual understanding by the communication partner, punctuation marks should be used correctly. The ability to punctuate correctly is a skill you should possess in order to climb the executive ladder.

Use punctuation for understanding.

Read the following paragraph that contains no marks of punctuation *within* the sentences.

The office manager has many areas of responsibility to superiors subordinates and self. Responsibilities to superiors include 1 keeping them informed about office conditions that could affect the superiors decision making 2 furnishing reports and numerical data and 3 interpreting management policies to subordinates. Responsibilities to subordinates include 1 planning office work 2 directing office activities 3 communicating policy decisions when these decisions will directly affect the subordinates work and 4 evaluating and controlling the work of the subordinates. The responsibilities to self include 1 periodic self analysis 2 job evaluation and 3 upgrading of management skills. The common denominator in performing all of these duties is clear complete communication.

Now read the same paragraph with punctuation marks added. Is it easier to read and understand?

The office manager has many areas of responsibility—to superiors, subordinates, and self. Resonsibilities to superiors include (1) keeping them informed about office conditions that could affect the superiors' decision-making, (2) furnishing reports and numerical data, and (3) interpreting management policies to subordinates. Responsibilities to subordinates include (1) planning office work, (2) directing office activities, (3) communicating policy decisions when these decisions will directly affect the subordinates' work, and (4) evaluating and controlling the work of the subordinates. The responsibilities to self include (1) periodic self-analysis, (2) job evaluation, and (3) upgrading of management skills. The common denominator in performing all of these duties is clear, complete communication.

The most commonly misused marks of punctuation are commas, semicolons, parentheses, and apostrophes. With the possible exception of parentheses, few business communications can be written without using these marks.

Apply rules for punctuating.

A brief review of the correct usage for commas, semicolons, parentheses, and apostrophes, and some examples of each, follows.

Eight Guidelines for Comma Usage

1. Use commas to separate independent clauses (that do not contain commas within) joined by *and, but, or, nor,* or *for.*

The secretary typed the letters, and her assistant sealed and mailed them.

2. Use commas to separate items in a series of three or more when the items do not contain internal commas.

Don Robinson took a copy of his data sheet, a shorthand pad, two ink pens, and a letter of recommendation with him when he went for the job interview.

3. Use commas to separate an introductory dependent clause or phrase from the independent clause that follows.

a. When Mrs. Thompson called yesterday (introductory dependent clause), she asked for an appointment.

b. Because of a bad telephone connection (introductory phrase), I had to call Ed White back to verify his appointment time.

4. Use commas to take the place of an obvious word or words left out of a sentence.

a. In 1977, Smith and Rhodes, Inc. had a net income of $70,000; in 1978, $78,000; and in 1979, $89,000.

Commas replace "Smith and Rhodes, Inc. had a net income of."

b. The manager of Smith and Rhodes, Inc. is a perceptive, conscientious man.

The comma between *perceptive* and *conscientious* takes the place of *and.*

5. Use commas to separate parenthetical remarks and nonrestrictive clauses from the rest of the sentence.

a. Ms. Wilma Gossett offered a perfectly logical reason for the mixup in the payroll department. The office personnel, however (parenthetical), continued to protest.

b. Mr. Conner's secretary, who is married and has two children (nonrestrictive clause), asked for extra vacation time to go to California with her family.

c. I think, Mrs. Kitt (parenthetical, noun of address), that you should consider the rental of computer time for the new project.

6. Use commas to set off nonrestrictive appositives.

The personnel director, Donna Gossett (nonrestrictive appositive), interviewed ten people to fill the vacancy in the research and development department.

7. Use commas to separate the city name from the state name.

My supervisor is originally from Lake Charles, Louisiana.

8. Use commas to separate parts of a date.

a. I was born on July 23, 1947.

b. My appointment was scheduled for Monday, February 5, 1980.

Four Guidelines for Semicolon Usage

1. Use a semicolon to separate two independent clauses connected by a coordinating conjunction when a comma appears in either or both of the independent clauses (unless the independent clauses are short and easy to understand).

Last week Marie Weaver, our newest employee, inventoried all of the equipment in the office; and, beginning Monday, she will inventory the office supplies.

2. Use a semicolon to separate two independent clauses when a coordinating conjunction is not used.

Last week Arthur Johnson inventoried all of the equipment in the office; beginning Monday, he will inventory the office supplies.

3. Use a semicolon to separate items in a series when the items either are very long or contain commas.

I have lived in four cities in the past twenty years: Lake Charles, Louisiana; Houston, Texas; Tulsa, Oklahoma; and Denver, Colorado.

4. Semicolons or commas may be used to separate parts of a *complete* address, but commas are preferred by most authorities.

Please send the order to Dr. Hu Robinson; 1868 Conover Ridge; Beaumont, TX 71213.

Two Guidelines for Parenthesis Usage

1. Use parentheses to enclose words, phrases, or clauses that are parenthetical or explanatory.

a. The programmer (the most efficient we have ever had) ran her program in less than two hours.

b. The readability (the ease with which something can be read) of business letters is an important factor to consider.

2. Use parentheses to enclose figures for numbered items within the text.

The three steps you should take when filing business papers are to (1) classify, (2) code, and (3) place in the appropriate file.

Three Guidelines for Apostrophe Usage

1. Use an apostrophe in contractions to take the place of a letter or letters left out of a word.

can't (cannot); it's (it is); you're (you are)

2. Use an apostrophe to show possession. When used with a singular subject, the apostrophe precedes the *s;* with a plural subject, it follows the *s*. (The possessive case is also discussed later in this chapter.)

girl's books (one girl's books)
girls' books (more than one girl's books)
people's choice (a large group of individuals)
members' resolution (more than one member's resolution)
the Collinses' house (belonging to all members of the Collins family)
Mr. Mayes's car (the car belonging to Mr. Mayes)

3. An apostrophe *may* be used to form the plural of a single letter or a number expressed as a figure.

a. The girl made two *A*'s, three *B*'s, and one *C*.
   The girl made two *A*s, three *B*s, and one *C*.

b. Among the scores on the test were three 85's, two 87's, and two 90's.
   Among the scores on the test were three 85s, two 87s, and two 90s.

Punctuation marks can totally change a communication message. Therefore, they are as much communication tools as are the words you use.

Use punctuation as a communication tool.

1. The receptionist *who has red hair and freckles* gave me the letter from Tom.

No punctuation before and after *who* and *freckles* indicates that this description is necessary to identify the receptionist. The omission of commas also implies that the company employs more than one receptionist and the description is necessary for identification.

2. The receptionist, who has red hair and freckles, gave me the letter from Tom.

The commas before *who* and after *freckles* indicate that the dependent clause is nonrestrictive—not needed for identification of the receptionist. In this case, the company probably has only one receptionist.

Use punctuation sparingly, but use it when needed to ensure clarity and readability.

Grammar Essentials

Grammar is defined in *Webster's New Collegiate Dictionary* (8th ed.) as "the study of the classes of words, their inflections, and their functions and relations in the sentence." One of the first requirements for communication is that the communication partners speak the same language. *Language* is defined as "the words, their pronunciation, and the methods of combining them used and understood by a considerable community." The effective business communicator, in order to relay information and understanding, should know the accepted, uniform methods of combining words to form messages.

The six grammar functions most commonly used and most often misused are:

1. Subject-verb agreement
2. Verb tense
3. Noun and pronoun case and person
4. Pronoun reference
5. Dangling modifiers
6. Parallel construction.

Subject-Verb Agreement

The subject and the verb in a sentence should agree in number. Use the nine guidelines that follow to accomplish this objective.

1. Nouns or pronouns intervening between the subject and the verb have no effect on the rule that the subject and the verb agree in number.

a. The *contract* (singular subject) containing ten clauses *is being considered* (singular verb) by the committee.

b. The *skills* (plural subject) needed by an efficient secretary *include* (plural verb) typing, filing, shorthand, and human relations.

2. Use a singular verb with a collective noun when the collective noun is regarded as a unit. Use a plural verb with a collective noun when the collective noun is regarded as a group of *separate entities*.

Use conventional grammar to ensure mutual understanding.

Select a verb that agrees in number with its subject.

a. The committee discusses (singular subject/singular verb) the transportation problem every time it (singular pronoun reference) meets.

This sentence emphasizes the committee as a single unit.

b. The committee discuss (plural subject/plural verb) the transportation problem every time they (plural pronoun reference) meet.

The sentence emphasizes the committee as a group of individuals.

   3. Use a singular verb with nouns that end in *s* or *es* but that are singular in meaning.

Politics is an interesting profession.

The singular subject, *politics,* uses a singular verb, *is.*

   4. When a relative pronoun is used as the subject, use a singular or plural verb depending on the antecedent for the pronoun.

a. The *girls* from Louisiana Tech *who are* my roommates are planning to visit me next week.

The relative pronoun, *who,* has a plural reference; you have more than one roommate.

b. The *girl* from Louisiana Tech *who is* my roommate is planning to visit me next week.

This relative pronoun, *who,* has a singular reference; you have only one roommate.

c. My sorority *sisters* are the only ones at the Panhellenic meeting *who seem* to know what is going on today.

The relative pronoun, *who,* has a plural reference.

   5. In sentences that contain predicate nouns, the verb should still agree with the subject in number.

a. The *dancers are* a product of the Jay LeBourgeois School of Dance.

b. *Mary Friezen is* public-relations director, personnel director, and office manager.

   6. Use a singular verb when the subject is *each, either, neither, anyone, anybody, someone, somebody, everyone, one, no one,* and *nobody.*

a. *Each has* her own preferences.

b. *No one is* perfect.

c. *Everyone is* unhappy at one time or another.

7. Use a singular verb when a sentence has compound singular subjects connected with *or* or *nor*.

a. *Bill or Sue is* always in the coffee shop.

b. Neither the *table nor* the *desk is* in good repair.

8. Use a plural verb with a compound subject connected with *or* or *nor* when the subject closer to the verb is plural.

a. Neither the *father nor* his *sons are* interested in the auto-mechanics class to be offered this semester.

b. Either the *two accountants* or their *supervisor is* going to the seminar tomorrow.

9. Use a plural verb when a sentence contains two or more subjects connected by *and* or arranged in a series.

a. *Bill, Charles,* and *Edward are* being considered as possible replacements for Martha Allen.

b. The *secretary* and the *treasurer are* both out of the office today.

Verb Tense

Use appropriate tense to convey time.

To achieve clarity when communicating, use the proper tense in each sentence. If you are writing about something that happened yesterday, use the past tense; something that is happening now, the present tense; or something that will happen tomorrow, the future tense.

a. I *saw* the report yesterday (past tense).

b. I *see* the report lying on your desk (present tense).

c. I *will see* the report at the meeting tomorrow (future tense).

Avoid confusing changes of tense, a pitfall for every communicator.

a. The secretary *typed* (past tense) the letter and *gives* (present tense) it to Mr. Johnson to sign.

This sentence has a confusing and unnecessary change of tense.

b. The secretary *typed* (past tense) the letter and *gave* (past tense) it to Mr. Johnson to sign.

Both actions occurred in the past.

c. The secretary *typed* (past tense) the letter and *will give* (future tense) it to Mr. Johnson as soon as he gets back from lunch.

The sequence of events in business is often very important to you and your communication partner. The tense you use in communicating relays valuable information. Suppose you receive a letter from a customer who owes you $150. If the customer says in the letter that he *mailed* (past tense) his check to you, you would assume that the check was mailed before the letter and that you will receive it soon. If, instead, the customer is planning to mail the check in two weeks when he receives a cash dividend on some stock he owns, the word *mailed* is incorrect. The customer should say *will mail* so you will not be expecting the $150 check to arrive in the next mail delivery.

Noun and Pronoun Case and Person

When selecting noun and pronoun forms, analyze their function in the sentence. A noun has the same form whether it is a subject or an object. However, the noun form changes when it is possessive (refer to the discussion of the apostrophe earlier in this chapter). The pronoun form is different for the nominative, objective, and possessive cases. Table 7–1 shows the various forms for these cases.

Use the *nominative-case* pronoun when it is used as the subject. Use the *objective-case* pronoun when it is the direct or indirect object of a verb or the object of a preposition. Use the *possessive-*

Analyze the function of nouns and pronouns in your sentences.

Based on function, use nominative-, objective-, or possessive-case pronouns.

Table 7–1
Noun and Pronoun Forms for the Nominative, Objective, and Possessive Cases

	Nominative	Objective	Possessive
Nouns (singular)	James	James	James's
	letter	letter	letter's
Nouns (plural)	Joneses	Joneses	Joneses'
	letters	letters	letters'
Pronouns (singular)	I	me	my, mine*
	he	him	his
	she	her	her, hers*
	it	it	its
Pronouns (plural)	we	us	our, ours*
	they	them	their, theirs*
Pronouns (singular and plural)	you	you	your, yours*
	who	whom	whose

*The first form of the possessive pronoun is used when it appears before a noun or gerund. The second form is used when the possessive appears in a noun position.

case pronoun when it shows possession. The possessive pronouns differ in form when they are followed by a noun or gerund, except *his, its,* and *whose.*

1. Mary's book was stolen.

Mary's is a possessive noun.

2. The *book's* most outstanding feature is *its* marginal notations.

Book's is a possessive noun; *its* is a possessive pronoun. Use *it* only to refer to inanimate objects and animals.

3. The stranger took the book from *Mary.*

Mary is in the objective case, the object of a preposition.

4. Mary tried to hide the book from *him.*

Him is in the objective case, the object of a preposition.

5. *He* found *her* locker and stole *her* book.

He is the subject and is in the nominative case; *her* shows possession in both uses and is in the possessive case.

6. *You* took *my* book.

You is the subject and is a nominative pronoun; *my* shows possession and is a possessive pronoun.

7. *I* gave my book to *you.*

I is the subject and is a nominative pronoun; *you* is the object of the preposition and is an objective pronoun.

8. *I* will sell *my* book to *whoever* wants *it.*

I is the subject and is a nominative pronoun; *my* shows possession and is a possessive pronoun. *Whoever* is the subject of the clause (whoever wants it) that is the object of the preposition *to* and is a nominative pronoun; *it* is the direct object of the verb *wants* in this clause and is an objective pronoun.

Use first-person pronouns (we, us, our, ours, I, me, my, mine) when you are speaking or writing about yourself or about a group to which you belong. Use second-person pronouns (you, your, yours) when you are talking or writing directly to someone. Use third-person pronouns (they, them, their, theirs, he, she, it, him, his, her, hers, its) when you are talking about someone who is not present or when you are writing about someone whose name does not

Select the appropriate pronoun person for relaying intended meaning.

appear in the inside address of your letter. Nouns do not have person.

1. *They* owe *me* $150.

They is the third-person subject; *me* is the first-person object.

2. *I* need to send *them* a letter before *you* and *I* discuss this matter further.

I is the first-person subject; *them* is the third-person object. *You* is in the second person, *I* is in the first person, and both are subjects of the verb *discuss* in the dependent clause that is the object of the preposition *before.*

3. *We* are so proud of *our* record.

Both pronouns are in the first person, one used as the subject, the other showing possession.

4. The *girls* checked the *book* out of the *library.*

Nouns do not have person.
    To achieve clarity and understanding in your communications, choose the correct case and person for both nouns and pronouns.

Pronoun Reference

A pronoun is used in place of a noun. Accepted grammar rules dictate that a pronoun be used *only* when the noun to which it refers is clearly understood. Therefore, the pronoun must agree in number with its antecedent.

Use a pronoun only when its antecedent is clear.

1. *Mary* told *Sally* that *she* was not going to be able to go to the dance.

Because the pronoun *she* is the singular form, it has two possible antecedents (confusing pronoun reference).

2. *Jerry* and *Allen* made plans to go to the dance, but *he* could not get *his* car.

The pronouns *he* and *his* have no clear antecedent because, again, the subject is compound. If *Jerry* and *Allen* are both antecedents, the pronouns should be plural.

3. *George* went to the meeting for *me*. When *he* got there, the meeting was over.

George is the antecedent for *he.* The antecedent for *me* is not expressed in the sentence, but the meaning is clear because it is a first-person pronoun.

4. The *secretaries* had a meeting with *their* union representative yesterday afternoon.

Secretaries is the obvious antecedent of *their.*

To achieve clarity and understanding in your communications, use pronouns only when their antecedents are obvious and clear.

Dangling Modifiers

Eliminate confusing dangling modifiers.

Dangling modifiers are participial, infinitive, or gerund phrases that do not clearly refer to any word in the sentence. When you recognize a dangling modifier in your communications, revise your sentence so the verbal phrase clearly modifies some word in that sentence.

1. To get rid of his headache, aspirins were taken.
   To get rid of his headache, Tom took two aspirins.

The infinitive phrase *to get rid of his headache* clearly does not modify *aspirins.* Revised, it obviously modifies *Tom.*

2. Before going to bed, the radio was turned off.
   Before going to bed, Jane turned off the radio.

Did the radio go to bed? The gerund phrase *going to bed,* the object of the preposition *before,* is confusing because it cannot apply to *radio.* Revised, it clearly indicates that Jane turned the radio off.

3. Opening our books, the lecturer entered the room.
   Opening our books, we prepared to take notes when the lecturer entered the room.

Did the lecturer open the books? Obviously the participial phrase *opening our books* cannot modify *lecturer,* so it is confusing. Revised, it clearly modifies the subject, *we.*

To achieve clarity and understanding in your communications, carefully eliminate or revise those sentences that contain dangling modifiers.

Parallel Construction

Use parallel structure for ideas of equal importance.

Ideas of equal importance should be expressed in parallel form. Coordinating conjunctions are used to connect words, phrases, or clauses expressed in similar form.

1. I told my supervisor *that I would type all the letters she dictated today* and *to send Mary to the post office to buy stamps.*

A dependent clause and an infinitive phrase are incorrectly connected by the coordinating conjunction *and.*

I told my supervisor that I would type all the letters she dictated today and that I would take them to the post office on my way home from work.

The revised sentence contains two dependent clauses of equal importance and structure joined by the coordinating conjunction *and.*

2. Mr. Johnson told me *to make a list of the supplies needed in the office, that a purchase order needed to be typed,* and *to inventory the present stock of photocopy paper.*

The first and third infinitive phrases *are* parallel, but the meaning of the sentence is confused by the dependent clause stating the second action in the series.

Mr. Johnson told me to make a list of the supplies needed in the office, to type a purchase order for the supplies, and to inventory the present stock of photocopy paper.

In the revised sentence, three infinitive phrases are connected by commas and the coordinating conjunction *and.*

3. Either Margaret will call the service representative or Tom will attempt to repair the typewriter.

The correlatives, *either* and *or,* connect two complete clauses in parallel construction.

To achieve maximum readability and clarity, use parallel structure in your sentences.

Several helpful books on grammar and writing are listed in Table 7–2. Your personal library should include one or more. (See also Table 9–1 listing style manuals in general use.)

You should periodically review and continually apply good grammar rules when speaking and writing. Only by presenting your messages in acceptable, uniform style can you expect to become an effective communicator.

Transition Methods

Transition methods help to move the thoughts of your reader smoothly from one idea to another. These methods help your reader follow your line of thought, your thought patterns. You can further reduce the possibility of miscommunication because of misunderstanding. Good transition techniques decrease the necessity

Use transition methods to help your communication partner.

Table 7—2

Helpful Books on Grammar and Writing

Jacques Barzun. *Simple and Direct: A Rhetoric for Writers.* New York: Harper & Row, 1976.

M. C. Butera, R. Krause, and W. A. Sabin. *College English: Grammar and Style.* New York: McGraw-Hill, 1967.

Eugene Ehrlich and Daniel Murphy. *Basic Grammar for Writing: A Step-by-Step Course in All the Essentials of Clear Writing.* New York: McGraw-Hill, 1971.

Rudolf Flesch. *Look It Up.* New York: Harper & Row, 1977.

H. W. Fowler. *A Dictionary of Modern English Usage.* 2nd ed. Rev. and ed. by Sir Ernest Gowers. New York: Oxford University Press, 1965.

Lewis Jordan. The New York Times *Manual of Style and Usage.* New York: Quadrangle/The New York Times Book Co., 1976.

William Strunk, Jr., and E. B. White. *The Elements of Style.* 2nd ed. New York: Macmillan, 1972.

Rufus P. Turner. *Technical Writer's and Editor's Stylebook.* Indianapolis, Ind.: Howard W. Sams & Co., 1964.

William Zinsser. *On Writing Well: An Informal Guide to Writing Nonfiction.* New York: Harper & Row, 1976.

for backtracking and rereading and thus shorten the time your communication partner must spend reading your communications.

The transition methods most often used are:

1. Parenthetical words
2. Repetition
3. Introductory and summary statements.

Parenthetical Words

Use parenthetical words to bridge thoughts.

Parenthetical words are not necessary to understand the sentence. Why, then, should you clutter your communication with parenthetical words?

Use parenthetical words only when justified.

Since every word you write in a business communication costs your company money in the form of dictator time, secretarial transcription time, and supplies and equipment, you should have a valid reason for adding parenthetical words. Every word in your communication should have a definite purpose for being there. The only true justification for these parenthetical words is that they serve as transition devices to make your writing smoother and easier to read.

The Miller Automotive Corporation spent $450,000 on its newest building. *Therefore,* the management is planning to sell an additional thousand shares of stock to cover the cost.

Therefore connects the $450,000 expenditure to the sale of additional stock. *Therefore* is used to carry the thoughts of the reader from one concept to another and enables the reader to more easily understand the relationship between the two ideas.

Other parenthetical words you can use for transition are listed in Table 7–3. Such a list can go on and on, but the important thing to remember is to use parenthetical words sparingly and only when needed for transition purposes. Although these words capture the attention of the reader only briefly, your communication partner will surely become distracted when reading your communication if every sentence contains a parenthetical expression. Overuse of any writing device tends to draw attention away from the purpose of your message.

Avoid overuse of parenthetical transition words.

Repetition

You can bridge the thoughts in your communication by occasionally repeating a key word or phrase.

Table 7–3
Transitional Words and Phrases to Smooth Your Writing

accordingly	in addition
after all	in other words
again	moreover
also	neither . . . nor
and	nevertheless
at the same time	next
because	nonetheless
before	only
besides	on the other hand
but	similarly
consequently	so
either . . . or	still
finally	therefore
for	thus
for example	too
for instance	with this thought in mind
furthermore	yet
however	

One of the biggest problems we have in our office is the *abuse* of morning and afternoon break times. This *abuse* is costing our company thousands of dollars.

Repeat a key word or phrase to bridge thoughts.

The idea of abuse is carried from one sentence to another and emphasized through repetition.

Introductory and Summary Statements

Summarize the topic of the preceding paragraph.

Introductory and summary statements used at the beginning of a paragraph, referring to either the preceding or several preceding paragraphs, can serve as a very effective transition method. The introductory/summary statement is particularly useful when the message contains a large number of details that the reader needs to absorb to arrive at the conclusion that you, the writer, intend. In essence, you are briefly summarizing (in one sentence) the points in the preceding paragraph or paragraphs. Then, you are ready to proceed to the next concept or idea you wish to present. When your introductory statement is a summary statement, the paragraph should be written in inductive order; the topic sentence is the last sentence in the paragraph. Assume that three paragraphs precede the following example paragraph. Paragraph one contains information about the debts of the company; paragraph two contains information about the company's accounts receivable value; and paragraph three contains information about operating costs. Paragraph four might read:

Operating costs, at $825,000 last year, are not out of line when you consider that our debts are approximately one-third of the value of our accounts receivable. The largest operating expense for fiscal 19— was for office equipment. Our office equipment was outdated and slowed down work in the office. Job performance, morale, and production are on the increase as a result of recent equipment purchases.

Use recurring introductory statements to stress one idea.

A little-used, but sometimes effective, transition device is the recurring introductory statement. This technique may be effectively used only when the message has a single purpose, one that is so important that it is repeated as an introduction to every paragraph. The remainder of each paragraph should contain a different reason, argument, or discussion that supports the recurring introductory statement.

A word-processing center is a much needed innovation in office organization. . . . Companies are able to take full advantage of specialization in office personnel.

A word-processing center is a much needed innovation in office organization. . . . Equipment purchased for the center is expensive, but production increases offset equipment costs.

A word processing center is a much needed innovation in office organization. . . . All of the noisy word-processing equipment is centrally located, leaving office areas quiet and allowing maximum concentration by the decision-makers in a business organization.

A variation of this transition method is to place the recurring statement at the end of each paragraph.

Use transition devices (1) to tie ideas together; (2) to help your communication partner to understand your message better, and (3) to ensure that your reader will arrive at the hoped-for conclusions. Transition devices are important tools for constructing effective business messages.

Proofreading and Revising

To ensure that all parts of the communication puzzle fit together precisely, you must carefully proofread your message and revise it if needed. The accuracy with which you proofread will depend on how critical a reader you are; on your ability to be objective enough to recognize your own errors; and on your knowledge of correct spelling and correct sentence, paragraph, and message structure. Proofreading is certainly not an easy task, but it is a necessary one.

Be objective when proofreading.

The proofreading and revising process includes recognizing errors, marking them, and making necessary changes. To reduce proofreading time, you should use standard proofreader's marks. Your typist, too, should understand proofreader's marks and be able to make the indicated corrections from rough-draft copy. Table 7–4 shows standard proofreader's marks. They can also be found in most dictionaries and style manuals (see Table 9–1).

Revise communications to eliminate errors.

Before beginning the revision of your message, gather any additional information needed, look up the correct spelling of any words thought to be misspelled, rewrite any paragraphs that seem illogical or disorganized, and delete unnecessary words and sentences. Revision actually begins when the typist retypes your corrected message. You must be equally conscientious about proofreading and revising the second, third, or even fourth rough drafts.

Use proofreader's marks to speed the revision process.

Table 7—4

Proofreader's Marks (Instructions to the typist are generally circled.)

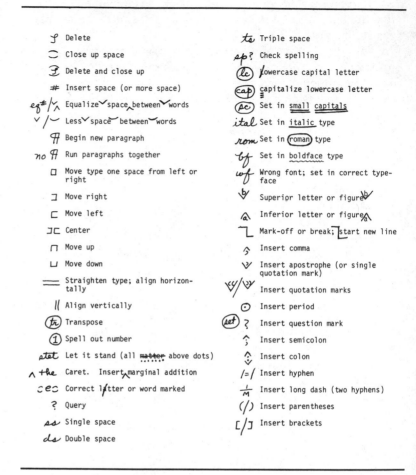

ℒ	Delete	ts	Triple space
⌒	Close up space	sp?	Check spelling
ℒ	Delete and close up	(lc)	lowercase capital letter
#	Insert space (or more space)	(cap)	capitalize lowercase letter
eq #/⋏	Equalize space between words	(sc)	Set in small capitals
∨/⌣	Less space between words	ital	Set in italic type
¶	Begin new paragraph	rom	Set in roman type
no ¶	Run paragraphs together	bf	Set in boldface type
□	Move type one space from left or right	wf	Wrong font; set in correct typeface
⌐	Move right	⋁	Superior letter or figure
⌐	Move left	⌐	Inferior letter or figure
⌐⌐	Center	⌐	Mark-off or break; start new line
⊓	Move up	⌣	Insert comma
⊔	Move down	⋁	Insert apostrophe (or single quotation mark)
⎓	Straighten type; align horizontally	⋁/⋁	Insert quotation marks
‖	Align vertically	⊙	Insert period
(tr)	Transpose	(set)?	Insert question mark
①	Spell out number	⌃	Insert semicolon
stet	Let it stand (all matter above dots)	⌃	Insert colon
∧ the	Caret. Insert marginal addition	/=/	Insert hyphen
c e ⌐	Correct letter or word marked	⌐/M	Insert long dash (two hyphens)
?	Query	(/)	Insert parentheses
ss	Single space	[/]	Insert brackets
ds	Double space		

The number of proofreading and revision processes for a clear, concise, complete message depends mostly on how important and lengthy the message is. When all the needed proofreading and revising is completed, you are ready to have the final copy typed. However, you still have to carefully proofread the final copy to eliminate typographical and spelling errors.

"A word to the wise." Each new rough draft of a message should be numbered—first draft, second draft, final draft. This procedure will help to prevent your typist from inadvertently using the wrong rough draft for typing the final copy.

Number each rough draft.

Summary

To prepare your communication, you have:
1. determined your message objective
2. analyzed your communication partner
3. outlined your message
4. written topic sentences to convey your message
5. developed paragraphs from your topic sentences
6. organized your paragraphs in a logical sequence
7. applied punctuation and grammar rules
8. used appropriate transition methods to promote clear meaning and to enhance readability
9. selected up-to-date words that your reader will understand
10. proofread carefully, using a dictionary
11. marked and corrected errors in your revision process
12. finally produced a communication that satisfies its reason for creation.

The communication puzzle is complete! As Confucius, the great Chinese philosopher said: "For one word a man is often deemed to be wise, and for one word he is often deemed to be foolish. We should be careful indeed what we say."

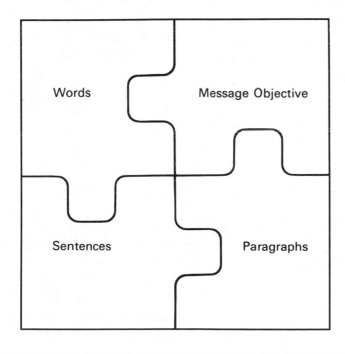

Figure 7—1
The communication puzzle is complete!

Exercises

Punctuate the following sentences correctly.

1. Please ship the merchandise that I ordered by Tuesday October 18.

2. Our big fall sale is scheduled to begin Friday October 21 and I need at least two days to price mark and display the merchandise.

3. Please ship immediately the following items 1 six dozen $3/4$'' wrenches 2 ten pounds #2 roofing nails and 3 six cartons $7/8$'' wood screws.

4. If you cannot ship my order by October 18 call me at 318-478-2212 between 8 A.M. and 5 P.M. at that time we can discuss alternative arrangements.

5. The committee chairperson who has been with our company for ten years is a capable industrious worker.

6. When the chairperson Rhonda Calhoun called me to take her place I told her I would be out of town at the time of the meeting however my plans have changed and I will attend the meeting.

7. The problem that I have more to do than I can accomplish during office hours is affecting the quality of my work.

8. The IBM MTST magnetic tape Selectric typewriter arrived yesterday but the new word processor who will operate the typewriter was at home with his sick child.

9. As soon as the word processor returns to work the IBM representative will conduct an orientation training session.

10. My secretary did not sign up for the orientation however I hope she will be able to attend.

11. Please send the catalog to Mr. Marcus V Blackmon 5156 Nelson Road Wheeling WV 26003.

12. Marshas coat was stolen from the cafeteria while she was eating. Its hard to believe that anyone could be so cruel.

13. My son Jerry made two As two Bs and two Cs on his report card but he made a U in deportment.

14. I called his teacher Mr. Vallot and asked for an appointment for Friday April 2 at eight oclock.

15. Charlotte called the plumber this morning the electrician at noon and the architect after lunch.

16. The plumber said he could meet with Charlotte tomorrow morning the electrician tomorrow afternoon and the architect Monday.

17. Collect everything you will need for the meeting pencils paper agenda minutes of the last meeting and by-laws of the organization.

18. The typewriter would not print Ws As Xs or Cs.

19. The service representative told the secretary that the extreme temperatures in the building caused the typewriter to malfunction.

20. Its hard to keep the typewriter operating properly because the sudden changes in temperature cause condensation to form on its moving parts.

Analyze the following sentences to determine whether the subject and verb agree in number. Revise the sentences in which you find verb-subject disagreement.

21. The library full of books, newspapers, and magazines are used by many business and professional people.

22. The rules for conducting a business meeting is set forth in the organization's by-laws.

23. The board meet in the second floor coffee shop on the first Monday of every month.

24. The Senate is composed of two elected delegates from each state.

25. Top management have issued a fair promotional policy for women.

26. The man who rent the office next door operate a telephone answering service.

27. Each of the members of the Board of Realtors have been asked to meet with the director at 9:30 A.M. tomorrow.

28. Parliamentary procedures are a set of rules used by an organization to conduct orderly meetings.

29. The "Seven Pops" is a barbershop singing group.

30. The "Seven Pops," in real life, is a doctor, two attorneys, two teachers, and two insurance agents.

Analyze the pronouns in the following sentences. Identify the pronoun case needed in each sentence, and make corrections if the incorrect case is used.

31. Mrs. Harlingen assigned the financial research to Edward and I.

32. Us career women must band together in our struggle for equal opportunities.

33. The top management of Mesu, Inc. has been more than fair in its promotional policies for we women.

34. George and me were selected as delegates to the state convention this year.

35. When I left the office yesterday, I saw you new car in the parking lot.

36. You and I must meet to discuss the project; Mr. Jones asked me to give you this message.

37. Mr. Conrod discussed his problems with the company psychologist and decided to continue in its present job.

38. Very few of the secretaries are interested in the new plan, but my am very interested in it.

39. I am planning to call you Monday, December 12, to remind you of the meeting to be held at my house.

40. Please send me a new telephone book; my neighbor and me are doing a telephone canvass of area merchants to determine their personnel needs.

Revise each of the following sentences to correct the pronoun shown in italics.

41. Frank Tullery is the office manager, but Montgomery Parish is responsible for hiring personnel. *He* has a degree in business from Harvard.

42. Martha Johnson and Joan Nelson are in charge of ticket sales, but *she* has to get permission to sell the tickets in the downtown mall.

43. George called Bill and told him that *he* was elected to represent the office at the secretarial conference in Denver, Colorado.

44. The dog and the cat that belong to my neighbors got into a terrible fight last week. *It* had to have stitches taken and stayed at the animal hospital four days.

45. The secretary to Mrs. Greene, Ellen Ellzey, was run over by a car last year; *she* was so upset.

46. Last year I took a vacation trip to Colorado, Nevada, California, and New Mexico! *It* is so nice to look at the pictures and remember all the fun we had.

47. Mr. Henry has asked me to be the secretary and to type the minutes for all the board meetings. I am afraid *it* is going to be boring.

48. I have always wished that I had finished my college education before Linda and Judy entered college. *She* spends so much money at college that I will have to wait until *she* gets *her* degree.

49. I wonder whatever happened to Victor Mancuso and Frederick Tarasewitcz. *He* was our senior-class president.

50. *It* has been a long time since I worked in the mailing services department.

Revise each of the following sentences to correct confusing dangling modifiers.

51. Walking the dog, the leash broke.

52. Before typing the manuscript, the typewriter was oiled and cleaned.

53. To prevent further thefts in the office, locks on all doors were changed.

54. Carrying a 16-gauge shotgun and wearing a ski mask, the owner of the store on Orchard Drive was held up by a robber.

55. To provide more comfortable working conditions, the air-conditioning system was cleaned, oiled, and repaired by the maintenance department.

Revise each of the following sentences so ideas of equal importance are parallel in form.

56. My boss asked me to hold all of his calls, to bring him a cup of coffee, and asked that I type a memo to Roger.

57. Before you can become an effective communicator, you must be proficient in English-composition skills, a good organizer, perceptive, and empathetic.

58. If you make a typographical error while typing a ditto master, you scrape the carbon off the back of the sheet, place an unused piece of carbon over the correction, and you take the carbon piece out after you type your correction.

59. Either call Alyce and make the appointment for tomorrow, call Juan to talk to Edward about the job, or I will have to make the appointment for you.

60. I recommend Virginia Woodley for the new management position. She is dependable, capable, and always likes to do jobs that require a lot of thought and creativity.

61. Rewrite the following paragraphs making the corrections indicated by the proofreader's marks.

Businesses are continually searching for ways too save time and money and for ways to produce data more accurately and more rapidly. the dictation process saves both time and money and makes possible the processing of greater volume of usable information.

Dictation takes less effort and and expends less energy than longhand composition. holding a microphone and taking are considerably less tiring than holding a pin and writing pages and pages of words and figures. The energy you save can best be put to use in collecting and organizing information and in coordinating men, money, materials, methods, machnes, and morale.

**Part Four   Your Role in Creating
Business Messages**

Chapter 8 Types of Business Letters

"The ablest writer is a gardner, first, and then a cook. His tasks are, carefully to select and cultivate his strongest and most nutritive thoughts, and, when they are ripe, to dress them wholesomely, and so that they may have a relish." — J. C. and A. W. Hare

Introduction

The business communicator writes many types of business letters, each one tailored to fit a specific need. Careful planning; a knowledge of business-letter-writing techniques; a thorough study of each situation; and the use of tact, honesty, perception, and empathy will help you write effective business messages to meet every need.

Why do you *write* business letters? Writing business letters has a threefold purpose:
1. to communicate
2. to provide a concrete, accurate, business record
3. to promote and maintain goodwill.

This threefold purpose indicates why you *write* letters instead of communicating in person or over the phone. Granted, you can promote and maintain goodwill and relay information and understanding in person or on the phone; but you will rarely have a concrete, accurate record of your conversation. Without a written record, the information, understanding, and goodwill may soon be forgotten, lost in the hurried pace of the business world.

When should you write a business letter? Here are some of the circumstances you may face in which a business letter would be appropriate.

1. You receive an order for a product your company manufactures, but the item ordered is temporarily out of stock.

2. You work in the bookkeeping department and are charged with the responsibility of persuading charge customers to pay their overdue bills.

3. You receive a request for information about the models, characteristics, and prices of a product sold by your firm.

4. A close business associate's brother dies.

Adapt your communications to specific needs.

Determine the purpose of each business message.

5. You work in the personnel department, and you receive a letter asking for a recommendation for a former employee of your company.

6. As manager of the sales department, you are asked to prepare a promotional letter for a new product your company is going to market.

7. A business associate in another city gives you valuable information about a client of yours who lives in that city. You are very grateful for that information.

8. As office manager, you ordered fifty reams of letterhead paper that arrived yesterday. You open one of the packages to examine the quality of the paper and notice that the wrong ZIP Code is printed on the letterhead.

9. In last night's newspaper, you read that a former college classmate of yours is moving to your city as the manager of a local retail store.

10. You are the office supervisor in a small branch office in Reno, Nevada, and have recently detected a feeling of insecurity and low morale among your office employees. You believe this general unrest in the office may be caused by rumors that your company is planning to centralize all computer operations in its home office in San Francisco. Most of the work in your office centers around its computer facility.

Hundreds of sometimes unique, sometimes routine situations similar to those listed above will require a written business message. Are you prepared to meet this challenge?

Your first task, as a business communicator, is to carefully analyze each situation that requires a letter to determine the objective of the letter you will write. Once this objective is determined, your next step is to combine the guidelines provided in this chapter with your own creativeness to invent letters that will communicate and, at the same time, promote and maintain goodwill.

Business letters can be divided into five broad categories:
1. Routine
2. Persuasive
3. Positive
4. Negative
5. Management-to-employee
These categories are based on the objectives for writing letters; but, at times, these objectives may tend to overlap.

Use your creativity when composing business messages.

Routine Letters

A routine letter is written in response to regularly recurring office situations. The routine letter is written so often that the business writer may only have to select a preconstructed letter (or paragraphs); adapt it to the particular situation by inserting the appropriate inside address, names, dollar amounts, and dates; and have it typed. Every business has its routine letters used to inform, to inquire, or to relay goodwill.

Routine correspondence may be classified into the following general categories:

1. Acknowledgments
2. Letters of transmittal
3. Requests for information
4. Order messages (when forms are not available)
5. Thank-you letters
6. Hotel-reservation requests
7. Letters of congratulations
8. Letters of recommendation
9. Condolence messages

Acknowledgments

An acknowledgment letter should be brief and should be written to inform the receiver that you have received the order or the request for information. If you can send the order or the information immediately, an acknowledgment letter is *unnecessary*. However, if there will be a delay in satisfying the request or sending the order, an acknowledgment message should be sent.

Acknowledgment of the receipt of an order for merchandise might be worded:

Your order #_____ was received today and will be shipped to you on or about ____(date)____. The invoice for the merchandise will reach your office from one to three days before delivery.

Thank you for your order.

Acknowledgment of a request for information might be worded:

The information you requested about ___(subject)___ was referred to ___(name)___ in our _____ department. A report is presently being prepared and should reach you in about ___(time)___.

We are happy to serve you and look forward to hearing from you again soon.

Letters of Transmittal

A letter of transmittal is written to ensure clear, complete communication. When a check is mailed, the letter of transmittal provides information to its receiver about the name of the account, the account number, and any instructions about the disbursement of the check. When a report, a catalog, a brochure, or a form is mailed, a letter of transmittal informs the receiver of the purpose of the mailing, the instructions for use or completion, or the procedures used and sources of information being sent.

Use a transmittal letter to explain the purpose of an enclosure.

The letter accompanying the annual report to the stockholders might read:

The 19— Annual Report for the Colston Corporation is enclosed. The figures and information contained in the report were compiled by a staff of about eighty people in the accounting, research and development, marketing, and sales departments. The auditing firm of James, Cameron, and Rollins certified the accuracy of the data. Colston Corporation appreciates your investment in its future.

The letter transmitting a check in payment of invoice #866255 might read:

Check No. 8210 for $1,565.80 is enclosed. Please apply $565.80 to our account #6621258 and $1,000 to our account #6621260.
Thank you for the prompt delivery of our ____(date)____ order.

Requests for Information

Request letters should be specific and courteous. The business communicator must empathize with the receiver of the request by furnishing all the details necessary to fill the request and by saying "please" and "thank you" when appropriate. But, guard against thanking in advance for something not yet received; your communication partner may think you are presumptuous.

Be specific and courteous when writing a request letter.

When you write your request letter, use the following outline:
1. Make contact with the receiver.
2. Make your request being sure to include all details the receiver will need in order to satisfy your request.

3. Give reasons for the request, when appropriate.

4. End with a goodwill statement.

Example one:

Your office manager, Tom Allen, tells us you are very pleased with the operation of your new word-processing center. We have been considering the installation of such a center but, up to now, have been unable to collect any first-hand data. Your answers to the following questions will help our staff to organize a word-processing center here at Donaldson's.

1. How many people are employed in your word-processing center?

2. What equipment do you use in your center?

3. Did you purchase, lease, or rent the equipment?

4. What was the approximate cost of the equipment?

5. What are the duties of each of your word-processing employees?

Enclosed is an addressed, postpaid envelope for your reply.

I will be in Akron next Tuesday and Wednesday and will call to see if you can get away for lunch with me one of those days.

Example two:

Last spring our employees were very pleased with the uniforms we ordered through your catalog. Here it is February again and time to order new uniforms for the upcoming spring and summer seasons.

Please send us a copy of your latest catalog so we may make our selections and place our order before March 1.

Order Messages

Most business firms use printed forms for placing merchandise orders. Whether you use a form or a letter, you must be sure to include the following information in your order:

Make sure your order messages are specific and complete.

1. A complete description of the items ordered, including catalog numbers, size, color, and other identifying information.

2. The number of units being ordered.

3. The unit price and the total cost of the units ordered.

4. The date needed, when time of delivery is an urgent matter.

5. The shipping instructions.

6. The payment terms, including purchase order or account number.

Please ship, air express, the following items:

200 ea.	#160V, 21 brass spools @ $2	$400.00
6 ctns.	#88623K, round robin carbon rings @ $12	72.00
	Total	$472.00

Our account number is 62605F. Payment will be made within ninety days.

Please call Carl Villerd at 508/222–1010 if shipment cannot be made by March 1.

Thank-You Letters

Write a thank-you message when the favor granted was particularly important.

A thank-you letter is written to show appreciation for a favor granted and to create goodwill for your company. Saying "thank you" is a matter of courtesy and should be written in letter form when the favor granted was particularly important.

When writing a thank-you letter, use the following outline:

1. Say "thank you" and be specific about the reason for your letter.
2. Comment on the results of the favor granted.
3. Offer to return the favor.

Thank you for sending me the information about your word-processing center. We are only in the planning stages now, but Walton's hopes to set up a center similar to yours by June or July of this year. The organizational plan and the job descriptions for your word-processing center have been a big help to us.

Please call on us if we can return the favor.

Hotel-Reservations Requests

Furnish complete details when making reservations.

Business correspondents seldom write letters to request hotel reservations since most hotels have toll-free telephone service or hotel-to-hotel teletype service. Whether the reservation is made over the phone, through the teletype service, or in writing, the following information should be furnished to the hotel:

1. Dates and approximate times of arrival and departure
2. Number of people needing accommodations
3. Size of room(s) desired (suite, single, double)
4. Type of beds required (queen, king, twin, double, rollaway, etc.)

5. Price limitations, if any

6. The name of the company and the representative(s) needing accommodations, if a business trip.

7. Name of the individual or company that will be responsible for payment (or the credit-card number)

8. The address and phone number of the company (if a business trip) or of the individual (if a pleasure trip)

Letters of Congratulations

Letters of congratulations are important ambassadors of goodwill sent to business associates and clients. When you take time from your busy day to recognize in letter form the accomplishments of others, you are sure to reap many kind thoughts and lasting business friendships.

Use the following guides for your congratulations letters:
1. Establish contact.
2. Express your congratulations.

A letter of congratulations may be handwritten to distinguish it from the ordinary typewritten, profit-oriented letters received daily.

Create and maintain goodwill with letters of congratulations.

Your picture in last night's Enterprise was obviously that of a man with a bright future in the business world.

Congratulations on your promotion to Vice President of Operations!

Sincerely

Connie Allen

Enclosed is copy of the story for your scrapbook.

Letters of Recommendation

A business associate, a client, a personal friend, or a past employee may give your name as a reference for a new job or ask you to send a letter of recommendation to a prospective employer. In either instance, you will have an opportunity in the letter you write to influence the decision of the prospective employer to hire your associate or friend.

Use the following guidelines in writing your letter of recommendation:

1. Introduce yourself and establish your credibility.
2. Make your recommendations, giving specific reasons and complete details.

As Office Manager for Cormier's, Inc. for the past ten years, I have had the pleasure of working daily with Martin Jones, an accountant in our Payroll Department. Martin is a loyal, conscientious, hard-working person who desires advancement in his profession. He has an M.B.A. from O.S.U., and he passed his CPA exam this month. Cormier's wishes it had a job opening for Martin.

Please give every consideration to hiring Martin Jones as the new head of your Accounting Division. He will be an asset to your firm.

Condolence Messages

The condolence message sent by a business person to a business associate or a client often takes the form of a purchased sympathy card or a few words written on a card attached to a floral arrangement. When the association is very close and when the business person knows the associate's or client's family well, he may wish to send a *handwritten* condolence message. The message should be concise, sincere, and positive. Most important, it should convey a "you-attitude." The objective of the condolence message is to sympathize, encourage, and, when appropriate, offer a helping hand.

> Your friends at Millers are saddened by the news of your brother's death.
>
> Tom was a valued customer as well as a close friend. In fact, his understanding and support five years ago when Millers underwent a series of financial crises account for our present existence and well being.
>
> Please call me if there is any way that Millers can be of service to you.

This letter is concise and contains a brief statement of sympathy, a kind word about the deceased, and a concrete offer to help. The letter is totally reader centered and is void of ridiculously overdramatic statements that tend to lessen the credibility and sincerity of letters of condolence.

Persuasive Letters

A persuasive letter is written primarily to convince others "to do something they want to do because you want them to do it." Persuasive letters are written:

1. to advertise and sell a product or a service
2. to collect on an overdue bill
3. to convince the receiver to provide information about an individual or a firm
4. to convince a company to satisfy your request for an adjustment
5. to convince your communication partner to grant you a *special* favor
6. to convince the receiver to accept your invitation.

If the primary objective of your communication is to convince someone to do something, the letter is persuasive.

First, determine the individual reason for writing the persuasive letter; then, fit your ideas into the following letter outline:

1. Establish contact with the reader.
2. Present the details of your proposal.
3. Justify reader acceptance of your proposal.
4. Tell your reader exactly what action to take.
5. End with a goodwill statement that leaves the communication doors open.

Get Your Reader's Attention

If you will keep in mind that the word *business* was originally defined as "the state of being busy," you will empathize with your reader by beginning your letter with a concise statement that gains immediate attention. Whether you choose to ask a question, to tell a joke or an anecdote, or to make an astounding or interesting statement, your opening should relate to the specific purpose of your letter.

Open your persuasive letter with an attention-getting statement.

When you have written your opening statement, ask yourself which of the following reactions it will most likely receive:

1. "I want to read this letter now!"
2. "I'll just put this letter in the stack to read later when I have more time."
3. "I can't be bothered with such trivia. The trash can is the best place to file this one."

In example one, you are writing a letter to collect an overdue bill. The client's payments are five months behind, and you have sent three previous notices. To persuade your client to want to read your letter, you might use one of these opening statements:

Do you realize that you have $68.50 that belongs to us?

This statement uses a question to appeal to the receiver's sense of honesty and justice.

Our attorney, Mr. James Hale, will call on you Thursday, December 12, at 10:30 A.M. If you do not wish to visit with James, send us your check for $68.50, or plan to be away from your office on December 12.

In this opener, the writer uses a rather unusual statement to emphasize the seriousness of the overdue account while maintaining a sense of humor in the second sentence. The result is a subtle appeal to the receiver's fear of legal action without the use of unreasonable, goodwill-destructive threats.

"A stitch in time saves nine," and your $68.50 check in this office by Thursday, February 9, will save you more than $9. Court costs for collection litigations average $200—$400, depending on the amount of the account involved.

This opening appeals to the receiver's chance to *save* money by paying the bill.

In example two, you are selling a transcriber-recorder.[1] To persuade your reader to want to finish the letter, your opening statement might be:

Have you often wished for a twenty-four-hour secretary?

This opening uses a question appealing to a common need for additional help. Or you could say:

You can have an attractive, color-coordinated, 7 x 8 inch box on your desk. What's that? You don't want anything else on your already-cluttered desk?

You are selling a telephone-activated dictating device that sits on the *secretary's* desk. This opening uses a ridiculous statement and some hypothetical dialogue to describe a typical office problem. Since most offices have dictating equipment, the above attention-getter would serve a two-fold purpose: to remind the reader of one disadvantage of separate recorders and transcribers—space needs—and, therefore, to set the stage for convincing the reader to change to a new, more convenient dictation system.

---

[1] A transcriber-recorder is a dual-purpose machine that records and plays back enabling the user to record dictation and also to listen to the recorded dictation. For economical reasons, a secretary could also use the machine for transcription.

Once you have successfully made contact with your reader in your opening statement, you again need to plan your words carefully—your objective being to keep your reader interested long enough to finish reading your letter. Keep in mind always that you are attempting to convince someone to do something. Therefore, you must continually evaluate your words on the basis of how your reader will react. One ill-chosen word or poorly expressed sentence might push your reader into disregarding your message. Empathize and you may convince your communication partner to read your next paragraph.

Present the Details of Your Proposal

Transitional devices are important tools in persuasive letters. Use repeated words or phrases; parenthetical words, such as *therefore* and *however;* and/or introductory and summary statements to guide your reader's thoughts from the contact statements to the "nitty-gritty" part of your letter. Then, present your reader with concrete facts, something on which to base his or her decision to do what you want done.

Use transitional devices in your persuasive letter.

When your objective is to sell a product or a service, you must decide whether to include information on the costs involved in the details section. A word of advice: Discuss costs only when you can justify your discussion of the subject as being a central selling point. For example, the cost of your product or service is much lower than competitive products or services. But, if you believe cost figures may work against your proposal or are relatively unimportant, postpone the discussion of costs until you receive a direct inquiry from the communication partner or can present cost figures in a face-to-face conversation about the product or service.

Discuss costs in an initial sales letter only when costs will be a positive motivator.

Example one:

On July 6, 19—, you purchased a twenty-four-channel Ranx CB radio, Model #AS627T, from us. The radio cost $68.50, including tax, installation, and a three-month parts and labor warranty. This $68.50 charge appeared on your August 1, September 1, October 1, and November 1 bills. However, our bookkeeper, Dottie Pearson, tells us you have made no payments on your account in the past five months.

Example two:

Martin Office Machines can solve your space problem by equipping your office with *invisible* dictation equipment. Our newest

Model XL-110 Dictation/Transcription System uses your telephone as the dictating device. You merely press a button to make the connection with your secretary's transcribing machine. What is more, we can adapt your present equipment to our invisible system. The enclosed brochure describes the features and operation of the Model XL-110 in detail.

Justify Reader Acceptance of Your Proposal

Empathize with your reader.

Justify your message for yourself and for your reader.

Empathy is the key to justification. Select your words carefully. Anticipate your reader's reactions. Your communication partner will appreciate your honesty and forthrightness when you present both sides of the proposal. Furthermore, this section of your persuasive letter is particularly important because of the opportunity you have to establish your credibility and to lead your reader to a logical conclusion. Your objective is to show that acting on your request will benefit both your reader and you and your company.

Example one:

What would you do if your employer forgot to pay your salary for five months? Mill Street Radio Sales and Service operates on the profits it earns just as you live on the income you earn.

Example two:

The Model XL-110 is an economical way to make dictation-transcription equipment less noticeable and, at the same time, more efficient. Dictation time is shortened substantially by the voice-activated programming device. Secretarial time is saved because your secretary no longer needs to retrieve the recorded tape or belt from the dictating machine in your office.

In addition, your secretary can transcribe already-recorded dictation at the same time you are recording new dictation. We will remove the 7 x 8 inch box from your desk, but your secretary will still have one.

Martin Office Machines stands behind its merchandise and guarantees free service and parts for one full year after purchase. We maintain our own Service Department and promise same-day service if you need us. Consultations with our communications-planning experts are included in our service. You may call on us for advice as well as for service!

Indicate Exactly What Action to Take

Because the many barriers to communication may lead to miscommunication, tell your reader exactly what action to take. Giving your communication partner specific instructions leaves no doubt in either of your minds as to what action is expected. Thus, the action or inaction of your reader is the real test of your persuasive writing abilities.

Will your reader take the action you wish because he or she wants to do it? Have you established a need? Have you given enough information? Have you established your credibility and honesty? If you have done these things, give your reader a chance to act.

Example one:

Send us your check for $68.50 by Wednesday, December 1, so we can tell James Hale not to call on you. He's a "Good Buddy," and I know he would prefer not to have the unpleasant task of calling on you.

Example two:

Enclosed is a postpaid, addressed postal card. Please check your responses to the questions on the card and return it today. The information you give us will enable us to fit our service to your needs.

Complete your persuasive message with action for your reader to take.

End With a Goodwill Statement

Your goodwill statement may be a separate paragraph, a sentence at the end of your action paragraph, or your entire action paragraph. The key point to remember is that no matter how negative your message is (pay your bill or else), your obligation to yourself, your company, and your communication partner is to make a closing statement to confirm that you will welcome further communication with your reader. Always leave your communication partner with the feeling that you are basically a nice person who represents a good, reputable company.

Example one:

Enclosed is our sale catalog describing the many radio and stereo bargains you will find this month at Mill Street Radio Sales and Service. By paying your $68.50 bill now, Mr. Bostick, you will have the opportunity to take advantage of our January clearance-sale bargains.

Encourage feedback with your persuasive message.

Example two: Although the sales letter for dictating equipment is complete without adding a last paragraph, you may wish to close with a one-sentence paragraph in the form of a catchy statement or question.

What's that? You want us to come out right away?

Or:

Our communication-planning consultant is anxious to work with you.

Your Persuasive Letter Is Complete

As you read the completed collection letter (Figure 8–1), notice the communication devices used and their effects.

1. *Personal names* are used instead of titles and pronouns. The attorney is Mr. James Hale; the bookkeeper is Dottie Pearson. By personalizing the attorney and the bookkeeper, you humanize the collection request. The more personal you make the letter, the more likely Mr. Bostick is to pay the bill.

2. *Direct address* is used in the goodwill paragraph of the letter. Using Mr. Bostick's name in the closing goodwill paragraph emphasizes the pleasant part of the business message.

3. *Second-person pronouns* are used as much as possible. By using mostly second-person pronouns, you are again humanizing and personalizing your business message. You are talking directly *to* the reader, not *at* him or her. Humanizing written messages involves the reader in the details of the message. If you want to convince someone to do something, he or she must feel personal involvement in the situation being described. There are eighteen second-person pronouns (you, yours), ten first-person pronouns (us, we, our), and three third-person pronouns (he, it) in Ms. Kohler's letter. [In the sales letter, Figure 8–2, there are twenty-two second-person pronouns (you, yours), fourteen first-person pronouns (us, we, our), and two third-person pronouns (hers, its, it).]

4. *Specific information* is used. Ruth Kohler doesn't use the worn-out "our attorney will call on you" approach; she says exactly *when* the attorney will be at Mr. Bostick's office. Thus, Mr. Bostick will not be able to procrastinate much longer. Ms. Kohler is again very specific when she describes the events that led up to her writing this letter. If there has been some sort of misunderstanding, Bostick will be able to set Ms. Kohler straight. Any discrepancy in facts will be easily detected.

Figure 8—1
A persuasive collection letter.

5. *A sympathetic appeal* is used in the third paragraph. Ms. Kohler asks Mr. Bostick to put himself in her place and equates personal salary to business income.

6. *Subtle humor* is used judiciously. In the first paragraph, Ms. Kohler suggests as the only alternative to meeting with Mr. Hale or paying the overdue bill the age-old escape-from-the-office-and-evade-the-bill-collector technique. In the fourth paragraph, James Hale is referred to as a "Good Buddy," the CB name for a fellow CBer.

Read the complete sales letter, Figure 8–2, and identify the communication devices used and their effects on you.

MILL STREET RADIO
SALES AND SERVICE
810 Mill Street
Gladstown, WI 54625

(414) 224-8880

December 6, 19--

Mr. Allen Bostick
P.O. Box 188B
Gladstown, WI 84628

Dear Mr. Bostick

Our attorney, Mr. James Hale, will call on you Thursday, December 12, at 10:30 A.M. If you do not wish to visit with James, send us your check for $68.50, or plan to be away from your office on December 12.

On July 6, 19--, you purchased a twenty-four-channel Ranx CB radio, Model #AS627T, from us. The radio cost $68.50, including tax, installation, and a three-month parts and labor warranty. This $68.50 charge appeared on your August 1, September 1, October 1, and November 1 bills. However, our bookkeeper, Dottie Pearson, tells us you have made no payments on your account in the past five months.

What would you do if your employer forgot to pay your salary for five months? Mill Street Radio Sales and Service operates on the profits it earns just as you live on the income you earn.

Send us your check for $68.50 by Wednesday, December 1, so we can tell James Hale not to call on you. He's a "Good Buddy," and I know he would prefer not to have the unpleasant task of calling on you.

Enclosed is our sale catalog describing the many radio and stereo bargains you will find this month at the Mill Street Radio Sales and Service. By paying your $68.50 bill now, Mr. Bostick, you will have the opportunity to take advantage of our January clearance-sale bargains.

Sincerely

Ruth W. Kohler

wm

Enclosure

```
                        MARTIN OFFICE MACHINES
                          1010 Boston Avenue
                           Chicago, IL 60605
                                                      (312) 439-5050

         August 18, 19--

         Miss Helen Jacobs
         Jacobs, Johnson, and Jenkins, Inc.
         Seventh Floor Adler Building
         8256 Sale Street
         Chicago, IL 60645

         Dear Miss Jacobs

         You can have an attractive, color-coordinated 7 X 8 inch box on your desk.
         What's that?  You don't want anything else on your already-cluttered desk?

         Martin Office Machines can solve your space problem by equipping your office
         with invisible dictation equipment.  Our newest Model XL-110 Dictation/
         Transcription System uses your telephone as the dictating device.  You merely
         press a button to make the connection with your secretary's transcribing
         machine.  What is more, we can adapt your present equipment to our invisible
         system.  The enclosed brochure describes the features and operation of the
         Model XL-110 in detail.

         The Model XL-110 is an economical way to make dictation-transcription equipment
         less noticeable and, at the same time, more efficient.  Dictation time is
         shortened substantially by the voice-activated programming device.  Secretarial
         time is saved because your secretary no longer needs to retrieve the recorded
         tape or belt from the dictating machine in your office.  In addition, your
         secretary can transcribe already-recorded dictation at the same time you are
         recording new dictation.  We will remove the 7 X 8 inch box from your desk, but
         your secretary will still have one.

         Martin Office Machines stands behind its merchandise and guarantees free
         service and parts for one full year after purchase.  We maintain our own
         Service Department and promise same-day service if you need us.  Consultations
         with our communications-planning experts are included in our service.  You may
         call on us for advice as well as for service!

         Enclosed is a postpaid, addressed postal card.  Please check your responses to
         the questions on the card and return it today.  The information you give us
         will enable us to fit our service to your needs.

         What's that?  You want us to come out right away?

         Sincerely

         Mark K. Collins
         Mark K. Collins

         wm

         Enclosures
```

Figure 8—2
A persuasive sales letter.

Positive Letters

Analyze your purpose for writing. Will your reader be happy about your message?

A positive letter anticipates a positive reader reaction. You are saying "yes" to an application for credit. You are sending the information someone requested. You are answering "yes" to someone's adjustment request. You believe that what you have to say will make your communication partner happy.

Again, start by determining the individual reason for writing the positive letter; then fit your ideas into the following letter outline:

1. Present the good news.
2. Present the details of your message.
3. End with a goodwill statement.

Present the Good News

Avoid negative words when answering positively. Don't say "yes" while shaking your head "no." Your reader's pleasant feelings about your letter are derived not only from your answer but also from the positive words you use. Say "yes" at the beginning of your message when you anticipate a positive reader reaction.

Example one:

Your credit request received *no bad* comments from any of your references. *No one* on our credit board voted *against* you. So your credit request has been accepted.

This reply is wordy and employs many negative words (in italics). Also it postpones the good news. How much better it is to say:

Your credit request has been approved.

Example two:

We *checked* with some of our other customers, and they said they had *never* had any *trouble* with their Model 1070 calculators. We are *sorry* you had *trouble* with yours, and we *cannot* understand why. I guess if it just *won't* work, send it back to us and we will give you your money back.

This is another wordy reply filled with negative words. The writer has forgotten the "you-attitude" completely. A much better reply is:

Yes, we are happy to refund your money. Caldon's stands behind its merchandise and is happy only when its customers are happy.

Example three:

We will fix the calculator, *but* the labor charges are *not* covered in your warranty.

The begrudging "yes" emphasizes the negative part of the warranty. This information could be included in the details paragraph of your letter. Why not start your letter:

Yes, your warranty is still in effect.

Example four:

If your fire loss is less than $100, your policy does *not* cover it.

Again, the opening emphasizes the negative. How much better to say this in a positive way in the details paragraph of your letter. Open with the positive statement:

Say "yes" at the beginning of your positive message.

Your fire loss is covered under your present home-owner's policy.

Example five:

We *don't* have any more brochures for our Model 592 Mason electronic calculator, but I've *tried* to answer *most* of your questions.

The negative tone of this opening paragraph conveys the feeling that the writer isn't very interested. Again the "you-attitude" is missing, and the statement is wordy. This opening is much better:

We are happy to answer your request for information about our Model 592 Mason electronic calculator.

Open the positive letter with a concise statement saying "yes" immediately and using a positive tone.

Present the Details

Provide your reader with concrete details.

Once you have relayed the good news, your objective is to provide the concrete details surrounding the situation. Almost any business transaction has some rules that must be followed or some qualifications that must be understood.

Example one:

You may charge up to $850 worth of merchandise at any of Gardiner's five locations. You pay $10 a month on amounts up to $200; $15, on amounts from $201 to $300; $20, on amounts from $301 to $400; and $25 a month on account balances of $401 to $850. Your monthly bill will never exceed $25.

Example two:

Just fill out the enclosed refund-request form and mail it to us in the enclosed postpaid envelope. You will receive your refund within ten days after we receive the completed form.

Example three:

You purchased your Dalton electric pencil sharpener on October 12, 19—, four months ago. The Dalton guarantee covers all parts and labor for the first ninety days after the purchase and parts only for sixty additional days. Our serviceman, Edward King, estimates that the labor charge for your sharpener will amount to approximately $3.85. With your permission, we will repair your pencil sharpener and send it to you C.O.D.

```
                    GARDINER'S
                  2562 Janis Boulevard
                   Tulsa, OK 74120
                                        (918) 882-3939


        June 21, 19--


        Mrs. Linda Cain
        Cain Investment Services
        P.O. Box 8261
        Tulsa, OK 74126

        Mrs. Cain

        Your credit request has been approved.

        You may charge up to $850 worth of merchandise at any of Gardiner's
        five locations.  You pay $10 a month on amounts up to $200; $15, on
        amounts from $201 to $300; $20, on amounts from $301 to $400; and
        $25, on account balances of $401 to $850.  Your monthly bill will
        never exceed $25.

        Gardiner's will look forward to seeing you at its special sale for
        credit customers only that begins July 1 and ends July 14.
        Enclosed is a list of the items available at sale prices and a red
        pen to use in marking those items which particularly interest you.
        Gardiner's is proud to have you join its family of fine customers.


        Sincerely


        Carol K. Lyons
        Carol K. Lyons
        Manager


        wmn

        Enclosures
```

Figure 8—3
A positive letter granting credit.

Be specific, concise, and honest when you present the details your reader wants to know.

End With a Goodwill Statement

The closing paragraph of a positive letter should be used for two purposes:
1. to keep communication channels open
2. to provide an opportunity for you to promote your company, your service, and your product—resale (additional sales).
   Example one:

Use your positive letter for more sales.

```
                              CALDON'S
                          885 Sanford Avenue
                          Phoenix, AZ 85028
                                                        (602) 625-0453




        December 28, 19--


        Mr. Todd Moore
        Moore Office Products
        P.O. Box 2020
        Phoenix, AZ 85030

        Mr. Moore

        Yes, we are happy to refund your money.  Caldon's stands behind
        its merchandise and is happy only when its customers are happy.

        Just fill out the enclosed refund-request form and mail it to us in
        the enclosed postpaid envelope.  You will receive your refund within
        ten days after we receive the completed form.

        The enclosed brochure is an announcement of our semiannual sale
        which begins January 9 and ends January 19.  Caldon's offers its
        finest merchandise at greatly reduced prices to only its best
        customers.  We look forward to seeing you January 9!

        Sincerely

        Mike A. Johnson

        Mike A. Johnson

        wm

        Enclosures
```

Figure 8—4
A positive letter granting a refund.

Gardiner's will look forward to seeing you at its special sale for credit customers only that begins July 1 and ends July 14. Enclosed is a list of the items available at sale prices and a red pen to use in marking those items in which you are particularly interested. Gardiner's is proud to have you join its family of fine customers.

Example two:

The enclosed brochure is an announcement of our semiannual sale which begins January 9 and ends January 19. Caldon's offers its finest merchandise at greatly reduced prices to only its best customers. We look forward to seeing you January 9!

Example three:

```
                      DALTON OFFICE MACHINES
                         888 Princeton Road
                       Montgomery, AL 36111
                                              (205) 925-1780



        February 10, 19--


        Miss Joyce Lawson
        Lawson Bookkeeping and
        Tax Service
        P.O. Box 5051
        Montgomery, AL 36110

        Miss Lawson

        Yes, your warranty is still in effect.

        You purchased your Dalton electric pencil sharpener on October 12,
        19--, four months ago.  The Dalton guarantee covers all parts and
        labor for the first ninety days after the purchase and parts only
        for sixty additional days.  Our serviceman, Edward King, estimates
        that the labor charge for your sharpener will amount to approximately
        $3.85.  With your permission, we will repair your pencil sharpener
        and send it to you C.O.D.

        The Dalton semiannual sale begins in two weeks.  Our store will be
        open from 0 A.M. to 0 P.M. from August 1 through August 5 for your
        shopping convenience.  And, delivery is free for purchases over $75.
        All merchandise in our store will be sold at a 25% discount during
        those five days only.  Dalton's looks forward to doing business with
        you!

        Sincerely

        Blanche Bowling

        Blanche Bowling
        Manager


        wm

        Edward King will repair your pencil sharpener just as soon as he
        gets an OK from you.
```

Figure 8—5

A positive letter granting an adjustment request.

The Dalton semiannual sale begins in two weeks. Our store will be open from 8 A.M. to 8 P.M. from August 1 through August 5 for your shopping convenience. And, delivery is free for purchases over $75. Dalton's looks forward to doing business with you!

Your Positive Letter Is Complete

As you read the complete letters in Figures 8–3, 8–4, and 8–5, ask yourself the following questions:

1. Does the first statement motivate you to continue reading the letter?

2. Do you understand that the writer is granting your request?
3. Is the resale portion of each letter tactfully stated?
4. Does the letter reflect a "you-attitude"?
5. Is the general tone of the letter positive or negative?
6. Are the details clear, complete, and easy to understand?

Negative Letters

Anticipate the reader's disappointment in negative letters.

A negative letter anticipates the reader's disappointment or displeasure. You have to deny a credit request, a request for information, a request for an adjustment, or an order for merchandise. You realize that the person making the request expects a "yes" answer, or they would not have made the request. Therefore, a "no" answer will almost always disappoint your reader.

A negative letter presents a special challenge to the business communicator. You have to relay the information and understanding that the answer is "no." Yet, you have to say "no" in such a way that the reader will understand the reasons for your refusal—if goodwill is to be maintained. What if the letter writer fails? The receiver has a written record of the failure! Tact, courtesy, empathy, and honesty are necessary for the writer of negative letters.

Remember to relay goodwill, even in negative messages.

Begin by determining the individual reason for writing your negative letter; then, fit your ideas into the following letter outline:

1. Open your letter with an interesting, relevant statement.
2. Present the details of the situation and the reasons for your refusal.
3. State your refusal.
4. End with a goodwill statement.

During the planning and rough-draft stages of your letter writing, use the following guidelines to ensure letter effectiveness:

1. Use transition words and phrases to lead your reader to the same logical conclusion that you reached—refusal.
2. Use persuasive tactics to help your reader *understand* the reasoning behind your refusal.
3. Avoid negative words in your letter. Negative words coupled with the refusal almost certainly override the persuasive, goodwill aspects of your letter.
4. Use positive words and concepts to offset the negative objective of your letter—the refusal. Show your reader how your "no" answer can be beneficial to him or her.

5. De-emphasize the refusal. Subordinate your refusal by placing it in a dependent clause or by using the passive voice in the refusal sentence.

6. Use the goodwill paragraph of your letter to keep the doors to further communication open. Tell the reader what you can do for him or her.

7. Make your letter reader centered instead of writer centered.

Open Your Letter With an Interesting Statement

The first sentence of your letter should say something that will produce the response: "I want to read this letter now." You may open with a question, an astounding fact, a hypothetical situation, or an interesting or amusing story. You will very rarely make the refusal statement at the beginning of your letter. State your refusal first *only* when your receiver will not take "no" for an answer and bluntness is the only method for getting your point across.

Explain first; refuse second.

Example one:

Did you watch the CBS special on consumer credit at 9:00 P.M. last Wednesday? Tom Carter did a really fantastic job of explaining the effects of credit buying on individuals and on businesses that are less than two years old. CBS collected a tremendous amount of data on the subject, and I have asked them to send me some copies of their report. If you would like to have a copy, let me know; I'll see that you get one.

Example two:

Congratulations on your new business venture! Lake Allen has needed a good sporting-goods store that specializes in equipment for water sports for a long time. The accessibility of nearby lakes and streams attracts residents and tourists who like to participate in water skiing, boating, sailing, and fishing. You picked a great area in which to locate your business.

Example three:

Last week. I ran into a mutual friend of ours, Leslie Crowe, at the Conover City National Bank. He was telling me about an innovative loan program the bank is starting this month. According to Les, the economy in our area is on the upswing, and Conover City National Bank has created a low-interest-loan incentive program to attract new businesses and to help existing ones.

Review the Situation and the Reasons for Your Refusal

Present reasons for your refusal in a convincing manner.

If you put yourself in the place of the reader, you will be able to present reasons for refusing the request that your reader will find acceptable and logical. Make sure that the details in this section provide *reasons* for the refusal, not *excuses* for the refusal.

Example one:

The gist of the CBS special was the responsibilities that lending institutions and businesses accepting credit purchases have to their customers. Carter pointed out that when credit purchasers get into trouble financially and cannot pay their bills, their creditors may be at fault. Creditors must make certain that their customers are allowed to charge only what they can afford. Mr. Jackson, Coastal Electric recognizes and accepts this responsibility.

Example two:

This morning I received your order for 18 dozen Champion fishing rods. Three days ago, I shipped 40 dozen of the same rods to a sporting-goods store in Akron. Champion makes a very popular rod that is used by many fishermen in your area, and Barton's is happy that you are planning to stock your store with this item.

Example three:

Mr. Carl Johannsen, our credit manager, reminded me about Les's low-interest-loan incentive program when he brought in your credit application today. Johannsen commented that because of your good references and broad capital base he wished that Antone's could make an exception to its rule to sell on a cash basis only to businesses less than two years old. Actually, Barbara, you would save money by borrowing from Les at 8% and paying cash for the merchandise you order from Antone's. Most wholesale typewriter firms in this part of the country charge at least $9\frac{1}{2}$% on credit-account balances.

State Your Refusal

Say "no" tactfully.

Say "no" as tactfully and as positively as you can. When possible, say "no" by telling your communication partner what you *can* do for him or her. After you write the refusal paragraph of your letter, ask yourself if the refusal is a logical conclusion your reader will certainly understand.

Example one:

Kate Elison, our bookkeeper, sent me your $2,856.50 order, dated October 6. The memo she attached to it tells me that your $5,000 credit limit with us would be exceeded by $1,500 if we add your October 6 order to your existing balance. For this reason, you will need to send us a $1,500 payment on your account so we may charge and send your October 6 order to you.

Example two:

Unfortunately, the Akron order almost depleted our stock of Champion rods, leaving us with 10 dozen in our warehouse. I called the Champion factory in Mission, Wisconsin, this morning, and they assured me that the remaining 8 dozen rods needed to complete your order can be delivered directly to you from the factory in four to five weeks.

Example three:

Antone's will be happy to fill your orders for merchandise on cash terms.

End With a Goodwill Statement

Your closing statements are particularly important to the success of a negative letter. You will either leave your reader with good thoughts about your company and an invitation to further communications or leave your reader with unpleasant "how-can-they-do-this-to-me" thoughts about your company and closed doors to further communication.

Leave the doors open to further communication.

Example one:

Enclosed is a postage-paid envelope to speed your payment to us and thus to allow us to fill your order promptly. We, at Coastal Electric Company, look forward to serving your electrical needs.

Example two:

In the meantime, may we send you the 10 dozen rods we have on hand now? Barton's looks forward to hearing from you soon.

Example three:

Antone's will be happy to fill your orders for merchandise on cash terms. Enclosed is our sale catalog from which you may order 1981 typewriters at 1977 prices!

Figure 8—6
A negative letter refusing a credit order.

The letter reads:

COASTAL ELECTRIC COMPANY
8506 Common Street
Jacksonville, FL 32202

(904) 739-3333

October 8, 19--

Mr. Carl Jackson
Jackson Office Supplies and
Equipment
P.O. Box 1816B
Pearl, FL 32305

Mr. Jackson

Did you watch the CBS special on consumer credit last Wednesday? Tom Carter did a really fantastic job of explaining the effects of credit buying on individuals and on businesses that are less than two years old. CBS collected a tremendous amount of data on the subject, and I have asked them to send me some copies of their report. If you would like to have a copy, let me know; I will see that you get one.

The gist of the CBS special was the responsibilities that lending institutions and businesses accepting credit purchases have to their customers. Carter pointed out that when credit purchasers get into trouble financially and cannot pay their bills, their creditors may be at fault. Creditors must make certain that their customers are allowed to charge only what they can afford. Mr. Jackson, Coastal Electric recognizes and accepts this responsibility.

Kate Elison, our bookkeeper, sent me your $2,856.50 order, dated October 6. The memo she attached to it tells me that your $5,000 credit limit with us would be exceeded by $1,500 if we added your October 6 order to your existing balance. For this reason, you will need to send us a $1,500 payment on your account so we may charge and send your October 6 order to you.

Enclosed is a postage-paid envelope to speed your payment to us and thus to allow us to fill your order promptly. We, at Coastal Electric, look forward to serving your electrical needs.

Sincerely

Frank Atkinson
Frank Atkinson

wm

Enclosure

Your Negative Letter Is Complete

Is your letter a success? Are the facts presented logically and persuasively? Read the completed letters in Figures 8–6, 8–7, and 8–8, and evaluate their effectiveness.

Management-to-Employee Communications

Management-to-employee communications can be divided into two general categories: informative letters and letters for employee files.

```
                    BARTON WHOLESALE HOUSE
                       33612 Mountain Road
                      Lake Allen, OH 44501
                                                  (216) 774-4142


  September 14, 19--


  Mr. Roy Franklin
  Water Sports, Inc.
  P.O. Box 404
  Lake Allen, OH 44501

  Mr. Franklin

  Congratulations on your new business venture!  Lake Allen has needed a good
  sporting-goods store that specializes in equipment for water sports for a long
  time.  The accessibility of nearby lakes and streams attracts residents and
  tourists who like to participate in water skiing, boating, sailing, and
  fishing.  You picked a great area in which to locate your business!

  This morning I received your order for 18 dozen Champion fishing rods.  Three
  days ago, I shipped 40 dozen of the same rods to a sporting-goods store in
  Akron.  Champion makes a very popular rod that is used by many fishermen in
  your area, and Barton's is happy that you are planning to stock your store with
  this item.

  Unfortunately, the Akron order almost depleted our stock of Champion rods,
  leaving us with 10 dozen in our warehouse.  I called the Champion factory in
  Mission, Wisconsin, this morning; and they assured me that the remaining 8
  dozen rods needed to complete your order can be delivered directly to you from
  the factory in four to five weeks.

  In the meantime, may we send you the 10 dozen Champion rods we have on hand?
  Barton's looks forward to hearing from you soon.

  Sincerely

  H. H. Barton

  H. H. Barton

  wm

  Enclosed is our newest catalog of high quality water-sports equipment.
```

Figure 8—7
A negative letter advising the customer why the order cannot be shipped.

Informative letters may concern company profits, physical expansion, reorganizational plans, new products, fringe benefits, and the introduction of new members of the management team. Letters for employee files may be letters of commendation, promotion, or reprimand.

Use management communications to inform, commend, promote, or reprimand.

Management-to-employee communications may take any one of several forms:

1. Letters sent to individual employees
2. Memorandums sent to departments
3. Memorandums sent to individual employees
4. Supervisory newsletters sent to each employee
5. Letters placed on bulletin boards for all employees to read.

MARTIN ANTONE OFFICE MACHINES
2212 Bayou Boulevard
Conover, TX 78510

(512) 366-0945

February 4, 19--

Ms. Barbara Coleman
O. and A. Office Products
P.O. Box 1414
Conover, TX 78581

Ms. Coleman

Last week, I ran into a mutual friend of ours, Leslie Crowe, at the Conover City National Bank. He was telling me about an innovative loan program the bank is starting this month. According to Les, the economy in our area is on the upswing, and Conover City National Bank has created a low-interest-loan incentive program to attract new businesses and to help existing ones.

Mr. Carl Johannsen, our credit manager, reminded me about Les's low-interest-loan incentive program when he brought in your credit application today. Johannsen commented that because of your good references and broad capital base he wished that Antone's could make an exception to its rule to sell on a cash basis only to businesses less than two years old. Actually, Barbara, you would save money by borrowing from Les at 8% and paying cash for the merchandise you order from Antone's. Most wholesale typewriter firms in this part of the country charge at least 9½% on credit-account balances.

Antone's will be happy to fill your orders for merchandise on cash terms. Enclosed is our sale catalog from which you may order 1981 typewriters at 1977 prices!

Sincerely

Rod Jeffers

Rod Jeffers

wm

Enclosure

Figure 8—8
A negative letter refusing a credit application from a new business.

When writing your management-to-employee messages, use the following guidelines:

1. Messages should be sent regularly.

2. Messages should be factual and concise.

3. Messages may occasionally be sent to the employee's home instead of to the office.

4. Messages may occasionally be sent to the family of an employee.

5. The vocabulary used should fit the level of understanding of the receivers of a management message.

6. Consider sending different messages containing basically the same information to personnel on different organizational levels.

(This procedure will enable you to adapt information to the responsibility and interest areas of the different levels of employees.)

7. Executives on all levels of management should write messages to their subordinates.

8. Management should empathize with and anticipate the reactions of employees.

9. Messages should encourage feedback.

Some problems that the business communicator should recognize in planning management-to-employee communications are:

1. You should try hard to overcome the traditional authoritative, autocratic status of management that closes many doors to communication.

2. You should understand and consider your firm's history of management-employee relations.

3. You should recognize that the amount of respect employees have for their supervisors will have a significant effect on the success of management-to-employee communications.

4. You should understand that you and your company are accountable, both legally and morally, for any messages you write to your employees.

Messages Sent to All Employees

This message announces an upcoming expansion project to all employees:

On July 1, 1980, Taylor Oil Company will begin construction of a new petrochemical facility in Cory, Illinois. This construction project will be completed some time in the summer or fall of 1981. Approximately 1,200 employees (craftsmen, operators, and management personnel) will be needed to run the new facility. As a present Taylor employee, you will have the first choice of job openings in Cory should you desire to relocate.

Taylor Oil Company has come a long way during its fifty-two years in operation—from 25 employees in 1927 to approximately 11,600 in 1979. And, we're still growing! You are helping to make our continued growth possible through your dedicated work at and your loyal support of Taylor Oil Company.

We welcome your suggestions for the construction of employee facilities at Cory. Enclosed is a questionnaire and an addressed, postpaid envelope for your use in letting us know your wishes.

This message introduces a new executive to the employees:

Your new Personnel Director is Mrs. Helen Bedford.

Mrs. Bedford moved here from Alexandria, Louisiana, where she was Office Manager for an insurance firm for the past eight years. She recently earned her M.B.A. degree from Louisiana State University in Baton Rouge, specializing in personnel management. We are proud to have someone with such good qualifications to direct our Personnel Department here at Vallot's.

You are invited to have coffee and refreshments and to get acquainted with Helen Bedford, Wednesday, March 18, from 9:30 A.M. to 11:00 A.M. in the second floor coffee shop.

R.S.V.P.: Regrets only to Ext. 480

This message explains a new medical-insurance benefit that will take effect in one month:

On July 1, 19—, your medical-insurance coverage can be expanded to include dental benefits. For a number of months, many of you have been asking for this additional coverage.

Enclosed is a brochure explaining the costs and details of these dental benefits. Please refer to the chart on page 2 that explains the monthly cost based on the number of dependents you have. For example, a family of four will pay $11.80 a month in exchange for full coverage in excess of $75 each year for each family member. This new coverage will include costs of extractions, fillings, checkups, X rays, surgery, and braces.

The dental clause is optional and will be added to your individual coverage only if you sign and return the enclosed card.

Letters for Employee Files

Letter of Commendation
The original commendation letter generally is sent to the employee, and a carbon copy is placed in her or his personnel file for consideration when promotional opportunities arise.

Taylor Oil Company commends you for your excellent work performance during the recent operators' strike. Without your expert help and untiring efforts, the continued operation of our chemical facility would have been impossible.

You are a valued member of the Taylor management team.

Letter of Promotion
The original promotion letter is sent to the employee and a carbon copy is placed in the employee's personnel file to keep the file current.

Congratulations on your promotion to Mechanical Superintendent! Your twenty years service to Taylor Oil Company, your recent completion of the M.B.A. degree in personnel management,
and your excellent record as a Unit Supervisor contributed to your
promotion.

Your new office will be ready for you on March 1. Call Tom
Pearly for assistance in moving your things and for any redecorat-
ing you wish to do.

Taylor Oil Company is proud to have you join its middle-manage-
ment team.

Table 8—1
Checklist for Effective
Business Letters

1. What is the primary purpose of your message?
   Persuasive
   Positive
   Negative
   Routine
   Management to employee

2. What will be your reader's reaction?
   Positive
   Negative
   Neutral

3. What information do you need in order to write the message?
   Facts
   Figures
   Documents
   Enclosures

4. Does the rough draft of your message contain these elements?
   Clear wording
   Logical presentation
   Accurate figures
   Accurate statements
   Correct spelling
   Correct grammar
   Correct punctuation
   Ethical and legal statements

5. After the letter is typed in final form, did you take these steps?
   Proofread the letter carefully
   Revise the letter, if necessary
   Send the letter (or copies of it) to the appropriate people

Letter of Reprimand

The original letter is sent to the employee and a carbon copy is placed in the employee's personnel file for consideration when promotional opportunities arise.

For the past twenty-five years you have been a loyal employee of Taylor Oil Company. Your good work habits and excellent attendance record are appreciated.

However, during the week of November 12, the unit you were in charge of suffered several unnecessary malfunctions. The pressure rose to fifty pounds above the recommended level. The feed stock piled up to the extent that lines going to the unit were blocked and in danger of exploding. And Number Two tank filled to a dangerous two feet above the recommended level. In every instance you were the operator in charge and were responsible for the malfunctions.

In the future you must take special care to avoid such malfunctions. You should check all instruments in your unit at fifteen-to-thirty-minute intervals, realizing the danger to yourself and others when you do not follow safety procedures.

A copy of this letter will be placed in your personnel file. Should a similar incident occur in the future, disciplinary action will be taken.

The employee should be called in for a private conference with his or her immediate supervisor any time a letter of reprimand is placed in the personnel file. An opportunity for feedback to the letter is given in the conference instead of in the letter.

Summary

Plan and analyze your business communications carefully.

Careful planning and analyses are the keys to effective business-letter writing. Use the checklist in Table 8–1 to organize and complete your business messages.

Questions for Discussion

1. What are the three purposes for writing business letters?

2. Into what five categories can business letters be divided? Why should you categorize the letters you write?

3. Define a routine letter. List at least five communication situations that may be classified as routine in an office?

4. When is an acknowledgment letter necessary? When is it unnecessary?

5. Why should the business person always send a transmittal letter with a check?

6. What information should be included in a request (oral or written) for hotel or motel accommodations?

7. What are the characteristics of a good condolence message?

8. What should be included in an effective letter requesting information?

9. Why should the business writer avoid thanking the communication partner for information not yet received or favors not yet granted?

10. When is a handwritten business letter both acceptable and preferred?

11. What information should be included in an order letter?

12. What five steps should you follow when writing a persuasive letter? Explain each step briefly.

13. What are the three reactions the recipient may have after reading the opening sentence of a letter?

14. How is empathy the key to persuasion?

15. What is the real test of your persuasive writing abilities?

16. Why should you try to humanize your written messages?

17. Define a positive letter. Give an example of a business situation that would be handled by writing a positive letter.

18. Give three examples of good opening sentences for a positive letter.

19. Define a negative letter. What is one example of a business situation that would require a negative letter?

20. Why are negative letters particularly difficult for the business communicator to write?

21. Why should you provide reasons, not excuses, in your negative letter?

22. How can you test the effectiveness of your refusal statement in your negative letter?

23. Name and describe the two categories of management-to-employee communications.

24. What are the nine guidelines for preparing management-to-employee messages?

25. Why should an employee be called in for a conference when a letter of reprimand is placed in his or her file?

Business Situations

Read each of the following business situations, and react to each situation by writing an appropriate business communication. Analyze and categorize each problem; then use your own creative abilities to respond to these business situations by following the suggested outlines for writing business letters.

1. Mr. A. Charles Broderick, Personnel Director, V and L Chemicals, P. O. Box 8588, Wilmington, DE 19899, requested a recommendation for Mrs. Alice V. Polechec who is applying for a secretarial position at V and L. Your records show that Mrs. Polechec worked for your company for one year, seven months. She left your employ voluntarily and moved to Wilmington two years ago. Your records also show that Mrs. Polechec was a diligent worker when she came to work but she missed at least four days each month. Answer Mr. Broderick's letter.

2. Caruso T. Valentine has worked in the accounting department for five years. In the past three years he has not been absent a single day and has missed only two days in five years. Write a letter to Mr. Valentine commending him for his excellent attendance record.

3. You are the office manager in a large legal office — Jackson, Arnold, Dunn, and Robinson. You have been asked to gather information about word-processing centers in operation in other law firms for presentation at a meeting to be held in two weeks. The purpose of the meeting will be to determine the feasibility of setting up such a center in your firm. Compose a letter requesting information about the organization of, equipment used in, personnel requirements for, training programs needed for, and approximate cost of the word-processing center at Carlston, Frederick, and Youngblood, Attorneys at Law.

4. Write a thank-you letter to Ms. Rhonda Bedford, office manager, Carlston, Frederick, and Youngblood, Attorneys at Law, relaying your appreciation for the information she sent you about their word-processing center and her prompt reply.

5. You are the sales manager for Speedy Data Processing Equipment, Inc. Your Research and Development Division has just announced the development of a new electronic calculator that has three memory banks, uses one-third less calculator tape than the average electronic calculator, and comes equipped with a ribbon that produces dark, readable figures for one year (or 2,000 hours of operation). The normal life of a calculator ribbon is approximately one month or 100 hours of operation. The new calculator can be battery operated or electrically operated. Write a sales promotion letter to market your new product.

6. You are the administrative assistant to Alton P. Harmon, vice president of Alton Oil Company in Tulsa, Oklahoma. Mr. Harmon will attend a professional meeting in San Francisco, California, next month. He will take his wife and ten-year-old son with him. Mr. Harmon will be in San Francisco for ten nights and eleven days. Write to the Emerald Hotel in San Francisco and request reservations for the Harmon family.

7. You are the office manager for the Springfield, Kentucky, Chamber of Commerce. Five years, two months ago the Chamber purchased a ten-ton air conditioning unit from a local dealer. The air conditioning unit carried a five-year warranty on the compressor. About six months ago you called the local dealer, who had installed your air-conditioning unit, and complained that the Chamber offices were very uncomfortable. The service representative diagnosed the problem as a low Freon level. He put $25 worth of Freon in the air conditioner. Now

the air conditioner has quit cooling and the local dealer says your compressor is not operating properly. Write a letter to the factory explaining the past events and requesting a new compressor without charge. You believe that when you called the local dealer six months ago, the problem was a faulty compressor rather than a low Freon level.

8. Pick a product or service of your choice — either factual or fictional. Write a sales promotional letter to a prospective customer. Convince the customer that he or she needs your product or service.

9. As supervisor of the mailing services department, you must counsel each employee in your department twice a year. For each counseling session, you are responsible for writing a status letter designed to commend or reprimand each employee. These letters are placed in the employees' files for use in promoting, demoting, discharging, or determining merit increases. Vance Compton is a clerk in your department. He has been late for work a total of fifteen times in the last six months. Write a letter for Compton's file.

10. You are the manager of the credit department at Salomes Department Store. You have four employees who work under your direct supervision. Each of these employees, from time to time, composes and sends collection letters to customers who have overdue balances. Your policy for sending collection letters includes three stages: reminder, request for payment, and strong request for payment. In the past two years collection letters have produced less than desirable effects — a low collection rate on overdue balances and a number of disgruntled good-pay customers who were angered by the collection letters they received when their balances were only a few days overdue. Write three model letters for use by your four subordinates — one letter for each collection stage.

11. You are the manager of the insurance department of LaSalle Textile Manufacturing Company, Inc. As a result of a recent collective-bargaining session, a new union contract was signed providing for dental-insurance coverage that can be added to other group medical-insurance plans available to employees at LaSalle. The dental-insurance premium will be paid by the company and is, therefore, a new fringe benefit offered by LaSalle. Write a letter informing all employees of the availability of the dental insurance and the procedures they should follow to take advantage of the insurance.

12. You received a letter yesterday from Ms. Burns, office manager for Tom-Tom Electronics. She asked that you send her a copy of your Office Manual to use as a model for preparing an Office Manual for Tom-Tom Electronics. Your company policy prohibits you from sending your manual to her. Write a letter to Ms. Burns telling her you cannot satisfy her request. Remember that you always tell your communication partners what you can do for them when you write a refusal letter.

Chapter 9 Research for Business Communication

Library Research
Types of Libraries
Categories of Materials
Evaluation of Secondary
  Sources

Primary Research
Company Records
Observation
Experimentation
Surveys

Documentation

Summary

"Every fact that is learned becomes a key to other facts."
—E. L. Youmans

When someone mentions communication, is the response ever *research?* Research! What is research? How does communication and the collection of data fit into research? Does research have anything to do with the business investigator? How can the average business-communication student deal with a research problem?

Research can play a major role in the communication process. Research is the collecting and reporting of data in an objective and systematic manner. Now, reread this definition of research. "Collection of data" is where the research process begins. Business organizations of today are constantly seeking solutions to complex problems. These problems may be in marketing, personnel, sales, organization, or an administrative upheaval in the Hong Kong office. The problem may be too complicated to be solved by information that is easily accessible. Thus, a hunt for data is initiated, and the search—or research—is on.

Research begins with the collection of information.

When the problem is one that others in the business world have already encountered, the business investigator may be able to benefit from the findings of someone else. Research through published material is called secondary research. If the investigator has been asked to blaze a new trail, then the person has to find her or his own data. Research based on the initial experiment, diverse company documents, or surveys and questionnaires is primary research.

The Sue Starks Oil Company (SSOC) was preparing for an expansion program. Because of the energy crisis, which had been publicly acknowledged in the early seventies, the company had to diversify or go out of business. Years before most people in the United States were aware of the impending shortage of oil and its by-products, the SSOC was quietly researching the international marketing situation. The company knew that if their researchers did a good job, the company could look forward to years of growth and expansion.

Primary research in action.

The company's research experts were turned loose on the business community. They were looking for anything and everything that might possibly indicate the direction or directions their company should consider. The research included thousands of hours of secondary research—reading what other companies were doing, checking government documents, and comparing data from different companies. When possible, other companies' records were checked. Critical observations were made. Experimentation with new products was carried out on a limited basis. A survey was conducted among the stockholders to determine their reaction to some of the contemplated business ventures.

On the target date assigned to the research team, a complete report was presented to top management. Included in this report were conclusions, recommendations, and supporting data for the diversification of a multimillion-dollar oil company. The research was so thorough and so carefully conducted that the report provided the foundation for the SSOC's first billion-dollar production year.

Secondary research in action.

Henry L. Davis, Incorporated is being held in contempt of court for noncompliance with a court order to bring the company's hiring practices in line with the federal sex-discrimination laws. The company president, Henry L. Davis, is concerned that the company will lose its federal contracts if the court feels that the hiring practices are still discriminatory. Consequently, he has instructed the company's legal department to research law cases dealing with sex discrimination and to gather information about the hiring practices of other companies. After researching the law books and other companies' practices, the department is to present a proposal for revisions in the company's hiring practices to Mr. Davis. The court will evaluate this proposal and will decide whether Henry L. Davis, Incorporated is still in contempt or if it is eligible to receive federal contracts.

The Sue Starks Oil Company and Henry L. Davis, Incorporated, are just two illustrations of how the business community needs and uses research. Research is not only an integral part of making proposals and writing reports, but research may also be necessary to write a business letter. Every business letter that has been written contains at least one mutual component—information. How does the writer get the information? Some form of research is conducted. The research may not be as extensive as if a report were to be prepared, but often the letter writer will consult company records (which we will discuss later in the chapter) and/or some type of reference materials.

The business-communication student who is introduced to the business world as a new employee may be asked to collect data for a letter or report concerning some problem management wants investigated. The new employee may be assigned the research because no one else is interested. Or the old employee (five years later, that is you) is asked to perform similar research because he or she has been doing such a superb job for five years that it would be troublesome to ask someone else to do it.

A word to the wise: The business world needs people who can conduct good research. This skill, which can be acquired, is one of the best ways for an intelligent person to climb the corporate ladder. Top executives are always on the lookout for the bright, new employee who is on the ball, and being on the ball might mean putting in many extra hours doing research. The bright, new employee could become the junior executive who is ready with a solution to the problem or who has a well-documented answer to a very complex question. The junior executive who becomes the president's protégée is often selected as a result of *unassigned* research that is well done.

Before writing your letter or report, reliable and complete facts should be collected. Basically, five methods of securing information may be used: library research, company records, observation, experimentation, and surveys. Library research is secondary research. This method is the process of searching through the results of someone else's investigations. The other four methods of research are primary research; investigators uncover their own materials or data.

The business community needs effective researchers.

Research is a skill.

Research: secondary and primary.

Library Research

The search for information usually begins with the investigation of all published material that is pertinent and available. Published material will provide you with data that other people, hopefully experts, have researched and reported. Many times professional people use their own references—possibly their college textbooks. But sometimes they find that their personal reference books do not hold all the answers. They must find other sources.

A library, in all probability, will supply the needed sources. Not only will a library search provide you with relevant information for your immediate project, but it provides background information as well as acquainting you with the whole spectrum of the problem.

Your search begins in the library and may also end in the library.

Types of Libraries

The business researcher may have several types of libraries from which to choose, and knowledgeable investigators will acquaint themselves with those that are available for their use.

Public Libraries
The library with which most of us are familiar is the public library. Most cities and towns have at least one. This type of library contains information in most of the familiar disciplines (areas of study). Public libraries are easily accessible to the business researcher.

University and College Libraries
These libraries are maintained for the faculty and students of the school. However, in most instances they are open to the general public. General information is housed in these libraries; usually a large volume of business information can be found in university and college libraries. The business investigator using these libraries should be able to collect sufficient data to solve ordinary business problems.

Company Libraries
The information available in company libraries is usually limited to the special area in which the company operates. In most instances such libraries provide an excellent source of specialized information. Company libraries are not open to the general public, but the researcher may be able to use the library facilities, especially if there is a benefit to the company.

Specialized Libraries
Professional and trade associations, labor unions, chambers of commerce, etc., often maintain their own libraries. Although these libraries may be maintained for the benefit of the organization's membership, most reputable researchers would be welcome. These libraries will have in-depth coverage of the special areas each particular group represents. Because of the many specialized libraries that have been established, guides have been published to assist in locating them. One of the most frequently used guides is the *Directory of Special Libraries and Information Centers.*

Library of Congress
The top library in the United States is the Library of Congress in Washington, D.C. By law, this library receives a copy of everything copyrighted in the United States. The Library of Congress has a

Why do companies have libraries?

214

printed catalog of its books; most public libraries have a copy. The reference department of the Library of Congress provides service to researchers in all fields except law.

Interlibrary Loans
Interlibrary loans is a system designed to provide librarians with information for a researcher from other libraries throughout the nation. By using a union list showing where the material is stored, the librarian can determine which library has the needed material. A loan request for the original material or a copy may be made to the appropriate library. These loans are governed by rules and regulations set up by the American Library Association and are an interlibrary courtesy.

Books can be borrowed from libraries throughout the country.

Information Retrieval Services (Computer Search)
Commercial, computer-based, bibliographic services have been available to libraries since the late 1960s. This service is not a library, but the researcher should know that this service is obtainable. It provides a very sophisticated method of searching for information to the person who is doing in-depth research. Bibliographic abstracting and indexing services use computers to provide bibliographies and abstracts of articles from selected files or data banks. Most of these services charge a fee for the information. Two of the best-known, commercial, search services used by business and industry are Lockheed Information Systems' DIALOG and System Development Corporation's ORBIT. Most libraries can provide further information to the researcher interested in pursuing this topic.

This service can save time and effort.

Categories of Materials

Published materials, that is, secondary sources, are usually divided into four broad categories: reference works, general collections of books (books in library stacks), periodicals, and government documents.

Reference Works
When beginning a search through secondary sources, the first step is usually to consult reference books. A great deal of information can be secured from these sources, and sometimes the researcher will not have to look any further. An infinite number of reference books are available. Here are just a few of the kinds that can be found in most libraries.

Knowing where to look is the "key."

Encyclopedias. Encyclopedias are probably the best-known and most widely used source for general knowledge. These reference books provide broad general information. However, because of their wide range of information, coverage is usually extremely brief. Most libraries have both general encyclopedias, such as the *Encyclopaedia Britannica* and the *Encyclopedia Americana,* and specialized encyclopedias, such as the *Accountant's Encyclopedia* and the *Encyclopedia of Banking and Finance.*

Almanacs. Almanacs are perhaps the best source for recent factual and statistical information. *The World Almanac and Book of Facts* is a very familiar general almanac; specialized almanacs, such as *The Economic Almanac,* are also available.

Trade directories. Trade directories contain information about products, type of operations, addresses of offices and plants, names of officers and executives, etc., of various types of businesses. A researcher can find information about a particular company easily by using the proper directory. One of the best known is the *Guide to American Directories.* Dun & Bradstreet publishes two directories that are especially valuable to the business researcher. The *Million Dollar Directory* identifies companies with a net worth of $1 million or more, and the *Middle Market Directory* identifies companies with a net worth of $500 thousand to $1 million.

Biographical directories. Information about noteworthy people can be found in these directories. They range from directories that attempt to include the entire world to specialized works relating to a particular locality or a profession. The *Dictionary of American Biography* (prominent Americans of the past) and *Who's Who in America* (review of the lives of living Americans) are two biographical directories that might be used in research on famous Americans. Prominent business people are listed in *Standard and Poor's Register of Corporations, Directors and Executives.*

Geographical reference books. These books generally are published in three forms: atlases, gazetteers, and guidebooks. As a business researcher, you might need an atlas or a gazetteer. Atlases are books that contain collections of maps, as Rand McNally's *Commercial Atlas and Marketing Guide.* Gazetteers are alphabetical dictionaries that supply minimum basic data on specific geographical areas, cities, states, or countries. Two examples are *Webster's New Geographical Dictionary* and *Columbia Lippincott Gazetteer of the World.* Guidebooks may be just the reference books you need. They contain information not found in atlases or gazetteers—maps of small towns and areas, information about communications, transportation, natural resources, etc. *The American Guide Series* and *Reference Guide for Travellers* might have that little bit of information you need to complete your project.

Yearbooks.   These books include a wide variety of information relating to events, progress, and conditions during one particular year. Many encyclopedias have yearbook supplements. *Americana Annual* is a supplement to the *Encyclopedia Americana. The United States in World Affairs,* a survey of America's international involvement, is an annual record of events in this special field.

Handbooks.   These books contain detailed facts and statistics on specialized subjects. They are generally arranged for convenient use, and most are well indexed and well organized. The *Business Executive's Handbook* and the *Personnel Handbook* are two that will be found in most business libraries.

Bibliographies.   Bibliographies direct you to specialized reference books or provide lists of books published on a given subject during a period of time. They can often save hours of searching. The *Cumulative Book Index* and the *Encyclopedia of Business Information Sources* can supply you with bibliographies on a variety of subjects.

Business services.   A wide assortment of published information is made available to business people by business services. Two of the more widely recognized are Moody's Investors Service and Standard and Poor's Corporation Services. These services supply financial information of particular interest to investors, but business researchers may find their publications helpful.

Financial information.

General Collections of Books

Most library books are in the general collections of the library. Books are housed on shelves and are arranged according to a definite plan. The plan uses groups of numbers and letters to indicate a given subject. The numbers and letters represent the classification system; each book in the library is assigned a call number. The two major classification systems employed by libraries in the United States are the Dewey Decimal system and the Library of Congress system.

Card catalog.   In order to use the general collections of books (and, in most instances, reference works), researchers consult the card catalog. This catalog is a complete list of all the books in the library. Each book is listed on a 3 x 5 inch card, and the cards are filed alphabetically by author, by title, and by subject. The card catalog is centrally located for easy accessibility.

The library's roadmap.

658.85
G441h

Girard, Joe.
　　How to sell anything to anybody / Joe Girard with Stanley H. Brown. — New York : Simon and Schuster, c1977.
　　191 p. ; 22 cm.
　　ISBN 0-671-22651-7

　　1. Girard, Joe.　2. Sales personnel—Biography.　3. Selling.　I. Brown, Stanley H., joint author.　II. Title.

HF5439.5.G57A33　　　　　　658.85　　　　　　77-21683
　　　　　　　　　　　　　　　　　　　　　　　　　MARC

Library of Congress　　　　　77

Figure 9—1
The author card from the card catalog.

For example, you have been assigned the project of selling "Daffodil Soap." For this project, you want to read *How to Sell Anything to Anybody* by Joe Girard. You have no idea where to locate Girard's book. No one in the office has a copy so you make a trip to the public library. First you check the card catalog. You find the book listed under *Girard.* The call number in the upper left-hand corner of the card is your key to pinpointing the location of the book in the library stacks. Figure 9–1 is a sample of the author card in the card catalog.

Open or closed stacks. After you find the call number for *How to Sell Anything to Anybody,* you go to the part of the library where the books are shelved. Most libraries today have open shelves; you go directly to the shelves (stacks) and find the book(s) you need. If you are not familiar with the library or the arrangement of the books, do not hesitate to ask the librarians for help. If you find a librarian who is not helpful, be insistent. Closed stacks require that you request the book by call number and have someone (librarian or aide) get it from the stacks for you.

Open stacks are convenient for everyone.

A special note: Directional and other signs are posted in the library for your convenience. Just look around; you are sure to benefit.

Periodicals

The greatest source of current information is periodicals. Information about new ideas and developments in most fields often appear in a magazine before being published in book form. However, there

Periodicals have the most current information.

is one small catch—how many periodicals can you name? In order to find and use the information published in these often specialized sources, three types of guides are available that can help you find what you want in the mass of published materials: directories, indexes or abstracts, and union lists. The two most often used by business researchers are directories and indexes.

Directories.   Directories publish a list of periodicals by title, frequency of publication, and major subject matter. Directories can be very helpful when you are not acquainted with the publications in the field being researched. A well-known directory is *Ulrich's International Periodical Directory.*

Indexes.   Periodical indexes list the articles that have appeared in certain periodicals. Researchers have general and special indexes available. The most commonly used general indexes are the *Readers' Guide to Periodical Literature,* the *Humanities Index,* and the *Social Sciences Index.* The latter two indexes were originally published as one volume, the *International Index to Periodicals.* Among the specialized indexes are the *Accountants' Index and Supplements,* the *Business Periodicals Index,* and the *Engineering Index.*

Daily newspapers are the best source of information on day-by-day events. An index is not available covering all newspapers, but several special indexes can be helpful to the business person: *The New York Times Index, The Wall Street Journal Index, Facts on File,* and *Keesing's Contemporary Archives.*

Union lists.   These lists enable researchers and librarians to determine which libraries hold certain periodicals. If a periodical is not available in the library you are using, your librarian can ascertain from the union list which library has the needed publication. The librarian can also request a copy of the periodical or a copy of the article you need.

Government Documents

Publications by various governmental agencies are among the oldest of our written records. Perhaps libraries were first established to preserve this body of knowledge. Almost every nation publishes information relating to its governmental activities.

The United States government is our nation's most prolific publisher—publishing books, pamphlets, periodicals, reports, bibliographies, and reference books. Adding to the wealth of government information are state and local agencies. These sources are so voluminous and so immensely rich in information that the business

Government publications contain a wealth of information.

researcher should become well acquainted with the guidebooks that list and classify such documents.

The United States government has printed, since 1895, the *Monthly Catalog of United States Government Publications.* This monthly publication has an index in each issue. Semiannual cumulative indexes are compiled in separate volumes. The catalog contains the complete list of currently issued government publications, arranged alphabetically by issuing agency. Both the novice researcher and the experienced one will find that checking the index for the subject being researched is quicker and easier than going through the alphabetized agencies.

The *Index to U.S. Government Periodicals* is an index of selected periodicals published by different agencies of the United States government. Until this publication was started in 1974, some of these articles were inaccessible to many researchers. This is a quarterly publication with an annual cumulative index.

If information concerning material published by one of the states is needed, the best guide is the *Monthly Checklist of State Publications,* published monthly by the Library of Congress. A guide that lists data published by municipalities is the *Municipal Year Book.* However, if detailed information from either a state or municipal publication is needed, check the central library for that state or municipality.

Evaluation of Secondary Sources

The knowledgeable investigator should be discriminating when working with secondary documents. Remember the old saying, "Don't believe everything you read." When using secondary sources, ask yourself:

1. *Who is the author?* Is this person a respected authority in the field? What are the author's credentials? In other words, have the author's conclusions been tested; is the material reliable?

2. *Do statistics lie?* You have often heard, "numbers do not lie." But numbers are like words—they can be manipulated to prove *any* point. Learn to question figures; they can be deceiving and misleading—perhaps purposefully.

3. *Who is the publisher?* Is the publishing house well known? Established publishers evaluate what they publish and their decision may be based on the credibility of the author. However, do not always eliminate the use of material just because you are not familiar with the publisher. Do some objective evaluating.

4. *What is the publication date?* Certain types of material can become outdated quickly. Be sure your research is up to date. However, remember that the most recent information is not necessarily the best. Einstein's theory on relativity has been the basis for many research projects; it was published in 1905 and verified in 1919.

5. *Did you read the original material?* Be sure that you read and understand the original writing. If you are using someone else's version, an abstract, or a summary, the material may be quoted out of context.

Primary Research

A problem that has little current published material requires primary research to find a solution. Primary research requires that researchers locate their own information. After the data are collected, they must analyze, evaluate, and interpret the information in terms of the problem to be solved. The information and analysis may be objective if the research has been carefully done. The opinions, conclusions, and recommendations may be objective—or subjective, if the researcher's approach is not carefully considered.

Thomas Alva Edison was a famous researcher who had 1,093 patents issued to him. These patents included the incandescent electric lamp, the phonograph, the carbon telephone transmitter, and the motion-picture projector. His lifetime was devoted to primary research, and you have benefited from his research.

Edward L. Thorndike conducted several vocabulary studies in which he identified the 10 thousand, 20 thousand, and 30 thousand most widely used words. The 10 thousand word list was selected from over 7 million words taken from elementary-school textbooks, children's literature, English classics, the Bible, personal correspondence, newspapers, etc. The longer word lists were essentially a continuation of his first study. Thorndike's research led to the careful choice of words used at each grade level. It was also the basis for subsequent research in readability (discussed in Chapter 4).

The research you do may not have the far-reaching results of Edison's or Thorndike's, but it could provide your company with some answers to questions that are very important to your company's future—and your own. What methods of primary research are available to you? In general, there are four widely used primary sources of business data: company records, observation, experimentation, and surveys.

Company Records

Records contain vital information.

The management of the Green Fox Company wants to know if their sales are increasing and the percent of increase so they can evaluate the company's progress for the past five years. You are the junior sales executive, so you receive the assignment to compile and prepare the information. Where will you get this material? In most instances the best source for this information will be the records of the company. Another resource that can be used is older employees. Usually they have a storehouse of information.

Because of the varied types of records that companies keep, an explanation of how to research each type would be almost impossible. Just a gentle reminder, never underestimate the ability of those familiar with the company or the files to render help when you are working with company records. The beginning researcher can get invaluable help by discussing the problem with someone who has been with the company for a long time and also with the person who is in charge of the files.

Observation

Observation is the second type of primary research. As the name implies, observation is a method of carefully watching a physical occurrence and recording the occurrence in an organized manner. To be considered true research, the observer *must* remain uninvolved and record *exactly* what takes place. No attempt can be made to direct the results.

The observer must be an accurate recorder.

Observational research may be as simple as counting the amount of different flavors of ice cream purchased in convenience stores in various neighborhoods for a week. Or it may be as complex as the psychologist Arnold Gesell's observation of the developmental phases of human beings from infancy to sixteen, including observation of motor and physical development, emotional expression, philosophic outlook, adaptive behavior, language, interpersonal relationships, and personal-social behavior. His observations extended over a half century from 1911 to 1961.

Observation employs one or more of the five senses. Usually research conducted for the business world uses the sense of sight. However, in some industries other senses are utilized—cheese tasters, yarn inspectors, tobacco experts, audio specialists.

What are the advantages of this method?

The advantages and disadvantages of observation should be understood when considering the use of this method. If conducted objectively and accurately, observation is very dependable. No intermediary can affect the information that is gathered (unless you allow it). This information has not been gathered or influenced by other humans.

The major advantage of the observation method of research is that it is as reliable and as accurate as its observers. If the person planning the research is thorough and knows the job, a system of checks and balances can be adopted to insure the accuracy and objectivity of the observations, eliminating the subjective factors. Such a system greatly reduces the chance of human error.

The limitations of the observation method should be carefully considered before a decision is made to use this method. First, only the physical activity being observed can be recorded. The researcher cannot know what is happening in the mind of the person being observed. Observation cannot measure opinions, beliefs, attitudes, or motives. Observation may answer the *what* of the action but not the *why*.

Cost is a second consideration. The cost of conducting the ice-cream survey would not be excessive, but think of the cost that was involved in the Gesell study. Before the observation method is employed, the researcher should consult the budget.

Other problems exist and should be studied before embarking on observational research. The decision must be made as to exactly what is to be observed. Lee's Department Store is interested in conducting a market survey on women's fashions. They want to know what their customers are wearing. The marketing director must decide whether the complete ensemble is to be observed and recorded or just the accessories. If only the accessories are to be recorded, exactly what accessories are to be included.

The researcher will have to keep in mind that good data depend on the frequency of occurrence. If the investigator is not careful, too much emphasis may be placed on a few isolated happenings that could distort the whole effort. If research is not objective, *any* point can be proved.

Frequency of occurrence and time span are important factors.

How long is the activity to be observed? Will a week be long enough to observe the sales of the different flavors of ice cream? In comparison would a week be long enough to study the effects of the price of gold on the international-trade market? A decision on the length of time covered by the study must be made before the research begins.

Two other considerations concerning the observation method should be mentioned: where will the observers be stationed, and how many observers will be needed. If several observers are to be used, all must be trained in the recording procedure to ensure that the observations are recorded as uniformly as possible. Of course, the type of product or the goal of the observations will affect the decision of where the observations are performed. Both factors should be very carefully determined.

Experimentation

When most of us in the business community think of experimentation, we usually conjure up a mental picture of a scientist in a white coat working with test tubes in a laboratory. This image has been strengthened by the physical-research scientists, but it has not been widely associated with the behavioral sciences. When we think of a scientific experiment, we generally think of exact measurement, but exact measurement is not always possible in the behavioral sciences. When dealing with people, exact measurement is a hope at best.

Experimentation consists of working with several factors, called variables, changing one of these factors, but keeping the other factors constant. The results are then measured.

How might a researcher use experimentation in business? Suppose the marketing specialist of the Green Fox Company wants to know the best color for the outside packaging of a new toothpaste the company is ready to put on the market. The specialist decides that the packaging should be manufactured in three colors. Red, blue, and yellow are the colors chosen, and each color will be introduced in a different city. New Orleans will receive the red containers; Chicago, the yellow; and Denver, the blue. If the toothpaste sells better in Denver, the company may assume that the blue package was the deciding factor. If the experiment is conducted again using the same three colors but sending them to different cities, and if the same results are obtained, then the company could assume that blue is the color that should be used to package the new toothpaste.

Surveys

Many times the information a company needs can be obtained only by asking questions and recording the information given in response to the questions. This survey method of research can be conducted very formally by personal interviews with twenty company presidents or conducted informally through on-the-job discussion with fellow employees.

In the introductory stages of the survey, two decisions need to be made: *who* will answer the questions, and *what* questions will be asked. The serious investigator will understand that even the

Is experimentation feasible in business?

Who and *what* must be answered.

simplest and smallest of surveys are frequently involved and time-consuming.

Once *who* will answer the question is decided, a small group is selected from the entire group of people (the universe) around whom the problem is centered. The small group is representative of the whole. For example, if you are interested in how women college graduates react to the new toothpaste, would it be possible to interview every female college graduate? Theoretically, you would find it impossible to interview all women college graduates. Therefore, a group—the sample—must be selected from all women college graduates. If the research is to be valid, the sample must be representative of the entire group, the universe.

If the research is to be objective, the sample must be selected without bias. Several means of selecting an unbiased sample are available for the business investigator's use: random sample, area sample, quota, systematic sample, etc. A statistician or a market analyst can be consulted about which technique will be best suited to the research design.

Objectivity is the goal.

After deciding *who* will answer the questions, you must decide *what* questions are to be asked. The survey instrument (questionnaire or interview questions) must be carefully constructed. The questions asked and the way in which they are asked will have a decided effect on the quality or value of the answers and how many answers you receive. These answers will provide the data from which your report will be made. Therefore, when a researcher constructs the questions to be used in the survey instrument, the following principles should be used as guides.

Questions must be carefully constructed.

1. *Questions should be easy to understand.* The language used in the questions should be clear, direct, and simple. Keep the people who will answer the question, the respondents, in mind. The question may be clear in the author's mind; however, the respondents cannot be expected to reply consistently where there might be a possible variation in meaning. Ask the question so it cannot be misunderstood. The best (and probably the only) way to test a question is to try it out on several people. If any doubt exists, rewrite the question until only one possible meaning can be construed.

2. *Avoid questions that involve biases, prejudices, or pride.* Because we are human, we cannot be expected to answer certain personal questions accurately. Even though the woman's movement has prompted many women to give their age with pride, many others feel that this is privileged information and prefer not to report their birth dates. Other areas that might cause a slight shading of the truth are income, personal hygiene, and morals. If some personal information is necessary for the research, ask for the information in

Be careful when asking personal questions.

the least offensive way possible. For instance, perhaps you can determine the person's age by asking what year they graduated from high school. This answer would give you an approximate age, which is all that is necessary in most cases.

3. *Avoid leading questions.* These questions suggest specific answers. Do not ask: Is your favorite vacation spot Las Vegas? Instead, you should ask: What is your favorite vacation spot? The answers you receive will be more objective.

4. *Ask for current information.* Most humans have limited memories; consequently, questions should be those that the respondent can answer accurately. Several factors affect our memory: recency, importance, frequency, duration, vividness, interest, meaningfulness, setting, etc.

5. *Avoid using needless technical terms.* Economists know the meaning of money flow and gross national product. But most of us understand more readily if the question is worded "payments made by consumers to producers for goods" and "payments made by producers to owners of resources" rather than "money flow." Or the question asks about "the nation's total production of goods and services" rather than "gross national product."

6. *Avoid using general expressions.* Do you visit your dentist often? Do you eat fast? What is often? Once a month, twice a year, once every two years? How fast is fast? Two seconds, two minutes, two hours? *Often* and *fast* mean different things to different people.

7. *Stick to facts.* People may not always know how they feel; therefore, they are not accurate reporters of their inner feelings. Questions that involve motives, opinions, or attitudes need special handling to give objective and consistent results, and the wise interviewer will avoid this type of question.

8. *Avoid multiple-meaning questions.* Each question should cover only one point. If more than one point is questioned, the researcher cannot know which answer to assign to which question. Would you like to have movies on commercial air flights at a slight extra charge? How should the respondent answer this question? If the answer is "no," does it mean that he or she wouldn't like them even if they are free? If the respondent would like to see a movie on a long flight but not on a short one, what is the answer? If the respondent doesn't want to see a movie at all, charge or no charge, how does he or she indicate that preference?

The preceding guidelines should be followed whether the questions are designed for a personal interview or for a questionnaire to be returned. In any type of survey, if the research is to be valid, all questions must be the same. If the survey is the personal-interview type, all the interviewers should follow the same procedure and ask the questions in the same manner.

In constructing a questionnaire to be mailed, the researcher must consider the physical appearance of the form and the length. No questionnaire will obtain the desired results if the receiver throws it away. With the tons of mail that individuals and business firms receive daily, the person interested in a questionnaire return of 50 percent or more should follow the example of those who have gone before. You have at your disposal the experience of others who have constructed questionnaires. They have established guides to aid you in the construction of your instrument.

Benefit from the experience of others.

1. *The size of the form will depend to some extent on the nature and scope of the survey.* The best way to decide on size is to assess what type of instruments are successful today. As a general rule, most people will answer a questionnaire that is one to four pages in length. Usually the respondent will consider more than four pages to be too time-consuming. *Time* is too important to most people to be spent filling in questionnaires. This, of course, applies to the general public; if the questionnaire is to be sent to professionals, then the forms can be more detailed.

2. *The color of the paper on which the questionnaire is printed is important.* If the questionnaire is to be mailed, the researcher might consider colored paper. Color attracts attention and might be the deciding factor to persuade the respondent to fill in the blanks. However, a word of caution, check to see which colors create the most favorable response. The following associations are usually credited to certain colors.

Color makes a difference.

Red excites nerves; arouses feelings
Orange is heating, soon causes irritation
Yellow arouses joy and gaiety
Green is restful, soothing; neither warm nor cool
Blue is cooling, quieting

Some factor associated with the product may influence the choice of color of the questionnaire. For example, suppose you are designing a survey to market Daffodil bath soap. You might have the questionnaires printed on blue paper—blue is the color people usually associate with water. Or, since the brand name suggests yellow, you might have the form printed on yellow paper.

3. *Arrangement of the items on the page should be given careful consideration.* The design should be uncluttered, and the questions should appear uncomplicated. All persons involved (interviewer, researcher, and respondent) should be able to glance over the form to see if all the questions have been answered. Related questions should be grouped together. If a question is dependent on the answer to the preceding one, it should be given a subordinate place.

```
                THE SELECTED LIFE HISTORY ITEMS OF MIDDLE MANAGERS
                             ON THE PACIFIC COAST

          INSTRUCTIONS:  Please mark only one blank (X)--the blank which best describes
                         you--under each question.

          BIOGRAPHICAL BACKGROUND

          1.  In what age group do you fall?
                    20-24              40-44              55-59
                    25-29              45-49              60-64
                    30-34              50-54              65-69
                    35-39

          2.  What is your marital status?
                    Single             Widowed            Divorced
                    Married            Separated

          3.  Do you have children?
                    0                  3                  6
                    1                  4                  (If more than six, please
                    2                  5                  give number.)

          4.  What is your ethnic identification?
                    White              Asian or Pacific Islander
                    Black              American Indian or Alaskan Native
                    Hispanic

          FAMILY BACKGROUND

          5.  How many years of education did your parents have?
                    Mother             Father

          6.  How many siblings in your family?
                    Sisters            Brothers
                    1                  1
                    2                  2
                    3                  3
                    4                  4
                    5                  5
                    (If more,          (If more,
                    please             please
                    state.)            state.)

          7.  The place in which you spent the most time during your early life was a
                    1.  Farm
                    2.  Town of less than 2,000
                    3.  Town of 2,000 or more but less than 10,000
                    4.  City of 10,000 to 100,000
                    5.  City larger than 100,000
```

Figure 9—2
A questionnaire used in research on job satisfaction.

4. *Be sure that sufficient space has been provided for all possible responses.* In most instances the obvious responses are listed. The final selection could be "Other—specify." For example, in designing a question about the primary duties performed by a supervisor, the format might be:

_____ Formulate detailed plans

_____ Direct day-to-day operations

_____ Assign tasks to personnel

_____ Evaluate personnel

_____ Other (please specify) _____

(Indicate percent of time spent on each major duty you perform.)

Figure 9–2 is part of a questionnaire used in a research project dealing with job satisfaction.

After deciding what questions need to be answered and wording them to secure accurate, objective answers, the decision must be made as to what type of survey will do the best job. The three choices are personal interview, telephone interview or mail questionnaire. Each type has its strong and weak points.

Personal Interviews

Most people enjoy talking about themselves, and this enjoyment can be a decided advantage for face-to-face interviewers. Longer questionnaires can be administered and sensitive areas can be in-

People enjoy talking about themselves.

vestigated. Usually people are much more willing to tell personal information than they are to write the information.

During the session the interviewer also may change a question if the situation warrants a change. However, to do this, the interviewer must be skilled or the results may be changed enough to influence the data. The personal interview also has the advantage of securing answers the same day the interview is conducted. Naturally the number of answers received will depend on the number of interviews conducted.

Costs must be considered.

The cost of personal interviews can be quite high. Training interviewers or hiring experienced ones can send the cost of the research soaring. If the respondents are scattered across the United States, travel expenses should be considered. Personal interviewing is used at its optimum when the sample is located in a small geographic area.

Bias can affect the interview.

Most experts will agree that the greatest weakness of the personal interview is the human element involved. Even though competent people are hired as interviewers, the interviewer's personal bias may have an effect on the answers. Also the respondents, because of personal bias, personal importance, desire to please, etc., may shade their answers.

Telephone Interviews

The major advantages of telephone interviews are the speed with which you can reach people and the large number of people that can be contacted. However, unless the interview group is located in a small geographic area, cost would be a consideration.

Several disadvantages might influence a researcher to disregard this type of survey. Questions must be brief and few in number. Most people do not want to spend any length of time being interviewed on the telephone. Because the telephone has been used quite widely during the last decade for selling and promotion, the general public has been turned against the use of the telephone for interviews. Another frequent limitation is people's reluctance to give personal information over the telephone to someone they do not know. In addition, the interviewer is not able to accurately assess the respondent's physical reaction to a question (as can be done in a personal interview).

Mail Interviews

Mail interviews have several advantages that should be considered when the decision is made concerning the type of survey research that will be conducted. Perhaps the strongest advantage of this type of survey is the low cost per response. A wide geographical area can be surveyed at any given time. The United States Postal Service has access to many places that a personal or telephone interview might not be able to reach. The human element is cut in half because personal interviewers are not injecting their bias.

However, you must remember that the questionnaire must be short and to the point or the respondent will not bother to answer the questions. The researcher can expect a certain amount of bias in the returns because only those people who feel strongly one way or the other will take the time to fill in and return the form. Consequently, not many returns will be received from the middle-of-the-roaders. Furthermore, when a questionnaire is mailed, the investigator cannot know whether the intended recipient answered the questions or whether someone else did. Another point to consider, the postal service is not always fast nor is it always reliable. The respondent may delay answering the form; if time is a factor, this possible delay should be considered.

Disadvantages must be considered.

Documentation

Documentation provides your communication partner with the source of your information. Researchers have a responsibility to their readers to properly document the information contained in the communication. If primary research (company records, observation, surveys, or experiments) is used, an explanation of the research procedures used to collect the information will provide the necessary documentation. When secondary sources are used, credit should be given to the person who provided the information. Credit can be given in the text of the letter or report or with a footnote.

Proper documentation is essential.

Give credit!

A word of warning to all who tend to be procrastinators: As you gather information for your project, be sure that all the necessary information about the source is recorded. If you do not have accurate documentation in writing where you can find it, you may find yourself spending hours looking for a lost source.

Record vital information.

Footnotes are used for two reasons. They give credit to the original source of the material, or they explain something in the text of the communication. This explanatory type of footnote is used when putting the explanation in the text would distract from the main point of the paragraph. Documentation gives information to the reader, but it also gives credit to the source of the information. Footnotes should be placed conveniently for the reader. If the company president is extremely demanding about sources and frequently checks on them, you would be wise to have your footnotes placed at the bottom of the page. However, if your supervisor is not as hard to satisfy, you may prefer to place all of the footnotes at the end of the section or report. If the footnote information does not provide publishing information, the researcher should be sure to include a complete bibliography.

What information needs to be footnoted? This question has been a problem for years. The general rule is that if the information is from the common body of knowledge in a particular field, a footnote is not needed. For example, Columbus discovered America in 1492. Who should receive credit for this information? What is the original source of the seven "C's of communication"? If the information is based on personal knowledge or research and is not from the common body of knowledge, credit should be given to the person from whom the information was drawn. The rule of thumb is: when in doubt, give credit.

The researcher will find many forms of documentation available for use. Actually the choice is left up to you, unless your company has a preferred style. Some subjects or disciplines have documentation methods and other styles that are standardized for those subjects. Table 9–1 lists a number of general and specialized style manuals you may find helpful. Choose one style and use it consis-

Table 9–1
Style Manuals and Guides

William G. Campbell and Stephen V. Ballou. *Form and Style: Theses, Reports, Term Papers.* Boston: Houghton Mifflin, 1974.

Eugene Ehrlich and Daniel Murphy. *Writing and Researching Term Papers and Reports: A New Guide for Students.* New York: Bantam, 1968.

John C. Hodges and Mary E. Whitten. *Harbrace College Handbook.* 8th ed. New York: Harcourt Brace Jovanovich, 1977.

Marigold Linton. *A Simplified Style Manual: For the Preparation of Journal Articles in Psychology, Social Sciences, Education and Literature.* New York: Appleton-Century-Crofts, 1972.

Modern Language Association. *MLA Handbook for Writers of Research Papers, Theses, and Dissertations.* New York: MLA, 1977.

Kate L. Turabian. *A Manual for Writers of Term Papers, Theses and Dissertations.* 4th ed. Chicago: University of Chicago Press, 1973.

————. *Student's Guide for Writing College Papers.* 3rd ed. Chicago: University of Chicago Press, 1976.

University of Chicago Press. *A Manual of Style.* 12th ed. Chicago: University of Chicago Press, 1969.

Mary-Claire van Leunen. *A Handbook for Scholars.* New York: Knopf, 1978.

tently. The best documentation style is the simplest style that contains all the necessary information. Carefully check article and book titles. Double-check the spelling of all author's names.

Use a style that you can remember.

Summary

This chapter is an introduction to library research, primary research, and documentation. Volumes have been written on each of the three areas, so this discussion is just a beginning. If you need more information on research, you will find books covering the subject in more detail available in most libraries.

Questions for Discussion

1. Define secondary research. Define primary research.

2. How can secondary research help you write a letter or report?

3. As a researcher, why should you know how to use the library?

4. How can the knowledge of sources of business information simplify the researcher's task?

5. How can an evaluation of secondary sources help to maintain the objectivity of a project?

6. What is a computer search?

7. What are the four types of primary research? Present a business situation in which you might employ two of the four primary research methods.

8. Define the observation method of research. What are the advantages and disadvantages of this research method?

9. What two questions must be answered before survey research begins?

10. How important is the form of the questionnaire in conducting a survey? What influences the form to be used?

11. List four principles for constructing the questions included on the survey instrument.

12. Describe the three types of surveys.

13. Why should researchers document their reports carefully?

14. What is the general rule for documentation?

15. Which form of documentation is better? Why? Under what circumstances would you use the other form of documentation?

Exercises

1. As a research assistant for the American Bank and Trust Company of Greeley, Colorado, you have been asked to gather information and report on the feasibility of adding a 24-hour automated teller machine to the bank's full-service program.

   a. Gather secondary information on this equipment.

   b. Prepare a short questionnaire to survey bank customers. Questions might include: (1) age, (2) yearly income, (3) frequency of using bank services, (4) types of bank services now used, (5) length of association with bank, (6) etc.

   c. Decide which type of survey to use.

   d. Conduct the survey among the members of your class.

   e. Summarize the results of your survey.

2. Using *Moody's Manuals* or *Standard Corporation Records,* compile a financial profile or financial history of a company that has been in the news during the past year.

3. Prepare a biographical sketch of a prominent business person in your state or a person mentioned in your local newspaper using a biographical directory.

4. Using the observation method of research, determine what the current fashions are this semester on your campus.

5. With the permission of your dean or department chairperson, use university records to analyze the enrollment in your department, school, or college for the past five years. Summarize your analysis and state your conclusions.

Chapter 10 Justification and Preparation of Reports

The Why of Report Writing

Establishing the Purpose

Defining the Problem

Classifying and Organizing the Data

Preparing Your Outline
Inductive or Deductive Order
Past or Present Tense

Preparing the Rough Draft

Personal or Impersonal Style
Formal or Informal Style

Preparing the Report

Format
Prefatory Pages
The Body of the Report
Appended Parts of the Report

Summary

"That writer does the most, who gives his reader the most *knowledge, and takes from him the* least *time."* — C. C. Colton

The Why of Report Writing

A large manufacturing plant is considering the addition of a word-processing center. The office manager believes that a centralized system for dictation and transcription will increase efficiency and maintain control of paperwork. As the assistant office manager, you are asked to study the existing system, to determine the cost of installing the word-processing center, and to recommend whether or not the addition of such a center is feasible. Your findings will be presented as a report to be circulated to the plant executives. This initial report could require further reports if addition of the center is feasible. For example, a later study may be conducted to ensure proper transfer from the existing system to the new word-processing system with a minimum amount of employee frustration.

Reports aid in decisions.

As the researcher for this study, you will need to examine such factors as available space for the center, the effects on the personnel involved in the change, the costs of implementing the system, and the effects on productivity.

You may begin your research by reading up-to-date articles about word-processing centers, which may be found in professional and trade magazines. You may visit firms in your industry that utilize word-processing centers. Such visits would allow you to report on the advantages and disadvantages of word-processing centers from a realistic and practical viewpoint. These visits would also be helpful in determining whether your company is suited for such a center. Talking with sales representatives from companies that manufacture equipment for word-processing centers will acquaint you with the available equipment, its prices, and practical uses. This information will help you decide if the equipment meets the objectives of your management. You will study your firm's facilities to determine if a center could be installed at a reasonable cost.

How do you begin your research?

You may observe the current practices followed in your office under normal operating conditions. You may project the effects on productivity of the installation of a word-processing center. You will make comparisons, and, finally, you will present your recommendations whether or not installation of a word-processing center is feasible. Your report will be used by management as a basis for their decision. To make this report, your research will use both secondary and primary sources. Reading printed material in periodicals is the secondary research. Primary research will consist of formally questioning people who are well acquainted with word-processing centers and observing what is being done in plants with word-processing centers.

Such a study to consider the installation of a word-processing center represents a need for a business report. However, all business reports are not as complex or need not take as much time as this example would. Installation of the word-processing center was a special problem that required conducting a study.

Many business reports are prepared solely to present information. The size and complexity of modern businesses demand written reports, prepared so management can make efficient decisions and transmit information throughout an organization. Sufficient information can no longer be circulated throughout most companies by word of mouth. Data is conveyed through reports for several reasons:

1. Written reports can be kept on file for reference and/or follow up.

2. Written reports help the researcher adhere closely to the original assignment.

3. Written reports serve as proof of assignment completion and are safeguards against miscommunication.

4. Written reports point out strengths and weaknesses in an organization.

5. Written reports allow management to make difficult decisions with a minimum of effort and time.

Management's role is to plan, organize, activate, and control. Therefore, management must constantly make decisions—decisions that should be based on factual data carefully gathered, assimilated, and presented in understandable terms. Data must be organized and presented briefly to enable the reader to see relationships, interpret meanings, and effectively *use* the information the report contains. Management is interested in concrete, unbiased, and orderly information that can be utilized easily and quickly. You, as a report writer, must demonstrate your ability to communicate data so as to earn the confidence of management.

Reports present solutions to problems.

Reports present needed information.

Reports serve as a basis for decisions.

Reports must contain usable information.

The steps involved in preparing your report will depend on the particular situation under study. Many reports in business require only a few handwritten notes and need not follow a detailed, formal outline. However, if you are presented a complicated problem such as the feasibility study for a word-processing center, you should consider following these steps:

What are some possible steps in preparing reports?

1. Establish the purpose of the report.
2. Define the problem to be solved.
3. Determine the best sources of data.
4. Select the appropriate methods of research.
5. Specify the scope and limitations of the problem.
6. Conduct the research.
7. Classify and organize the data.
8. Prepare the report.

This chapter focuses primarily on establishing the purpose of the report, defining the problem to be solved, classifying and organizing the data, and preparing the report in final form.

Establishing the Purpose

Before any research is initiated, the purpose for a particular assignment should be established. The feasibility study for the word-processing center was assigned by your supervisor. If you had only received one segment of the assignment, your research might result in a limited view of a much broader problem. Instead, you knew the final objective of your research. Although you did not determine the purpose, you were informed by the office manager what the end result of your research would be—management's decision whether or not to install a word-processing center.

Because reports usually travel upward, the need for a report will probably be recognized by someone other than yourself. Your assignment may be oral or written, but it is necessary to determine the purpose so you understand where your research fits into the management scheme. You will fulfill your obligation better when you know the overall goal.

Who recognizes the need for a report?

By stating the purpose of the study in your report, the reader knows:

1. how the findings will meet management's objectives, and
2. how and by whom the results of the research are to be used.

The purpose should catch the reader's attention and interest. The purpose of the report could precede the statement of the problem in some studies; in others, the problem might precede the purpose. In certain situations, the purpose and the problem could be combined. The placement will be determined by the characteristics of the research.

Your assignment, or problem, was to determine the effects and costs of installing a word-processing center. The purpose of the study was to enable management to decide whether or not a word-processing center would maximize efficiency, reduce costs, and meet company objectives. In your research, the problem and the purpose were not the same.

Reports present factual information.

The purpose also depends on the function of the report. All business reports should present factual information. Some reports not only present information but interpret the information to aid the reader. Other reports interpret the information, analyze the data, draw conclusions, and make recommendations or suggestions.

Whatever the assignment, do only what you are requested to do. While this may contradict past recommendations about doing more than is asked, sometimes you are not in a position to do anything except present information. You may be involved in only a small phase of a project, and your suggestions might not be appropriate until all phases are complete. For example, if your assignment were to study the costs and effects of a word-processing center in only one department, recommendations should not be made for the entire company until the effects in all departments are determined.

Defining the Problem

After the purpose of the study is clearly established, your specific task should then be stated. By clearly defining the problem to be solved, your mind should begin to react to your assignment. Seldom, if ever, will you be allowed uninterrupted time on any report. Daily routine tasks continue. The statement of the problem will keep you from digressing even though other work tends to interfere. The problem should be stated as concisely as possible without omitting any relevant information. You will then have available a clear, permanent record of your assignment.

Clearly define your problem.

The way in which you state your problem is not as important as the fact that you have a clear statement of the problem in writing. The problem can be defined in a declarative statement or as a question. The purpose of a report is general; the problem statement is specific.

Your problem statement might read:

The problem is to determine the effects and costs of installing a word-processing center in our plant.

Or the problem might be stated:

What will be the costs and effects of installing a word-processing center in our plant?

From a clear statement of the problem, you can set up tentative assumptions or hypotheses to be accepted or rejected. Your hypotheses must be verified or proven before they can be accepted. In other words, hypotheses are tentative answers or educated guesses. You may make the assumption that a word-processing center will increase efficiency, or you may make the assumption that a word-processing center will decrease efficiency. You must then prove or disprove your hypothesis about efficiency.

What is a hypothesis?

The statement of the problem should establish the delimitations and limitations of the study. Delimitations are conscious, intentional controls or restrictions set up by the researcher for purposes of accuracy. The researcher intentionally places boundaries to suit the purposes of the study. If your company has plants located across the country, your study will not determine if word-processing centers should be installed in all plants, only in the one in which you work. Thus, you have delimited your research to one specific place.

Limitations are those conditions over which there is little control; they are given or inherent in the situation. For instance, your superior will probably allot a certain amount of money and time for the study of the word-processing center. Your study may also be limited by the available suppliers of word-processing equipment in your area. As the researcher, you are limited by these conditions. Therefore, you may wish to control certain data and restrict certain areas of your research to fit the limitations.

With your problem clearly defined, you are ready to find the best way to reach a solution. If your research can be done satisfactorily by using secondary sources, you will save your company both time and money. However, solutions to all problems are not available through secondary sources. Observing word-processing centers in action, talking with representatives of companies that manufacture equipment, and studying the existing system within your company are all forms of primary research. In the preceding chapter, you learned that the proper selection of research methods is extremely crucial in arriving at the optimum solution to your problem. Then, after you have collected your data, you need to determine how to best organize your findings.

Classifying and Organizing the Data

Whether you conduct secondary research, primary research, or a combination of the two, the information must be classified in order to organize the facts into an understandable form. If only secondary research is involved, classifying and organizing the data will be relatively simple. As the research is conducted, notes placed on index cards should be kept on each topic. By separating the cards into the main subjects, you are classifying your data. Next, the cards are arranged by major and minor classifications into a logical order.

The criteria you use to classify and organize your data is an essential and critical step in presenting your report. The reader should not be presented with a jumble of facts and statistics that must be sorted out to reach the solution to the problem. The results of your research are the most important part of your report. A workable outline is needed so you may logically present your findings. Because your final outline will become the table of contents in your report, all sections should be parallel in the outline.

Data must be sorted.

Preparing Your Outline

Although short reports of a routine nature do not generally require written outlines, you should mentally think through your problem and decide on the order in which you will present your information. An outline helps you to structure your thoughts to better analyze the problem. Your thinking is clarified, and you are better able to evaluate your ideas objectively. An outline establishes the relationship between the parts and the whole. Emphasis can be achieved by placing key points in positions of importance. Subpoints will flow easily from key points.

Your principal objectives in outlining are:
1. to carry out the purpose of the report
2. to develop the problem statement to show relationships or comparisons revealed by your research
3. to save time in writing.

Any acceptable form of outline will suffice. Whether you use Roman numerals, decimals, or a combination of letters and numbers makes little difference as long as you separate your information into logical, workable sections that may be expanded to include all of the important elements of the problem. Break down your purpose into sub-purposes. These sub-purposes can act as objectives for sections and paragraphs. For example, a study of the role of the college-educated secretary in selected business firms in Chicago might have an outline similar to the one shown in Table 10-1.

All items in the outline merely identify each section to be discussed. A more complete outline would further identify the sections by describing the information to be discussed. As the outline expands into the table of contents, you might develop the findings section as shown in Table 10-2.

Descriptive outlines aid the reader.

All parts of this expanded outline are complete sentences. However, noun phrases could have been used instead, as in Table 10-1. Regardless of the form you choose for your outline, it must be consistent. Each section must be parallel in construction. If one part of a section in your outline is in sentence form, all parts of the

C. Business Firms Recognize the Abilities of College-Educated
Secretaries
1. The returns indicate a preference for hiring college-educated secretaries.
2. The majority of business executives are aware of the courses studied by the secretary in college.
3. The majority of secretaries utilize business courses studied in college in their work.
4. Job status, as well as remuneration, is higher among college-educated secretaries.
5. College-educated secretaries assume more responsibility and are given more authority.
6. Duties of college-educated secretaries include administrative tasks rather than just routine skills.

section should be expressed in sentences. A part labeled *A* should be followed by a part labeled *B;* a part labeled *1* should be followed by *2*.

Good organization with the help of a good outline will provide structure to your writing. You have a starting point from which you can proceed through the beginning, the middle, and the end.

Inductive or Deductive Order

As you organize the information for your report, you must decide whether to write in inductive or deductive order. When you write in inductive order, you begin with an introduction to the problem and work through the problem, step by step, until you reach a conclusion. The facts build up to your conclusion. This follows the logical process of reasoning.

Why then would you choose the deductive order? Returning to one of the reasons why reports are written, you will remember that management needs to make decisions with the least amount of effort and time. When you employ deductive order, you begin with a general statement and proceed to the specific facts; you state your conclusions first. The reader of your report could reach a decision by reading only the beginning. Later, the entire report may be read. Or you may get the reputation of being an expert in research and logic, and the entire report may never be read.

The decision to use inductive or deductive order also depends on the formality of the report. In longer, more formal reports, induc-

Deductive order can save time for the reader.

tive order is traditional. Shorter reports are often more routine, and consequently the conclusions are usually given first. Thus, time is saved for the reader. The reader does not have to read background information before seeing the conclusions or recommendations.

A feasibility report would appropriately be written in inductive order. Although business reports should be objective rather than persuasive, if you think your conclusions will be accepted more readily if someone reads through your reasons first, present your report in inductive order. You will be more likely to convince someone to accept your ideas if you begin with an introduction to the problem, present your findings, and then draw your conclusions based on the findings.

Decide how you think the reader will react to what you have to say, then determine whether to use inductive or deductive order.

Past or Present Tense

If you approach your writing with the idea that all the research was prepared in the past, you might choose to use verbs in the past tense. However, using the present tense is a more logical way of writing. But, it does not mean that you use every verb in the present tense. Events that clearly occurred in the past should be put in the past tense; events that will occur in the future should be put in the future tense. For example, compare these statements:

Less than one-half of the respondents (40 percent) received additional salary as a result of their education (past tense).

Less than one-half of the respondents (40 percent) receive additional salary as a result of their education (present tense).

Changing the tense within a sentence should be avoided. Regardless of whether you write in the present or past tense, be consistent in your report.

Preparing the Rough Draft

Perhaps the most difficult part of your report will be to put the first words on paper. A rough draft will actually save you time.

Drafts save time!

Any section may be written first. After you have gathered, classified, and organized your data, you may know what your conclusions will be. In that case, you could write the conclusions first. Or background material may be assembled and written while you are waiting for the results of a questionnaire. The order in which the report is written is not important. Your confidence will grow if you write the parts with which you feel most comfortable first.

Prepare familiar material first.

The more you write, the easier writing becomes; and, after all, you have to begin somewhere! Expressing your ideas on paper when you know you have an opportunity to change words, check statistics, verify spelling, and rephrase sentences is helpful in keeping the thought processes flowing. Do not worry about redundancy at this stage. This is your working copy, and you will have time later to consult a thesaurus for synonyms or a dictionary for spelling and accurate meaning. Concentration can be broken if you stop to check how to spell a word or to correctly word a sentence.

Write something, remembering that you can go back and make changes. Whether you dictate to your secretary, use a dictating machine, or actually handwrite or type your rough draft, you will have written words that can be edited and improved. If your secretary types the draft, request that space be left for editing. Few writers can prepare a final draft the first time. A good suggestion to follow is to prepare the rough draft, put the draft away for a day or longer, then read your draft again, and revise what you have written before the final copy is typed. You may find that extensive changes are needed. If so, have a second rough draft typed, and repeat the review steps as before. Your report will be improved every time it is revised.

Personal or Impersonal Style

The third person is used when you write in an impersonal style. Doctoral dissertations, proposals to the president of a company, and most reports over 100 pages are written in formal style using the third person, usually the standard report form.

Personal writing uses first-person pronouns. Reports distributed within the company among employees of the same rank or lower are usually written in informal style, using the first or second person.

Several considerations before choosing the personal or impersonal style of writing include:

1. Who will receive the report?

2. Does the subject matter lend itself more to a conversational or to a formal style of writing?

3. Will the report be so long that the third person would be the acceptable form of writing?

If your report contains routine information intended for employees on the same level of authority as you or will be sent to your subordinates, an impersonal style would probably be out of place. How you present your information has a definite effect on the way it is received. Writing in the third person to a fellow employee with whom you share an office could well create an uncomfortable situation and possibly cause resentment.

When you are on a first-name basis and the report is informal, use first-person pronouns. Addressing a memorandum to Mrs. Roy A. Moore, III, when you normally call her Wilma, might not cause a breakdown in communication, but the tone would be rigid and impersonal. The same message could be conveyed by addressing the memorandum to Wilma Moore, and a much more relaxed atmosphere for receiving your message would be established. A conversational style of writing, unless company policy dictates otherwise, is more natural and easier to read.

Determine your relationship with the reader.

Formal or Informal Style

When you transmit reports upward in the company, your formality will increase. If your assignment is complex, you should probably prepare your report formally just as you would dress for a formal occasion. In fact, your report assignment can be compared to an invitation to a party. When you receive an invitation to a party, you intuitively recognize from the appearance of the invitation whether you are expected to come in a formal dress or tuxedo or in very casual clothes. If you receive an engraved invitation, you can generally assume that the dress is formal. A handwritten note or a telephone call will most likely imply that casual dress is in order.

The feasibility study for the word-processing center is to be prepared for the office manager, your supervisor, who, in turn, will present the report to upper management. This assignment warrants a formal report. Because of the length and formality of the report, certain prefatory and appended parts (illustrated later in this chapter) will probably be required.

The nature of the problem and the recipient of the report help determine the formality or informality of the report format. Policies established by your company should be considered first. If your company always uses a formal plan of presentation and you use personal pronouns, first names, or slang, you could create an unfavorable impression. Formality and informality, of course, have no effect on spelling, punctuation, or grammar. Even the shortest handwritten note is a reflection of your ability to communicate.

Preparing the Report

How your report is received depends upon how well you present the package.

A long, formal report generally has all or most of the parts listed in Table 10-3. As the formality and length of the report increase, the need for prefatory and appended pages increases. If formality so dictates, add the appropriate prefatory and appended pages.

There are no cut-and-dried rules for the format of your report. Check the company files for reports prepared by others or discuss with your supervisor the most effective format for your report.

Format

When a standard format is not used by your company, the following plan offers acceptable ways to prepare your report. An attractively prepared report should catch your reader's eye and pave the way for easy reading.

Cover
You may bind your report with staples or by punching holes into the pages and using metal or plastic fasteners. A cover of cardboard, plastic, or leather will protect your report. The appearance of the

Table 10-3
Parts of Long, Formal Reports

Prefatory Pages
   Title fly
   Title page
   Letter of transmittal
   Table of contents
   List of illustrations, tables, or charts
   Summary

Body of the Report
   Introduction
   Findings
   Conclusions and/or recommendations

Appended Pages
   Bibliography
   Appendix
   Index

report is impressive if bound in leather. If the report will be retained for a number of years, choose a durable cover. Sections or chapters may be marked with labeled tabs.

Spacing

Business reports may be either single-spaced or double-spaced. Conventionally, reports are double-spaced as most people prefer a space between each line for reading ease. When reports are double-spaced, paragraph indentions are necessary because no additional space is added between paragraphs. Paragraphs are almost always indented five spaces. Single-spaced reports may have blocked paragraphs with a double space between the paragraphs.

Margins

The margins for your report will depend on the form in which the report is submitted. Set the typewriter guide on zero. The margins may then be set according to the following guides.

Top margins. The first page of the report body (and of any main sections, if they are used) and all special pages (such as the table of contents, lists of tables and figures, appendixes, bibliography, and the index) should have a top margin of 2 inches. For example, the title of your report or its first section will begin on line 13 of the first page of the report body. If the report is bound at the top, the first page and special pages should have a top margin of $2\frac{1}{2}$ inches.

Regular pages should have a top margin of 1 inch (six blank lines); regular pages in top-bound reports should have a top margin of $1\frac{1}{2}$ inches.

Left margins. The left margin for unbound and top-bound reports should be 1 inch. If the cover of the report fastens on the left, the left margin should be approximately $1\frac{1}{2}$ inches to allow for the binding. If you are using a pica typewriter (10 spaces to the horizontal inch), set your left margin on 15. If you are using an elite typewriter (12 spaces to the horizontal inch), your left margin should be set on 18.

Right margins. There should be a right margin of at least 1 inch on all reports, regardless of binding. The right margin should be set at 75 for pica type and at 90 for elite type.

Bottom margins. The bottom margin should be approximately 1 inch. An $8\frac{1}{2}$ by 11 inch sheet of paper has sixty-six vertical spaces. Text copy should end as close to line 60 as possible. Using a guide sheet behind your original helps you know where to end the page correctly without having to count lines. A guide sheet, illustrated in

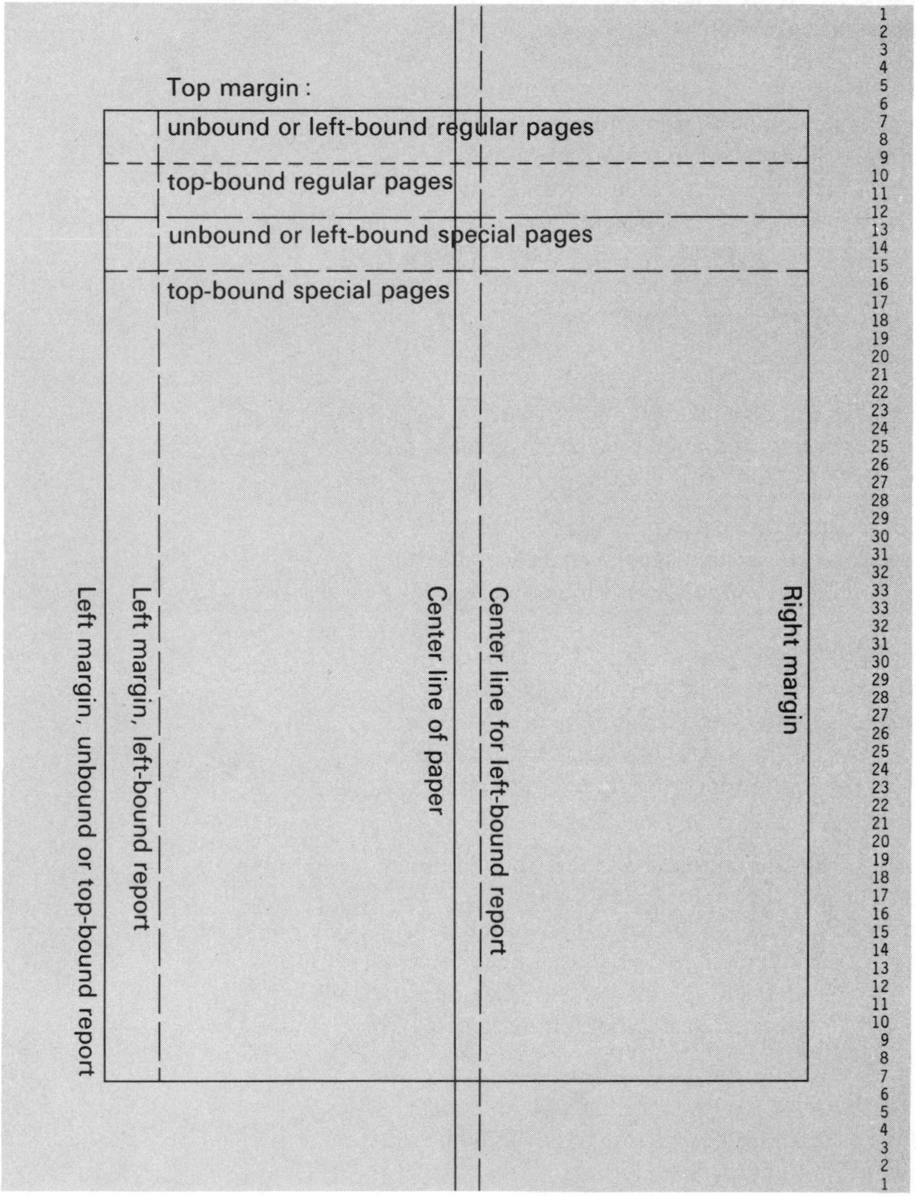

Figure 10—1
A guide sheet for typing reports.

Figure 10–1, helps you or your typist know where you are on the page. A light pencil line near the left side of the paper (that can be erased when the page is checked) can also be helpful.

At least two lines of any paragraph should be carried over to a new page. If there is only a short line left when the last line is typed, it is much better to have a slightly longer page containing the whole paragraph. Do not put a heading on the last line. Leave the page shorter than normal, and start the new page with the heading.

Center line.   If you have added an extra half inch to the left margin for binding, the center point of the page will be three spaces to the right of the physical center. The corrected center line will be at 45 for pica type and at 54 for elite type.

Headings or Captions

Dividing your report with headings is very helpful for the reader. Imagine reading a textbook without any break! Headings not only break the reading but identify the different sections of the report. Most headings follow the outline you made and indicate the various points to be stressed in your report. Headings are guides for the reader. They are generally differentiated by capitalization, underlining, and position on the page. Headings of the same importance should always be typed the same way and be put in the same position. Short, simple reports may only use one type of heading. Longer, complex reports may use two or even more types of headings. The following suggestions should be helpful in differentiating between the headings in your report.

1. The title of the report may be typed in all capital letters, centered between the margins, and underscored, as the first typed line on the page. Put at least two spaces (triple-space) between the report title and the first main heading or the first line of the body of the report.

2. The main headings are typed with the important words capitalized, centered between the margins, and underscored. Two blank spaces (triple-space) should be used above all main headings; triple-space below all main headings to the text of the report that follows. Two types of main headings can be used by underlining the more important head.

3. The second-level headings begin at the left margin, the important words are capitalized, and the heading is underscored. Two blank spaces (triple-space) should be used above all second-level headings; double-space below them to the text. Additional types of second-level headings can be designated by not underlining or by indenting the headings the same as the paragraph indention, with or without underlining.

4. Run-in headings may begin at the left margin or be indented the same as a paragraph. This heading generally has an initial capital letter with the balance of the heading typed in lower-case letters. There is always a period at the end of the run-in heading, the only heading that has any terminal punctuation. Two spaces always follow this period. Run-in captions are generally underlined to make them stand out in the report. Figure 10–2 illustrates the first page of a report and shows the spacing around the heads used.

Page Numbers

The body of the report and any appended parts generally have arabic page numbers. Using a page number on the first page of the report body is optional. If a number is used, place it approximately $\frac{1}{2}$ inch from the bottom of the page in the center. Other special pages in the report are numbered in the same location. All page numbers in a top-bound report are also centered at the bottom of the page.

Regular pages in a left-bound or unbound report will have the page number typed at the right margin, $\frac{1}{2}$ inch from the top of the page (on line 4).

The numbers used on the prefatory pages are typed in small Roman numerals. Most of the prefatory pages are not numbered, but counting begins with the first page. For example, if you have a title fly (i), title page (ii), letter of transmittal (iii), a two-page table of contents (iv and v), and a summary, the summary page will be numbered vi. Numbering the contents pages is optional; the summary or synopsis is generally numbered. The number is placed about $\frac{1}{2}$ inch from the bottom of the page in the center.

Quoted Material

Material written by others is often used in report writing. Through continual usage, many principles have become part of the common body of knowledge of a given subject. Specific acknowledgment of the sources of this common knowledge (if they are known) is not necessary.

However, if you summarize or even paraphrase (restate in your own words) the findings of other researchers when their work has made a contribution to your report, you should acknowledge their work. This acknowledgment may be made in one of two ways: by a footnote (discussed in the next section) or by an acknowledgment within the text.

When the work of others is acknowledged in the text, it is generally done by putting the name of the author, the title of the work, and the number of the page in parentheses following the reference

```
                    A REPORT ON REPORTS

                     The Main Heading

        The main headings are typed with the important words
   capitalized, centered between the margins, and underscored.
   Two blank spaces (triple-space) should be used above and below
   all main headings.

   Second-level Headings
        Second-level headings begin at the left margin, the important
   words are capitalized, and the heading is underscored.  Two blank
   spaces (triple-space once) should be used above all second-level
   headings; double-space below them to the text.
        Run-in headings.  Run-in headings may begin at the left margin
   or be indented the same as a paragraph.  This heading generally
   has an initial capital letter with the balance of the heading typed
   in lower case.  There is always a period at the end of the run-in
   heading.

                     The Second Main Heading

        All headings may be varied by changes in capitalization,
   underlining, or indention to differentiate between them in a very
   complex report.
```

Figure 10—2
The various types of report headings and the spacing around them.

in a location that will not interrupt the flow of the text (for example, Turabian, *Student's Guide for Writing College Papers,* p. 77). If this method is used, a bibliography is necessary at the end of the report to include publication information for the works acknowledged.

If you are quoting the writings of someone else verbatim, the material should be placed in quotation marks. "Written statements of policy are an important means of transmitting management attitudes" is a direct quotation from a book. If the source of the quotation is important to your report, the information is generally given in a footnote. The footnote reference is indicated by following the quotation with a superscript number (a number raised slightly above the base of the type, for example [1]).

If the quoted material is four typewritten lines or longer, it may be single-spaced with the margins of the quotation indented five spaces on both the left and right sides. When quoted material is set off this way, no quotation marks are used at the beginning and end of the quotation. A footnote reference to the source of such a quotation is again indicated by a superscript.

> The Clean Air Act of 1970 was enacted with the noblest intention—to make the air good to breathe. Nine years later, the act is choking industrial development, and the Environmental Protection Agency promises even more restrictive enforcement in the future. The trade-off is: How much pure atmosphere should be sacrificed to ensure a growing economy?[2]

An omission from a direct quotation is indicated by using three periods separated by a space, called ellipses. If the omission falls within a sentence, there is a space before and after the ellipsis dots. If the omission is at the end of a sentence, and the quoted portion is a complete sentence, four dots are used with no space before the first dot (indicating the period for the sentence, followed by the ellipses).

Except in legal or very technical work, the first word in a quotation follows grammatical rules for capitalization. Punctuation within a quotation that contributes to understanding the meaning is generally included. If the quotation is shown in your report in quotation marks, any quotation marks in the original will be changed to single quotation marks in your report, following the normal punctuation rules.

Footnotes

Footnotes, sometimes called endnotes, are used for two major purposes: to show the source of quotations or acknowledgments of the work of others, and to enlarge on a statement made in the text when the information would be distracting if placed in the text. Ideally footnotes should be placed at the bottom of the page on which the citation appears because the reader does not have to flip through the report for the reference. Because of the time involved in putting the footnotes on the page where the citation occurs, some authorities recommend that they be typed on a separate page. If this method is followed, the footnote page should be set up as a special page, should be the first page in the appended parts, and should also be listed in the table of contents.

When footnotes appear at the bottom of the page, they are separated from the text by a divider line 1½ inches long, made with the underscore key. This line should be typed a single space below the last line of text on the page, beginning at the left margin. Double-space below the line before typing the footnote. The footnotes generally follow the indention of paragraphs in your report and are generally single-spaced.

The footnote begins with a superscript matching the one in the text. If you have quoted from a book, the footnote contains the full name of the author; the title of the book, underlined; the publication information, enclosed in parentheses, giving the location and name of the publisher and the date of publication; and finally the page number or numbers where the original quotation is found. Quotations from a periodical are footnoted by showing the name of the author of the article; the title of the article in quotation marks; the name of the periodical, underlined; the volume, number, and year of publication (the year is put in parentheses), or the month and year of publication; and finally the page number or numbers where the quotation is found. For example, the two quotations given above are footnoted:

---

[1]Alton R. Kindred, *Data Systems and Management* (Englewood Cliffs, N.J.: Prentice-Hall, Inc., 1973), p. 193.

[2]John M. Eddinger, ''Business Needs a Breather From the Clean Air Act,'' *Nation's Business,* June 1979, p. 83.

Further information about proper footnote form can be found in the style books shown in Table 9–1.

Prefatory Pages

Internal reports in the form of memorandums and external reports in the form of letters require no prefatory pages because, by their nature, they are informal and short. As the length of your report increases, add pages to indicate formality and aid the reader in previewing your report. All pages will not be necessary for every report; usually, as the formality increases, so do the number of prefatory pages.

Title Fly
The title fly serves no purpose except to indicate formality. The official title of the project is typed, perhaps on colored paper, slightly above the center of the page (see Figure 10–3). If no cover is used, the title fly protects the title page and the text. As the formality decreases, this page would be eliminated first. The title used on the title fly is exactly the same as the title on the title page.

```
THE SELECTION OF A PLANT SITE

        FOR LEISURE LIFE
```

Figure 10—3
A title fly for a long formal report.
Place the title slightly above the center of the page (three or four vertical spaces).

The title may appear in all capital letters or with only the important words capitalized. Neither quotation marks nor a period at the end of the title are used.

Title Page

The title page is necessary for any report other than a memorandum or letter report. Four types of information should be included:

1. A clear, concise, and complete title, preferably not more than ten words in length.

2. The name and position of the person or organization for whom the report is being prepared.

```
                  THE SELECTION OF A PLANT SITE

                        FOR LEISURE LIFE




                          Prepared for

                         John A. Spivey

                      President, Leisure Life







                          Prepared by

                        Robert W. Alden

                      Marketing Department


                        October 21, 1981
```

Figure 10—4
Illustration of the title page of a
report.

3. The name and position of the person or persons who are preparing the report. If the report is to be sent outside the company, include the name of the company.

4. The date on which the report is completed.

Figure 10–4 illustrates the title page of a report.

Letter of Transmittal

The letter of transmittal, addressed to the person who receives the report, is your opportunity to communicate with the reader even if your report is extremely formal. This letter follows the same format as any other letter written by your company and is written in the

LEISURE LIFE
318 West Charles
Alpine, CA 96070

916-903-8727

October 21, 1981

Mr. John A. Spivey, President
Leisure Life Corporation
1423 West LaGrange Street
Alpine, CA 96070

Mr. Spivey

Subject: Selection of a Plant Site for Leisure Life

Attached is the report you asked me to prepare for the new location for a plant. This study, authorized on August 1, 1981, was completed with the assistance of John Byrnes, Ralph Martinez, and Constance Masters.

Available plant sites in Georgia were in the cities of Beauregard, Marksville, and Gingerton. Factors considered were availability of raw materials, of labor, of land and tax concessions, and of transportation. Gingerton proved to be the best prospect for the new site.

My staff and I appreciate your confidence in us. If you have any questions concerning the study, please contact me.

Sincerely

Robert W. Alden

Robert W. Alden

cp

Attachment

Figure 10–5
Illustration of a letter of transmittal.

first person. The contents of the letter identify the nature of the report. If the report was authorized in writing, a copy should be included.

An expression of appreciation for the assignment or to the people who helped you in preparing the report is appropriate, unless you choose to have a special page for acknowledgments. You could also include the purpose of the study, the highlights of your findings, and/or the major conclusions drawn from your research. Any introductory or explanatory information that would be helpful to the reader could be included. If you feel the reader will not agree with your conclusions until he or she has read the findings of your report, avoid including the conclusions in the letter of transmittal.

Your delimitations, limitations, and any personal remarks you may wish to express not included in the body of the report would also be appropriate in the letter.

Begin with a positive paragraph to catch the reader's interest, and close with a statement of goodwill. Type the letter on company stationery in the appropriate style. Be sure you refer to the date the report was authorized, and include any other data necessary to remind the reader of the assignment. Figure 10–5 illustrates a letter of transmittal.

Table of Contents

The reader will be helped by a contents page if the report is over five or six pages long and the sections have been broken down into subsections. Your final outline becomes your table of contents with each section and subsection listed with the appropriate page number. Show the page number on which the section or subsection begins in the table of contents. Leader lines (dots with a space between) may be used between the title of the section or subsection and the page number. If leader lines are used, align the dots by placing them on either the odd or even spaces of the typewriter scale.

The titles of the sections and subsections should be emphasized in the table of contents just as they are in the report body. The summary of the report will generally be the first entry in the table of contents. Figure 10–6 illustrates the table of contents for a report. Since this table of contents is rather long, it requires two pages. These pages are numbered iv and v, and both page numbers are centered at the bottom of the page.

Also note that this example is single-spaced, with a double space between each item. Since the list of tables and figures is included on the second page, there are two spaces above this title and two spaces below it.

Lists of Illustrations, Tables, or Charts

Usually illustrations, drawings, tables, and charts do not require a separate contents section. However, if your report contains quite a few of them, you could list them separately following the table of contents. Always consider your reader. If a specific illustration or chart might be used independently of the report, place the list in the prefatory pages to permit easy reference to the material. In Figure 10–6, the list of tables and figures was combined with the table of contents. A separate page could have been used, but because the list was not long, the combination was effective.

Illustrations, tables, and charts are usually numbered throughout the report with arabic numbers. Although some style authorities

Figure 10—6
Illustration of a two-page table of contents including a list of tables and figures.

accept tables only being numbered with capital Roman numerals (I, II, etc.), the modern trend is away from this usage. Obviously, the numbering must be consistent. If the report is exceptionally long or sections of it may be circulated to different executives or departments, your illustrations, tables, and charts may carry a double number, as 4.1, 4.2, etc. The first number indicates the chapter or section of the report; the second number indicates the order within the chapter or section, always beginning with 1.

Summary
Your entire report should be condensed into a summary. Sometimes called the epitome, abstract, brief, or synopsis, the summary

saves your reader time and gives an insight into the findings and conclusions of the report. The summary can be used to make quick decisions. Confidence in you as a writer and researcher will allow your reader to examine the summary, make a decision, and perhaps delay reading the entire report until a more convenient time.

Even for the reader who goes on through the whole report, the synopsis gives a bird's-eye view which helps in reading the rest more easily and more intelligently because already knowing the final results makes clearer how each fact or explanation fits.[1]

[1]J. H. Menning, C. W. Wilkinson, and Peter B. Clarke, *Communicating* *Through Letters and Reports,* 6th ed. (Homewood, Ill.: Irwin, 1976), p. 500.

Summary

Gingerton, Georgia's ample labor force, availability of free
land, raw materials, and tax concessions provide the best location
for a new plant site. Possible sites were narrowed to Beauregard,
Marksville, and Gingerton. Factors considered in making the
decision were the availability of the following: raw materials,
labor, land and tax concessions, and transportation.

Beauregard has a thriving textile mill and is ideally located
for the market. The likelihood of high labor costs, however,
reduces the desirability for a plant site. Another factor that is
a disadvantage is the high cost of land in the area.

Marksville ranks lowest in all factors considered except for
the availability of free land. Property taxes are unusually high.
Obtaining raw materials and labor would be costly.

The cotton industry in Gingerton is an outstanding factor in
Gingerton's favor. Free land and no taxes for five years are added
enticements for locating here. As labor and transportation present
no problems, Gingerton should provide a profitable and productive
center.

vi

Figure 10—7
Illustration of the summary for a
report.

The summary is also often sent to interested people who would not
need to read the entire report but could gain needed information
from reading the condensed portion.

Although the summary should contain parts of all sections of the
report, major emphasis should be placed on the conclusions and
recommendations. Highlight your important findings. The factual
data that lead to the conclusions should be stated in the summary.
The "how" and "why" are not as important in this section as the
"what."

The summary can be single-spaced with a double space between
each paragraph. Keep the condensation to one page, if possible.
Although either inductive or deductive order is acceptable, most

writers use deductive order as the reader is interested in the conclusions. If a positive reaction is not expected, however, inductive order would better prepare the reader for the results. Figure 10–7 illustrates the summary of a report.

The Body of the Report

Correct grammar and punctuation are essential for all sections of your report. Check your beginning carefully to avoid any errors that might raise communication barriers. Although technical words are sometimes necessary, their overuse may not be met with total acceptance even though each one is defined. Whenever possible, use words familiar to the reader for easier communication.

Three major sections comprise the body of the report: the introduction, the findings, and the conclusions. If recommendations have been requested, include them in the conclusion section.

Introduction

The first few paragraphs of a report often determine acceptance or rejection. Therefore, catch the reader's attention quickly. The purpose of the report should be explained as well as any background material that would be helpful in leading your reader to the heart of your report, the findings. Clearly define your problem if it differs from the purpose.

Catch the reader's attention.

Your methodology, how you conducted your research, should be clearly and completely explained. Indicate any delimitations and/or limitations in this section. You may define any technical words that might be unfamiliar in the introduction, or you may wait until the words are actually used in the report.

Findings

Your findings represent the time and effort spent on your research. To neglect proper preparation of this section ignores the reason why you were given the assignment. Present your findings clearly, concisely, yet completely to retain confidence in your research. Your reports are one basis for evaluating you as an effective employee.

Your opinions should not be expressed in the findings section. All data should be factual and objective. If an issue has more than one side, show all sides. Sometimes, opinions of others will be your only sources of data. If so, be sure to include the sources of the opinions cited in your findings and your reasons for using these sources.

TABLE 2. SOURCES OF RAW MATERIALS - BENNETT

Sources	Types of Raw Materials		
	Woven Cotton	Assembly Threads	Garment Attachments
National suppliers	5%	35%	70%
Statewide suppliers	76%	42%	28%
Local suppliers	19%	23%	2%

Figure 10—8
Illustration of a table.

Graphics help to explain.

If illustrations (drawings or photographs), tables, or charts will help the reader understand your ideas clearly, by all means use these aids. Discuss the information contained in each illustration, table, or chart in the text. A table or graphic aid should appear as soon after the discussion starts as possible. Small illustrations, tables, or charts may be placed in the body of the report. A separate page is necessary only if the size requires a full page.

Comparisons can often be made more easily by presenting your findings in tabular form, rather than in a long textual discussion. Figure 10–8 shows research information presented as a table. The word *table* and the caption are generally typed in all capital letters. A period may follow the table number, or at least two spaces should separate the number and the caption if they are on the same line. A table contains at least two columns (unless it is a special form, as many of the tables in this book are). Each column is labeled to identify the information included. A line is generally placed above

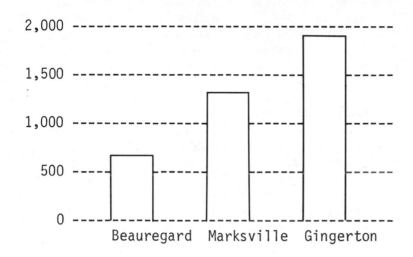

Figure 1. Labor Force Projections for 1980.

and below the column heads and at the end of the table to set off this information.

Relationships among quantities are usually understood better when shown in graphic form. The material may be presented in any one of several ways. Figure 10–9 shows a bar chart comparing the projected labor force in three towns of the report example. The height of the bar conforms to the amount to be shown. Line charts are often used to show changes over a period of time, often with two lines on the same chart. If more than one line is used, differentiate between the lines in some way (line width, dotted line, etc.). Pie charts can illustrate differences in percentages. Figure 10–10

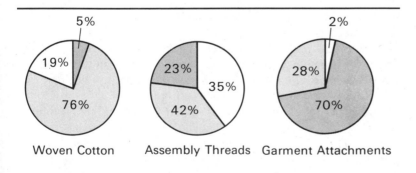

Woven Cotton   Assembly Threads   Garment Attachments

illustrates in pie-chart form the material presented in the table shown in Figure 10–8. The word *figure* and the important words in the caption are generally capitalized. As with tables, a period or at least two spaces should separate the figure number from the caption. The number and caption are generally placed below the figure.

Conclusions and Recommendations

Your conclusions, of course, will be based on your findings. Each conclusion should be backed by factual data that you have presented in the findings section. Enumerating your conclusions and/or recommendations is effective in making each stand out for the reader. Your recommendations reflect your personal opinion but should flow naturally from your findings and your conclusions.

Use factual data as the bases for conclusions and recommendations.

Appended Parts of the Report

Although many reports do not require appended parts, some do. If you have cited any information from other sources, you should include a bibliography. Your working papers, supplemental graphic information, observation sheets, questionnaires, and cover letters are appropriately placed in an appendix. Definitions of special terms used may be included in a glossary. An index is an important aid only in extremely lengthy projects.

Bibliography

Reports that contain contributions of other writers require a bibliography. Although you have properly documented your sources, either by footnotes or by text citations, a bibliography lists all published material you consulted, including books, magazines, and other sources. All sources footnoted or cited must be included; all works consulted can be included. If your research involved personal interviews, the names, company positions, and addresses of those interviewed can appear in the bibliography. If your bibliography is lengthy, you may wish to separate your sources into different sections for books, magazines, government publications, and other references. The cards prepared during your research can be placed in alphabetical order for ease in typing the bibliography. The first page of a bibliography is illustrated in Figure 10–11.

The form of the bibliography is similar to the form for footnotes, but there are some differences. The author's name begins at the left margin. The second and succeeding lines are generally indented five spaces. The bibliography contains complete publishing information in three parts.

BIBLIOGRAPHY

Books

Crowningshield, Gerald R. Cost Accounting: Principles and
    Applications. Boston: Houghton Mifflin, 1962.

Keller, I. Wayne, and William L. Ferrara. Management Accounting
    for Profit Control. New York: McGraw-Hill, 1966.

Lynch, Richard M. Accounting for Management: Planning and
    Control. New York: McGraw-Hill, 1967.

Moore, Carl L., and Robert K. Jaedicke. Managerial Accounting.
    Cincinnati: South-Western, 1967.

Tucker, Spencer A. The Break-Even System: A Tool for Profit
    Planning. Englewood Cliffs, N.J.: Prentice-Hall, 1964.

Villers, Raymond. Dynamic Management in Industry. Englewood
    Cliffs, N.J.: Prentice-Hall, 1960.

Welsch, Glenn A. Budgeting Profit Planning and Control.
    Englewood Cliffs, N.J.: Prentice-Hall, 1971.

Periodicals

Battista, G. L., and G. R. Crowningshield. "Cost Behavior and
    Breakeven Analysis--A Different Approach." Management
    Accounting, October, 1966, pp. 3-15.

Bell, Albert L. "Break-Even Charts Versus Marginal Graphs."
    Management Accounting, February, 1969, pp. 32-35.

Chapin, Ned. "The Development of the Break-Even Chart: A
    Bibliographical Note." Journal of Business, April, 1955,
    pp. 148-149.

Dow, Alice S., and Orace Johnson. "The Break-Even Point Concept:
    Its Development and Expanding Applications." Management
    Accounting, February, 1969, pp. 29-31, 48.

76

Figure 10—11
Illustration of a bibliography
separated into books and periodicals. A single alphabetical
series may also be used.

1. The author's name is listed alphabetically, last name first.
When two or more authors' names are shown, reverse only the last
name of the first author. The name or names of the editor(s) of a
book are followed by a comma and *ed.* If no author's name is
shown, alphabetize by the name of the book or article or the organization publishing the reference. End with a period.

2. The title of the article or book follows. Titles of articles are
enclosed in quotation marks, ending in a period. Titles of books are
underlined. Give the complete title of a book including the subtitle.
End with a period.

3. Complete publication information follows the title. For books,
give the location of the publisher (including the state if the city is

not well known), followed by a colon. Next is the name of the publisher, which may be shortened if no confusion will result, and a comma. The date of publication is last, followed by a period. Information for a magazine article begins with the name of the magazine, underlined, followed by a comma. Next is the date of issue (month and year) or the volume and number and the year (enclosed in parentheses). The final part of the entry is the inclusive pages for the complete article, preceded by *p.* or *pp.,* and ending in a period. Page numbers are not given for books.

Further information about proper citation of other publications or additional information that may be required in the bibliography for clarity and correctness may be found in any of the various style manuals listed in Table 9–1.

Appendix

Any information that might contribute to the understanding of your report but that is not vital to your findings should be placed in the appendix. Supporting tables, charts, or graphic aids, as well as raw data from questionnaires and observation sheets, often are included in the appendix. If more than one exhibit is necessary, type each on a separate page, using arabic numbers. Figure 10–12 shows a portion of a questionnaire used in research that could be included in the appendix of the report.

Index

Few business reports require an index. In a long, detailed report, an index would help the reader locate specific pieces of information.

To index your report, determine the important concepts and identify them with key words used in the report. Put these words on 3 x 5 inch index cards. Add to the cards the page numbers on which these words appear. Give inclusive page numbers. Each time the key word is used throughout the report, the page number(s) should be included in the index. For example, if your key words are *inductive order,* and those words and a discussion of that concept appeared in your report three times, your index entry should read:

inductive order, 9, 16–17, 33

Index entries generally begin at the left margin. Subentries may be indented several spaces (often three). If a second line is required, it is indented five spaces if there are no subentries (or five spaces to the right of the indention of the lowest subentry) so the level of all entries is perfectly clear. All indentions must be the same throughout the index.

Index entries are alphabetized by the first word (or the first important word if an article or preposition precedes the first word).

THE QUESTIONNAIRE

THE ROLE OF THE COLLEGE-EDUCATED SECRETARY
IN BUSINESS FIRMS IN SELECTED CITIES
IN NORTH LOUISIANA

	Yes	No
1. Does your present secretary have a college degree?	____	____
2. If not, have you ever employed a college-educated secretary?		
3. Was your secretary's education in secretarial science?	____	____
4. Was your secretary's education in business education?	____	____
5. Were you aware of the college program studied by your secretary when she/he was employed?	____	____
6. Are you aware of this program now?	____	____
7. Do you value experience more than education for initial employment?	____	____
8. Do you consider your secretary as a part of your management team?	____	____
9. Do you encourage professionalism, such as participation in seminars and workshops and membership in professional organizations?	____	____
10. Does your secretary understand how her/his job relates to the industry as a whole?	____	____
11. Does your secretary receive any additional salary because of education?	____	____
12. Is your secretary classified as an executive secretary?	____	____
13. Is your secretary classified as an administrative assistant?	____	____
14. Does your secretary have a stenographer?	____	____

Figure 10—12
Illustration of a portion of the questionnaire used in research to be included in the report appendix.

The terminal period is generally not used in an index entry. Key words may be cross-referenced if such a reference would contribute to the understanding of your report. Cross references generally follow the last page entry:

equipment, 10, 12—15, 17, 25. *See also* dictating equipment; transcribers; typewriters

The index entry with a cross reference following generally ends in a period. The words *see also* or *see* are underlined. The cross-referenced entries are capitalized only if they are capitalized in the index; they are generally separated by a semicolon.

Summary

Your expertise is required in preparing clear, objective, and logical reports to help management make efficient decisions. Your ability to communicate effectively through report writing is basic to your career in the business world. The necessity for quick decisions by management demands that you have know-how to prepare a report that will leave no doubt about the best alternative for solving your company's problem.

A clear definition of the purpose of the report is your first step toward a finished report that communicates necessary data for decision-making. Your work will reflect your concern for your company. A well-planned, well-organized, carefully documented report is your goal. By following the steps outlined in the chapter, you will reach that goal!

Questions for Discussion

1. What are three reasons for written reports?

2. Why is it important to know the purpose of a report?

3. What are the advantages and disadvantages of writing in a personal style and an impersonal style?

4. Explain the difference between inductive and deductive order. Give an example of when you would use inductive order and when you would use deductive order.

5. Report writing includes a statement of purpose and a statement of the problem. These statements provide important bits of information to both the writer and the reader. Define a statement of purpose and a statement of the problem and explain the differences between them.

6. Why should report writers use a personal writing style when writing for subordinates and equals?

7. Assume that you are employed by a new, dynamic advertising firm whose president sees himself as ''one of the boys.'' What style of report presentation would you employ for a report to him? Explain why you would use this style.

8. What is the difference between a title fly and a title page? When would both be included in a report?

9. Distinguish between the delimitations and the limitations of a report.

10. Why should an outline be prepared for all but the very shortest of reports?

11. In *The Wizard of Oz,* the good witch of the North told Dorothy to ''follow the yellow brick road.'' That was the beginning of Dorothy's trip to see the wizard. In report-writing situations should you always start at the beginning? Should you always ''follow the yellow brick road'' in the report-writing process? Why or why not?

12. Why is an accurate report title important?

Exercises

1. Write two paragraphs, one using inductive order and the other using deductive order.

2. Prepare a title for one of the following report situations that has been assigned to you. Be careful to use concise language and complete thoughts.

a. Examine the feasibility of franchising a health spa in your company's building.

b. Study the cost of establishing a mail and duplication room on each floor of your company's fifty-story office building.

3. Develop a report outline and statement of the problem for the following assignment: Your company is considering the purchase of automobiles for the use of its top executives. You are to review the costs of such a program in terms of purchasing price, insurance costs, and operating expenses. You are to consider only automobile dealers in your city.

4. Write a letter of transmittal for the report assignment in exercise 3.

5. From one of the following situations, develop a statement of the problem, a report title, and a tentative report outline.

a. An investigation by the chamber of commerce of a number of shoplifting incidents in your city's largest shopping mall.

b. A feasibility study for establishing group-insurance coverage for your company's employees.

c. A study of the effects of pollution-control devices on your company's profits.

Part Five   Your Role in Employment

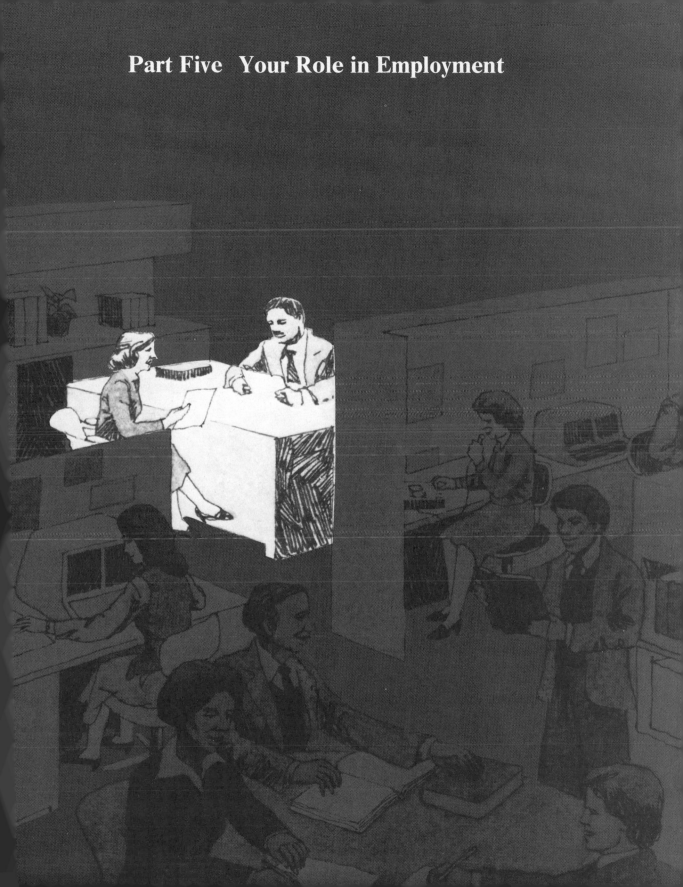

Chapter 11 Research for Employment

"There are two kinds of men in the world: Those who sail and those who drift; those who choose the ports to which they go and skillfully and boldly shape their course across the seas with the wind or against it, and those who let winds and tides carry them where they will. The men who sail in due course arrive; those who drift, often cover greater distances and face far greater perils, but they never make port. The men who sail know where they want to go and what they want to do." — Bishop Charles Henry Fowler

By sharpening your skills of perception, including observation, reading, listening, and feedback, you become a more effective communicator. Then, through your skills of organization and interpretation, including synthesis and analysis, you are able to use the deductive and inductive processes of logic to avoid many of the fallacies of ineffective communication. Finally, you use your functions of perception, organization, and interpretation to apply your abilities to effective correspondence.

Possibly the most important and personally rewarding demonstration of your communication power is your use of words to get *the job* you want. You are not interested merely in obtaining *a job,* you want *the job* for which you have been preparing. First, you must analyze yourself, the occupation, and specific jobs in relation to your goals in life. You need an interest in and an aptitude for your career choice. Your habits, character, willingness to work, ability to get along with others, health, and personality traits are tremendously important to your success—no matter what occupation you select.

You are preparing for *the job* you want—not just *a job.*

Making an appropriate vocational choice actually involves two concurrent processes: a study of your interests, aptitudes, mental abilities, personal traits, and other related abilities along with a study of occupational opportunities. Then, you need to match your traits and the opportunities in the vocation you choose with appropriate career direction and planning toward your goals.

However, in making occupational choices, some persons fail to follow these processes and often have very unrealistic job expectations. Vocational decisions are sometimes based on pressure from others, emotional appeals, and a lack of information about individual interests and aptitudes and the broad requirements of occupations as well as specific vocational goals. Therefore, you should be especially careful as you analyze yourself and evaluate vocations, specific positions, and job markets before you make your employment choice and create your *application package.*

Know Yourself in Relation to Your Occupational Goals

No one can tell you what job you need to make you a happy person in the world of work. Before you start looking for a position, you first need to ask yourself some questions.

1. What type of job will make me most happy and useful?
2. Where would I like to live or locate?
3. What do I do best?
4. What are the personal, professional, educational, and social requirements for the life-style I choose?

When you know the answers to these questions, you are ready to analyze your interests, aptitudes, and mental abilities so you may make an intelligent choice of a position in which you will be productive and find personal satisfaction.

Your Interests

Tests are available that will help you distinguish your real interests and reveal your preferences for certain types of tasks and work environments. However, the results of these tests are valid only if you measure your own interests further by considering the way you feel about yourself and by relating the test results to your occupational preferences. Two well-known tests to measure interest are the Strong-Campbell Interest Inventory and the Kuder Occupational Interest Survey. The Strong-Campbell test matches your responses to those given by happily employed persons in the various occupational categories. The Kuder Survey is designed for use by college students to assist you in making decisions about potential occupational choices.

Your Aptitudes

Similarly, analyze your aptitudes through tests that include verbal reasoning, numerical ability, abstract reasoning, spatial relations, clerical speed and accuracy, mechanical reasoning, and artistic and musical ability. The U.S. Employment Office uses the General Aptitude Test Battery. You may take this or a similar aptitude test. Again, a measurement of your aptitudes through testing only provides guidelines to help you relate your aptitudes to the occupation that you desire. For example, after taking numerous tests, if you are extremely deficient in numerical ability, you will probably not choose to become a statistician or an accountant. Remember, however, these examinations merely measure your aptitudes; you must relate them to the occupations you choose.

Your Mental Abilities

Intelligence tests (IQ) are usually used to measure general mental ability. Your mental ability may be directly related to your choice of vocation. A short-form IQ test often used is the Otis Quick Score of Mental Ability (published by Hartcourt, Brace, and World, Inc.). However, no one or even two tests can predict your mental ability or achievement in work. Attitude, aptitude, and self-determination all enter into the picture of what you can do.

You may have mental characteristics other than your intelligence quotient, such as memory, imagination, unusual ability to concentrate, creative ability, accuracy, strong reasoning facilities, natural ability for problem solving, analytical ability, observation powers, and visualization. These mental characteristics combined with your intelligence quotient, skills, personality traits, and interests may strongly influence your choice of vocation. However, if your IQ is average, you probably will choose to work toward obtaining a subordinate position such as the manager of a local branch office rather than to become a top business executive.

Your Other Personal Attributes

Personality tests, such as the Edwards Personal Profile or the California Test of Personality, are available to help you find yourself in relation to your career goals. However, a checklist of your own likes and dislikes may be equally effective. For example, if you enjoy working alone, you would probably prefer some other job than that of a receptionist or a sales person. Furthermore, if you dislike being away from home, you would choose a position as an inside sales person rather than one requiring a considerable amount of traveling.

Understand the Importance of Occupational Goals

You should know yourself as best you can in order to achieve your occupational goals. You will be happier if you remember that people differ in their abilities, and occupations differ in the abilities required for acceptable performance. Therefore, choose your occupation by considering your strengths and weaknesses as well as your limitations. Be especially careful, however, to avoid narrow job choices. When you have finished your education, you should be able to fill a variety of positions in your occupational field.

Your success is determined by your ability, your aptitudes, your intelligence, and your personal attributes. But luck, knowing the right person or being at the right place at the right time, may help you as you enter the world of work.

Your occupational choice influences every phase of your life. For example, your occupation predetermines many of the following:

Your occupational choice can influence every phase of your life.

1. Occupational choice determines where you and your family will live.

2. Occupational choice determines your chances for marriage and your marital status.

3. Occupational choice determines your economic status.

4. Occupational choice determines the cultural status of your family.

5. Occupational choice determines how a democratic society will utilize its manpower, especially you.

6. Occupational choice helps to determine the development and economic growth of your nation.

7. Occupational choice helps to determine the productivity of your nation in times of economic crisis, stress, or war.

8. Occupational choice helps to determine your development as a good citizen.

Use Research to Prepare for Your Employment Application

Because many thousands of different occupations are available to you, you should study as many of them as possible before making a choice. As Elbert Hubbard said: "The truth is that in human service, there is no low or high degree; the person who scrubs is as worthy of respect as the person who preaches."

Of course, as a trained and educated person, you will want to be able to choose the entry-level job that offers you the most opportunities and begins at your highest level. However, be careful that you do not narrow your choice by a lack of research leading to a lack of understanding about the world of work.

Importance of Research

Research allows wide and wise educational and occupational planning that can help to ensure your personal success, happiness, and satisfaction. If you are happy in your work, you will probably be a better citizen and a more productive member of society with a higher standard of living. Research will also help you avoid poor occupational decisions that could bring you personal failure, unhappiness, and dissatisfaction.

Occupations are usually grouped according to one of two major classification systems, *The Dictionary of Occupational Titles* or the *U.S. Census Classification System.* By studying the broad fields in each system, you can learn something about a great many occupations. Then, you can concentrate on those that interest you, narrowing your choice within those families of jobs on the levels that fit your education, abilities, personality, interests, and chances for obtaining employment.

Although the U.S. Census classification was developed first and based on an agrarian society, these two occupational classifications are similar. Both systems have many subdivisions that should be studied at length before you narrow your job choices. Table 11–1 compares the major classes of occupations under these two systems.

Why should you study each occupation in one of the classification systems? By doing so, you can get an overall picture of the work done by the occupational group, the overall requirements, and the advantages and disadvantages. Furthermore, through a thorough study of several occupations in each classification group, you will be able to investigate in the shortest time available many ways of making a living. You can see how your education and training can give you additional choices, many of which you may not have considered. Your outlook will be broadened in your selection of occupations, and you will not be hampered by lack of knowledge of the various career opportunities that do exist for you.

Also, you need to research the changing world of work because many jobs exist today that were not available three or four years ago. Some recent changes include:
1. increased industrial mechanization and automation

Wise occupational planning can aid the nation's manpower and development.

The *Dictionary of Occupational Titles* and the *U.S. Census Report* are helpful in your employment analysis.

Table 11–1

Comparison of the Two Major Occupational Classification Systems

Dictionary of Occupational Titles	U.S. Census Classification System
1. Professional and managerial	1. Professional, technical, and kindred workers
2. Clerical and sales	2. Farmers and farm managers
3. Service	3. Managers, officials, and proprietors
4. Agriculture	4. Clerical and kindred workers
5. Skilled	5. Sales workers
6. Semi-skilled	6. Craftsmen, foremen, and kindred workers
7. Unskilled	7. Operative and kindred workers
	8. Private household workers
	9. Service workers, except private household
	10. Farm laborers and foremen
	11. Laborers, except farm and mine

2. increased job specialization
3. increased power of union organization
4. increased government regulations
5. changed Social Security and welfare laws
6. a shorter work week
7. an increased number of women in industry and of jobs available to women
8. increased employment opportunities
9. an increased number of jobs never before available in the world of work.

Furthermore, recent trends show occupational shortages in many areas, increased educational requirements, and a need for occupational mobility. All of these will influence you as you choose your job career. Possible changes in the future include work in environmental protection and other areas that will come into existence during your working years. You may be faced with increased specialization. Certainly, improved methods of production and increased automation will affect you.

Therefore, research before you make an employment application is more than a necessity as you enter the world of work. You will also need to use the techniques of research that give you the most information in the shortest period of time as you evaluate yourself, your occupation, your position, and the job market.

Occupational research includes personal, vocational, position, and market evaluations.

Techniques of Research

How can you use research in the employment-application process? Research techniques include *listing* your skills in relation to occupational choices. Assessing your personality, including how you look, how you feel, what you say, and how you act, is also important. You can even make a numerical evaluation of your plus and minus personality assets in relation to your career choice.

Similarly, evaluating your health, your work habits, and your personal habits can be a vital part of your research. For example, if you have visual problems, you will probably not want to be an accountant who is subject to constant eye strain. You must relate your health to your occupation. Also, your physical characteristics are important as you assess yourself. Your size, strength, dexterity, and appearance are all important aspects to consider in choosing your occupational goals. Your hobbies or leisure-time activities, such as your methods of self-expression, your use of safety valves, and appreciation of various activities, will help you as you choose your job.

Research and list your personal attributes. Study yourself, analyze yourself; formulate the purpose of your job application, plan methods of fulfilling that purpose; collect, analyze, synthesize, and truly interpret the information you have. Then, record, report, and use your findings.

Evaluate Your Findings

You are now ready for your personal evaluation, occupational evaluation, position evaluation, and market evaluation as you study the world of work to determine the job for you.

Personal Evaluation

You should begin now to assess your personal qualifications, your characteristics, your attitudes, your abilities, your personality, and your skills as they relate to your job decision. You are the only person who understands "you." And, strangely enough, even you may not see yourself as others see you!

Unless you know and understand yourself, however, you will have difficulty in finding out how other people see you and in using your aptitudes, interests, and intelligence to study the careers in which you might be most successful. Again, any personal appraisal should include completing a vocational-interest test, an IQ test, an aptitude test, and a personality assessment or an informal self-analysis. These tests, combined with your favorite activities and extracurricular activities and your education and experience, will help you understand yourself as you prepare to fill out an application blank or write an application letter and data sheet, and schedule your interview.

Apply the checklist in Table 11–2 to your self-evaluation. Since all of these traits help determine the type of work that fits you best, this checklist along with all of the other tools for self-analysis will

Table 11–2
A Self-Evaluation Checklist

1. Evaluate your education.

2. Consider your past work experience.

3. Analyze extracurricular or academic activities. Do these still interest you? Why?

4. Review projects, awards, hobbies, and other things that have used your basic skills and abilities in the last three to five years.

5. List the activities that give you the most satisfaction.

6. List the activities in which you excel.

7. List your favorite activities in order of preference and compare them. What specific skills did each use (such as managing money, working with people, organizing, or taking responsibility)? Do you seem to prefer one type of environment over another?

8. Evaluate and add things in terms of your past history and current feelings. Do you enjoy working with concrete, physical things or abstract ideas such as time and space? Do you like to have your assignments detailed for you, or do you prefer to work independently? Are you an indoors or outdoors person? Do you work well under deadline pressure? Are you most comfortable spending time in a large group, with just a few people, or by yourself? Do you like to be in charge?

9. Have others review your checklist.

10. Make a checklist to see if you can find the "real you" in relation to options in the job market.

help develop a rough sketch of the real you. Then you will be much more capable of locating your special options in the job market.

After you have made a self-evaluation, you will want to study the numerous occupations that are available to you. If you know what you want out of life after your personal evaluation, you will find it easier to plan for a career that will make you happy. As Jonathan Swift said: "It is an uncontroverted truth that no man ever made an ill figure who understood his own talents nor a good one who mistook them."

Therefore, after your personal evaluation, you should make an intensive study of two or three broad occupational groups before making a decision based on your specific evaluation of the job you have chosen.

Occupational Evaluation

Planning a career is a special process that should begin before or, at the latest, while you are in college. You need to prepare for broad occupational choices and opportunities in order to narrow your goals as you find yourself in the job market.

Prepare yourself for broad career goals.

However, in studying careers, you must compare your career expectations with job realities. For example, for several years the government has forecast "some good news and some bad news" for college graduates. The good news is that 98 percent of all graduates

In planning your career, keep your expectations realistic. Consider your future in making your choice.

who want jobs are able to find them. The bad news is that one out of every four graduates does not get the kind of job desired. However, stated positively, three of four graduates do find the job they want.

Although the value of a college education has been questioned in the past few years, the monetary rewards are still encouraging. The average university graduate can expect lifetime earnings 35 to 40 percent greater than the average earnings of a high-school graduate. Fortunately, a degree in a business-related field can be a passport to success in the job market. As a college graduate, you can expect higher-than-average starting salaries, and usually you can find *the job* instead of *a job*.

Remember, however, your vocation should be chosen with care because the law of supply and demand will always prevail. A strong growth rate in any field—even business—may be quickly counteracted by a flood of qualified graduates. Therefore, you should prepare to do several things you enjoy doing and that you are capable of doing well.

The difference between being able and not being able to get a job after graduation, in 99 percent of the cases, usually involves planning. Some students realize they need a job and haphazardly begin to look for work. Choosing a line of work demands a great deal of energy—far more than that in choosing a musical sound system or a new automobile.

Moving toward the right career is a vital part of your education—a process to begin long before you leave the campus. This preparation involves not only finding out as much as possible about yourself but also studying occupations that meet your needs and interests in the job markets available. For example, a career in office administration requires different preparation, abilities, and interests from a career in marketing. Similarly, a career in accounting requires different knowledge, skills, and interests from a career in technical writing. Therefore, if you know yourself and the demands for employment in the various careers, you will be better prepared for the world of work and more likely to find job satisfaction.

The main reason for planning and making your vocational appraisal is not only to give you a competitive edge over all the other job-seekers but also to help you find the right position—an occupation that uses your skills and satisfies your goals most effectively. "The happiest and most successful person," Mark Twain once said, "works all year long at what he would otherwise choose to do in a summer vacation."

As a matter of fact, the average American adult spends approximately 10,000 days on the job. These 10,000 working days could end up as forty years of hard labor if you are unhappy in your work. You need to be career conscious. A vocational appraisal will help you choose whether you should take a position involving the solitude of research or one involving the public-relations skills of the chairman of the board.

As with a personal appraisal, an occupational appraisal is an effort to fit yourself into your world of work. You should examine the following factors carefully in preparing your occupational evaluation:

Career appraisals are vital in fitting yourself into the world of work.

1. The general requirements of the occupation
2. The educational requirements necessary for success
3. The specialized training required
4. The personality characteristics considered essential
5. The personal attributes considered desirable
6. The experience required for entry positions
7. The relationship between the career and your education, experience, interests, attributes, etc.

By analyzing the occupation itself as well as talking with others in the career field, you may find the demands, limitations, satisfactions, and opportunities for advancement this field offers. As you look at a career in the light of your preferences, you must be as truthful in your occupational evaluation as in your personal evaluation.

Your occupational evaluation should be a private record. However, if you make an effort to write, study, and prepare an evaluation, you will be better able to evaluate the occupation to plan for a career that will bring you maximum productivity, fulfillment, and self-realization.

Position Evaluation

After you have studied yourself and several occupations, and chosen a broad career area in which you are interested and seem to fit, then you make a specific job or position analysis. Again, you follow basic guides in preparing this special analysis so you may remain flexible in the job market as positions change and as you change your opinions concerning the job you want.

Basically, a position analysis is more specific than a general occupational analysis. You need to consider definite details and facts rather than generalities; you study concretely what the position requires and what you do well.

In your special position and occupational analysis, you might

Table 11—3
An Outline for Studying an
Occupation

I. The Occupation or Position
  A. Name or title of the occupation or position
  B. Description of the position
  C. Physical demands or requirements
  D. Methods of entry
  E. Relation to other jobs
     1. Entry jobs leading to this particular position
     2. Jobs to which you may be promoted from this position
     3. Chances for your promotion
     4. Related occupations to and from which you may shift with reasonable ease
  F. Employment opportunities—supply of and demand for workers such as you
     1. Factors that might affect your future prospects for employment
     2. Present local employment outlook and opportunities
     3. Present regional and national outlook and opportunities
  G. Level of difficulty—the level of task complexity characterizing the position and the necessary requirements to perform the various tasks. The level of difficulty may be determined by:
     1. Responsibility
     2. Knowledge
     3. Resourcefulness
     4. Mental alertness
     5. Thinking and decision-making
     6. Dexterity
     7. Accuracy
     8. Other factors essential to the position
  H. Earnings, fringe benefits, hours, and working conditions
     1. Average hourly earnings
     2. Average weekly earnings
     3. Average monthly earnings
     4. Average number of hours worked per day
     5. Average number of hours worked per week
     6. Average number of weeks worked per year
     7. Vacations and leave provisions
     8. Educational and in-service training possibilities
     9. Working environment—nature of the surroundings
     10. Work or supervision
     11. Health and accident hazards
     12. Seasonal effects on the position

13. Economic effects of depressions and prosperity
14. Security provisions
15. Union and/or professional representation for you as the employee

II. You as the Worker
  A. Personal qualifications
    1. Age preferences
    2. Men or women preferred
    3. Physical requirements
    4. Special ability requirements
    5. Desirable occupational-interest pattern
  B. Educational and training requirements
    1. Minimum level of education
    2. School courses especially important
    3. Special training desirable or required
    4. On-the-job training
    5. Relationship of advanced education and training to promotion
  C. Other requirements
    1. Specialized tools or equipment furnished by employer or worker
    2. Memberships in unions, professional organizations, or associations required or elected by you, the employee
    3. Licensing or legal requirements
    4. Examinations or special tests required, such as the CPA or CPS
  D. Reactions of workers presently employed in this occupation. In other words, you should try to talk with several persons now working in this field to get information about what they like most and dislike most about the position. If you can make a job-inspection trip you will be most fortunate.

---

prepare a study guide to give you information about the particular requirements, benefits, levels of difficulty, and other factors regarding your relationship to the occupation or the special position you are considering or applying for. Table 11–3 outlines the information you need for your occupational analysis.

    After you collect the information from this guide, you can summarize the advantages and disadvantages of the occupation or position in relation to your aptitudes, interests, and abilities to meet the requirements of the position. Then, you should also make a market evaluation using the research material gathered from your personal, occupational, and position evaluations.

An occupational study guide will help you prepare for a specific position.

Market Evaluation

When you begin your market evaluation in your job campaign, you should be professional. The most successful job candidates are those who know that positions will not fall in their laps. You are a sales representative who can sell yourself to the prospective employer. You have studied yourself, analyzed your occupational goals, and evaluated desirable positions. You have considered the job you want in the light of your experience, education, attitudes, interests, and mental abilities. You finally fit all these together by making a market evaluation using resource tools, analyzing the positions available, and determining the sources of job leads that will be most helpful to you.

Resource Tools For Market Evaluation

Many excellent publications can help you find more information about careers and employment possibilities. Most of these publications are available through your placement office or the college library. Table 11–4 describes a few publications that may help you.

Make comparisons by checking the past history of each business, its financial balance sheet, the number of divisions or companies it holds and the employees in each one, and the locations of branches and subsidiaries. Try to evaluate its future growth patterns, profits, and sales. Such business magazines as *Forbes, Barron's, Fortune,* and *Business Week* are usually available to you at your library. They often discuss the outlook for various industries, or they may publish an article about a company in which you are interested. When you research a company, you can write more effective letters of inquiry, find out which executive should get your résumé, and be more knowledgeable should you obtain an interview.

Always contact the career planning or placement office on your campus. Relatively few students check on jobs available at college placement centers. Yet, these centers maintain sources of information for choosing your career and supply help in getting the position you want. Many of the necessary research tools are available from these centers.

Sources of Job Leads

Even after researching yourself and the career you have chosen and analyzing the position you want, you will find that approximately 50 percent of job hunters find their employment through people they know. Yet, you may consider *pull* or *contacts* as dirty words.

You often hear that a person got a job because of contacts or pull, disparaging remarks like "John got that job because of his father."

Table 11—4
Publications Providing Career
Information

1. *Dictionary of Occupational Titles*—A guide (previously discussed) published by the U.S. Department of Labor listing the thousands of general jobs available that can give you a broad spectrum from which to choose.

2. *United States Census Report*—A source of job listings and groupings (previously discussed) that will give you an insight into various occupations in your chosen field of work.

3. *Occupational Outlook Handbook*—Brief descriptions of occupations grouped into clusters explaining job duties, educational requirements, employment outlook, and earnings for approximately 300 occupations in thirty-five industries. This handbook is available at most libraries or can be obtained for a minimum fee from the Superintendent of Documents, U.S. Government Printing Office, Washington, DC 20402.

4. *The Occupational Outlook for College Graduates*—A booklet that contains occupational listings about more than 100 jobs for which an education beyond high school is necessary or helpful. This booklet is available at most libraries or it can be obtained from the U.S. Government Printing Office for a minimum fee.

5. *College Placement Annual*—An occupational directory on career information from approximately 1,000 employers. Your college placement office usually has this directory; otherwise, you can obtain it for a small fee from the College Placement Council, Inc., P. O. Box 2263, Bethlehem, PA 18001.

6. *Occupations in Demand at Job Service Offices*—A monthly bulletin highlighting occupations for which large numbers of job openings are listed with the public employment services. A special edition is compiled in the fall for students and recent graduates. You can receive these bulletins by writing the Employment and Training Administration, U.S. Department of Labor, Washington, DC 20213.

7. *The Encyclopedia of Associations*—A listing of professional organizations and trade journals that are useful sources of information about prospective careers and job opportunities. Most professional groups offer information on jobs, training, and scholarships.

8. U.S. Civil Service Commission pamphlets—These pamphlets give information on Civil Service tests scheduled to be given in the area. Contact any placement office that gives Civil Service Tests.

9. *Career*—The annual guide to business opportunities available at your college placement office or library.

10. *The Wall Street Journal*—A weekday newspaper that carries help-wanted ads and discusses a wide variety of business subjects including the worldwide outlook for most industries.

However, using your contacts or pull is not cheating. To misuse a contact when you are unqualified is unfair. However, when you use your common sense and empathy as you put yourself into the employer's shoes, you realize that to hire someone who is recommended is easier and less risky than to take a chance on someone unknown.

Government studies show that only one out of five jobs is likely to be advertised or listed with an employment agency. Often, company insiders are your best bet for keeping informed of job possibilities. How can you make contacts or obtain pull? Try some of the strategies listed in Table 11–5.

You will notice that newspaper advertisements are placed last. Often many desirable jobs are filled from a waiting list and, therefore, are not advertised. However, if you want to answer a newspaper advertisement, you must be prompt. Your letter should be written carefully and be well planned to arrive as early as possible.

All of these sources of job leads are helpful. However, if you are interested in more information about your prospective employment possibilities, you should prepare a prospect list that you can study in order to learn more about the available positions and also so you can make an analysis of the positions available.

Analysis of Desirable Positions Available
After you have used your research tools and sources of job leads, you may want to research the market and seek out prospective employers who may need your abilities and for whom you would like to work. Probably, you will find several positions that interest you. Your responsibility, therefore, will be to show that you have the attributes necessary to fill these positions.

To evaluate and analyze the positions available, you should consider the following points:

1. You should determine the history, character, products, and services of the company to which you are applying.

2. You should understand, as much as possible, the company's needs so you can relate them to your qualifications.

3. You should analyze the company's standing within its industry and community.

4. You should determine the nature of the company's products and how they are accepted in the market.

5. You should know the company's hiring, firing, and promotion policies.

6. You should determine the employee-turnover rates as well as why people leave.

Table 11—5
Making Contacts for Job
Opportunities

1. Become active in school activities.
2. Become active in alumni associations after you graduate. These people are established in the working world and can give you an inside track for job openings.
3. Join a local civic group especially if you would like to remain in the community where your school is located. Local contacts can provide good references and even a starting point in your field.
4. Join the student division of the professional association in your field. When you graduate, join and become active in such an association. You may find regular members who can provide the contact that will lead to career opportunities.
5. Listen carefully when job opportunities are discussed in general conversation. Knowledge of many positions becomes available to you if you establish a wide circle of acquaintances who know your special abilities and interests.
6. Keep checking back to see if a job has become available. Remember that sometimes the hardest part of obtaining success in a position is getting the right job.

Some additional sources of job leads are:
a. Tips about vacancies from friends and relatives.
b. Contacts of parents or relatives.
c. Contacts with former employees.
d. Tips about employment opportunities from teachers.
e. Personal applications for jobs.
f. Written applications for jobs.
g. School or college placement offices.
h. State employment agencies.
i. Private employment agencies.
j. Factory or office representatives looking for graduates.
k. Nonprofit employment agencies.
l. Unions or professional associations.
m. Industrial directories that give names of firms hiring workers.
n. Walk-in interviews.
o. Employment advertisements in newspapers.

7. You must determine the specific needs of the position and your future possibilities in that position.
8. You should try to interview other employees concerning the company. However, be sure you are selective in choosing the people to whom you talk so you may have valid and reliable answers.

Preparation of a Prospect List

After this research, you should actually prepare a prospect list. You do not want to send application letters indiscriminately to companies or persons in which you are not interested or to those who are not interested in you. Use your research tools and job-information resources to help you as you list the prospective employers who may need your abilities. However, again, try not to be too specific. Remember that mobility is a problem or an asset depending on the way you use it. Also, starting salary is often less important than promotional possibilities. Therefore, gather all of the information about the position before applying in order to make your application blank, application letter, data sheet, or interview most effective.

Summary

In summary, as you prepare for employment, you must first try to understand yourself so you can consider an occupation that meets your needs and is beneficial to your employers. Second, you must realize the importance of occupational goals and understand that careers do not just happen to people. Third, research is necessary in order to find the job you want—not just a job. The techniques of research will include personal evaluation, position evaluation, and market potential. After this research to prepare for an appointment about employment, you are now ready to use the verbal and written communications that will help to ensure your successful future in the profession that you choose.

Questions for Discussion

1. Explain the differences between realistic and unrealistic job expectations. Give examples applicable to your personal situation and goals. Why are unrealistic vocational choices sometimes made?

2. Discuss the concurrent processes that are involved in making your vocational choice. Include such factors as interests, aptitudes, intelligence, etc.

3. Name at least three of the factors that should be considered before you start looking for a position. Discuss several factors applicable to your choice of a position that will make you most happy, productive, and successful.

4. Name at least three tests that will help you to distinguish between various aspects of your interests, aptitudes, mental abilities, and personality traits. Explain how these tests relate to your occupational or positional goals in the world of work.

5. Why is knowing yourself important in achieving occupational goals? Explain the relationship of your personal analysis to success in your chosen position.

6. Name and discuss at least five ways through which your occupational choice will influence other phases of your life. Which are the most important? Why?

7. Discuss the importance of research in your occupational choice. What factors are involved? How can research help you to avoid too narrow job or occupational choices?

8. Name the two major occupational classification systems. List the occupations from the *Dictionary of Occupational Titles* and the United States Census. Discuss the importance of each system in analysis of the job market. Compare and contrast the two systems, including the advantages and disadvantages of each.

9. Name and discuss various changes in the world of work in the past ten years. What other changes do you envision in the future?

10. List and discuss the factors necessary in making a personal evaluation. Discuss how this personal assessment can help you choose options in the career market.

11. Discuss the importance of early planning in *finding "the" job you want.* How do preparation and career consciousness fit into your analysis?

12. Explain the advantages of making an occupational and positional evaluation. List the factors necessary in completing each one. Compare and contrast the two evaluations as they relate to your final vocational choice.

13. What factors should be considered in making a market evaluation? Discuss these aspects as they affect your entry into the job market.

14. List and discuss at least ten resource tools and sources of information that can be helpful in your employment research. Make a detailed analysis of at least five of these tools, library materials, or other sources of information showing their usefulness in relation to your vocational goals.

15. List and discuss sources of job leads. Explain the use of pull in the job market—its advantages and disadvantages.

16. Explain the advantages of analyzing desirable positions available and of making a prospect list. Describe the factors and guides you would follow.

17. Explain the advantages of keeping an up-to-date occupational-history file. How could this file be of value to you ten years from now?

Exercises

1. Prepare a self-appraisal that includes an assessment of your personal characteristics, interests, aptitudes, mental abilities, education, experience, etc. Although you should prepare this record in writing for your own evaluation, you need not submit it as a class exercise as this information could be extremely personal. Compare your assessments with the requirements for several of your occupational choices. As you prepare this appraisal, be honest with yourself in relation to your qualifications and the positions you are considering. You may want to share this appraisal with your instructor, the testing center, the placement director, or others who are interested in helping you find the job you want for which you are most qualified.

2. Make an appointment with the director of testing at the university. Ask what interest, aptitude, mental ability, personality, and other tests are available to aid you in your assessment of the feasibility of your vocational choices. Ask to complete as many of these tests as possible. Request an analysis of the results. Write and present a complete but concise report describing your experiences in the testing process and the results of your analysis. Although you need not divulge the results, you should use the interpretations in making your final career and position choices.

3. Make a list of prospective jobs available to you. List jobs available in the local community, out-of-state positions, and governmental positions that you might obtain after passing the required tests. Report your findings, listing the advantages and disadvantages of each position.

4. Write and talk to people in companies or positions that interest you. Ask for an exploratory appointment to learn more about the position, its advantages and disadvantages, what the job involves, and the method of entry into the field.

5. Visit your college placement center. Discuss your interests and qualifications for the job you want with the director. Fill out any forms that are necessary. Ask to complete a placement file and to arrange meetings with recruiters who can consider your qualifications. Follow up on these activities. Make a written report of your activities to your instructor.

6. Go to your library. Inspect and analyze the occupations listed in the *Dictionary of Occupational Titles* and the United States Census in relation to your occupational choices. See what other facilities are available to you through the library. Make a written report.

7. Study the requirements of the job you desire. Does this position require a graduate degree? If so, list the admission requirements of the best schools in your field. If you decide to work for an advanced degree, you should contact the person in charge of graduate studies or advanced programs in a nationally accredited school and begin now to prepare to meet the prerequisites you need to enter graduate school. Graduates of the schools that interest you may be of help. Your university professors can give assistance. Be sure that you need an advanced degree. Consider whether you should take an entry-level job in the field before entering graduate school. Write a short report on your research.

8. Consider the work experience you already have. Then, make an analysis to determine if you need to or can gain additional experience while in school. Remember that many business students work to gain experience while in school or during summer breaks.

9. Using the outline given in Table 11—3, prepare and present to your instructor an occupational study guide that can help you to decide on your qualifications for the position you are interested in as related to requirements.

Business Situations

1. Too Anxious for a Promotion

Your friend, George Alex, was hired as an accountant clerk with the XYZ Construction Company. George obtained the job through the university placement service. George was more than qualified for the position that he held. His salary was acceptable; his employer was excellent. After six weeks, however, George left the company. He called the placement director to report that he left because he did only routine work—not the type of work for which he had been trained at the university. George felt that he would never get ahead in this job.

The university placement director called to check with George's supervisor at the XYZ Construction Company. The supervisor stated that George was "too anxious to be the president and that he wanted to get ahead too fast." The supervisor further stated that George's chance was awaiting him if he could have shown some patience.

Analyze the problem. Take into consideration George's attitude toward getting ahead fast. Consider a beginner's attitude toward routine work as well as the length of time necessary to advance. As a manager or supervisor, how would you have handled this problem? Use the steps in decision-making to answer this question:

1. State the problem.
2. Analyze all the facts.
3. List several alternative decisions.
4. Decide on the best decision.
5. Follow through and evaluate the decision you chose.

2. Too Underemployed

Your friend Mark Schmidt majored in accounting at your university. After analyzing the job market, he decided to accept a job as a bookkeeper for a large legal firm. Mark would have preferred to work as a financial analyst, but he could find no jobs available in that field.

Mark likes his job; the physical surroundings are excellent; his salary is satisfactory. He feels that the routine bookkeeping work he is doing may not allow him to keep in touch with financial analysis, especially with current laws and developments, although he uses some of this knowledge in the legal area in which he works.

In empathizing with Mark, what would you do? Since he likes his job, his employers, and his surroundings, what can he do? Should he look for another job after a year? Should he strive for advancement within the firm? Would advanced planning have helped him to avoid this situation? Use the steps in decision-making to help Mark find a solution.

3. Flexibility in the Job Market

Your friend, Juanita Lopez, will be graduating next month with a degree in business education. After analyzing the job market carefully, she finds that no teaching jobs are available. However, she has excellent skills in shorthand, typewriting, and accounting. Furthermore, she has taken office and personnel management courses that will qualify her in time for a managerial position in an office.

Miss Lopez has been offered a job as an executive secretary for the Acme Oil Corporation. She feels that promotional opportunities exist for her in this corporation.

However, since teaching was her first choice, she has two other decisions she could make. First, she could try to secure a business-education teaching job in another town although she prefers to remain in her college town or a neighboring area. Second, she could enter the Master of Business Education program at the university with the expectation of securing a job a year from now.

Using the steps in decision-making, what would you do? List the advantages and disadvantages of your choices.

Chapter 12   Communications for Employment

"A man's success in business today turns upon his power of getting people to believe he has something they want."
— Gerald Stanley Lee

After you have finished your research of yourself and your broad career goals and made your position and market evaluations, you are ready to apply your written and oral communication skills to your *application package.* Your search for the job you desire may be difficult. However, you have an excellent chance to obtain the position of your dreams through your effective communication skills.

You are the commodity you wish to sell. Furthermore, since business is essentially people, you must be able to show that you can be part of the team. Your prospective employer is also interested in your attitude toward work and your enthusiasm for the job, the people in the company, and the organization itself. The company must make a profit from your services. You must be able to show that *what you can do* fits *what must be done.* The art of a good application package is to show how these two can work together.

The actual verbal and written application package may contain several or all of the following:
1. Letter of application
2. Data sheet
3. Application blank
4. Interview
5. Follow-up messages.

In some cases, you may need to complete all parts. Ordinarily, you will more likely submit your letter of application and your data sheet or an application blank. As a prospective employee looking for the job you want, you should be skilled in communicating in all these areas, however.

You are the commodity in your application package.

Letter of Application

Before you write your application letter, you should adopt a plan that is individual and personal as well as flexible. Actually, *your application letter is you!* No letter is more important than the application letter that you write to persuade an employer to give you an interview. This letter shows what you think of yourself and presents a picture of your attributes. Strangely enough, many applicants submit letters that are deficient in form, neatness, and content.

Prospective employers in every business like to picture you, the applicant, through the application letter before the interview. They actually want to know whether you are worth taking the time to see. In fact, your application letter presents your first image to your prospective employer. Therefore, be sure you prepare this letter so you can compete with other applicants who want the same position just as earnestly as you do.

Through a thorough research of yourself and an analysis of the job opportunities and the market, you can be competitive. In fact, to make your preparatory steps of research count, use the following summary:

The commodity is you—your skills, your abilities, your education, and your experience.

The market is your prospective employers whose locations, job opportunities, and needs you have studied.

The sales promotion is your application package.

Your application may be solicited, a response to an announcement of an opening such as a classified advertisement; or your application may be unsolicited, written in the hope that an opening may exist.

For example, you might write an unsolicited application to a large company that often has a vacancy; or you might write an unsolicited application at the suggestion of another person who may know that a definite job is open. This person may be a friend, an employment agent, or a representative of the company.

In either case, your solicited or unsolicited application is a reflection of you and is highly important in reaching your goal of obtaining an interview. Therefore, as you plan your application, you will want to be flexible. However, you should narrow your application to several specific jobs; you do not want to ask for just any job.

As a persuasive writer, you may not need to follow any specific plan in your application letter. This letter is often only your transmittal for your résumé. However, the four A's of the application letter will guide you through the main steps of your application procedure. This four-step plan is:

Your application letter is your ambassador to your prospective employer.

Your application is you.

298

1. *Attract Attention*
2. *Assure Awareness*
3. *Analyze Achievements*
4. *Anticipate Action*

These four A's are not necessarily separated into distinct parts. However, they are convenient and persuasive tools in your application package. Actually, the A's of application fit together like building blocks.

These four A's of the application letter—evident in all management areas, especially in persuasion—can give your reader a more subjective and personal view of your motives, goals, personality, and ability of expression. Attention, awareness, and achievement are all functions of your persuasive application package from which you hope to obtain action by gaining an interview.

Attract Attention

Of course, the more attractive your letter is, the higher attention value it will have. A neat, well-placed, and attractive transmittal letter shows that you really care about yourself as well as the job for which you are applying.

You should type your letter on the best quality bond paper; you should avoid detectable typewritten corrections; you should proofread your material carefully and avoid misspelled words. A picture-frame effect with an inch or more of white space at the top, bottom, left, and right will add to your letter's effectiveness. Your stationery reflects your image. Therefore, you should not use social, organizational, or letterhead paper from the firm where you are presently employed.

The main purpose of your application letter is to obtain an interview. However, you cannot obtain a conference with a prospective employer if the first impression made through your application letter is negative or detrimental.

The primary purpose of your application letter is to obtain an interview.

Your application letter or covering letter for your data sheet will probably be the first thing a prospective employer or interviewer will see from you. Therefore, the four A's are extremely important as the opening part of your persuasive application package.

If possible, you should address your letter to the person in the company responsible for screening applicants—either the personnel manager or the head of the department in which you hope to work. Specific names and job titles can be found in many company publications or directories or through college placement offices. You may simply telephone the company to get the name of the person to whom you should address your letter. Your letter must first secure favorable attention; prospective employers prefer that you know the correct names and titles.

Use a point of contact to secure attention.

In securing attention, you might want to indicate your point of contact. This is a statement telling about how you learned of the position. Suppose your college professor informed you that an opening existed in the XYZ Company. In this case, you could open your letter by saying: "Dr. Joe H. Black, chairman of the Department of Accounting, has told me that a position is available in your company. Please consider me as an applicant for this position."

Sometimes, you may use a different approach by explaining an attribute you have that others do not. Perhaps you have exceptional education or experience. If so, include this in your attention-getting paragraph. You may want to ask a question such as: "How much would it be worth to your organization, in time and money, to have a managerial assistant who has worked forty hours a week while attending college and has developed the ability to make decisions and communicate effectively with others?"

Remember, you must always apply for the position. Never leave the prospective employer up in the air as to whether or not you want to be considered an applicant. In fact, you should make a

Make a definite application for the position.

definite statement such as, "Please consider me as an applicant for the position." Then, if you have other ties that might put your prospective employer in an embarrassing situation, these will be removed by your simple statement that you are applying for the particular position.

An interesting statement may also create the attention factor you desire. For example, you might say: "The position you have vacant in your payroll department interests me because I have had similar experience for four years while I worked my way through college." Your story may strike a parallel between you and your interviewer and help to arouse the interest you desire.

The interest level that follows your attention-getting opener is vital to you as a prospective applicant. In following the four A's, you must first gain attention; then you should show interest in and awareness of the requirements of the job before you list your achievements in order to ensure favorable action—your goal of obtaining an interview to secure the job you want.

Assure Awareness

When you assure the employer's representative that you have an awareness of the requirements of the position and the organization's needs, you are more interesting to your prospective employer.

```
                 2914 North Lake Shore Drive
                 Chicago, IL 60657
                 May 11, 19--


                 Mr. Roger N. Watkins
                 Personnel Director
                 XYZ Insurance Company
                 213 South Wacker Drive
                 Chicago, IL 60606

                 Dear Mr. Watkins

                 Miss Lisa Smith, one of your employees who attended Ford High
                 School with me, told me that there will be an opening for a
                 stenographer on July 3.  Please consider me as an applicant for
                 this position.

                 I understand that you need a person with the finest secretarial
                 skills who can meet the public and answer the telephone.  I should
                 like to apply for the position as I feel my secretarial qualifica-
                 tions meet the high standards of your company.

                 I graduated magna cum laude from college.  During the fall term, I
                 plan to take the Certified Professional Secretaries review course
                 in the evening division of Chicago University.  My application for
                 admission has already been approved.

                 During the past two summers I have had experience as a clerk-typist
                 with the State Farm Insurance Company, as listed on the enclosed
                 data sheet.  The office manager, Mr. Rod L. Johnson, has given me
                 permission to use his name as one of my business references.

                 I enjoyed my work with the State Farm Insurance Company  and should
                 like to continue in the insurance field.  Please call me at 478-
                 2333 for an interview.

                 Sincerely yours

                 Susie Kaye Poole
                 (Miss) Susie Kaye Poole

                 Enclosure
```

Figure 12—1
An application letter in block style with open punctuation.

You need to assure the interviewer, the employer, and the company how they will benefit from hiring you. Choose words that will supply concrete evidence of your performance or ability. Show that you are aware of their needs and that you have the training and education necessary to fill the position.

Your data sheet should list in tabular form your educational and experience qualifications. However, state your information about your education and experience from your employer's viewpoint. Try to find what you can do relative to the needs of the position. Fit your experience and educational qualifications to the needs of the company. Sift the facts that focus on the employer's needs.

Paraphrasing John Kennedy's famous statement, remember that

After you have obtained attention, you should assure awareness of the company's needs.

10334 Airline Highway
Baton Rouge, LA 70816
April 28, 19--

Mr. John Knight, Personnel Director
Import Services Unlimited
402 Pujo Street
Lake Charles, LA 70601

Dear Mr. Knight:

As a secretary in your import division, I could take your dictation at a rapid 130 words per minute and transcribe it accurately in attractive letters and memos at 60 words per minute--whether it is in English or Spanish. In fact, because I have been thoroughly trained in grammar and letter writing, I can create your letters for you.

In secretarial courses during my four years of study at Louisiana State University, I have consistently demonstrated by ability to handle material at these speeds. I have practiced my Spanish by recording what my teachers and classmates say. I have no difficulty transcribing these notes later.

I learned a good deal about your markets and your clientele while doing research for a report I submitted this semester in marketing, "Some Recent Developments in Latin-American Markets." During my research I became familiar with such publications as European Exports, Imports, and The American Yearbook.

I am neat and conservative in appearance. On the telephone or in person, I could greet your clients pleasantly and put them at ease. Courses in management, law, and decision-making have prepared me for the time when I may become an administrator or supervisor.

Please call me at 504/436-8134 and tell me a time when I may come to your office and show you how well my preparation will fit into your firm.

Sincerely yours,

Jackie Jones

Jackie Jones

Figure 12–2
An application letter in modified block style with mixed punctuation.

your attitude should be: "Ask not what the company can do for you; instead, ask what you can do for the company."

Convince the persons involved of your interest, awareness, education, experience, and abilities, thereby creating a strong desire for your services.

Analyze Achievements

Give additional qualifications to increase interest and create desire.

You may intensify interest in many ways. For example, you may present additional personal qualifications and human-interest images that portray you as more valuable than other applicants.

```
130 Herby Drive
Athens, GA 30602
March 12, 19--


Personnel Director
Shell Oil Company
1509 Springhill Avenue
Mobile, AL 36604

APPLICATION FOR POSITION IN PUBLIC RELATIONS

Most businessmen agree that success in business is determined to a
large extent by what the public thinks of the organization and that
business is judged by the quality of its products, advertisements,
and employees.  With my experience and education, I can be an asset
in developing public relations for your organization.

I have gotten considerable public relations experience while
selling insurance and radio advertisements.  Through my work I
traveled extensively through the South and met and communicated
with all kinds of people.  Because I am well aware of what a direct
bearing public relations has on success and profit, I am very
active in business clubs and civic organizations.

While earning my degree in marketing at Jacksonville University, I
also studied management, consumer behavior, and psychology.  I took
extensive courses in communications also.  The enclosed resumé
gives further details of my education, experience, and personality.

Please call me at 404/567-3418, or write me and let me know when I
may come to discuss with you, personally, just what I can bring to
Shell Oil Company in the public relations field.
```

Calvin Thomas
CALVIN THOMAS

dm

Enclosure

Figure 12—3
An application letter in AMS
simplified style (an unusual
style for an application letter).

You may want to include your extracurricular activities that show your leadership and managerial ability such as:

As president of Delta Sigma Pi, I was able to lead our group successfully in several fund-raising drives. This experience enabled me to help the departments in the School of Business as well as to assist several community and civic organizations. At the same time, the fraternity's financial statement at the end of my term showed an increase in our assets.

Similarly, you may analyze and state your achievements:

I gained excellent experience in office procedures while working as

```
                    5615 Arkansas Street
                    Austin, TX 78702
                    March 27, 19--


                    Mr. Bob Cook, Personnel Director
                    Red Manufacturing Company
                    1702 Congress Avenue
                    Austin, TX 78701

                    Dear Mr. Cook:

                    The placement office at Central University has told me of the
                    opening in your office for an associate degree graduate in office
                    administration with some stenographic experience.  I understand
                    that the position requires a large volume of dictation in addition
                    to routine office duties and provides an opportunity to assume
                    administrative responsibilities.  Because I believe I have the
                    necessary qualifications, I would like to be considered for this
                    position.

                    While taking secretarial training at Central, I had the opportunity
                    to tour a number of industrial firms in our city.  Of those that I
                    visited, your company offices, your operations, and the friendli-
                    ness of the staff impressed me the most.  My hope is to become a
                    part of your organization.

                    You will see from the enclosed data sheet that I have acquired a
                    high level of stenographic skills and have the ability to operate
                    a number of office machines.  You will also note that I have
                    supplemented my course work at Central with on-the-job experience
                    during the summers.

                    Since it may be difficult to reach me by telephone during working
                    hours, I shall call your office to see if I may arrange an
                    appointment with you for next Tuesday to discuss this position.

                    Yours very truly,

                    Lynn K. Jones
                    Lynn K. Jones

                    Enclosure
```

Figure 12—4
An application letter in block style with mixed punctuation (an unusual letter because the applicant will try to arrange the interview).

a student assistant in the Department of Office Administration during the four years I attended McNeese State University.

Another interesting statement that might show your achievements and create desire could be similar to this one:

I enjoyed meeting people and increased my ability to be cheerful, efficient, and helpful during the four years I spent as a secretary in Smith Hall where I worked on a scholarship to earn my tuition, room, and board.

Your steps to obtain attention and analyze your achievements will depend on the job for which you apply. However, if you can make your qualifications fit the needs of the position, you are far

```
                                    123 West State Street
                                    Lake Arthur, LA 70549
                                    December 1, 19--


        Ms. Susie James, Personnel Director
        A & R Food Distributors
        4567 Windsor Drive
        Baton Rouge, LA 70815

        Dear Ms. James:

            A & R Food Distributors is one of the largest and fastest
        growing food chains in the United States. Because of rapid
        expansion, it offers a real future for well-qualified people at the
        managerial level. As a recent college graduate in the field of
        business administration, I believe A & R Food Distributors offers
        me the future I am seeking as one of your managerial trainees.

            While earning my degree I gained a broad background in
        business through courses in accounting, marketing, management, and
        finance. While taking these courses I began to understand the
        problems of people and how they relate to this.

            I have on-the-job experience as I worked as a bag boy, stock
        clerk, and cashier at Super-L Super Market and at other stores
        between semesters, holidays, and weekends. I have also been
        involved with young people at the Lake Charles YMCA.

            Please read my résumé for more details about my education and
        preparation and then call me at 774-3705, or write me and tell me
        when I may come in to discuss personally a future with A & R Food
        Distributors.

                            Sincerely yours,

                            Mark Smith
                            Mark Smith


        Enclosure
```

Figure 12–5
An unsolicited application letter
in a modified block style with
mixed punctuation.

ahead toward obtaining the preferential treatment you will receive
as the best prospect and getting you the interview you desire.

Anticipate Action

By using the four-step plan, your present goal is to obtain an interview at the employer's convenience. Few people are hired before
being interviewed. You obtain an interview to reinforce your application letter and your data sheet. Therefore, you need to include a
clincher to remind your prospective employer that the company
will benefit from your services. You may give references or indicate

Include a clincher that will obtain the interview you need.

```
                                    Virginia Union University
                                    Richmond, VA 23220
                                    March 15, 19--

          Mr. Reggie J. Wilson
          Director of Personnel
          General Motors, Inc.
          3044 Grand Blvd. W.
          Detroit, MI 48202

          Dear Mr. Wilson:

          With graduation only two months away, I would like very much to
          apply for a position in this year's executive training program
          at General Motors.  My B.S. degree will be in computer programming.
          I will finish in the top 10 percent of my class.

          For the past three summers, I have been employed on the staff of
          the Norfolk Boy's Club Camp.  During the first two years, I served
          as a counselor.  Last summer I became a supervisor responsible for
          fourteen counselors and their campers.  The enclosed résumé will
          give you fuller details of this experience and the rest of my
          background.

          With my bachelor's work nearly completed, I see this year as a
          time of beginning.  The career that interests me most is one with
          General Motors.  May I hear from you regarding my qualifications
          and come to Detroit at your convenience for an interview?

                                    Sincerely yours,

                                    Richard J. Miller

                                    Richard J. Miller

          Enclosure
```

Figure 12—6
An application for acceptance
into an executive training program set up in a modified block
style with mixed punctuation.

the availability of references to increase your employer's confidence in your ability. Of course, references are given only with the permission of the persons named.

Your closing sentence should include suggestions that make obtaining an interview as easy as possible. Include your telephone number; give an approximate time and place where your prospective employer may reach you; or you may even suggest that you call and arrange an interview. However, do not be presumptuous; an interview is a privilege extended to you rather than a right that you may consider yours.

Application letters vary according to your education, experience, abilities, aptitudes, and special interests. Your goal is to present

Miller follows the recommended pattern for an application transmittal letter.

First, Miller indicates his purpose for writing.

Here, a really important idea is given its own isolated sentence.

Then, he highlights his background, making sure to mention its most impressive features.

Notice the extra detail to emphasize an interesting fact in Miller's background, his supervisory experience.

After highlighting his background, Miller makes explicit reference to the detailed resume.

Miller injects a note of personal aspiration into the letter. Employers want more than college degrees and experience in their applicants. They want seriously motivated human beings.

And, in closing, he asks for the specific response he desires.

Miller strikes a nice balance in this letter between confidence and humility.

Dear Mr. Wilson:

With graduation only two months away, I would like very much to apply for a position in this year's executive training program at General Motors. My B.S. degree will be in computer programming. I will finish in the top 10 percent of my class.

For the past three summers, I have been employed on the staff of the Norfolk Boy's Club Camp. During the first two years, I served as a counselor. Last summer I became a supervisor responsible for fourteen counselors and their campers. The enclosed resume will give you fuller details of this experience and the rest of my background.

With my bachelor's work nearly completed, I see this year as a time of beginning. The career that interests me most is one with General Motors. May I hear from you regarding my qualifications and come to Detroit at your convenience for an interview?

Sincerely yours,

your qualifications most favorably and show that you are the best person for the position. Several representative examples of application letters are shown in Figures 12–1, 12–2, 12–3, 12–4, 12–5, and 12–6.

Why is the letter in Figure 12–6 especially effective? Figure 12–7 analyzes what Miller has done in his letter. First, he follows the

Figure 12—7
An analysis of the application letter in Figure 12—6.

recommended pattern for a covering letter of application. Notice that by using opening modifiers, passive constructions, and one interrogative sentence, Miller has avoided opening his sentences with *I* in nine out of ten cases. This is one of the difficulties many applicants have in writing covering letters. Miller strikes a balance in this letter between confidence and humility.

In the first statement, Miller indicates his purpose for writing. This paragraph ends with a really important idea in its own isolated sentence.

Miller highlights his background, making sure to mention its most impressive features. He emphasizes one interesting fact in his background—his supervisory experience. Then, Miller makes explicit reference to the detailed résumé he is enclosing.

The last paragraph injects a note of personal aspiration into the letter. He recognizes that employers want more than college degrees and experience in their applicants. They want seriously motivated human beings. And, in closing, Miller asks for the specific response he desires—an interview.

You have seen examples of positive application letters. You should carefully watch for the tone you use. You do not want to appear arrogant or overaggressive; on the other hand, you must not imply timidity or self-abasement. You want to appear to be the rational, confident applicant that the company needs.

Use positive tone and the "you-attitude" when writing the application letter.

You should avoid the pronoun *I* as much as possible. However, you are talking about yourself; you must give information about your training and experience. Therefore, you should use the pronoun *I* when you need to do so; otherwise, the message may seem insecure and artificial.

On the other hand, repeating the word *I* should be avoided. Try to keep the I's down to a reasonable number. Especially try to begin as many paragraphs as possible with some word other than *I* to prevent negative attention through emphasis of yourself.

Avoid negative statements in your application letter.

Similarly, avoid negative statements or suggestions in applications. Do not broadcast that you have had no experience. In this case, do not mention experience at all. Do not suggest that salary is unimportant. However, do not emphasize salary until you have your interview.

You will want to make good word choices as you write your application letters. You need to use an outline such as the four A's plan to be sure that you have included all of the necessary information. However, you do not want to make your application sound like a carbon copy of everyone else's. In fact, the whole idea of your application letter is to show the extras that you can provide the company.

Data Sheet or Résumé

Many communication experts feel that the procedure for writing the application package has changed in recent years. For example, some authorities feel your application letter should be only a communication that includes some of your pertinent data while serving as a transmittal letter.

In fact, many authorities feel that the data sheet or résumé should be written first so you can understand your qualifications thoroughly. In that way you can present yourself to your best advantage when writing the letter concerning the position in which you are interested. Furthermore, these experts consider that your application letter should merely highlight your background by mentioning your qualifications and relating your background to details in your data sheet or résumé. In the past, the application letter was always written first; now, some employment experts consider that by writing your data sheet first, you may combine your self-analysis, your career and job evaluation, and your market analysis more successfully as you decide what goes in your résumé or data sheet. Most authorities still feel that your application letter is your most successful persuasive tool for getting the job you want. In any case, both must be able to stand alone as you work toward obtaining your job interview.

Your data sheet will show in tabular form the significant details of your personal history.

Regardless of the method you choose, the data sheet will outline, tabulate, and summarize the significant details of your personal history. Along with your persuasive letter of application, the data sheet will give detailed, concrete, and correct evidence of what your application message describes. Your well-written résumé, vitae, or data sheet—outlined to save your reader's time—will present your qualifications quickly under obvious headings in summary form.

For you, the most difficult part of preparing the résumé may be to tabulate and type the material so the details may be easily read and understood. The format of your data sheet, however, also provides evidence of your ability to organize. Many formats for data sheets or résumés are acceptable.

Your data sheet shows your ability to organize.

Your résumé makes a better impression if the typing is done so space is used economically without appearing crowded. Most of the headings should be obvious to make locating the information easy. Résumés usually include personal details, education, experience, extracurricular activities, and references. Your application letter will usually be less than a page. A carefully outlined and completely detailed data sheet of an experienced employee may run to two or three pages.

Your school placement office may use a standard data sheet which you will be asked to fill out. You may use this as a résumé of your activity and work experience. Some companies may ask you to fill out their own application blank. Because your data sheet may represent you to people who have never met you, appearance is most important.

Most companies prefer that you develop your own résumé, rather than using a form as a supplement to the face-to-face interview. The organization of your data sheet may vary according to the parts that you want to emphasize. Your main goal is not how you organize the separate elements of your résumé but your ability to show an orderly, reasonable process. You will usually want to organize the data sheet categories according to the priority of interest for the employer, rather than for yourself. List the most important categories first. Furthermore, when you organize the data sheet items within categories, again list the most important points for your employer first—usually in reverse chronological order.

A good résumé or data sheet helps you make an excellent impression; a poor résumé can seriously hurt your chances to show that you are a desirable applicant. Furthermore, a self-prepared résumé becomes increasingly important as you change jobs in the years after graduation and obtain more education and experience. The things you remember accurately today may be difficult for you to research or recall in the future.

Your résumé may be organized in one of many forms. In fact, if you are conventional, you will want to begin with personal details concerning yourself and end with references. Usually, personal details and education come first in the conventional form illustrated in Figures 12–8 and 12–9.

Your data sheet is employee-oriented to show your outstanding qualifications. You should present a neat, correct, accurate, and outstanding résumé that emphasizes what you can do in terms of the job for which you are applying. Complete sentences or paragraphs are not used to detract from its tabular arrangement, skillfully organized according to the attributes you possess. In other words, arrange the parts of your résumé to emphasize what you need to sell yourself.

Most résumés are organized in the conventional form.

Your Personal Information

The first section in a typical, model résumé usually consists of personal information. Your name appears at the top. It may be centered and typed in capital letters, and it is emphasized through

```
Rebecca Steinburg                    Home Address:
P.O. Box 202 - MSU                   1200 Avenue B
Lake Charles, LA 70609               Jennings, LA 70546


PERSONAL DATA:

     Birth Date:  January 19, 1959
     Height:  5' 1"   Weight:  120
     Marital Status:  Married
     Health:  Excellent

OCCUPATIONAL GOAL:

     My goal is a job in the field of business with the eventual
     aim of a management position.

EDUCATION:

     University of Southwestern Louisiana, Lafayette, LA 70501
     Degree:  Bachelor of Science, 1980
     Major:  Office Administration
     Minor:  English
     Major Subjects:
          Typewriting, Shorthand, Business-Report Writing, Business
          Communications, Secretarial Procedures, Office Management,
          Personnel Management, Economics, Psychology, Accounting,
          Business Organization, English Composition and Litera-
          ture.
     Grades:  3.5 overall average.

EXTRACURRICULAR ACTIVITIES:

     President, Phi Chi Theta, business women's fraternity.
     Secretary, Student Government Association.
     International gourmet cooking group.

WORK EXPERIENCE:

     Summer, 1976 - Mead Products, Inc., 700 Ryan Street, Lake
                    Charles, LA 70601, stenographer in Personnel
                    Department.
     Summer, 1975 - Kelly Girls, Inc., P.O. Box 100, Lake Charles,
                    LA 70602, temporary secretarial employment for
                    various firms including insurance agency, hospi-
                    tal, oil company, and law firm.
     Summer, 1974 - Camp Fire Girls Association, P.O. Box 27,
                    Lafayette, LA 70502, clerk in Accounts
                    Receivable Department.

REFERENCES:

Mrs. Brenda Cox, CPS     Mr. John Nix          Ms. Esther Roe
Ace Manufacturing Co.    Personnel Director    717 West Street
P.O. Box 3299            P.O. Drawer 2         Jennings, La 75046
Lafayette, LA 70502      Lake Charles LA 70602 318 289-2211
318 784-2729             318 478-5631
```

Figure 12—8
A conventional data sheet giving education first.

typographical placement. Your address and phone number are always included so you may be reached easily.

Age is usually included in your résumé; however, under the newer laws governing age discrimination, you are no longer required to disclose your age. Height and weight often are given as indexes of your personal appearance. Marital status is usually included although many women choose to omit this point as they feel this aspect is irrelevant to their ability to perform a job. Giving this information is a matter of your personal preference. Married applicants may often be considered to be more stable. However, single persons may be able to meet requirements of travel or irregular

In the personal section, you will want to emphasize your name, address, and phone number so you may be reached easily.

LAURA EDMONDSON

71 Serendipity Drive
Corona, CA 91720
(315) 356-3442

Age: 22
Ht.: 5'7" Wt.: 128
Single

Experience

Executive Secretary, Southwestern Life & Indemnity Company, Riverside, California, May 1981 to present. Responsible for scheduling all appointments for the president, hosting all public functions, and overseeing and assigning work to other office employees.

Corresponding Secretary, Hernandez-Foster, Inc., Pomona, California, May 1980 to May 1981. Responsible for typing all letters for the company and taking orders by telephone.

Education

Corona High School, Corona, California. Graduated in 1978.

San Jose City College, San Jose, California. Graduated in 1980 with an Associate degree in Office Administration.

College Course Work in: Typewriting, Shorthand, Composition, Business Communications, Report Writing, Office Machines, Economics, Management, and Business Law.

Personal Interests

Enjoy painting, travel, meeting people, participating in many sports activities, and sewing.

References

Mr. Marcus Foster
Hernandez-Foster, Inc.
3512 Pomona Boulevard
Pomona, CA 91768
Phone Number: (714) 456-7778

Mrs. Dorothy Lyman, CPS
Instructor, Secretarial Arts
San Jose City College
2100 Moorpark Avenue
San Jose, CA 95128
Phone Number: (418) 298-2181

Miss Evelyn Winterborn, Legal Secretary
Beverly Hills Law Associates
8502 Wilshire Boulevard
Beverly Hills, CA 90211
Phone Number: (213) 564-7896

Figure 12–9
A conventional data sheet giving experience first.

hours. In fact, a statement of willingness to relocate, if true, can be an advantage when applying to a company with regional offices.

In the personal section, indications of race, religion, national origin, or health need not be included. However, if these help your job application, you would mention them. Similarly, you may enclose a photograph, which is no longer required. You may include one if you think it will strengthen your résumé. Be sure, however, that you include a photograph that is representative and in good taste. A photograph similar to—but better than—a passport picture would be most suitable.

Your Education

If, as a college student or graduate, you have little experience in the kind of work you seek, education will probably be the next section of your data sheet. Your educational attainments are one of the best indexes of your job potential. You may want to include your specific degree, the name of the school, and your date of graduation. If you have an overall average of B or higher, a letter-grade translation might be included in this section. Sometimes, you will want to include a list of the specific courses you took in school that are related to the job for which you are applying.

If you have special skills, these may be listed either in the education section or in another section. Skills and educational attainment should be explained thoroughly to your prospective employers. Until recently, the name of the high school from which you graduated was always listed. However, unless your high-school graduation is your highest achievement, this is no longer necessary.

As a prospective college graduate, you may use the future tense in listing your educational qualifications by stating something like "will be graduated with a B.S. degree in accounting from the University of Northern Colorado in May, 1981."

> Your educational attainments may be one of the best indexes of your job potential.

Your Work Experience

Your work experience is an essential ingredient of any résumé. Almost any kind of honest, respectable work experience is an asset through which you show that you can handle responsibilities.

Ordinarily, your work experience should begin with the last job you held. The listings are in reverse order, ending with the earliest. You may impress a prospective employer by showing that you have held a job with a company for a considerable length of time. As a part-time employee, you might emphasize that you have been asked to return to the same company several summers or various times in succession. If your job has increased in responsibility, you should indicate this on your data sheet. Demonstrated ability and progress may mean more to an interviewer than the simple fact that you have held a certain job. As a beginning worker, significant minor experience that can help you should be included.

If you have worked as a student assistant in a bookstore, library, or office on campus, these facts should be emphasized in the résumé. The fact that you have worked during college indicates that you have initiative and can take responsibility. Students who really want an education enough to do additional work are inclined to

> Almost any work will show that you can handle responsibility.

> Your most recent job is usually listed first.

apply themselves on the job. Although job experience related directly to the position for which you are applying may be more desirable, any job experience will be helpful in showing that you have entered the world of work.

Working for others also shows a certain amount of independence and maturity. If you delivered newspapers, sold magazines, bagged groceries in a supermarket, or supervised young people at a summer camp, these activities may be listed by you as a young prospective employee.

In relating your experiences, use concreteness. In other words, give the dates, the position, name of the person or firm, address, the phone number of the company, and a brief description of your duties. If your actual experience in this job is similar to the one for which you are making application, you should enlarge this experience report with a longer description of job duties.

Your Extracurricular and Civic Activities

Include your extracurricular activities. Many jobs are especially fitted for a well-rounded individual. The fact that you have been a member of an off-campus organization will help to show that you are interested in your community. Demonstrated social awareness accompanied by awards or offices held shows your leadership ability, which is welcomed by your prospective employer. You should be involved in some extracurricular activities. Being chosen as a member of an honorary group or elected to a professional society in

Getting along with others is one of your most important business skills. From Steel Case, Inc., Grand Rapids, MI.

your field speaks well for your leadership abilities. A listing of social organizations may be helpful. In some firms, a large part of your success grows out of your ability to get along with other people. As Theodore Roosevelt said: "The most important single ingredient in the formula of success is the knack of getting along with people."

Leadership ability is demonstrated by your membership in civic and professional organizations.

However, do not overdo your personal interests when listing them on your résumé unless they relate directly to your ability. For example, you may want to exclude memberships in religious and political organizations if they bear little relation to your potential. Also, you might be wise to exclude such hobbies as skydiving, motorcycle racing, or sword swallowing. Any extracurricular activities that create an impression of temperamental irregularities, although not necessarily true, may hurt your chances of obtaining the job you seek.

Search for the something special that is *you*. Analyze any special abilities, any talents and interests, correctly. Stress your strong points because they may be the extra special abilities for which your prospective employer is looking.

Your References

At one time, references were always listed. In fact, at one time, you should have included at least three and no more than six references. When seeking your first "special" job, you will still probably list them.

Today, however, there are several ways that you can handle personal references on a résumé. One suggestion is that at the bottom of the résumé, you list the names, positions, addresses, and telephone numbers of three or four qualified people that are willing to recommend you on the basis of your education, experience, character, and your job potential. If you follow this suggestion, be sure to include the person's position, full address including the ZIP Code, and the telephone number for each reference. Figure 12–10 shows a résumé with the references listed.

You may list your references or indicate that they are available upon request.

In the other case, you may merely indicate that references are available. For example, you may list: "References available upon request." Then, you should have sufficient information should you be asked for these references. Figure 12–11 shows a résumé prepared this way. Employers prefer that your references be previous employers, teachers, and persons that know your ability rather than family, friends, doctors, and political leaders.

Before you list any reference, you should ask the person for permission to use his or her name. You may be overconfident and list

Ask persons for permission to use their names as references.

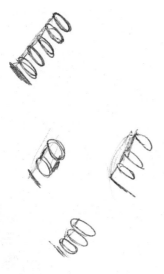

```
              RICHARD BROOK'S PREPARATION FOR EMPLOYMENT
                                 with
                       OZARK ENTERPRISES, INC.

   Address until June 1, 1980           Address after June 1, 1980

       P.O. Box 333                         713 Aster Street
       University of Arkansas               Little Rock, AR 72209
       Little Rock, AR 72201                501  722-3351
       501  783-6432

                          Professional Goals

   Initial:  Manager Trainee,        Eventual:  Vice President in
             Sales Department                    Charge of Sales

                      Manager-Related Experiences

   Assistant Manager                  Parts Department Manager
   Pizza Place, Inc.                  AAA Auto Parts, Inc.
   Little Rock, Arkansas              Little Rock, Arkansas
   1976 to 1979                       1974 to 1976, part time
       Supervised five                    Supervised two clerks,
       employees, handled                 responsible for
       work schedules and                 inventory control.
       payroll.

                     Manager-Oriented Education

   To receive a Bachelor of Science degree in Business Administration
   in May, 1980.  Among courses taken at University of Arkansas (B
   average):

   Business                           General Education

   Retail Management                  English Composition and
   Systems Management                     Literature
   Corporation Finance                Psychology
   Business Law                       Speech
   Personnel Management               Computer Science
   Sales and Advertising Management   Government
   Managerial Economics

                        Personal Information

   Age, 25 yrs.              Height, 6 ft. 3 in.    Special interests,
   Marital Status, single    Weight, 190 lbs.        astronomy and
                                                     swimming

                             References

   Ms. Marie Miles, Proprietor   Professor Lee Brown, CPA   Mr. George Fry, Manager
   Pizza Place, Inc.             University of Arkansas     AAA Auto Parts, Inc.
   P.O. Box 888                  P.O. Drawer VV             721 Westwood Drive
   Banks, AR 71631               Little Rock, AR 72203      Little Rock, AR  72204
   501  599-1234                 501  783-7722              501  783-7651
```

Figure 12—10
A conventional data sheet listing references including name, professional positions, company, address, and complete phone number.

as a reference a person who does not know you well enough to give you the glowing praise you expect. However, no prospective reference will object to being asked, "Will you be willing to write a reference letter for me?" If you feel that this prospective reference hesitates even a little to answer the question, consider asking someone else to recommend you. Remember that naming your references or indicating their availability strengthens your achievement evaluation—a plus in the application package.

```
                          JONATHAN E. HAYDEN

        1938 Ryan Street                Age: 25
        Lake Charles, LA 70601          Ht: 6'1"  Wt: 185
        318-477-0938                    Married

        Experience

            Department Supervisor, Continental Oil Company, Processing De-
              partment, Lake Charles, Louisiana, May 1980 to the present.
              Responsible for obtaining, scheduling, and overseeing work
              assignments of thirty engineering, planning, and administra-
              tive support personnel.  Also responsible for reconciling
              department budget.

            Technical Writer, Continental Oil Company, Communications De-
              partment, Lake Charles, Louisiana, July 1979 to May 1980.
              Responsible for writing and updating technical manuals on
              classified spacecraft and military projects.  Was granted
              "secret" security clearance.

            Technical Writer, Johnson-Adams, Technical Publications, Baton
              Rouge, Louisiana, August 1978 to July 1979.  Responsible for
              writing and updating Air Force Technical Orders.

        Education

            McNeese State University, Lake Charles, Louisiana.  Part-time
              night student since September 1979.  Will be graduated with
              B.S. in Business Administration in May 1982.  (Plan to con-
              tinue study as a part-time night student at McNeese State
              toward the M.B.A. degree.)

            Louisiana State University, Baton Rouge, Louisiana.  Electronics
              major, from September 1977 to June 1979.

            University of Southwestern Louisiana, Lafayette, Louisiana.
              Graduated in June 1977.  Associate of Arts Degree in Radio
              Technology and Radio Technician's Certificate.

        Personal Interests

            Play men's softball and basketball in city league; coach for
              Babe Ruth baseball team; Lake Charles Jaycees.

        References

            Will gladly be provided on request.
```

Figure 12—11
A résumé indicating that references are available on request.

Emphasize the Experience You Have

What can you do to overcome a lack of experience in jobs that directly contribute to the job you seek? A functional résumé emphasizes abilities, interests, and enthusiasm in working rather than your experience, as shown in Figure 12–12. Mr. Wilson has used good form; his résumé heading gives his full address and phone number so he can be easily and quickly contacted.

Because Mr. Wilson's experience is limited, he has positively emphasized the skills, knowledge, and transferable aspects of his rather

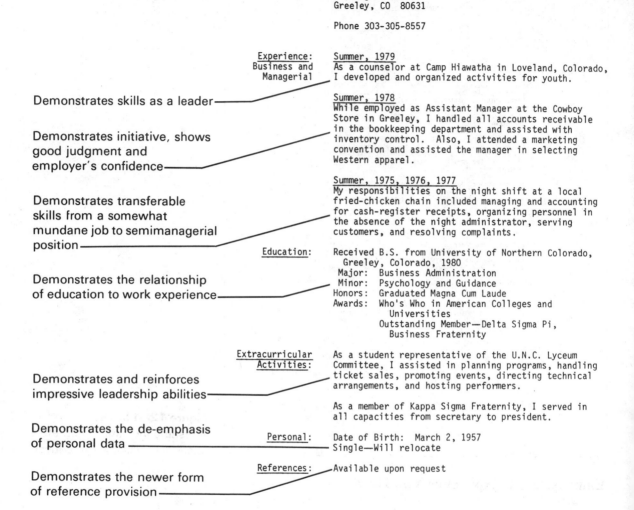

Andrew S. Wilson
501 Eighth Street
Greeley, CO 80631

Phone 303-305-8557

Experience: Business and Managerial

Demonstrates skills as a leader

Summer, 1979
As a counselor at Camp Hiawatha in Loveland, Colorado, I developed and organized activities for youth.

Demonstrates initiative, shows good judgment and employer's confidence

Summer, 1978
While employed as Assistant Manager at the Cowboy Store in Greeley, I handled all accounts receivable in the bookkeeping department and assisted with inventory control. Also, I attended a marketing convention and assisted the manager in selecting Western apparel.

Demonstrates transferable skills from a somewhat mundane job to semimanagerial position

Summer, 1975, 1976, 1977
My responsibilities on the night shift at a local fried-chicken chain included managing and accounting for cash-register receipts, organizing personnel in the absence of the night administrator, serving customers, and resolving complaints.

Demonstrates the relationship of education to work experience

Education:
Received B.S. from University of Northern Colorado, Greeley, Colorado, 1980
Major: Business Administration
Minor: Psychology and Guidance
Honors: Graduated Magna Cum Laude
Awards: Who's Who in American Colleges and Universities
         Outstanding Member—Delta Sigma Pi, Business Fraternity

Demonstrates and reinforces impressive leadership abilities

Extracurricular Activities:
As a student representative of the U.N.C. Lyceum Committee, I assisted in planning programs, handling ticket sales, promoting events, directing technical arrangements, and hosting performers.

As a member of Kappa Sigma Fraternity, I served in all capacities from secretary to president.

Demonstrates the de-emphasis of personal data

Personal:
Date of Birth: March 2, 1957
Single—Will relocate

Demonstrates the newer form of reference provision

References:
Available upon request

Figure 12—12

A functional résumé that might be used by recent graduates with a degree but little significant work experience.

unimpressive or mundane job experiences. As a recent graduate, he has demonstrated how his education related to these job experiences. Similarly, he has reinforced his image of leadership by showing how his extracurricular activities enhanced his education and experience.

Following the newer employment guidelines, Mr. Wilson minimizes his personal data. Also, he has followed the more modern approach of subordinating references by mentioning that these are available on request.

However, when you or Mr. Wilson use the functional data sheet, you will need an especially well prepared application letter to reinforce this résumé. This form of résumé is especially effective for a young graduate with minimum work experience. This application and its covering letter can show you to be an impressive young man or woman with qualities that employers seek.

In summary, you must remember that perhaps the most important communications you will write will be your résumé combined with your application letter. Your résumé probably has about ten seconds to make an initial impression on an employer, according to manpower expert Tom Jackson, author of the *Hidden Job Market* and *Guerrilla Tactics in the Job Market*.[1] Jackson feels that most student résumés are a "document of mediocrity" which do not communicate positive skills and results. Although sometimes controversial, his tips to keep your data sheet from landing in corporate wastebaskets are given in Table 12–1.

Use a checklist to keep your data sheet from landing in the wastebasket.

The Application Blank

Many firms have their own application blanks, data sheets, or résumés that they often prefer you to use. These should be filled in carefully and correctly—preferably typed. These blanks are easier because you do not have to design the form and you can merely fill in the questions that are asked. However, the application blank is employer-oriented and does not give you as much flexibility in answering questions. Furthermore, an application blank is not specifically designed to show your best abilities. Figure 12–13 illustrates a two-page application blank showing the information generally requested.

The application blank is employer-oriented; the data sheet is employee-oriented.

Completing application blanks demonstrates your ability to follow instructions, the time it takes to fill out the blank, and the completeness of the answers recorded on the blank. However, the time taken to fill in the blank is not as important as the accuracy. If you make an error on the blank, ask for another one. In fact, if you can take an application blank home with you, you may make a copy on which you can make a rough draft before you complete the actual application form. Furthermore, returning this filled-out

Your ability to fill in an application blank correctly may be considered indicative of your ability to fulfill the requirements of the job.

[1] Tom Jackson and Davidyne Mayles, *The Hidden Job Market* (New York: Quadrangle/New York Times, 1976); Tom Jackson, *Guerrilla Tactics in the Job Market* (New York: Bantam, 1978).

application form will give you an opportunity to make another contact with your prospective employer.

Remember that your completed application form gives a great deal of information about you—your penmanship, accuracy, carefulness, and neatness. Make it an image of you and your work.

The parts of the application blank are much the same as those of the data sheet. These include personal data, education, experience, extracurricular activities, and achievements. The same rules of privacy and rights of individuals apply. You need only complete the parts that you choose to fill in. However, be extremely careful because you may not be considered for the position if you have not

Table 12—1
Keep Your Data Sheet from Landing in the Wastbasket

1. *Take stock.* Don't start writing until you have compiled a list of your skills, accomplishments, and experiences. This inventory will help you pick and choose the most relevant aspects of your background to use for a particular job target.

2. *Present your accomplishments.* Let your employer know about things you have done that could relate to his or her needs—not just the job titles you have had or the duties you were supposed to perform.

3. *Eliminate unnecessary information.* Leave out personal data like height and weight, race, religion, or salary desired.

4. *Limit your résumé to one page.* This is the format most employers say they prefer. There are few young people whose job qualifications can't be summed up in one page. [Some need more, however.]

5. *Use action verbs.* Get sentences and paragraphs off to a brisk start with verbs like *created, organized, managed, took responsibility for,* and *built.* Don't bury your abilities and achievements behind long, stuffy windups. Don't use [an unusual] style unless you are applying for a job in a field (like advertising) where it could be appropriate.

6. *Make your data sheet look beautiful.* Your résumé should exude professionalism and competence. If possible, have it printed (not Xeroxed) on good-quality white or cream-colored bond paper. If you are not a good typist, have a friend or professional do it on an electric typewriter.

7. *Don't expect a résumé to land you the job.* A résumé is merely a direct-mail technique to help you get your foot in the door. It's no substitute for face-to-face contact with an employer. After you send out résumés, don't sit around waiting for employers to call. Get on with your job-hunting campaign.

From "The Most Important Piece of Paper Is Your Resume," *Ford's Insider* (Knoxville, Tenn.: 13—30 Corp., 1978), p. 23; quoting *Guerrilla Tactics in the Job Market,* by Tom Jackson (New York: Bantam, 1978).

320

filled in the details requested. Figure 12–14 illustrates one page of an application blank with a section for personal data that may be required of an applicant for business reasons. In using this form, the company checks the questions to be answered by the applicant.

Following these steps in filling in an application blank may help you:

1. Write or print neatly and legibly. (Type if a typewriter is available.)

2. Answer every question asked. If the question does not apply to you or is one that you do not want to answer, draw a line to show that you have read and considered the question.

3. Do not overstate or understate the facts. Any misstatement may be considered cause for rejection. Tell the truth.

4. Be specific.

5. Fill in each blank quickly yet carefully.

6. If you have had no experience whatever, fill in this section with "In school."

7. Have names of references ready with complete addresses and telephone numbers.

8. Spell correctly and use good English.

9. Read and check blanks carefully.

10. Review the application blank to be sure that you have followed directions exactly.

The Interview

The interview is the *action* that you desire from your letter and résumé. Formal interviews are really *conversations with a purpose.* The interview is a real-life test of how well you have been trained and how well you can apply what you have learned. In addition, you may need specific knowledge and skills in order to succeed in getting exactly the job you want. Business is highly competitive, and the person who is most successful in presenting her or his qualifications will be more likely to get the position.

In the interview, follow the rules of good conversation.

As a prospective candidate, your appearance, manner, and speech must be outstanding. Your employment interview is one of the most important events in your experience. The twenty or thirty minutes spent with the interviewer may determine your entire future if you have the training for the job you want.

Interviewers are constantly amazed at the number of applicants who drift—more or less—to job interviews without any apparent preparation and with only a vague knowledge of what they are

CONOCO
Continental Oil Company
Application for Employment

Equal Employment Opportunity — It is our policy to provide equal employment opportunity throughout the Company for all qualified persons without regard to race, color, religion, age, sex, national origin, or handicap.

Name (Last, First, Middle)	Over 18 — Under 65 ☐ Yes ☐ No	Social Security Number

Present Address (Street, City, State, Zip Code)	Telephone (Area Code First)

Permanent Address (Street, City, State, Zip Code)	Telephone (Area Code First)

Minimum salary expected	Date available for employment	Employment desired ☐ Permanent ☐ Temporary	Would you accept temporary employment? ☐ Yes ☐ No

Type of work desired — First Preference	Second Preference	Willingness to travel ☐ Occasionally ☐ Infrequently ☐ Frequently

State Nature of Related Work Experience	Will you perform shift work? ☐ Yes ☐ No

Geographical Location preferred	Location where you will not consider employment

State the nature of any Physical Defects or Limitations:	If not a U.S. Citizen or Permanent Resident what type of Visa do you have?	Valid Drivers License ☐ Yes ☐ No	State Issued
		License Number	Date expires

United States Military Service Record

Branch	Total length of Active Service	Highest rank or rating attained
Major duties		

Employment Record (List last Job first)

From Mo. Yr.	To Mo. Yr.	Employer / Address	Supervisor's name / Most Responsible Position Held	What were your major duties	Reason for Leaving

List those machines and/or equipment you are qualified to operate and any other skills you possess.

References (Give three references other than immediate family familiar with your work and/or academic background)

Name	Occupation	Address

12-21 PA, 11-75

Figure 12—13

A typical two-page application blank.

Reproduced with permission of the Continental Oil Company.

Education — Circle Highest Grade Completed	Dates Attended		Course of Study Major — Minor	Degree Received	Grade Average		Degree Date
1 2 3 4 5 6 7 8 9 10 11 12	From	To			Overall	Major	
High School Attended and Location				Diploma ☐Yes ☐ No			
Vocational or Technical School Attended			— — — — — — —	Completed ☐Yes ☐No			
College or University			— — — — — — —				
College or University			— — — — — — —				
College or University			— — — — — — —				

Other — (Include special training, military courses, apprenticeships completed and any other education you believe important)

Foreign Languages Spoken	Written	Read

Titles of Theses and Special Research Projects

You may omit references to activities in this section which might reveal age, race, color, sex, national origin, or handicap.

Name and description of scholastic honors received including scholarships

Name honorary, technical and professional organizations of which you have been a member, or other extra-curricular activities in which you have participated, including offices held. (List Professional licenses held)

Indicate source which referred you

☐ Campus Placement Office   ☐ Walk-In   ☐ Private Employment Agency   ☐ Published Advertisement
☐ Employee Referral   ☐ Write-In   ☐ Governmental Employment Agency   ☐ Other (Specify)
   ☐ Rehire

Additional Information

This form will usually provide the necessary information. It may be supplemented, however, by a letter or personal resume. **Permanent employment is subject to your passing a company prescribed physical examination and qualifying for a fidelity bond.**

I understand that an investigative consumer report may be made whereby information is obtained through personal interviews with third parties, such as family members, business associates, financial sources, friends, neighbors, or others with whom I am acquainted concerning information as to my character, general reputation, personal characteristics, and mode of living as the company may determine and I consent to and authorize any person to furnish information for such report. I further understand that I may request in writing a complete and accurate disclosure of the nature and scope of the investigation requested. I further declare that all information furnished in the attached application, signed and dated by me this date, is true to the best of my information and belief and that any willful misrepresentation herein shall be sufficient cause for termination.

Signature _____   Date _____

MILITARY SERVICE RECORD

Were you in U.S. Armed Forces? Yes _____ No _____ If yes, what Branch? _____

Dates of duty: From _____ To _____ Rank at discharge _____
　　　　　　　　　　Month　Day　Year　Month　　Day　　Year

List duties in the service including special training _____

_____

Have you taken any training under the G.I. Bill of Rights? _____ If yes, what training did you take? _____

PLEASE READ AND SIGN BELOW

The facts set forth in my application for employment are true and complete. I understand that if employed, false statements on this application shall be considered sufficient cause for dismissal. You are hereby authorized to make any investigation of my personal history and financial and credit record through any investigative or credit agencies or bureaus of your choice.

In making this application for employment I authorize you to make an investigative consumer report whereby information is obtained through personal interviews with my neighbors, friends, or others with whom I am acquainted. This inquiry, if made, may include information as to my character, general reputation, personal characteristics and mode of living. I understand that I have the right to make a written request within a reasonable period of time to receive additional, detailed information about the nature and scope of any such investigative report that is made.

_____
　　　　　　　　　Signature of Applicant

> To Applicant: READ THIS INTRODUCTION CAREFULLY BEFORE ANSWERING ANY QUESTIONS IN THIS BLOCKED-OFF AREA. The Civil Rights Act of 1964 prohibits discrimination in employment because of race, color, religion, sex or national origin. Federal law also prohibits discrimination on the basis of age with respect to certain individuals. The laws of most States also prohibit some or all of the above types of discrimination as well as some additional types such as discrimination based upon ancestry, marital status or physical or mental handicap or disability.
> DO NOT ANSWER ANY QUESTION CONTAINED IN THIS BLOCKED-OFF AREA UNLESS THE EMPLOYER HAS CHECKED THE BOX NEXT TO THE QUESTION, thereby indicating that for the position for which you are applying the requested information is needed for a legally permissible reason, including, without limitation, national security requirements, a bona fide occupational qualification or business necessity.

☐ How long have you lived at present address? _____

☐ Previous address_____ How long did you live there?_____
　　　　　　　　　　No.　　　　Street　　　　City　　　　State　　　　Zip

☐ Are you over the age of eighteen? _____ If no, hire is subject to verification that you are of minimum legal age

☐ How do you wish to be addressed? Mr.____Mrs.____Miss____Ms.____

☐ Sex: M _____ F _____　☐ Height: _____ft _____in.　☐ Weight: _____lbs.

☐ Marital Status: Single _____ Engaged _____ Married _____ Separated _____ Divorced _____ Widowed _____

☐ Date of Marriage _____ ☐Number of dependents including yourself _____ ☐ Are you a citizen of the U.S.A.? _____

☐ What is your present Selective Service classification?_____

☐ Indicate dates you attended school:

Elementary_____ High School _____ College _____
　　　　　　From　　　To　　　　　　　　From　　　To　　　　　　　　From　　　To
Other (Specify type of school) _____
　　　　　　　　　　　　　　　　　　　　　　　　　　　From　　　To

☐ Have you ever been bonded?_____ If yes, on what jobs? _____

☐ Have you been convicted of a crime in the past ten years, excluding misdemeanors and summary offenses?_____ If yes,
describe in full_____

☐ Do you have any physical defects which preclude you from performing certain kinds of work?_____ If yes, describe such
defects and specific work limitations._____

☐ Have you had a major illness in the past 5 years?_____ If yes, describe_____
_____

☐ Have you received compensation for injuries?_____ If yes, describe_____
_____

Employer may list other bona fide occupational questions on lines below:
☐ _____
☐ _____

—3—

Figure 12—14

One page of an application blank with a section for personal data that can be adapted to the specific job conditions. From V. W. Eimicke Associates, Inc., Bronxville, NY 10708. © Copyright 1955, 1962, 1968, 1971, 1972, 1973, 1976, 1978.

going to be asked and how they are going to answer. As a prospective employee, you certainly do not want to give the impression, "Here I am, world; what do you plan to do with me?"

By acting too casually, you may unconsciously create an impression of indifference. You should attempt to control any nervousness that you feel. Try not to answer the questions of the interviewer in monosyllables. An experienced interviewer will realize that you may be slightly uneasy and will try to help you through the situation. Nevertheless, marks of your inexperience can be avoided by knowing what is actually expected of you and by making a few simple preparations before the interview.

Preparing for the Interview

First of all, hopefully you know what type of interview to expect. Second, be sure that you know the exact time and place. This may sound basic, but many unfortunate applicants assume that the interview is to be held in a certain place and then discover several minutes before the time that the appointment is somewhere else. Therefore, note and write down the time, the name and position of the person you are to see, and the full name and address of the company; keep this notation with you. Never rely on your memory.

Be certain that you have the interviewer's full name and the correct pronunciation. Often seemingly unimportant details such as correct pronunciation of a name, the physical setting (seating, temperature, lighting), the social setting (the nature of occasion), and the difference between you and your interviewer will affect the *climate* and perhaps the *climax* of your interview. The lack of adequate preparation for an interview is the greatest single fault you can make in interviewing—the final part of your application process. You should not consider an interview as a threat to your self-image, but you need to prepare for each interview on an individual basis. You should consider it as an opportunity to understand how an organization receives you and your qualifications.

Consider each interview on an individual basis.

Your job-application letter and résumé will help your interviewer ask you further questions. The purpose of the interview may be to gain information about how you present yourself, express yourself, and conduct yourself. Your interviewer will evaluate how your particular abilities will fit into the needs of the organization. Your cooperation is necessary in reaching these goals.

Before the interview, you will need to prepare yourself mentally and physically, as well as to think about questions that you might be asked and that you might want to ask.

Be sure that you are mentally and physically prepared for the interview.

Mental Preparations

Use the following checklist to help you make your mental preparations for your interview.

1. Know the company to which you are applying.
2. Research all the details of the organization—its products, services, locations, plant offices, growth, and prospects for the future.
3. Know your qualifications thoroughly.
4. Sell yourself on your merits.
5. Have all information about yourself ready. Be prepared to talk about yourself and the facts mentioned in your application letter or data sheet.
6. Know your work record in detail.
7. Know your school records in detail.
8. Have all necessary papers ready.
9. Learn as much as you can about why you want to work for this company.
10. Decide your prospective goals as an entry employee and as an employee ten years from now.
11. Learn as much as possible about the specific job for which you are applying. Don't ask for just *anything*. However, keep enough flexibility to fill a related position that you can handle.
12. Be able to relate your qualifications to the job.
13. Anticipate the questions that your interviewer might ask.

Physical Preparations

The essentials of neatness and cleanliness when appearing for an interview scarcely need to be mentioned to a university student. Your good taste will be your guide as you consider that you are looking for the position you want—not going to a party or an athletic event. Your sincerity, friendliness, and honesty, as well as your personal appearance, will help you to make a good impression. Follow this checklist in making your physical preparations for the interview.

1. Decide before the interview what you will wear. Appearance is vitally important. Plan to dress very neatly, appropriately, and somewhat conservatively.
2. Be sure that you are well groomed.
3. Be sure that you have a full night's sleep before the interview.
4. Be prepared to relax and enjoy yourself, as much as possible, in the interview situation.
5. Use your conversational methods of goodwill in communicating what you have that is necessary for the company.

Conducting Yourself in the Interview

You cannot really rehearse your role in an interview because you do not know what cues will be given to you. Your best guide is to rely on courtesy and good common sense.

Greet the interviewer by name as you enter the office. Take your cues from the interviewer. For example, you shake hands only if the interviewer makes the first gesture. Normally, wait until a chair is offered before you sit down. Never smoke unless invited to do so. Even then, you would probably be wise to refrain. Never chew gum; repress habits that could possibly offend others, especially an older person.

There are some basic rules to follow during most interviews. If you think about them before your interview, you will be well prepared.

1. Be on time or a few minutes early for the appointment.

2. Be calm; try not to be nervous. Relax! For people to be tense during interviews is normal. A little nervousness is expected. However, you can control this situation by placing your hands in your lap and keeping them still if you experience extreme anxiety.

3. Be well groomed and attractively and appropriately dressed.

4. Follow the lead of the interviewer who is your host or hostess. Wait for an invitation before seating yourself.

5. Follow the principles of good conversation. Be tactful and gracious. Listen earnestly and eagerly, and don't interrupt. Don't bore the interviewer with long, overly detailed answers to questions; but do give him or her more than a mere "yes" or "no" in answer to the questions asked.

6. Be frank and use common sense in answering questions.

7. Appeal to your interviewer's self-interest.

8. Stress your qualifications for the job and your interest in it. Highlight your abilities.

9. Pick up clues given by the interviewer's questions or statements and use these to point out that you fit the requirements.

10. Avoid mention of your personal, domestic, or financial problems. Discuss only matters related to the job.

11. Have your papers arranged for easy reference: the identification data, summary of work experience, references, etc.

12. Ask questions about the job and the company. Be sure the questions are intelligent.

13. Ask for specific types of jobs rather than *anything*. Be flexible and willing to make changes as the job requires, but also indicate preferences.

14. Have a definite understanding as to what is required of you should you accept the job.

15. Be realistic in discussing wages. Remember that chances for advancement are often more important than salary.

16. Be prepared to take tests. If relevant, know your approximate typing and shorthand speeds. Know all other specific abilities.

17. When the interviewer is ready to end the conversation, he or she will indicate the fact in some way. Do not try to prolong the interview. Leave quickly. Show appreciation for the time and interest that the interviewer has given you.

18. Keep up your courage if the employer doesn't hire you. You may not get the first job you seek.

If you don't get the first job you want, don't let discouragement show.

Anticipating Questions an Employer Might Ask

Most interviewers follow a rather simple question-and-answer formula. If such is the case, your ability to answer quickly and intelligently is very important. If your answers are confused and contradictory, your opportunity is lost. The best guard against contradictory answers is the plain, unvarnished truth. A frank answer or admission can be turned to your advantage.

You should be ready for unexpected and seemingly irrelevant questions. In fact, you may expect and should be prepared to answer at least one surprise or shock question. A favorite one is, "What would you like to be doing ten years from now if you are hired by this company?"

This seems to be an easy question, but actually this query is difficult to answer. This is where your preparation counts. In every case, try to be as specific and honest as you can.

Follow your interviewer's lead; use the principles of good conversation in answering his or her questions. Table 12–2 gives some of the questions you might be asked by an interviewer. If you have thought through your answers, you will be thoroughly prepared.

Be prepared to answer at least one surprise question.

Table 12–2
Questions Often Asked by Interviewers

1. What type of position do you want with our company?
2. Why do you want this job?
3. Why do you want to work for our company?
4. What do you know about our organization?
5. What do you think we have to offer you?
6. What do you think you have to offer us?
7. Why did you become interested in this type of work (accountant, manager, secretary, administrative assistant, engineer, etc.)?
8. How much education have you completed? Did you receive your degree?

328

9. What was your major in college? Your minor?

10. Did you change your major or minor? Why?

11. What courses did you like best? Least?

12. What are your future educational plans or goals?

13. How does your educational background qualify you for the job for which you are applying?

14. What experience have you had? Was it full-time or part-time work?

15. Why did you leave your last job?

16. How do you feel about your last employer?

17. Would your previous employer recommend you?

18. Can you supply other references?

19. How can you relate any experience you have had to the job for which you are applying?

20. Were you employed while attending school? How much? How do you feel about this employment?

21. What extracurricular activities did you participate in while in school?

22. Which were most meaningful? Why?

23. Did you receive any special honors or awards?

24. What accomplishments in this area pleased you most?

25. How do you spend your spare time?

26. What are your hobbies? Special interests? Activities?

27. Do you like people? Do you feel that people like you?

28. Would you prefer working primarily with people or alone?

29. Do you have a sense of humor? If necessary, can you laugh *at* yourself and / or *with* others?

30. Can you accept constructive criticism?

31. Can you work without close supervision?

32. Can you work under pressure?

33. Do you cooperate with others? Would you help a co-worker after you had completed your assigned tasks? Would you make a sincere effort to get along with other employees and supervisors?

34. How would you describe yourself as a person?

35. What is the one most important factor that you are looking for in a job?

36. What salary would you accept?

37. Would you relocate?

38. Would you object to working as a trainee for six months?

39. Would you object to working overtime or doing shift work if operations are conducted around the clock and you are needed?

40. Would you object to travel?

41. If you had your choice of job and company, what would you most like to be doing ten years from now? Why? Where?

```
                                    1544 Rose Street
                                    Lake Charles, LA 70601
                                    March 19, 19--

                                    Ms. Cecelia Hayden, Personnel Director
                                    Royce Manufacturing Company
                                    3233 Broad Street
                                    Lake Charles, LA 70601

                                    Dear Ms. Hayden:

                                    Thank you very much for talking with me Wednesday, March 17,
                                    19--, about job opportunities with Royce Manufacturing Company.
                                    The program you told me about sounds very interesting, and I am
                                    eager to discuss this with you further.

                                    After our talk, I remembered that the very first thing I ever
                                    earned, when I was about seven or eight, was a fishing rod.  I sold
                                    three cases of mail-order Rockchester Ointment to family, friends,
                                    and neighbors.  Of course, it's quite a step up from selling Rock-
                                    chester Ointment to selling for Royce Manufacturing Company, but I
                                    will wager I am one of the few applicants for the job who can
                                    honestly point to a successful career in sales spanning more than
                                    a decade.

                                    Once you've had a chance to evaluate the results of your campus
                                    interviews, I will be looking forward to hearing from you again.

                                    Cordially,

                                    Fred Mauler

                                    Fred Mauler
```

Figure 12—15
A good example of a follow-up letter.

Deciding What to Take to the Interview

Take necessary materials with you to the interview.

Although you cannot anticipate everything that you might need during an interview, you should take some items with you. For example, you should have the following:

1. A filled fountain pen or an attractive ball-point pen. Most pens for public use are not dependable.

2. Your Social Security number.

3. Two copies of your data sheet showing a list of all available references with correct addresses and telephone numbers, plus the usual material about education, experience, etc.

```
                              2202 Contour Drive
                              Dallas, TX 75248
                              April 2, 19--


        Mr. William R. Smith
        Union Oil, Inc.
        Suite 535, Zigler Building
        413 Lark Street
        New Orleans, LA 70124

        Dear Mr. Smith:

        Enclosed is the completed application blank that you
        requested.  Thank you for your encouragement.

        I had intended to find a permanent position soon after
        graduation.  However, if a definite arrangement can be
        made for my joining your firm early in the spring, I
        shall find temporary employment for the fall.

        Please tell me what other information you require for
        a mutually satisfactory arrangement.

                              Sincerely,

                              Robin J. Estes
                              Robin J. Estes


        Enclosure
```

Figure 12—16
A follow-up letter returning a completed application blank.

4. Photos—wallet size—and other information that might be useful in getting the job.

Each company has an image, a character, and a personality. You will want to consider whether you can be part of that personality. If not, you should look for opportunity elsewhere. However, regardless of how you feel at the end of the interview, don't forget to thank the interviewer for his or her time and the opportunity to apply for the opening.

Show appreciation for the interviewer's time.

Few employers have the right to hire on first impressions. Therefore, don't burn your bridges behind you. Try to keep the channels open to future communication. One way of doing this is by writing a follow-up letter as part of your total application procedure.

```
                                        413 St. Ann Drive
                                        New Orleans, LA 67046
                                        August 28, 19--


        Mr. Jean M. Hebert, CPA
        Hebert, Lafayette, and Soileau Accountants, Inc.
        238 Government Street
        Baton Rouge, LA 70802

        Dear Mr. Hebert

        Thank you for your job offer of August 25.  However, because of my
        recently completed degree in Administrative Services, I accepted a
        managerial position in an office-supply company in Baton Rouge in
        which my administrative training should be more fully utilized.

        Certainly, many opportunities exist for any person in your innova-
        tive firm with the growth potential that you project.  Your
        personnel are friendly, enthusiastic, and energetic.  I would have
        been delighted to be a member of such an organization.

        Please accept my appreciation for the interview, the time you
        spent with me, and your genuine concern for my future.

                                        Sincerely

                                        Karl Broussard
                                        Karl Broussard
```

Figure 12–17
A letter refusing a job offer.

Follow-up Letters

After a job interview many applicants go home and quietly await the good or bad news. You gain a psychological advantage through an effective follow-up letter, one that expresses appreciation for having been given the opportunity for the interview, re-expresses the desire for the job, and reasserts the self-confidence necessary to handle it. Figure 12–15 shows a good example of a follow-up letter. Note that the second paragraph refers to an experience of possible interest to the interviewer.

Both the courtesy and the initiative shown by you in writing this

```
                    WORD PROCESSING, INC.
                    45 Sherwood Forest Drive
                    Baton Rouge, LA  70815
                                              504/463-1300



     August 26, 19--


     Miss Jane White
     413 St. Ann Drive
     New Orleans, LA 70116

     Dear Miss White

     Congratulations!  Welcome to Word Processing, Inc.

     You will begin your career as the manager of Group B on September
     15, here at our Baton Rouge office.  Your beginning salary is
     $950 a month.  We are confident that your progress will justify
     a higher salary within a short period of time.  We are pleased
     to have you as a member of our word processing management team.

     Sincerely

     Ed Robinson

     Ed Robinson
     Personnel Director

     jf
```

Figure 12–18
A letter confirming your job offer and welcoming you to your new job.

follow-up letter may impress your interviewer. Whenever you have an interview with an organization that you would like to work for, you are wise to follow up with a well-written letter of thanks.

Sometimes, you may need to supply additional information such as a completed application blank or data sheet. Figure 12–16 gives an example of a follow-up letter returning a completed application blank. Ms. Estes also refers to the interview discussion about the time the job opening will occur.

If you have applied for several jobs and received more than one job offer, you may need to write a refusal letter similar to that shown in Figure 12–17. Refusal letters require your best communication techniques using courtesy, clarity, frankness, and positive

Supplying additional information helps you to remind your prospective employer of your application.

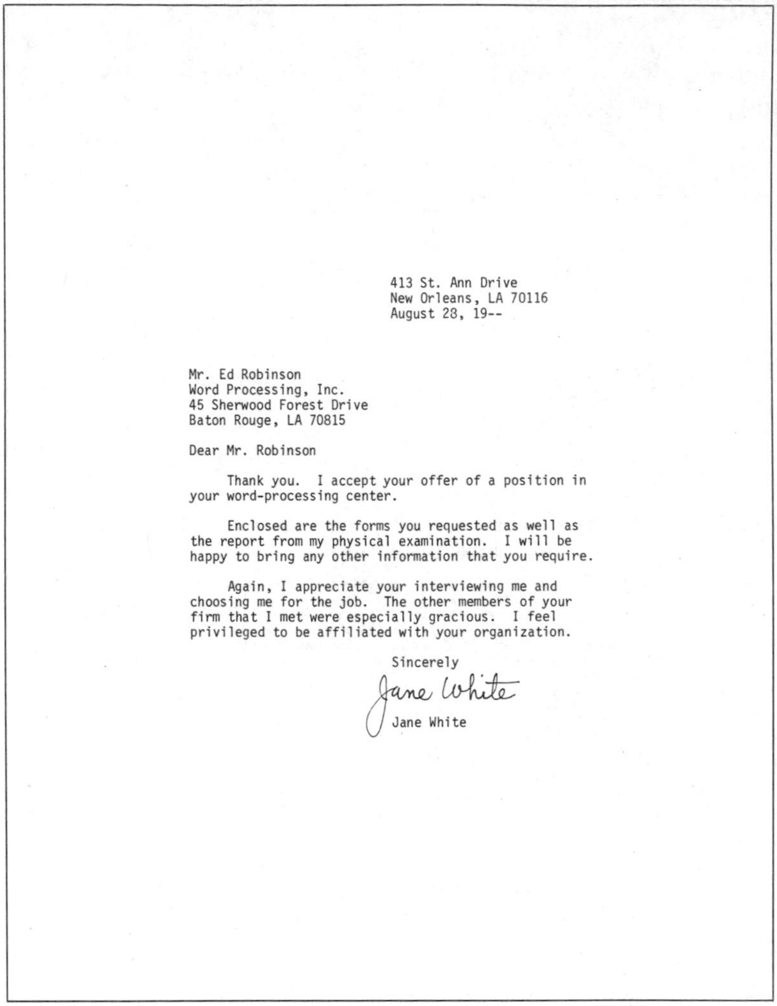

```
                              413 St. Ann Drive
                              New Orleans, LA 70116
                              August 28, 19--


        Mr. Ed Robinson
        Word Processing, Inc.
        45 Sherwood Forest Drive
        Baton Rouge, LA 70815

        Dear Mr. Robinson

             Thank you.  I accept your offer of a position in
        your word-processing center.

             Enclosed are the forms you requested as well as
        the report from my physical examination.  I will be
        happy to bring any other information that you require.

             Again, I appreciate your interviewing me and
        choosing me for the job.  The other members of your
        firm that I met were especially gracious.  I feel
        privileged to be affiliated with your organization.

                              Sincerely

                              Jane White

                              Jane White
```

Figure 12—19
Your letter accepting the job offer.

tone. You should give a reason for your refusal, refer to the positive aspects of the company, and end with a friendly note of appreciation.

When your job quest has been successful, you will receive a letter similar to the one shown in Figure 12–18 indicating that you have been hired. Notice that this letter confirms the position, the date you are expected to report, and your salary. Then you may write your acceptance letter, similar to the one in Figure 12–19. This good-news letter should begin by accepting the job in the first sentence and end with a courteous statement of appreciation. Your acceptance letter should reinforce your selection as the right person for the job.

Summary

A persuasive technique is your key to your successful job application from its conception or research to your final placement. Your résumé, your application letter, your application blank, your interview, and your follow-up letters all serve specific purposes and build your detailed application package.

Questions for Discussion

1. "*You* are the commodity in your application package." Discuss this statement and show how it affects the various parts of the application package.

2. Discuss the purpose and importance of the application letter.

3. List the parts of the application package and discuss why each one is important.

4. Discuss the difference between solicited applications and unsolicited applications in terms of your application letter.

5. The commodity, the market, and the sales promotion are parts of the application process. Discuss each one and point out how it fits into the whole process.

6. List and discuss the four "A's" of the application letter.

7. Why is it important to create a good impression in all stages of your application procedure?

8. Why should you indicate your point of contact in your application letter?

9. Discuss the importance of applying for a definite position.

10. How can you convey your awareness of the needs of the company?

11. Why is all work experience important?

12. Discuss ways of presenting personal qualifications and human-interest images that portray you as a more valuable employee than other applicants. Explain how these procedures help to increase interest and create desire on the part of your prospective employer.

13. What should you include in the closing paragraph of an application letter? Why?

14. Explain why a positive tone and the "you-attitude" are important in writing an application letter.

15. What is the purpose of the data sheet or résumé?

16. List at least four categories to be included in the data sheet and discuss each category.

17. Discuss the importance of good organization of your data sheet.

18. Describe the conventional form of a data sheet.

19. Data sheets with unusual layouts may get attention. When is it appropriate to use an unconventional form?

20. "Your data sheet is employee-oriented." Explain this statement.

21. Newer discrimination laws do not necessitate your disclosing certain personal information. How can answering some of these questions be beneficial to you?

22. Sometimes you may benefit by listing educational qualifications before experience, and sometimes you may want to list experience first. What determines the order of these two parts of your data sheet or résumé?

23. Your educational attainments may be one of the best indexes of your job potential. Why is this true?

24. As a beginning worker, significant minor experience should be included in your data sheet or résumé. When should you include this experience, and why?

25. Explain the importance of being involved in extracurricula activities in terms of your job application.

26. Some personal interests and activities should not be included on the data sheet. What are they, and why should they not be shown?

27. Discuss the two ways of handling the reference section of the data sheet.

28. Why should you ask a person's permission to use his or her name as a reference?

29. List and discuss at least four ways to keep your data sheet from landing in the corporate wastebasket.

30. Why is the application letter employee-oriented and the application blank employer-oriented?

31. "Application blanks take into consideration your ability to follow instructions." Explain why this statement is true.

32. How is the application blank similar to the data sheet? How is it different?

33. List and discuss at least five steps you may follow to help in filling in an application blank.

34. Your ability to fill in an application blank correctly may be indicative of your ability to fulfill the requirements of the job. Explain.

35. Discuss the purpose of the interview.

36. Why is it important to know what type of interview to expect, the exact time and place of the interview, and the interviewer's full name and the correct pronunciation?

37. How can you mentally prepare for an interview?

38. How can you physically prepare yourself for an interview?

39. List and discuss ten of the basic rules for conducting yourself in an application interview.

40. You should be prepared to answer at least one surprise question. What is the best way to handle surprise questions?

41. Discuss at least two items you should take with you to an interview. Why should you take them?

42. What is the purpose of a follow-up letter as part of your total application procedure?

43. What are the advantages of preparing a data sheet or résumé before writing a letter of application? After writing a letter of application?

44. Explain how your résumé, your application letter, your application blank, your interview, and your follow-up letters all serve as specific parts to build your detailed application package.

Exercises

Write a critical analysis of the following sentences. Then, strengthen them by making the necessary corrections.

1. Because of the serious illness of my wife and the expense of raising three preschool children, I need a job. Please give me an interview on Monday, May 23, 19—.

2. You advertised a job for a salesman in Sunday's *Gazette.* I am the person for the position.

3. As you know, business people must relate with each other. I can. (Used as the opening statement.)

4. I know that you will agree that I can handle any job in the area of business administration.

5. Although I have had no experience in marketing, I am willing to learn. My marketing degree plus my personal observation of the work of my friends in this field should qualify me for the job.

6. Although I know that changing jobs is risky, I am willing to accept the challenge of a job with your new, unknown firm.

7. I know that I can fulfill your requirements, but I am interested in the salary and fringe benefits your company offers.

8. My references will prove that I am the person you need. You may contact them if you are considering me for the job.

9. Please consider me as an applicant for any job you have open at Gulf's States.

10. I shall expect you to write me at the above address for an interview.

11. Compose two opening paragraphs for an application letter. Write the first one for a solicited application. Write the second one for an unsolicited application.

12. Write an effective closing paragraph for one of the application letters in exercise 11.

13. You have had experience in the college bookstore. You are applying for a job in sales. Write a paragraph showing how this part-time experience will help you meet the requirements of a sales position for the XYZ Publishing Company.

14. Assume that you are a graduate with a degree in business administration. You have taken enough courses for a minor in accounting. The job you want is that of an entry-level accountant with a CPA firm. Write a letter showing how your education can fit the needs of this position.

15. As a student anticipating graduation next semester, you have been a leader in several business, civic, and student-government organizations. You desire a position as a public-relations assistant with the ABC Advertising Agency. Write a paragraph about your activities to show your abilities in human relations and working with people and relate your extracurricular activities to the requirements of this position in public relations.

16. Because you plan an intensive job-hunting campaign, you do not want your references contacted by every company to which you apply. Write a paragraph showing that your references are available upon request.

17. Because a primary purpose of your application letter is to get an interview, write a paragraph asking for an appointment with a prospective employer. Make it easy for the employer to contact you.

18. Visit several companies in which you are interested. Secure application blanks. Make copies of these to complete in rough-draft form. Then, neatly type and submit the original to the company for which you prefer to work.

19. You have had considerable experience in marketing as you have worked in your father's store and accompanied him to market many times during the past five years. You are applying for a job in marketing. Use your experience to show that you have an awareness of the needs of a buyer. Write a paragraph to convince the prospective employer that your education as well as your experience would be helpful to this company.

20. You have excellent skills in secretarial procedures and will receive your degree in office administration. Your avocation is music. You have performed frequently with university choral and concert groups serving as their accompanist. An excellent opportunity for an executive secretary, which also requires occasional part-time selling, is open at Hebrew's Music Corporation. In a letter to this company, show how your education, avocation, and achievements make you a desirable person for this job.

21. As an outstanding student with a grade point average of 3.8 out of a possible 4.0, you are able to secure the recommendation of your college professors. You have also been extremely active in campus, civic, and religious organizations. Many persons have offered to help you in obtaining a job. Write a paragraph in which you choose and list references that are willing to recommend you.

22. You are interviewing for a position with the Bank of the Rock Insurance Company as a prospective accountant. Decide and list the apparel you would wear for the interview.

Business Situations

1. Assume that a $1,000 scholarship is available to an agri-business major with a 3.5 grade point average. This person must be a college junior who lives on a farm and is actively engaged in part-time agricultural work. Assume that you meet these qualifications. Type a scholarship application letter to the Future Agriculture Leaders, Inc., 2013 Midtown Street, Sulphur, LA 70663. Attach a data sheet emphasizing your educational achievements and qualifications first; then indicate your experience and other qualifications. (In your letter, use the modified block form and mixed punctuation. Use the traditional data-sheet form.)

2. Apply for a summer job in an area in which you feel qualified. Consider your major field of study, your educational qualifications, and any experience you may have had. Be truthful. Write your letter of application emphasizing part-time experience, if possible. List the college courses you have completed in this area and related courses you have taken. Prepare an interesting data sheet that represents you well.

3. Write a solicited application letter in answer to an advertisement in a newspaper or trade journal. You may assume that you are completing your university's requirements for a degree. Select an advertisement for a position for which you are qualified. Although you may assume the completion of educational goals, you should be truthful and realistic when reporting all other aspects. Include a data sheet that will attract attention to you as one of many persons answering this advertisement. (Use the AMS letter form with open punctuation.)

4. Compose and type an unsolicited application letter to a large company that has frequent vacancies. Assume that you have completed educational goals in a field such as management, marketing, or advertising. Include a data sheet that will convey your creativity. Be truthful concerning all personal aspects except the completion of educational qualifications.

5. Assume that you are in your last semester or quarter of school and are seeking a job in the field of your choice. You have learned from a professor in your major field, who will recommend you, that a suitable job is available for you. In order to compete with others who desire this position, you must write a letter of application and send a data sheet that refers to your qualifications and to the specific position for which you are applying. When you write this solicited letter of application, assume your educational requirements are completed. Use extreme block form with open punctuation. Include your return address; address your letter to a person in the company; be specific, concrete, correct, and careful. Use factual experience and information except for educational qualifications. Compose and type the most tabular and concrete form of data sheet you can.

6. Assume that you have worked in your present position (the one chosen in situation 5) for five or more years. You have obtained additional educational training as well. However, the position you hold offers little chance for growth. Therefore, you plan to seek another similar position that offers advancement. In fact, you are applying for a position with a competitive firm. Write an application letter and a data sheet that will show your additional experience and education qualifying you for this job that would advance you in your career goals.

7. Assume that you have had an interview for the position in situation 6. You consider the interview to have been somewhat successful. Write a thank-you letter that will not only express your appreciation but will also remind the prospective employer of your application.

8. Assume that you were chosen for the job for which you applied. Write an appreciative acceptance letter to the company.

9. Assume that you have been offered a job for which you applied. You have decided to accept another position that you consider better. Write a refusal letter using a positive tone and expressing appreciation for the interview.

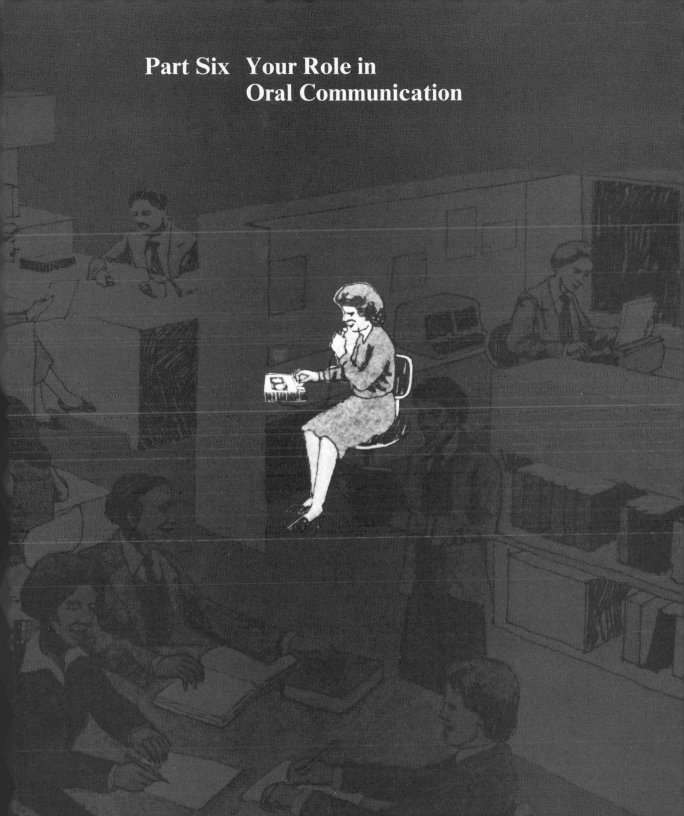

**Part Six Your Role in
Oral Communication**

Chapter 13 Speaking in the Business Environment

".   .   all the thefts and embezzlements that corporations suffer each year do not cost the economy as much as verbal incompetence." — Edwin A. Locke, Jr.

The study of human communication, as discussed in Chapter 1, has a long and dignified history. From the time of the ancient Greeks and Romans, effective oral communication has been a source of concern to civilized communities. To indicate how involved modern society is in all areas of communication, a recent survey showed that most people spend approximately 75 percent of their waking hours in listening and speaking situations.

The major portion—twelve chapters—of *Business Communication* has been devoted to written communication. Now, turn your attention to some oral aspects of business communication. You have been communicating orally in one way or another since shortly after you were born. Even before you uttered your first word, you were transmitting messages to other people. Your earliest needs for food or attention were met because you were able to convey to someone what you wanted through noises or nonverbal means.

That people need to communicate is undeniable. They must communicate in order to accomplish tasks—to work or to play. In today's world, human beings are interdependent. Think about this! What do you enjoy doing alone? You need others to help you do nearly everything. All communication springs from this fundamental need. No one can exist without communicating with others. Even when you want solitude, you must effectively communicate this message. So you are always actively involved in the process of communication with others.

Human beings must communicate.

When you need something or when you just want to be heard, you let others know. Perhaps you want a cup of coffee, you need information about car insurance, you wish someone would go jogging with you; whatever the situation, you are communicating.

If you are a part of the business world, you may be asked to explain some new equipment to your associates, to give an informative speech, to report on product research you have done. You may be asked to lead a conference or participate in one, to present an award, or to preside at a seminar.

Even though you express yourself to others in many ways, to most people, speech is their most important means of communication. The authors of an oral communication textbook made this observation: "Most people are sadly inadequate in situations that make more than minimal demands on their capacity to communicate."[1] The actual cost of oral miscommunication would be difficult to measure, but the fact that such a statement was made indicates the severity of the problem.

Effective oral communication can no longer be taken for granted, even as we can no longer take for granted that the air we breathe is fresh. In the swift-paced, crowded, and multifaceted world we live in, verbal utterance that are meaningless, misdirected, and inaccurate will only compound misunderstanding and confusion. As you strive to acquire a more effective method of oral communication, explore some of the areas that will help you improve this skill.

Oral communication is a skill that can be improved.

Oral or Written Communication?

Writing and speaking go hand in hand in most business environments. They can be used separately or in combination to help you achieve your objectives. However, some differences between the two exist. As you focus on oral communication, you will find the understanding of these differences beneficial.

Understanding writing and speaking helps you to communicate more effectively.

When you are writing, you can spend more time formulating your ideas. You may take two days to compose an answer to a request from a friendly competitor concerning your company's impending advertising campaign. If you were attending a convention and the same person asked about the plans, you would need to answer without taking time to plan what and how you should respond.

Because written communication can be studied with an eye for correctness, most people try to produce a manuscript that will stand up under the closest scrutiny. How correct should the mechanics of your oral communication be as compared to those of your written communication—grammar, punctuation, etc.? Can you recall how many times you or someone else has checked oral work? Very seldom is oral communication checked for accuracy. But when your thoughts and ideas have been uttered, they are stored in your mind

[1] James H. McBurney and Ernest J. Wrage, *Guide to Good Speech*, 3rd Ed. (Englewood Cliffs, N.J.: Prentice-Hall, 1965), p.1.

and in the minds of your receivers. The next time you are involved in a heavy discussion, listen closely to what is said. You will notice that the language standards in a discussion are much more flexible than the ones for writing. But you will also notice that spoken words can change minds and spur listeners to action. The spoken words of a Winston Churchill or an Adolph Hitler can change the course of history.

Written communication is more exact.

During oral communication, you receive immediate feedback. This response exists whether you are in a one-on-one situation or whether you are speaking before a group. With an immediate response—either nonverbal or verbal—you as the transmitter can take action to change your position or to correct a miscommunication. If you are attuned to the situation and your listeners, feedback enables you to utilize your whole personality and behavior to communicate more effectively with your audience. Messages that are transmitted by wire, telegrams, or cablegrams may be read minutes after they are written; routine letters, hopefully, are received and read in a day or two. In written communication, feedback is slow at best. You have only the written words to evaluate. The immediate feedback from oral communication helps the sender determine if the correct message has been received.

Immediate feedback helps.

In some cases a written document does not communicate the real you to the recipient. Many people think they can judge sincerity better in a face-to-face situation. When you are speaking, your actions speak *with* your words. Certainly you would be more effective if you asked your employer for a raise than you would if you wrote a request.

Are you a good actor?

Written and oral communication work together in the business world. A union does its negotiating with management concerning a new contract. The two parties sit down and talk until compromises and agreements have been reached. The new version of the contract is written, and both sides leave the bargaining table. The union representative takes the written document to the union membership and verbally explains the terms as they have been written—management does the same.

Best friends: the written and spoken word.

Types of Presentations

Four principal methods of delivering speeches are employed in our society today: impromptu delivery, speaking extemporaneously, reading from a manuscript, and memorization. However, you will more often use only two—impromptu and extemporaneous speaking. These two will be discussed in detail. Then, because the busi-

ness world revolves around the conference table, the area of conference communication will be explored.

Impromptu Speaking

Special knowledge equals impromptu presentations.

If you are asked to speak on the spur of the moment without advance notice or time for specific preparation, you will be giving an impromptu speech. Usually you will have some general knowledge on the subject. Many times, because of your special knowledge or experience, you will be called upon to say a few words. To help you handle the situation effectively, you might find it advantageous to have a mental outline ready. This type of preparation could save you from being caught completely off guard.

No magic formula is available to help you become a skillful impromptu speaker. However, since business people often find themselves in this type of speaking situation, these suggestions may help you communicate more effectively.

1. If you think you might be called on for an impromptu speech, try to second-guess the situation. Have your mental outline ready.

2. Use your experience as the focal point of your remarks. You will be more relaxed if you feel confident in what you are communicating.

3. Be brief. The more concise your remarks, the less chance you have to make mistakes.

4. Avoid overexposure. When you have made your point, quit. You may feel that you have not said enough or that your remarks were very successful, but do not be tempted to rattle on until your effective communication is destroyed.

5. Keep on track. If you lose your trend of thought, summarize. A quick review many times can help you regain your direction.

6. Decline. If you have nothing to say, then don't. As Abraham Lincoln said: "Better to remain silent and be thought a fool than to speak out and remove all doubt."

Extemporaneous Speaking

Prepare thoroughly. Be yourself.

Most speeches are presented in a relatively informal and flexible situation and are seldom governed by rigid rules of procedure. The types of speeches usually given on these occasions are unmemorized ones that you have prepared in advance. You prepare thoroughly, but you avoid rote delivery. What you actually do is rely upon your resources to supply the appropriate words at the moment you speak. The best extemporaneous speech you can give is built on a solid foundation of rigorous preparation. From this basis you will find the freedom, flexibility, and spontaneity to adapt your speech to the signals you will receive from your audience.

There are five key steps to remember in presenting an extemporaneous speech:

1. Select a subject in which you are interested and that you want to share with your audience.

2. Formulate your outline.

3. Prepare early. Start well ahead of the date you are to speak so you can sift through your ideas and discard the ones you will not need.

4. After you have formed your outline, practice. Practice by yourself in front of a mirror. Practice before a friend or a member of your family. Remember your purpose for making the presentation and the audience that will be listening—practice with these in mind.

5. Be yourself. Share your ideas and information with your audience. Keep your presentation relaxed and let your ideas flow.

Techniques of Delivery

The skills needed for delivering a speech are very similar to those you use in daily conversation. As with writing, the skill of effective oral communication can be acquired. As with other skills, effective speaking takes practice and preparation. One idea that might make your speaking easier is to remember that your audience is not expecting a performance. In a business setting you are only expected to produce usable information. However, you want to ensure that your message is received favorably and with interest. Several techniques will help you to share your ideas with your audience more effectively.

Practice and preparation are the keys.

Eye Contact

In order to communicate effectively, you must have some type of contact with the person(s) with whom you are communicating. One direct method of contact with your audience is through the eyes. When you talk with your friends, you look at them. You don't shuffle your feet, wring your hands, or look at a spot on the wall behind them. If you want to communicate with your audience,

Eye contact is a must.

make eye contact. Look at your audience as you share your ideas. Meet one person's eyes, then slowly move your head and make eye contact with another person. As you speak, continue to move your eyes over the group making contact with one person and then another.

The results are feedback.

Maintain eye contact and your audience will relate to you and your subject. This technique will provide you with important feedback. As your eyes move across the group, you will be able to detect what type of response you are getting. You will immediately know whether your reception is good or whether you have lost your audience's interest. Eye contact can do a great deal to strengthen an inept presentation, and an otherwise effective presentation can become dry and dull without it.

Posture

Do you remember when you were a kid and your mother insisted, "Hold your shoulders up!" Your mother knew that good posture would give you a better physical appearance and, at the same time, give your body a better opportunity to develop properly. Correct posture conveys a positive message to your audience. Mentally, the audience is saying, "Here is a speaker who is alert and interesting." A speaker with this positive technique also says, "I know what I'm talking about."

Eye contact and gestures help your audience share your ideas. Gary W. Cralle/ Freelance Photo Guild.

You probably know when you are standing or sitting correctly. But do you know when you are guilty of poor posture? Most people do not. Practice good posture all the time; then, when you have an occasion to speak, you will not have a problem. However, speakers have to be careful to avoid a studied posture. When you appear artificial and stiff, you are less appealing to your audience.

Stand straight and convey self-confidence.

Gestures and Movement

No special rules exist for making gestures or movements. The important rule is *be yourself.* If you are to be effective, you must be natural and comfortable. If you use gestures in normal conversation, you will be perfectly natural in using them in your speech. If you force yourself or use an unnatural gesture, your audience will recognize it, and your presentation will lose some of its punch. Most gestures do not have a definite meaning. A lowered head can indicate a moment of reverence or it can signify defiance.

Be natural.

Avoid excessive gestures or movements. Most business talks are crisp, but low key. Too much motion distracts from your presentation, and it also has a tendency to make your audience uncomfortable. Never pace up and down. Who is interested in listening to a "caged tiger"? If space is available, you might take a few steps to one side or the other; however, avoid turning your back to the audience. If you find you are not comfortable moving around, you can add some variety of movement by changing the angle at which you face your audience.

Create interest.

Hands! What should you do with them? You must find some place for them so you are comfortable. A lectern is a safe place to rest them, but don't lean on or clutch it. Perhaps the best advice is, "Don't have anything in your hands unless the item is needed for your speech." Even though you are not aware of playing with an object in your hands, the audience will notice. When you finish using the piece of chalk or anything else, put it down. Nervous hands are distracting.

Hands can be your ally.

In this age of advanced technology, many organizations have a video-tape unit as part of their equipment. If your company has such a unit, have an associate tape your presentation. Someone else can be more objective than you, so, if at all possible, have your colleague critique the tape with you. Be especially careful to see that your gestures and movements help you in delivering your message. If your company does not have video equipment, ask one of your associates to observe you and to offer criticism.

Voice

People who give business presentations are not expected to have professional voice qualities, but your voice is an instrument in putting your ideas across. You need to be heard, and your words need to be understood. Most people can give an adequate presentation; however, a few people might have special problems and should seek the help of a professional speech therapist.

Analyze your voice.

Most voice problems can be helped through self-analysis. Use a tape recorder to help you assess the quality and adequacy of your voice. Listen and analyze these voice qualities.

1. Volume. How well will your audience hear you? Will they have to strain to hear, or will they wish they had ear plugs? Do you need a sound system?

2. Pitch. Is your voice too high? A high-pitched voice will cause listeners to become disinterested. A moderately low voice is the most pleasing. If the pitch of your voice needs correcting, you change it by concentrated practice.

3. Tone. How is the tone of your voice? Your tone reflects your attitudes and feelings. Your listeners will know whether you are sincere and honest, how you feel about them, and if you are interested in your topic. Think about what you are saying, and adjust your tone to your ideas. By your tone ye shall be known.

4. Tempo. What about your tempo? Tempo is the rate of speed at which you deliver your talk. Tempo can present a problem because you want to speak slowly enough for your listeners to understand but fast enough to keep them from falling asleep. Vary your rate of speaking with the type of information you are presenting. Pauses will add emphasis and variation. However, be careful not to pause at a point that does not add to your message. An inappropriate pause can cause your listener's attention to fly away.

Appearance

Your physical appearance often determines whether your audience is going to listen to you. A good appearance is associated with success. If you convey the message of success with your appearance, your audience will be ready to listen to you. The person who radiates success is dressed appropriately, is well groomed, is alert, and has good posture.

Many people who speak in a business environment feel that their appearance is insignificant because of the importance of what they have to say. Remember that you are seen before you are heard and that before you begin to speak, the audience has already been affected by your appearance. As you know, human beings are very critical. When you walk before a group, you can be sure that every person is looking you over and sizing you up. You won't have a chance to defend your choice of clothing.

Visual and Auditory Media

"A picture is worth a thousand words." For this reason many speakers use visual information in their presentations. Communicating effectively with just the spoken word is very difficult. Statistics show that when words alone are used, an estimated 90 percent of the message is misinterpreted or entirely forgotten. A good presentation with effective visual assistance far outshines a good presentation without visuals. Visuals can depict clearly and quickly ideas that are difficult to convey orally. In addition, visual media create interest, generate variety, increase impact, and save time.

Visuals enhance the message.

However, effective visuals require preparation and creative thought. They can also divert attention away from your message and can be very costly. If they are not properly handled, the results can become a simple flop or a total disaster.

Visual and auditory media and equipment—charts, maps, graphs, diagrams, pictures, cartoons, posters, slides, transparencies, tape recorders, overhead projectors, models, and objects used for demonstration—work with you by reinforcing your words. Research indicates that retention can be increased as much as 50 percent with the use of visuals. Remember the following points as you plan your presentation and the visual assistance you will use.

Visuals are supports.

1. *Use the visuals as a supplement.* Visuals should be used to support the purpose of your presentation. They are a means, not an end. Never include them for their own sake. If your listeners feel that you are simply parading a set of gimmicks, you will lose their respect as well as their interest. Perhaps the best advice is: don't crowd your presentation with visuals, and *never* use them as padding.

2. *Plan simple and understandable visuals.* If your explanation or the visual information itself is so complex that you lose your audience, the visual is more harmful than helpful. The purpose of your visuals should be easily and quickly recognized by your audience. Do not become involved with equipment so technical that you cannot use it effectively. Keep everything as simple as possible.

Keep visuals simple.

Know your equipment.

3. *Synchronize visuals with your presentation.* Many times speakers find themselves competing with their visuals. To be effective, your visual should be seen at the right time. If you are too early, it will distract from what you are saying; if you are too late, it be-

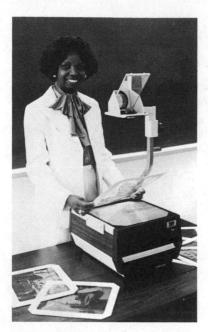

Figure 13—1
An overhead projector and transparencies ready for use.
Courtesy of 3M Company.

comes just something to show and not something that will add to your presentation.

4. *Check to be sure equipment is operating properly.* Equipment that does not function properly is an abomination to effective oral communication. Your presentation is coordinated; your first visual is a transparency. You turn the overhead projector on, and pop! If you have one of the new model projectors (as shown in Figure 13–1), you simply flip a switch to move the stand-by lamp into position, and your presentation goes on without interruption. However, if you have an older model, you should always have an extra bulb ready and know how to install it. If you are using slides, be certain they will project right side up and in correct order. Go through your entire presentation using your equipment. This practice will help you feel comfortable and can alert you to an unforeseen problem that might arise.

5. *Make sure your visuals can be seen by all of your audience.* Visuals should be clear and sharp. Even those sitting on the back row should be able to see without eye strain. Nothing is quite as distracting to a spectator as visual information that cannot be seen clearly.

You are a member of a visually oriented society. Use visuals in your presentation if they will help to convey your message. By simultaneously seeing and hearing your message, others can understand your ideas more easily and thus hopefully you can avoid miscommunication.

The Audience

Communication takes two.

"It takes two to speak truth—one to speak and another to hear." So the writer-philosopher Thoreau accurately stated one of the basic principles of effective communication—the process is a cooperative venture and requires a speaker with a purpose and one or more active listeners.

The speaker has the responsibility to present the topic in a way that will stimulate the attention and interest of the audience. Speaking is not a solo act, but is a combined effort of the speaker and the listeners. The audience—the listeners—should be fully aware of the speaker's purpose in making the presentation, and together they should fully participate in the sharing of information. To establish this sharing, speakers might consider several questions about their audience:

1. What are the audience's general characteristics?

2. What experiences and background do you and your audience share?

3. Will your audience be free to react to your presentation, or will something beyond your control affect their mood?

4. What is the occasion? How will you be received? How will your subject be received?

General Characteristics

Knowing the general characteristics of your audience should help you to predict how they will react to your message. Different factors—socioeconomic status, regions of the country, and climatic conditions—may pull people in diverse directions. However, beware of stereotyped thinking: women are more easily persuaded than men; senior citizens are less easy to persuade than teenagers. Try to develop a relationship built around your knowledge of the audience's general characteristics and your message.

Know your audience.

The size of your group can have an effect on your presentation. Certain topics and approaches are more effective when they are presented to a small group; others are more appropriate before a large group. The size of the group will influence the type and variety of visuals presented. And naturally, you will adjust your vocal and physical delivery to accommodate your audience. The formality of the occasion will also be affected by the number in the audience, the smaller the group, the less formal the situation.

Is group size important?

The educational level of the group is another item you will want to consider. Will you be talking to unskilled workers, skilled workers, white-collar workers, or top management? As an accomplished speaker, you will recognize that the ability of these groups to assimilate material may be vastly different. Remember to always gear your presentation to the lowest level of your group.

Although physical surroundings do not constitute a general characteristic of the audience, they represent an important factor that can have a decided effect on the audience, the speaker, and, consequently, the presentation. Attention to the seating arrangement, ventilation, lighting, and the sound system can help to provide a conducive atmosphere for a presentation. If the room is too hot or too cold or if your audience cannot hear you, you will have trouble getting and keeping their attention. If possible, check the meeting place before the scheduled time and make it as pleasant as possible.

Physical surroundings are important.

Background and Experience

Speak to your audience.

You may be a specialist in the subject you are presenting, but what is the level of knowledge of your listeners? To be an effective communicator you should know the background and experience of your audience. This knowledge can be used to help them understand your subject. A homogeneous group will not pose the same problems as a heterogeneous group. In working with the latter, you will need to provide more background information in order to arouse the interest of almost everyone.

In speaking to a group that is not familiar with your field or speciality, you might try a technique similar to that used by a certified public accountant. This professional was speaking to a group of homemakers. Realizing that many members of the audience would not understand such terms as *asset, liability,* and *capital,* simpler terms were used to help make the presentation easier to understand. When a discussion of assets was introduced, the speaker asked, "What do you own?" In working with liabilities, the question was posed, "What do you owe?" And when capital was introduced, "How much are you worth?" At the end of the presentation, the audience was just as interested as at the beginning—what could be easier for a homemaker to understand than *own, owe,* and *worth.* Many accountants might have delivered the same type of speech to the same audience and lost the group at the very beginning with the use of technical accounting terms.

Mood

Situations and events affect your presentation.

Many times the circumstances under which your speech is given will affect your audience. Perhaps a natural catastrophe has just occurred in your locality. A tornado hit a trailer park ten miles from your office building. Several lives were lost, and property damage was estimated in the millions. Will your audience feel the same as they did before the tornado? You are invited to speak at a conference; you are first on the program. You have been asked to deliver the concluding speech at a three-day seminar. Will your position on the program have an effect on the approach you use? The effective communicator will be aware of the audience's mood and adapt to the existing circumstances.

Speakers who want to communicate know as much about their audience as possible. As a business person who fits into this category, you will do most of your analyzing before your presentation. However, you will be cognizant of the fact that you will be analyzing the group as you give your speech and that you will make adaptations whenever you feel a need. Failure on your part to make desirable changes might make an otherwise well-organized and well-delivered speech ineffective.

The Occasion

The subject and the material to be used in the presentation are greatly influenced by the occasion. Are you to conduct a sales meeting or deliver a safety talk? Perhaps you have been invited by a local service club to explain your company's new antipollution policy. You may be asked to say a few words at the annual retirement banquet or to welcome the new staff members in an orientation program. Each of these presentations requires a different approach. Whatever the situation do not underestimate the impact the occasion can have on your topic and on the material you will use.

The occasion determines the approach.

Your Reception

When you face an audience, you want to know how you are being received. If possible, establish a rapport with them. If your reputation is known and the audience has confidence in you, then you will not have to be concerned with your reception. If you are not known or if the climate of the meeting is unfriendly, you may find it necessary to spend some time at the beginning of your speech winning the confidence of your listeners. Once the right atmosphere has been established, your audience will be more interested in and more receptive to what you have to say.

How do you establish this receptive atmosphere? Here are three suggestions:

1. Use some of your most interesting material at the beginning of your speech. Good information will command the audience's attention.

2. Use stories and illustrations that will indirectly tell your audience that you have expertise in your field. Statements such as these may qualify you indirectly as an authority: "during my twelve years in personnel, my workers have . . . ," or "the safety committee on which I serve has helped to establish . . . ."

3. Quote experts with whom your audience is familiar, and relate your ideas to their expertise. For example, if your presentation concerns investments, you might say: "Sylvia Porter and Richard Janaway are in accord with me that United States Savings Bonds will not bring the best return for your money."

Your Subject's Reception

You may think you have the most interesting subject in the world. But that does not mean your audience is going to be as enthusiastic. Audience attitude can create a serious problem for you. Never underestimate or overestimate the interest of your group. Audiences can be interested and believe in your idea, or they can be disinterested, hostile, or somewhere in between.

If the people in your audience are *interested* and believe in what you are presenting, background information will be less necessary. You will want to intensify their beliefs and move them to action. To accomplish this purpose, your material should be chosen with this objective in mind—you do not want to present material they already know. Usually an interested audience is easy to communicate with.

If your audience is *neutral,* the first thing you should do is to arouse their interest. The action or idea that you are trying to sell may be accomplished in one presentation, or it may involve several presentations. You may be trying to reorganize the procedures in the purchasing department. This change can mean fewer forms for the whole company. In the first meeting, you might establish the need for the change in procedures; in the next presentation, show the advantages of the new procedure; finally, you might tie the presentations together and sell the group on the reorganization. However you approach the situation, your first objective is to create interest.

The most difficult audience to speak to is the one that is *opposed* to your idea. This situation is very difficult and must be handled carefully. A very effective move in handling an opposing audience is to begin with areas in which you agree before moving into the areas of disagreement. If you will analyze your audience's reasons for disagreeing, you will often find that prejudice plays a major role in their position. Keeping this fact in mind, you might find it advisable to answer all possible objections at the beginning of your presentation rather than to open with positive statements. After you have answered all of the objections, you should find it possible to move on to more positive action. However, the best method of handling any objections is through a thorough and honest consideration of all ideas.

The above discussion of the various characteristics of your audience is primarily applicable in extemporaneous speaking situations, but some type of quick assessment should be made of the audience when you speak in impromptu situations. The more skillful you become in audience analysis, the more easily and quickly you will be able to evaluate your audience.

Is the audience interested in the topic?

Be honest. Explore all ideas.

Organizing Your Presentation

Planning is the key to success for any business. You, an oral communicator, share a common need with the company president, the district director of sales, or the office manager. The president needs carefully planned long- and short-term financing if the company is to grow and expand; the district director needs well-planned sales campaigns if the district is to meet its quota for the company; the office manager needs well-planned and efficient operating procedures if the work is to move smoothly. You, as an effective communicator, need a logical and carefully organized plan to follow in preparing your presentation.

Plan first.

Previous to most presentations, an effective business speaker will follow a definite plan in getting ready to communicate. As you become more skilled in the art of communicating orally, you probably will find that less time and attention is needed for advance preparation. However, wise speakers are seldom unprepared—no matter how many times they find themselves before an audience.

Even the experienced speaker prepares.

In organizing for an oral presentation you should
1. determine your purpose
2. gather the necessary materials
3. develop and outline your presentation
4. polish your speech.

Determine Your Purpose

Effective speakers first determine the general purpose for their presentation. Oral presentations are given to inform, to persuade, and to entertain—or a combination of these. After the general purpose has been established, a decision must be made about the specific purpose. To help achieve this objective, ask yourself the question: "What do I want my listeners to know at the conclusion of my presentation?"

Why are you giving this presentation?

If you are interested in marketing, you might start your speech preparation with the general purpose: informing your audience about marketing. The general subject of marketing is much too broad an area for a presentation. What specifically do you want your listeners to know about marketing? Your specific purpose could be to inform the group about the latest ideas resulting from market research on coffee and tea. The more specifically you state what you are going to present, the more systematically and intelligently your preparation can be made. Of course, the end result will be an interesting and informative speech.

Gather the Necessary Materials

Once you have decided your specific purpose, you must begin to locate and collect the materials and the details that will be included in your speech. Keep in mind that this material should closely relate to your topic and your specific audience. If your investigation turns up less information on the subject than you had expected, you will have to make the necessary adjustments in your speech plan.

The range of material you can use is vast. You may draw on your own knowledge and expertise. You may do serious research in the library (as discussed in Chapter 9) or you may simply skim a magazine article for an idea. Perhaps you will search through company records for a presentation designed to highlight the company's sales record. You may interview fellow workers and local experts for the preparation of a persuasive speech dealing with pollution control. Whatever your sources, you can present only what you know and remember. You must develop some form of acquiring information in an organized way so you can accurately pass it along to your listeners.

The information and material you collect will be used to support, to clarify, and to reinforce your presentation. If you are thorough in gathering your material, your speech will be more informative, more believable, and consequently more interesting.

Be thorough and objective.

Develop and Outline Your Presentation

When you first started thinking about your presentation, you decided on the general purpose, selected a specific topic, and then gathered the materials. Now you must develop the normal parts of the speech—the introduction, the body, and the conclusion—and fit these parts into an outline.

Body

Most professional speakers find it easier to work on the body of their presentation first. They find that after they have gathered their material they can concentrate on the main points to include in their speech. Select your main points. You derive these from your central and specific purposes. When you write your outline, these main points become your major headings. Your main points are the most important ideas you want to share with your audience. They should all be of the same importance and should not overlap or be repetitive. Be certain that your main points are brief, vivid, clear, important to your message, and stated to capture the interest and attention of your audience.

The heart of the speech.

After identifying your major points, select and organize the subpoints. These subpoints consist of information you have collected and organized to support your main points. Subpoints contribute strength, clarity, and substance to your presentation.

Subpoints support main points.

Everything you put into your speech should ultimately relate to the central purpose. Only if you present your materials in a consistent, comprehensive, logical, unified, and coherent manner can you hope that your listeners will follow and share in the achievement of your purpose.

An outline is to a speech what a pattern is to a tailor. A good, clear outline can help you discover mistakes, omissions, weaknesses, and superfluous information before your presentation. These suggestions may help you in constructing your outline.

An outline is a must.

1. Main points and subpoints are equal in importance as indicated by their number or letter in the outline.

2. Subpoints are directly related to their main point. They should be less important than the main point.

3. Each main point should express only one idea. Keep everything simple.

4. Each main point should be different; there should be no overlapping.

5. Proceed in an orderly, planned way.

If the body of your speech is organized efficiently, your audience will be able to follow you and understand all you say very easily. You will be communicating effectively.

Conclusion

After you have organized your supporting materials and established your main points, you are ready to prepare your conclusion. This part of your speech should provide your audience with a satisfying and effective culmination to your remarks. Your conclusion should reinforce the purpose of your presentation. Explicit directions can be given if you want your audience to take certain actions: "Write your representative about the pollution-control legislation. You will be handed a form letter as you leave the meeting room. All you have to do is fill in your representative's name and drop the letter in the mail chute." If your purpose is to inspire, you might need a more impressive conclusion. Here are four suggestions for developing an effective conclusion.

Listeners should feel satisfied.

1. *End forcefully.* Be certain that your ending reinforces your purpose. Use this moment to tie everything together.

2. *Do not introduce new information.* Instead, refer back to and emphasize your main points.

3. *Signal the end.* The audience needs some type of warning that you are about to conclude. A fast finish often leaves an audience

unsatisfied. You should close smoothly, and your tone should be very much like that of your speech—making it one unified message.

4. *Be positive.* Don't apologize for any of your shortcomings—maybe nobody noticed. Finish on the bright note that you enjoyed being with your audience.

Conclusions are generally shorter than either the introduction or the body. They serve to clarify and reinforce. Prepare your conclusion as carefully as the rest of your speech. And *quit while you are ahead.* Don't be guilty of ruining a good speech by an overly long, never-ending conclusion.

Introduction

Gain attention by offering a reason to listen.

The first few minutes—the introduction—of the presentation are extremely important. By planning your opening statements carefully, you gain your audience's attention, establish a reason for them to listen, create a need for them to know the information, and establish your own personal authority. After you have your audience's attention, you should clearly state your purpose. The majority of your listeners, especially in a business environment, are easier to talk to if they know what is going to happen. When the audience knows what your purpose is and what you plan to accomplish in your presentation, they are more likely to give you their complete attention and interest.

Good introductions relate to the subject.

A good introduction can be achieved in several different ways; regardless of your method, relate it directly to your subject. An unusual story concerning your problem in dressing for the meeting would be permissible, but only when you can relate the story to your topic. The same thing is true for humor. Although research is inconclusive, most experts in oral communication agree that if a speaker is going to use humor in the introduction of a speech (or in any other part), it should relate to the subject. Four suggestions to remember when you outline your introduction are:

1. Prepare for what will follow. Give the audience some idea about what they should listen for.

2. Establish the type of reaction you expect. Let the audience know what you expect them to do as the result of your message.

3. Avoid triteness. Strive for a fresh opening for your speech. Something new and different will let the audience know they are special to you.

4. Humor is unnecessary. Humor is *not* the only way to achieve rapport with your audience. If you must be humorous, be sure your audience will appreciate it.

Polish Your Speech

You have listened to presentations that seemed to be composed of totally different parts—parts that were completely unrelated. A well-organized, researched, and outlined speech that would do credit to any professional can become ineffective and a total disaster if the ideas and parts do not fit together. Your responsibility is to create a speech that flows from one part to the next with the use of properly placed techniques—pauses, gestures, voice inflections— and correctly used transitional words.

To keep your speech flowing smoothly, build bridges to your audience's understanding. Use clear transitions in moving from one point to another. Your presentation should convey completeness and should be coherent from beginning to end. As you know, every whole is divided into different parts. Your duty is to show your audience the connection between the parts as you move from one to the other. As an effective communicator, you may use transitional words and phrases similar to those in Table 13–1.

The list is incomplete, but you can readily understand that some words normally not considered important are vital to communication. Verbs, as you will recall, are the stars of the show, and nouns are their supporting players. However, most of the technical work is done by the little words listed below—and others like them. They enhance the flow and movement of your presentation. They show how ideas relate. Transitional words help you establish coherence and lead your audience in the direction that your thoughts are moving.

Transitions help the presentation to flow smoothly.

Table 13—1
Transitional Words and Phrases

accordingly	however
also	in the same way
and	moreover
as a result of	neither . . . nor
because	nevertheless
before	next
but	nonetheless
consequently	only
either . . . or	on the contrary
finally	so
for	still
for example	therefore
furthermore	thus
hence	

Words are not the only way you can direct your audience. The stress you place on words, the rate of your speech, the loudness of your voice, the pauses you make, the way you stand, and the gestures you use can help you to communicate effectively. Provide signposts for your listeners. Don't try to be subtle when you are switching from one aspect of your presentation to another—subtlety many times will just confuse your listeners. Why have a presentation if your audience cannot follow you?

Words can be signposts.

The Conference

One of management's most effective tools of communication is the conference. During the past two decades this tool has grown in importance and is helping management accomplish some communication objectives of the business community. A conference that operates properly and successfully combines the brainpower of those who attend for the purpose of searching out and finding solutions to the problems that confront the organization.

Conferences combine brainpower.

You will find that as a business person a great deal of your time is spent in group activities. Unfortunately, business people do not always know how to lead or participate in a conference. However, business and industry are making an effort to train their personnel in effective conference procedures. Management has learned that unless a conference is organized and operated efficiently, it can bog down in confusion and delay. Worse yet, it can end in arguments and dissention that can harm rather than help. As in all good planning, there are three stages to be organized.

Pre-Conference Activities

Certain activities must be performed before the conference begins.

Determine the Purpose
Key personnel should decide the purpose of the conference. Limitations should be established, and a clearly written purpose of the conference should be presented to those who will participate.

State the purpose in writing.

The purpose will indicate which one of the following types of conference will be held.

1. Informational—information is provided to everybody at the same time in the same way. Questions may be asked, and the information discussed, if necessary.

2. Problem Solving—the problem is presented, possible solutions are suggested and analyzed, and a final solution proposed.

3. Training—new skills, ideas, procedures, and methods are presented and discussed.

Select the Participants

Key personnel, keeping in mind the purpose of the conference, should determine who will participate. Only those people who can constructively contribute should be considered.

Only contributors are participants.

Arrange for Facilities

Everyone knows that a conference is to be held, but where? Arrangements should be made in advance for the room to be used. It should be large enough to hold the participants comfortably, but not so large that they are lost in it. Chairs and tables, if required, should be arranged to contribute to the conference. A round table stimulates discussion and makes note-taking easier. Check on the equipment that will be needed. Be sure the small details are worked out—keys, lighting, ventilation, refreshments. Nothing is as disagreeable as a locked conference room, no key, and a hall full of people.

Assemble the Necessary Materials

If special materials are to be handed to the participants at the beginning of or during the meeting, they should be ready. Be certain that the information is understandable and that each packet is complete. Supporting material might be needed during the conference. If so, this material should be available for ready reference. "When in doubt, bring it," is a good rule to follow in making decisions concerning material for a conference.

Choose the Conference Leader

The personnel that established the need for the conference should choose the leader. They should remember that the person who will be the most effective leader is the one who guides and directs—not the one who will be arbitrary or bossy. The leader must be able to create an environment of informality, but at the same time steer the meeting toward its goal.

Leaders guide and direct.

If you have been designated as a conference leader, you should do two things before the conference is held:

An *agenda* of the items to be discussed should be prepared. This agenda will help you to guide the meeting in the proper direction and will help to prepare those who will participate. The agenda should be sent or delivered to the participants several days in ad-

A written plan keeps business moving.

vance, generally not more than a week and not less than three days before. It should serve as a guide, something that is flexible.

Notify those involved as to the date, time, and place the conference will be held. An estimate of the amount of time to be spent in the conference would also be beneficial.

Activities During the Conference

Leader

The leader is responsible for keeping the conference in line. If the participants wander off the subject, gently bring them back to the topic by reminding them about the discussion.

Leaders have responsibilities.

Be sure that everyone has a chance to participate. Don't let one person dominate the whole conference. Watch for the person who interrupts; courteously remind him or her that another person has the floor.

Do not dominate the meeting yourself, and avoid giving your viewpoint too early. Let the participants comment on the ideas and suggestions that are proposed. If you are in the forefront, you might influence the outcome.

Listen, and keep the meeting moving. If you know what is being said, you can help make the meeting more productive by identifying the points and bringing them to the attention of the members. You can use the summarization technique to bring the group back into focus.

Appoint someone to keep the minutes. These minutes should summarize what was said, what was agreed upon, and what action was decided upon. Be sure time, place, date, and names of participants are included. (Chapter 14 discusses minutes in more detail.)

Participants

The conference leader has certain duties and responsibilities, but so do the participants. If you are a participant at a conference, prepare yourself to be an active one. Look over the agenda that was delivered to you. Think about what you will say. If you need material to strengthen your position, gather it. If visuals will help you to put your point across, have them ready. If you need copies of a statistical report, have enough for everyone. Be ready to work with the group instead of against it.

Participants have responsibilities.

Limits are generally not set on the amount of oral participation you are allowed during a conference discussion. If you have something to say, say it. Just be sure that your contribution is constructive, and give others the opportunity to express their views. Don't talk just to hear your own voice.

One of the key roles that you will play as a conference participant is that of listener. Actively participate by paying attention to the other members. Be alert and follow the ideas and suggestions of the others. As Harold P. Zelko said in his book *The Business Conference*: "Perhaps it should be remembered more that it is as valuable to absorb the other man's point of view as it is to expand on your own."[2] Zelko lists the participant's responsibilities:

1. Develop a proper attitude.
2. Have respect for other members of the group.
3. Help shape the goals and decisions of the meeting.
4. Participate appropriately.[3]

The success of a conference depends on both the leader and the participants. Both need to contribute actively. Norm Virag / Uniphoto.

Post-Conference Activities

After the conference, the leader has the responsibility of reporting the results of the conference. The personnel who were responsible for initiating the conference and each participant should receive a copy of the conference report. The participants should also be informed if there will be another meeting or if all business has been completed.

As a participant, you should follow through on any action for which you are responsible. If you have any ideas after the conference, be sure to relay them to the person who can take action.

[2] *The Business Conference* (New York: McGraw-Hill, 1969), p. 132.   [3] Ibid., p. 136.

Organizing and planning equal success.

Good conferences, like good speeches, don't just happen. Proper organizing and planning are the keys to success, and both leader and participants must be actively involved. All the members must know how and when to speak, as well as how and when to listen in order to achieve effective communication.

Summary

In this chapter, you have examined the types of presentations that are frequently a part of the business scene, and you have investigated the techniques that require special attention when you deliver your speech. Consideration has been given to your audience and to the organization of your presentation. Your knowledge of speaking in a business environment has been enhanced by the exploration of communicating in conferences, including how to lead and how to participate.

Questions for Discussion

1. Explain the differences between oral and written communication.

2. Do you prefer to express yourself orally or in writing? Explain your preference.

3. Discuss four ideas that will help you to give an effective impromptu speech.

4. What five steps will help you in preparing and presenting an extemporaneous speech?

5. Why is eye contact important to a speaker?

6. Why is the rule ''be yourself'' important in regard to gestures or movement?

7. In assessing the quality and adequacy of your voice, you must understand the meaning of *volume, pitch, tone,* and *tempo.* Explain each term.

8. What effect can appearance have on an oral presentation?

9. List and explain four points to remember in planning and using visuals in a speech.

10. How can knowledge of the general characteristics of the audience help a speaker achieve effective communication?

11. In developing a speech, why should you start with the body and end with the introduction?

12. What are the four suggestions that will help you to compose and then present a good introduction?

13. Your speech is ready! What can you do to ensure professional quality?

14. Why has the business conference become so popular?

15. Explain the three parts involved in planning an effective conference.

Exercises

1. Select a partner. Each person is to prepare a five-minute presentation of a business activity that is of particular interest. Each partner is to critique the other's presentation, either live or recorded.

2. After the critique, present your improved oral report to the class.

3. Give a one-minute speech on a current business event reported in your local newspaper, the *Wall Street Journal*, or a business periodical.

4. Analyze a professional presentation (a professor, a minister, a radio or television personality, a convention speaker, etc.). Special emphasis should be given to the voice quality and the delivery techniques. Be objective and sincere.

5. Watch television commercials for a three-day period for the purpose of observing the use of visuals. Employing the guides discussed in the chapter, determine if the visuals were effective.

6. Present an oral report on your findings from exercise 5.

Chapter 14   Techniques of Dictation

Please make two carbon copies of the following letter. One of the carbon copies will be mailed to Mr. C-l-a-u-d-e (Claude) C-o-l-l-i-n-s (Collins), 618 T-y-l-e-r (Tyler) Road, Rock Island, Maryland 20682. The second carbon copy will be placed in the Rock Island contract file. The original of this letter is to be sent to Mrs. A-l-i-c-e (Alice) V. (as in victor) S-m-y-t-h-e (Smythe), P. O. Box 8282B (as in boy), Houston, Texas 77004. Dear Mrs. Smythe. . . .

Dictation, Defined

Dictation, speaking for the purpose of having your words recorded for ultimate printing and transmittal to the recipients, is a team effort. The dictator speaks; the transcriber acts on the dictator's words in a prescribed manner. The product of the teamwork, the business message, depends on the communication abilities of the team members and on the objectives for communicating.

Make dictation a team effort.

The dictator may use one or all of the following dictation methods:

1. Dictation to a shorthand-writing secretary, word processor, or stenographer—called *face-to-face dictation.*

2. Dictation to a typist—called *typewriter dictation.*

3. Dictation by telephone to be recorded by a shorthand-writing secretary or by a recording machine—called *telephone dictation.*

4. Dictation directly to a dictating machine for subsequent transcription—called *machine dictation.*

What Should You Dictate?

The dictator may do routine dictation (acknowledgments, collections, transmittals, etc.); rush dictation (reports needed at once, urgent requests for information or supplies, etc.); printed-form dictation (insurance forms, personnel forms, etc.); confidential dictation (research and development projects, management-to-employee discipline or counseling messages, etc.); specialized dictation (medical, scientific, legal, etc.); and rough-draft dictation (long reports, detailed justifications, very important business messages, etc.). The transcriber takes the shorthand notes, the recording medium, or the typed rough draft and produces a mailable copy or carries out the dictator's instructions.

Dictate for mailable copy.

Why Should You Dictate?

Businesses are continually searching for ways to save time and money and for ways to produce data more accurately and more rapidly. The dictation process saves both time and money and makes possible the processing of a greater volume of usable information.

If you write a letter in longhand and give it to your secretary to type, you have wasted valuable time. The average person writes about 15–20 words a minute. Your secretary can type from well-written longhand about 35–40 words a minute. If you choose to dictate to a machine, you will use a slow-to-medium talking rate of about 100–120 words a minute, and your secretary will transcribe clear dictation at 55–65 words a minute. If you choose to dictate directly to your secretary, you will speak about 80–100 words a minute, and your secretary will transcribe about 30–35 words a minute. Dictation is, at its minimum, four times faster than longhand production. By dictating instead of writing in longhand, you can produce four times as much valuable data.

You also think faster than the 15–20 words a minute that you write in longhand. While your hand is trying to catch up with your mind, your mind is going on to other thoughts, leaving many good ideas unrecorded. Through dictation, you are able to get every valuable thought on record.

Dictation takes less effort and expends less energy than longhand composition. Holding a microphone and talking are considerably less tiring than holding a pen and writing pages and pages of words and figures. The energy you save can best be put to use in collecting and organizing information and in coordinating people, money, materials, methods, machines, and morale.

Dictation, recorded by a machine or in shorthand, insures greater confidentiality for business information. A longhand message left in a folder on a secretary's desk or in the secretary's desk drawer is much more accessible to a roving eye or a nosy employee or client than a shorthand or recorded message.

The newest and most promising innovation in data production in the office is the word-processing center.[1] The objective of this

Save your company money by dictating.

Dictate to keep up with your thoughts.

Dictate to save your energy.

Dictate to ensure confidentiality.

---

[1] A word-processing center contains dictating machines and special typewriters in one location. Dictators use telephones or private-wire connections to the dictating machines. Word processors transcribe on special computer-based typewriters on which corrections can be made before final copy is typed. This word-processing system also permits storage of form letters and reports and retrieval of stored material. Corrections or modifications can be made without changing other information. Appendix G provides additional information about word processing.

center is the production of mailable copy from the words and figures dictated by an originator (dictator). The success of the center depends heavily on the dictation skills of the originators and on the transcribing skills of the word processors. Many forward-looking companies with twenty-five or more employees are seriously researching the feasibility of word-processing centers and, once this feasibility is established, will begin staffing their offices with trained originators and word processors.

Dictate to keep up with current trends.

At General Electric's Erie, Pennsylvania, manufacturing division, word processing saves $40,000 a year in clerical overhead and executives' time. South Central Bell Telephone Company in New Orleans increased document output from 50 to 100 percent and saved $21,000 during the first year their word-processing center was used. At Lever Brothers' New York division a forty-two person typing team was replaced by ten word-processing experts.[2]

Why dictate?

1. Dictate to save time.
2. Dictate to save money.
3. Dictate to ensure more efficient recording of thoughts.
4. Dictate to ensure confidentiality.
5. Dictate to keep up with the current trend in information processing.

Who Should Dictate?

The originators and transmitters of internal and external information will need to develop dictating skills and use these skills efficiently. A basic understanding of English grammar, the ability to organize and present information orally, an understanding of the intimate workings of the business organization, a thorough knowledge of office and business terminology, and a knowledge of the psychology of communicating are necessary skills for the originators of business messages. The originators must also be alert, perceptive, intelligent, analytical, courteous, and cooperative. The originators must be able to work cooperatively with the transcribers to successfully complete the dictation process.

The wise office manager or training supervisor will develop a training program to increase the efficiency of the dictation-transcription process. The training should include:

Participate in dictation training programs.

[2]Walter A. Kleinschrod, *Management's Guide to Word Processing* (Chicago: Dartnell Corp., 1977), pp. 15, 16.

Figure 14—1
A dictator-rating form, to be completed by the transcribers.

1. Orientation to the mechanical aspects of using the dictating equipment and the recording medium.

2. A review of grammar and punctuation rules.

3. A concise study of the fundamentals of business communications.

4. Simulation and role-playing experiences to give the trainees opportunities to plan, organize, and dictate business communications. (The dictation script, as it appears at the beginning and end of this chapter, is a very effective, *initial* tool for learning to dictate.)

5. Periodic completion of evaluation sheets or checklists by both the dictators and the transcribers. (Figures 14—1 and 14—2 show

9. You give instructions about unusual format BEFORE you dictate the message.

   Always _____   Sometimes _____   Never _____

   Comments: _____

10. You give instructions about unusual sizes and kinds of stationery to use
    BEFORE you dictate the message.

    Always _____   Sometimes _____   Never _____

    Comments: _____

11. You are courteous.

    Always _____   Sometimes _____   Never _____

    Comments: _____

12. You are cooperative and helpful.

    Always _____   Sometimes _____   Never _____

    Comments: _____

sample rating forms that can be helpful in improving both dictation and transcription.)

The clerk in the purchasing department, the secretary to the vice president of operations, the supervisor of the records department, and the administrative assistant in the personnel department are only a few of the office workers who dictate letters, memorandums, and reports. With the continuing increase in automation, the office worker is freed from routine, repetitive tasks to engage in the more creative task—communication through dictation.

```
                          RATE YOUR TRANSCRIBER
        TO: _____        DATE: _____

        _____
                  Department
     FROM: _____

     1.  You complete the transcription in a satisfactory time period.

         Always _____        Sometimes _____        Never _____

         Comments: _____

     2.  You proofread and correct all typing errors.

         Always _____        Sometimes _____        Never _____

         Comments: _____

     3.  You make neat, unobtrusive corrections on my business messages.

         Always _____        Sometimes _____        Never _____

         Comments: _____

     4.  You follow directions precisely.

         Always _____        Sometimes _____        Never _____

         Comments: _____

     5.  You punctuate correctly.

         Always _____        Sometimes _____        Never _____

         Comments: _____

     6.  You present my business messages to me in an attractive format.

         Always _____        Sometimes _____        Never _____

         Comments: _____

     7.  You are courteous.

         Always _____        Sometimes _____        Never _____

         Comments: _____

     8.  You are cooperative and helpful.

         Always _____        Sometimes _____        Never _____

         Comments: _____
```

Figure 14—2
A transcriber-rating form, to be completed by the dictators.

When Should You Dictate?

To decide when you should dictate, answer the following questions:

1. Are you *capable* of typing your own business messages?
2. Do you have *time* to type your own business messages?
3. Can you *write* in longhand *or type* in rough-draft form as fast as you can dictate?
4. Do you have access to a shorthand-writing secretary or to a dictating machine to record your dictation?

If your answers to 1, 2, and 3 are "no" and your answer to 4 is "yes," you should develop and use your ability to dictate for mailable transcription. Your understanding of the benefits of dictation will "dictate that you dictate."

Plan your dictation time when you will have the fewest interruptions. Whether dictating to a secretary or to a machine, you are responsible for selecting an optimum time that is conducive to thinking, planning, organizing, and concentrating. Background noises should be kept to a minimum, someone should take over the responsibility of answering your phone and intercepting unexpected visitors, and sufficient time should be available for completing the dictation.

Plan your dictation time carefully.

If you use a machine, you may dictate before or after working hours, at home, in the office, in your hotel room while away on a business trip, or in the car. The availability of portable dictating machines makes dictation possible at almost any time that is convenient for the dictator. Figure 14–3 shows an ultrasmall Lanier portable dictation recorder.

Dictate by machine whenever the need arises.

Helpful Dictation Techniques

Proper techniques are necessary if dictation is to save time and money and result in the production of mailable copy. The following guidelines can help you be more efficient before you dictate, while you dictate, and after you dictate.

Before You Dictate

Be sure you follow these three guidelines before you dictate:

Follow these guidelines when preparing to dictate.

1. *Collect all resource materials you need.* You will need to have the letters you plan to answer; the instructions for the report you are going to write; your research findings for the preparation of reports, memorandums, and letters. You will need the files related to your dictation; copies of forms if you plan to dictate form fill-ins; and form books[3] if you plan to dictate form letters or form paragraphs. You should also have available at your desk a dictionary, policy manuals, a ZIP Code directory, and an English grammar handbook.

---

[3] Form books contain form letters and form paragraphs for use in writing routine business communications. The letters and paragraphs are written by communication experts and may be adapted to meet the objectives of a communication.

Figure 14—3
An ultrasmall Lanier portable dictation machine, the Vest Pocket Secretary™.
Courtesy of Lanier Business Products.

2. *Prepare the resource materials for your use.* Read and make notes on any letters and reports you will write. Outline the key points to be included in your dictation. Determine the priority of your dictation, and organize your resource materials in that order. Locate the form letters or form paragraphs that you plan to use for dictation in your form book.

3. *Prepare your machine or your secretary for recording your dictation.* If you do face-to-face dictation, ask your secretary to come in for dictation as soon as possible or at at specific time. Allow time for the secretary to ask someone to cover the phone and take care of necessary business at her or his desk. All confidential files and papers should be put away in a safe place before the secretary leaves her or his work station. If no one is available to answer the phone during your dictation, the secretary should notify the switchboard operator or the receptionist to hold all calls and callers and to take messages.

If you do machine dictation with a desk-top machine, make sure you have an adequate supply of the medium used by your machine—magnetic belt, cassette, or disk—and index slips (see Figure 14—6). If you are going to use a central dictation system[4] connected to a word-processing center, make sure that a channel is open to the center, and make your connection to the open channel. Figures 14—4 and 14—5 show new machine-dictation equipment that might be used in a central dictation system.

During Your Dictation

Follow these guidelines while dictating.

The procedures you use during your dictation can make the transcriber's work easier or more difficult. These guidelines will help you to dictate effectively for efficient, correct transcription of your messages.

1. *Before* you dictate each message, indicate how many carbon copies you will need.

2. *Before* you dictate each message, give special instructions for an unusual format.

3. *Before* you dictate each message, give special instructions for the use of an unusual size or kind of paper.

4. *Before* you dictate the message, indicate if you wish the transcription to be in rough-draft form. Thus, the secretary will not waste time producing a perfect copy, will use a cheaper grade of

---

[4]A central dictation system has a number of dictation recorders in one location made accessible to originators by telephone or private wire.

paper, and will double- or triple-space the transcription to give you space to rewrite.

    5. Dictate complete addresses.

    6. Spell all unusual or difficult names or words. (Enunciate the letters clearly.)

    7. Enunciate your words clearly.

    8. Talk at an even rate. If you are doing face-to-face dictation, watch for kinesic communications that will tell you if you are dictating too rapidly or too slowly.

Figure 14—4
A secretary inserts a cartridge into the recorder of a four-station IBM 6:5 Cartridge System. Courtesy IBM Corporation.

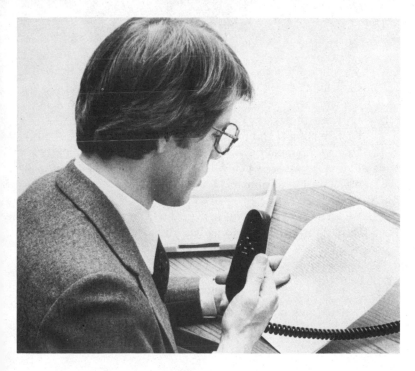

Figure 14—5
An executive dictates into a remote microphone of the IBM 6:5 Cartridge System. His dictation will be recorded on the machine shown in Figure 14—4.
Courtesy IBM Corporation.

Dictating your communications allows you to accomplish more work with greater efficiency in the same time. Peter Southwick/Stock, Boston, Inc.

9. Use your normal tone of voice so your secretary can hear you or your machine can record your words without distortion.

10. If a word is to be capitalized, indicate the capitalization *before* you dictate the word.

11. Dictate paragraph breaks.

12. Dictate punctuation only if punctuation is a natural part of your thinking processes when you communicate. (Your secretary or the transcriber should punctuate as a part of the transcription process.)

13. When dictating form fill-ins, dictate from top to bottom and from left to right. If you are doing face-to-face dictation, give your secretary a copy of the form to look at as you dictate the fill-ins.

14. When using form books, dictate the form letter or form paragraph numbers *after* you give special typing instructions and addresses.

15. When doing machine dictation, mark the index slip at the end of each dictated message. Your secretary will be able to determine not only the number of communications on the medium but

the approximate length of each one. Figure 14–6 shows two IBM index slips marked to show the length of the message (the top marks) and the corrections made by the dictator (bottom marks).

16. When doing machine dictation, mark the index slip for every correction, deletion, or special instruction you wish to relay to the transcriber. The marking device is activated by a switch on the microphone of the dictation machine. For telephone-connected central dictation systems, the dictator dials or presses a special number on the telephone to indicate corrections.

17. Emphasize the confidentiality of especially confidential materials. Your instructions will alert your secretary to be especially careful about where the finished copy of the letter, the carbon copies, and the carbon paper are placed.

18. Be sure to write your name and the date on the index slip before giving the medium and the index to your secretary. If you are dictating to a central system, record your name and the date at the beginning and the end of your dictation.

19. If you lose your train of thought while dictating to your secretary, ask her or him to read back your last sentence. If you are using a dictation machine, rewind it and replay your last sentence. If you are using a central system, dial or press the number that activates the rewind and playback mechanism.

20. As you dictate from source documents and files, stack them face down in the order in which you use them. You should make

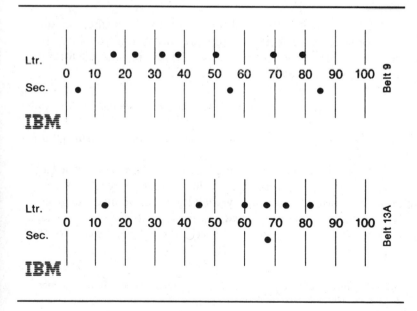

Figure 14—6
IBM index slips marked to show the length of the messages dictated and corrections made during the message.
Courtesy IBM Corporation.

these sources available to your secretary or to the word processor who transcribes your dictation so any information contained in these files can be checked.

21. If enclosures are mentioned in your letter, you should remind the transcriber at the end of the letter to type an enclosure notation.

22. Whether dictating face-to-face to your secretary or to a recording device, remember to humanize your message. Dictating can become such a mechanical operation that the dictator may lose the human touch, the empathy that all effective communicators must practice. Remember that a human being will read and react to the finished product of your dictation. Keep that person in mind as you dictate.

23. If you are doing typewriter dictation, the typist should produce a rough draft from your dictation. Do not expect the finished copy to be redone while you are standing at the typewriter. (Use typewriter dictation only when the matter is so urgent that you do not have time to dictate the message any other way.)

After You Dictate

Follow these guidelines when you have finished dictating.

If you made the proper preparations and dictated your messages for efficient transcription, you can follow these guidelines after your dictation has been completed:

1. Expect a mailable copy[5] from your secretary or the transcriber.

2. Proofread all transcribed copy carefully. Your signature on a letter or your name on a typed report indicates that you have approved the copy. *You,* not the transcriber, are responsible for any errors on the finished copy.

3. Read the communication first for correct content being sure to check for typographical errors; then read it for logical, clear organization.

4. Make sure all enclosures are attached to their transmittal messages.

5. If your dictation was done by a long-distance telephone call to a shorthand-writing secretary, ask the secretary to read back your entire communication before you end the call. Many times your long-distance dictation is typed and mailed without your having an opportunity to proofread or approve it. Therefore, the cost for the

---

[5] Mailable copy is ready to be mailed or distributed. The copy should be free from typing, grammar, and composition errors.

time your secretary spends reading back your communication is justified.

6. Sign all letters and initial all memorandums that are ready to be mailed or distributed and return them to your secretary for distribution and mailing.

7. Periodically evaluate the dictating and transcribing process (see Figures 14–1 and 14–2). Identify and correct any bad dictating and transcribing habits for more efficient and better business communication.

Unique Dictation Situations

Some less common dictation situations in which you may participate are: minutes of meetings, group-dictated communications, and impromptu dictation.

Minutes Dictation

Assume that you are on the Board of Directors for a local chain of equipment-rental establishments. You are elected secretary for the Board and, in that capacity, will take notes on the business conducted at all Board meetings. The corporate minutes book is in your charge. After each meeting, you use your notes from the meeting to dictate the minutes for transcription by your secretary. In your capacity as board secretary, you realize the necessity for accuracy and completeness of the corporation's minutes because such minutes become an important and necessary part of all financial audits of the corporation. You also realize the necessity of understanding and following Robert's *Rules of Order*[6] to ensure the clear organization and presentation of the minutes.

Review Robert's *Rules of Order* before dictating minutes.

Before dictating the minutes, you should specify the form you wish your secretary to use, whether you wish a final copy or a rough draft typed. You will need to indicate how many copies will be needed, the copy process you prefer for making the necessary copies,[7] and any special instructions about the kind and size of paper to be used. Many corporations specify that the original copy of the minutes be typed on pre-numbered, specially marked paper, used to prevent tampering with such records. In this case, you

Dictate specific instructions to your secretary.

[6] Henry M. Robert, *Rules of Order,* rev. ed. (Chicago: Scott, Foresman, 1970).
[7] Among the copy processes that could be used are ditto, mimeograph, multigraph, thermograph, photocopying (Xerox, IBM, Savin), and offset printing.

COMPUTER FEASIBILITY COMMITTEE
Wednesday, January 22, 19--

The meeting was called to order by the chairman, Alton Zauder, at 3:05 p.m.

Members present. Carol Elender, Robert Kinder, Miles Montgomery, Vera Crowe, Charles Lyons, and Alton Zauder.

Members absent. P. K. Tate and Marilyn Cory.

Low bid. Montgomery reported that the ACR Computer Corporation sent in a low bid of $48,510, $1,110 less than the Nelson Computer bid. He noted that installation, service, and equipment were comparable and recommended accepting the ACR bid. Crowe made a motion that the decision be tabled until the next meeting. Kinder seconded the motion. The vote was 4 FOR and 2 AGAINST; therefore, the motion to accept ACR's bid was tabled.

Meetings with employees. Elender reported that her meetings with personnel in the Purchasing and Transportation Departments appeared to be very effective. Most of the employees she talked with were favorably impressed by her explanation of how the computer installation could be beneficial to them. Elender stated that all but one employee indicated an interest in the proposed training classes and seminars scheduled for early March.

ACR promotion. Lyons announced that ACR had called him to see if their representative could give a promotional presentation to each department to explain to the employees how the computer can make their work simpler and more accurate. He noted that their presentation would be a bit premature since no bid has been accepted. No action was taken.

Field trip to Frost. Elender made a motion that the committee take a field trip to the nearby Frost Aluminum Corporation to look at its newly installed computer center and to talk with computer personnel there. Kinder seconded the motion. A brief discussion was held, and the vote was unanimous to contact the Frost Corporation's computer supervisor to set up a time for the visit.

Newsletter communication. Zauder asked for a volunteer to write an article on the feasibility study's progress for the company newsletter. Elender volunteered and will have the article ready before the next newsletter goes to press.

Adjournment. Lyons made a motion that the meeting be adjourned at 4:15 p.m. Kinder seconded the motion which was carried unanimously.

Next meeting. Zauder announced that the next meeting will be held one week from today, January 29, at 1 p.m. He asked that all committee members be ready to report on their projects.

Miles Montgomery ____________ Date ____________

Figure 14–7
Minutes with subdivisions indicated by paragraph side headings.

would probably be wise to ask your secretary to type a rough draft for your approval before typing the final copy on the special paper. If you are preparing minutes for a committee, club, or organization, you would probably prefer a final copy be typed from your dictation.

Two examples of acceptable forms for minutes are shown in Figures 14–7 and 14–8. Please notice how helpful the headings are in speeding your reading or for finding a specific subject. The headings achieve two objectives: clarity and transition.

Organize your notes before dictating minutes.

All minutes should contain the following information. You would be wise to organize your notes for dictation in this order.

1. Name of organization, committee, or group

```
                    COMPUTER FEASIBILITY COMMITTEE
                      Wednesday, January 22, 19--

                     The meeting was called to order by the chairman, Alton
                  Zauder, at 3:05 p.m.

Membership              Those present were Carol Elender, Robert Kinder, Miles
attendance        Montgomery, Vera Crowe, Charles Lyons, and Alton Zauder.  Ab-
                  sent were P. K. Tate and Marilyn Cory.

                              OLD BUSINESS

Low bid              Montgomery reported that the ACR Computer Corporation
                  sent in a low bid of $48,510, $1,110 less than the Nelson
                  Computer bid.  He noted that installation, service, and
                  equipment were comparable and recommended accepting the ACR
                  bid.  Crowe made a motion that the decision be tabled until
                  the next meeting.  Kinder seconded the motion.  The vote was
                  4 FOR and 2 AGAINST; therefore, the motion to accept ACR's
                  bid was tabled.

Meetings with        Elender reported that her meetings with personnel in the
employees         Purchasing and Transportation Departments appeared to be very
                  effective.  Most of the employees she talked with were favor-
                  ably impressed by her explanation of how the computer instal-
                  lation could be beneficial to them.  Elender stated that all
                  but one employee indicated an interest in the proposed train-
                  ing classes and seminars scheduled for early March.

ACR promotion        Lyons announced that ACR had called him to see if their
                  representative could give a promotional presentation to each
                  department to explain to the employees how the computer can
                  make their work simpler and more accurate.  He noted that
                  their presentation would be a bit premature since no bid has
                  been accepted.  No action was taken.

                              NEW BUSINESS

Field trip to        Elender made a motion that the committee take a field
Frost             trip to the nearby Frost Aluminum Corporation to look at
                  its newly installed computer center and to talk with compu-
                  ter personnel there.  Kinder seconded the motion.  A brief
                  discussion was held, and the vote was unanimous to contact
                  the Frost Corporation's computer supervisor to set up a
                  time for the visit.

Newsletter           Zauder asked for a volunteer to write an article on the
communication     feasibility study's progress for the company newsletter.
                  Elender volunteered and will have the article ready before
                  the next newsletter goes to press.

Adjournment          Lyons made a motion that the meeting be adjourned at
                  4:15 p.m.  Kinder seconded the motion which was carried unan-
                  imously.  The next meeting will be held January 29, at 1 p.m.
                  Each member should be ready to report on his or her project.


        _____     _____
               Miles Montgomery              Date
```

Figure 14—8
Minutes with marginal headings for each paragraph.

2. Date and time of meeting

3. A record of members present and members absent, either by name or number

4. Record of old business discussed and any action taken

5. Record of new business discussed and any action taken

6. Notice of time of adjournment

7. Announcement of the next meeting time, if one is scheduled

8. Name of official secretary (typed name and signature)

9. Date minutes were typed.

Some special parts of minutes dictation are motions and resolutions. You must always dictate resolutions and motions verbatim, complete with the names of those who made and seconded the

Dictate resolutions and motions verbatim.

motions. Be sure to spell any unusual words or names when dictating.

A sample dictation script for a resolution is:

RESOLUTION, adopted April 28, 19--. (In all caps) BE IT RESOLVED (now, in lower case) that the B-e-s-t-w-a-y (Bestway) Equipment Rental Corporation Board of Directors declares the payment of a dividend of $1.39 per share on all common stock, effective April 25, 19--, for stockholders of record on April 1, 19--. (Paragraph.) (In all caps) BE IT FURTHER RESOLVED (now, in lower case) that the form of the dividend payment will be at the option of the stockholder. The stockholder may choose to receive cash or to have the dividends reinvested.

A sample dictation script for a motion is:

Spell all unusual or difficult words.

E-l-l-e-n (Ellen) V. (as in victor) C-a-n-e-l-l-o (Canello) made the following motion: The Bestway Rental Equipment Corporation will authorize its stores to close at noon on Saturday, beginning Saturday, April 25, 19--. D-a-n-i-e-l (Daniel) T. (as in tank) G-u-i-d-r-y (Guidry) seconded the motion. The advantages and disadvantages of the proposed closing were discussed. R-o-y (Roy) R-o-b-i-n-s-o-n (Robinson) called for the question,[8] and the motion was accepted with a vote of 15 FOR and 2 AGAINST.

The keys to effective minutes dictation are preplanning and knowledge of parliamentary procedure.

Group Dictation

Assume that you and five of your business associates meet to compose an announcement of a billion-dollar expansion of your company. Your secretary attends the meeting to take notes and will be responsible for typing the announcement for publication.

Prepare your secretary for group dictation.

Before attending the meeting, you should brief your secretary on the purpose of the meeting and what will probably take place. For instance, you might tell him or her:

1. Six people will be offering suggestions for an announced billion-dollar expansion of the company.

2. Periodically you (the secretary) will be called on to read back what has been suggested.

---

[8]A member may *call for the question,* but the chairman generally *puts the question* by asking, ''Are you ready for the question?'' Either is a request to stop the discussion of the motion and take a vote (*see* Robert, pp. 36—37).

3. The final decision on the announcement to use is to be recorded verbatim and read back to those attending the meeting.

4. If no corrections or additions are made, you are to prepare the announcement for transmittal to . . . .

The key to effective group dictation is an efficient shorthand-writing secretary who can periodically tie loose ends together by repeating all suggestions made so a consensus can be reached.

Impromptu Dictation

Another unique dictation situation occurs when, for one reason or another, you must dictate in a hurry. You do not have time to alert your secretary to come to your office nor do you have time to use your dictation machine or the central dictating system. Your prime concern is the rapid, accurate production of finished copy because you have a short, unexpected deadline to meet.

Successful impromptu dictation requires the ability to organize your thoughts logically and quickly and your ability to convey these thoughts to your secretary. Your secretary should be capable of taking dictation at the work station, in the filing room, or in the coffee shop, on a piece of typing paper, a napkin, or even a telephone note pad. Impromptu dictation requires a highly skilled dictation team for successful use.

Use impromptu dictation only when you do not have time for regular dictation.

Obstacles the Dictator Must Overcome

Dictation ability is seldom an innate skill; very few people are "natural born" dictators. Because of individual differences and individual talents, some people find "thinking out loud" easier than others do. Some of the obstacles that may stand in your way when you dictate are listed below, followed by suggestions for overcoming them (identified by letters). Of course, the first step in solving any problem is to recognize that the problem exists. Knowing that you are not the only "klutz" in the world should motivate you to overcome any difficulties you may have as a dictator of business communications.

1. Fear of saying something you do not want anyone to hear, much less to record.

a. Practice is the best cure for overcoming this obstacle. Once you have developed the ability to think out loud and to organize your thoughts orally, and you realize how much time you can save,

Use these guidelines to overcome obstacles of dictation.

Practice dictating.

dictation will become a routine matter and a welcome aid in getting your work done.

b. Use a dictating machine until you gain more confidence in your dictation abilities. You can record, erase, and rerecord until you believe your dictation is suitable for your secretary or the transcriber to hear. You need not fear making grammatical or composition errors since you can play back what you have dictated and erase any such errors.

2. Lack of knowledge about the correct procedures to use for dictation.

a. Take this book from the bookcase in your office and review the guidelines for dictating under "Helpful Dictation Techniques" discussed earlier in this chapter.

b. Call a representative of the company that manufactures your dictating equipment and ask for his or her assistance.

Ask your secretary for suggestions to improve your dictation.

c. Ask your secretary what dictating procedures you should follow to make her or his job of transcribing mailable copy easier. At first glance, you may object to this solution, because you believe such a request would cause you to lose the respect of your secretary. But, this is the age of participative management,[9] and you would be following a current management trend by asking your secretary for input into the team effort of producing mailable copy from dictation. The best person to advise you about *effective* dictating procedures is the person who will have to transcribe your dictation.

3. Inability to operate your dictating equipment easily.

Ask for help in operating difficult-to-use dictating equipment.

a. Call the nearest manufacturer's representative for your particular dictating machine and ask him or her to send you an operating manual.

b. Ask the manufacturer's representative to demonstrate the use of the machine. If you are having trouble recording dictation, the fault may be in the machine, not in your ability.

4. Lack of confidentiality of messages dictated to a central dictating system.

a. Dictate confidential messages to your secretary.

Ensure confidentiality of dictated messages.

b. Make sure that you emphasize the confidentiality of the message when you dictate to the central system.

c. Suggest to your company that one or two long-time, trusted employees in the word-processing center be assigned to transcribe *all* confidential dictation.

5. Lack of personal contact with the transcriber when a central system is used.

---

[9] Participative management is a management process that emphasizes the participation of subordinates in decision-making about those policies that directly affect them in their work.

a. Suggest to your company that evaluation checklists for both dictators and transcribers be completed periodically, monthy or bi-monthly (see Figures 14–1 and 14–2).

b. Suggest to the word-processing-center director that the transcriber who completes each dictation unit call the originator when his or her dictation has been transcribed. The originator would then have an opportunity to talk to the transcriber and *could* go personally to the center, if time permitted, to retrieve the transcription.

. . . sure you can!

Use evaluation checklists to improve dictation and transcription.

Summary

The costs of an average business letter are now over $5.50 and increasing every year as salaries and expenses go up. To save both time and money, business executives increasingly need proficiency in dictating.

Charles Hall, vice president of Lanier [Business Products], says that anyone can learn to dictate and that learning to dictate is a necessity if office personnel are going to put dictation equipment and shorthand-taking secretaries to good economical use.[10]

Approximately 75 percent of managers' and supervisors' time is spent communicating,[11] and "85 percent of all business communication is handled by written correspondence."[12] Consequently, dictation for mailable transcription is, and will continue to be, essential to business success until someone figures out a way to record the *thoughts* of the business communicator!

Your request for information about the status of the Rock Island drilling lease was referred to me only yesterday. When your letter arrived last week, I was in O-t-t-a-w-a (Ottawa) on a business trip. (Paragraph.) The lease is dated June 18, 1976, and is effective until June 18, 1986. G-r-e-g-s-t-o-n (Gregston) Oil Company is the l-e-s-s-o-r (lessor) and is presently making plans to drill in the (lower case n) northwest corner of your property on Rock Island. A copy of the lease is enclosed. (Paragraph.) Please write or call me if you have further questions about the Rock Island drilling lease.

[10] Arnold Rosen and Rosemary Fielden, *Word Processing* (Englewood Cliffs, N.J.: Prentice-Hall, 1977), p. 112.
[11] Ibid., p. 102.

[12] *Transcription Skills for Word Processing*, Student's Guide (Franklin Lakes, N.J.: International Business Machines Corp., 1969), p. 79.

Sincerely yours, C-o-n-s-t-a-n-c-e (Constance) R. (as in rose) A-a-r-o-n (Aaron). Enclosure. This is the end of my dictation. 3:30 P.M., Monday, September 18, 19—.

Business Situations

1. Prepare a script similar to the example that follows for the letter below.

Example: Mr. Phillips called to say that he will be in Carencro, Illinois, on March 6 and will not be able to attend the Orthopsychiatric conference.

Script: Mr. P-h-i-l-l-i-p-s (Phillips) called to say that he will be in (capital) C-a-r-e-n-c-r-o (Carencro), Illinois, on March 6 and will not be able to attend the o-r-t-h-o-p-s-y-c-h-i-a-t-r-i-c (orthopsychiatric) conference. (Paragraph.)

February 18, 19--

Mr. Tommasi R. Rothchild
816 N. Ryan Street
Parish, TX 88206

Dear Mr. Rothchild

Your check for $180.55 was received by our bookkeeper today. She tells me that the balance due on your account is only $155.80. Enclosed is our check made out to you for $24.75, the difference between what you owed and what you paid.

LGJ, Inc. appreciates your business. To show our appreciation we are sending you a courtesy card that will allow you a 25 percent discount on purchases made at any of our eight locations during the month of March.

Sincerely

James C. Bolzonni
Enclosures

cc Mrs. Theresa Calais

2. Prepare a script of your actual dictation for the following business situation:

Purpose of the letter: Payment on overdue account belonging to Mr. and Mrs. Fred Nicholson.

Facts:
Amount owed: $652.42
Length of time overdue: five months
Number of collection messages already sent to the Nicholsons: three (May 1, reminder; June 10, reminder; July 10, appeal)
Type of message needed now: strong appeal
Type of business: department store
Type of account: revolving-charge account
Interest charge: 18% on unpaid balance
Payment policy: $10 a month on $100 or less; $15 a month on $101–$200; $25 a month on $201–$400; $40 a month on $401–$700
Maximum charges allowed: $700

3. Prepare a script of your actual dictation for the following business situation:

Purpose of the letter: Congratulations to a business associate for being elected to the Board of Directors of a local financial institution.

Facts:
Business associate's relationship to you: You have done business with him for twenty years.
Business associate's profession: purchasing agent, L and V Restaurant Supplies.

4. Prepare an outline from which you could dictate a business communication to satisfy the following communication needs.

Needed: A memorandum to all office personnel

Subject: Proposed computer installation

Facts:

The work presently done by ten out of the sixty employees will be done by the computer after its installation. Twenty employees will be given an opportunity to attend a six-week computer-training course on company time, on company premises, and at company expense.

Course will begin: one month from today

Date of computer installation: three months from today

Types of jobs available as a result of the computer installation: two programmers, four computer operators, two systems analysts, and two keypunch operators

Advantages of computer installation: chance to train to become skilled in some phase of computer operation at the company's expense; a decrease in the amount of repetitive, routine work; increased capacity to process information in the office; a long-term increase in company profits resulting from the computer's ability to process data in "real time" (in time for management to make decisions that will result in more efficient operations); and ultimate pay increases made possible by increased company profits.

5. Read the letter in Figure 8—7. Prepare a script that includes exactly what you would dictate when answering Mr. Barton's letter.

6. Read the letter in Figure 6—2. After carefully analyzing the communication needs, take the following steps:

a. Perform the necessary research to accurately answer Mr. O'Shonnassey's letter.

b. Prepare an outline from which you *could* dictate an answer to the letter.

c. Prepare a script that includes exactly what you would dictate when answering Mr. O'Shonnassey's letter.

d. If dictation equipment is available, record your dictation for presentation to the class. If dictation equipment is not available, make arrangements to dictate your letter in class to someone who can record your dictation in shorthand.

7. Read the first example letter in Chapter 8 under the heading "Requests for Information." After carefully analyzing the communication needs, take the following steps:

a. Perform the necessary research for answering the letter.

b. Prepare an outline from which you could dictate an answer to the letter.

c. If dictation equipment is available, demonstrate machine dictation procedures as a class presentation by dictating an answer to the letter, using the outline you prepared in step b.

8. Read the letter in Figure 8—6. After carefully analyzing the communication needs, take the following steps:

a. Prepare to dictate an answer to Mr. Atkinson's letter.

b. Using dictation equipment or a shorthand-writing person, demonstrate to the class the dictation of your answer to the letter.

9. You are the office manager at Carlston, Frederick, and Youngblood, Attorneys at Law. You have received a letter from Ms. Carolyn Pitre, office manager at Jackson, Arnold, Dunn, and Robinson (a law firm), requesting information about equipment used in your word-processing center, the approximate cost of such equipment, and the advantages and disadvantages of a word-processing center.

    a. Gather the information you will need to answer Ms. Pitre's letter.

    b. Prepare an outline for use in dictating your answer.

    c. If dictation equipment is available, record your dictation for presentation to the class.

10. You purchased a Ranx AM-FM radio from a local department store. The Ranx carries a ninety-day factory warranty. When the AM becomes inaudible because of excessive static, you send the Ranx AM-FM radio back to the factory in Chicago, Illinois. Prepare a script that includes exactly what you would dictate as a transmittal letter to the factory. Explain the problem you are having with the radio, and ask for some adjustment.

11. You will graduate from Compton State University in Compton, Kansas, in May, with a B.S. in Business Administration. You have decided to work on an M.B.A. before entering the job market. Kansas State University and Mississippi State University are the two schools that you are considering entering to study for your M.B.A. Outline a letter to both universities asking them to send you some information about entrance requirements, curriculum, and procedures to follow for applying to graduate school. In your letters express your desire to work as a graduate assistant. Ask if any such positions will be available next semester. If dictation equipment is available, record your dictation. If dictation equipment is not available, prepare a script that includes exactly what you would dictate.

12. You are employed by the Mason Office Efficiency Consulting Company. You recently studied the office procedures used at the Lake Hills Accident and Life Insurance Company. The purpose of the study was to analyze present office procedures to determine how the efficiency of personnel at the Lake Hills' office could be improved. While conducting your study, you discover, through questionnaires and observations, the following information:

Average per-person time spent answering or making personal telephone calls each day = 30 minutes ($\frac{1}{2}$ hour $\times$ 40 employees = 20 hours per day of nonproductive time).

Average per-person time per day spent idle at desks = 30 minutes ($\frac{1}{2} \times$ 40 employees = 20 hours per day).

Number of employees who were more than 15 minutes late two or more days a week = 15 (minimum lost time = 15 employees $\times$ 2 days $\times$ 15 minutes a day = $7\frac{1}{2}$ hours a week of nonproductive time).

Average number of times per week that employees were 15 or more minutes late returning from a lunch break = 2 (40 employees x 15 minutes x 2 times = 1,200 minutes or 20 hours a week lost productive time).

Twenty out of the forty workers admitted taking home for personal use paper clips, rubber bands, pens, pencils, and note pads. (No dollar estimate for the loss was determined.)

Fifteen out of forty workers admitted to using the office photocopy machine to copy an average of five or more pages a week for personal use. Every one of the remaining twenty-five workers admitted having used the photocopy machine for personal reasons at least once since being employed at Lake Hills. The only way the photocopy machine can be used is if one of the two machine operators employed by Lake Hills uses his key to unlock the machine and run the copies. This means not only incurring the expense of paper and machine time (approximately 12¢ a copy) but also the expense of employee time.

    a. Analyze your findings.

    b. Perform any research needed to organize and use the findings as the basis for a report.

    c. Prepare an outline from which to dictate a report to Lake Hills explaining the problem areas and making your recommendations for improving office efficiency.

    d. If dictation equipment is available, record your dictation for presentation to the class. (Use your outline, not a script.)

13. Prepare a script for your dictation of a transmittal letter for the consulting report you are sending to Lake Hills Accident and Life Insurance Company.

14. You are the supervisor of the Payroll Department at Lewis Oil Company. You have suggested to the top management of the company that payroll dates be changed from the first and fifteenth of each month to a biweekly payroll system. Hourly paid employees would be paid on alternate Thursdays; salaried employees would be paid on alternate Fridays. Top management agrees with your recommendations and has charged you with the responsibility of preparing a memorandum to be sent to all employees informing them of the change. You should include in the memo reasons for the change in payroll dates—reasons that emphasize the benefits to employees as well as to the company.

    a. Perform any research needed to provide logical reasons for the payroll-date change.

    b. Prepare an outline from which you can dictate your memorandum.

    c. If dictation equipment is available, record your dictation for a class presentation. (Use your outline, not a script.) If dictation equipment is not available, prepare a script that includes exactly what you would dictate.

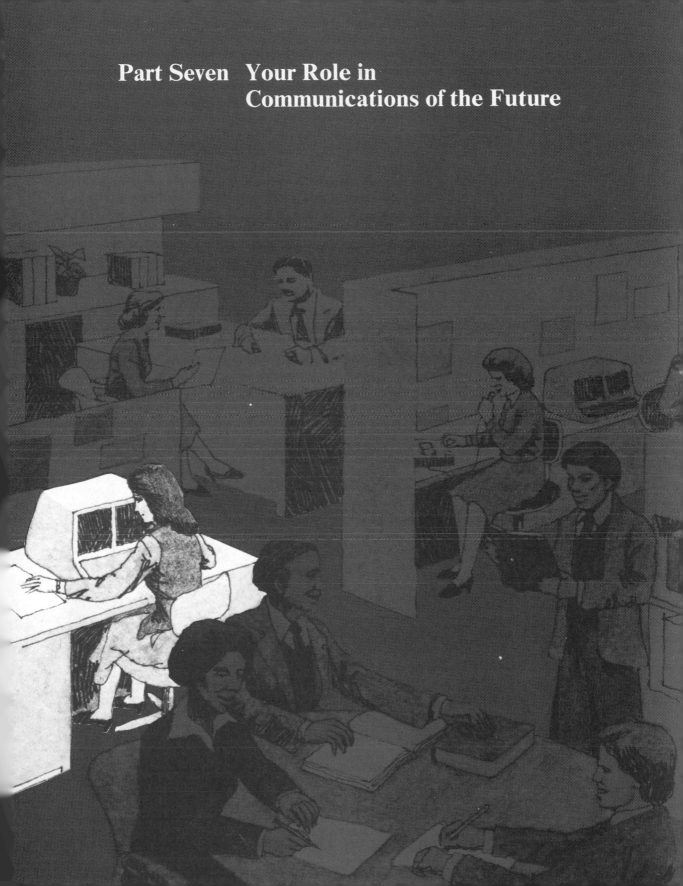

**Part Seven   Your Role in
Communications of the Future**

Chapter 15 Legality and Ethics in Business Communications

"Though it may be legally correct, is it ethically right?" — William A. Spurrier

The *future* of business communications must include a stronger emphasis on legality and ethics. The court dockets are overflowing with lawsuits, many of which are the result of *libel* or *slander charges*. An ethical approach to business transactions and a strong awareness of the possibility of libelous or slanderous actions will be necessary concerns for the business communicator of the future. Therefore, you should strive for both legality and ethics when planning, writing, or orally presenting your business communications. William A. Spurrier said, "Honesty, integrity, prudence, wisdom, truth-telling, and sincerity are guides" to the achievement of business objectives.[1] Empathy with your reader should motivate you to set ethical and legal goals.

Legality

The written record that you produce when you write a business communication is, in essence, a legal contract. The partners in this contract are you and your business as the "makers" and your communication partner and the business he or she represents as the "receivers." When you *write* business messages, consider the following factors:

Consider these factors when you write future business communications.

1. A written communication is acceptable as legal evidence in a court of law. You and your company may be forced to carry out your promises, or you and your company could be sued for breach of contract.

2. Your signature on a letter indicates that you agree with and approve of its contents.

[1]*Ethics and Business* (New York: Scribner's, 1962), p. 163.

3. You cannot legally change your mind once your written communication reaches the receiver unless you can prove that circumstances have changed enough to legally release you from previous commitments.

4. If your written statements indicate that a person is unfit to perform his or her job or that a company is unfit to carry on its business, you and your company may be sued for libel.

Libel

Libel is basically a written statement that is unjustly defamatory to a person or a business. That person or business may have grounds for a libel suit from which damages may be collected if your written statements:
1. hurt the reputation of a person or a company,
2. interfere with the earnings of a person or a company,
3. diminish the employment possibilities of a person,
4. disparage the character of a firm or its method of doing business.[2]

Truth is the only effective defense against libel charges. Defamation can seldom be proven when the written statements in question are factual. For example, a Louisiana resident filed a libel suit for $25,000 on the basis of a letter written to him with copies being sent to his brothers and sisters. The following statement, answering a letter written by the plaintiff to the defendant, was the basis for the suit:

> One can expect such a letter as you have written, in view of the fact that you failed in the filial devotion that you owed your late mother by refusing to pay your ⅕th of her funeral bill. Your excuse for not paying this bill was the ridiculous statement that you had not been consulted in making the funeral arrangements.[3]

The court found in favor of the defendant, who wrote the above statement, because the information was factual. No libel was proven.

On the other hand, Dun & Bradstreet had to pay very costly damages as a result of a libel suit because of mistakenly reporting that an electrical-supply company in Kansas had filed for bankruptcy. The information reported by Dun & Bradstreet was untrue; and even though this financial-reporting agency had not intention-

Avoid libel charges by writing truthful statements.

[2] Alice K. Helm, ed., *The Family Legal Advisor,* 2nd ed. (New York: Greystone Press, 1978), pp. 238–239.

[3] Ibid., p. 231.

ally falsified its reports, it was found guilty on the basis of negligence in checking its records carefully before publicizing credit information.[4]

Privileged communications between business partners are exempt from libel suits as long as the possibly libelous information is not shared with anyone outside the partnership.[5] Another example of a privileged communication is one written in response to a request for *factual* information about someone's credit or employment history. This type of written message becomes privileged when you include statements indicating that:

1. the information you are providing is being sent at the inquirer's request,
2. the information is to be kept confidential,
3. the information being sent by you is to be used only for the purpose stated in the request you received for the information.

Privileged communications also include "those of an attorney to his client, a doctor to his patient, a priest to his communicant, public officials to their superiors, or witnesses in a trial to a judge and jury."[6]

To avoid legal suits resulting from your written communications, follow these guidelines:

1. Proofread everything before signing your name.
2. When planning your communications, check all facts carefully, especially names, dates, dollar amounts, and all other figures.
3. If you are unsure about anything, do not put it in writing.
4. Make sure you can prove everything you write.
5. If what you state is your opinion, *not necessarily* something you could prove, be sure to indicate that the statements are *your opinion.*

Slander

Oral statements that you make to a business associate, a client, or a representative of the news media are sources of possible slander charges against you and the company you represent. *Slander* is an *oral* statement that damages the reputation of a person or a company; libel refers primarily to written materials that are defamatory. But, slander and libel are alike in that truth negates either charge unless malice can be proven. Also, the words, spoken or written, must be made public ("communicated to, and understood by, at

Negligence will invite libel suits against future communicators.

In the future, use privileged communication techniques to report someone's credit or employment history.

Follow these guidelines to avoid libel suits as a result of your future business messages.

Avoid slander charges by speaking the truth without malice.

[4] Ibid., p. 239.
[5] Ibid., p. 242.
[6] Ibid.

least one person other than the one of whom they are spoken or written"[7]). The state of New York held that the words heard by a stenographer as dictated by the originator make her or him the third party; therefore, the message being dictated had become a *public* statement.[8]

An Ohio hotel manager fired a waiter and stated: "You stole the butter and that is not the only thing you ever stole around here." The waiter filed a suit for slander against the hotel manager, but the courts found in favor of the hotel manager. No basis for slander existed because a third party was not present when the statement was made.[9]

Tomorrow's business communicator should become knowlegeable about state and federal slander laws.

To be classified as *slander per se,* slanderous because a third party heard the statement, your oral statements must fall within one or more of the following categories:

(1) words imputing the commission of a crime; (2) words imputing infection by a loathsome or contagious disease that excludes the person from society; (3) words proclaiming unfitness for office or employment or words derogatory of a person's fitness for a trade or profession; (4) words imputing unchastity (spoken of a woman).[10]

The plaintiff in a charge of slander per se needs only the testimony of a third party to win the case.

Few people are sufficiently skilled in impromptu communication to avoid an occasional foot-in-the-mouth. Therefore, impromptu communication provides the most fertile ground for slander charges.

To avoid the possibility of legal suits resulting from your oral communications, follow these guidelines:

Plan the words you speak carefully.

1. Keep up to date on information about your company, your services and products, the national economy, federal and state laws pertaining to the industry you represent, and the actions of competitive industries or companies.

2. Choose your words carefully, saying only what you *know* to be the truth. If you are unsure about the facts, either avoid the issue or make sure that you clearly indicate your uncertainty about the factual nature of your statements. Say you do not know if you do not. Say that the statements you are making are based only on your *opinion.*

Clearly distinguish between opinions and facts.

3. If you receive an unexpected call from someone requesting information about your products, your services, or a fellow em-

---

[7] Ibid., p. 235.
[8] Bruce D. Fisher. *Introduction to the Legal System,* 2nd ed. (St. Paul, Minn.: West Publishing Co., 1977), p. 329.
[9] Helm, p. 235.
[10] Ibid., p. 234.

ployee, tell the caller you will have to return the call after you have had time to check your records or files. This delay will give you an opportunity to gather the facts and to plan what you will say.

4. Unless you have *concrete* proof of the inadequacies of former or present employees, do not make any derogatory statements. Your *feelings,* with no factual basis, could result in a slander suit with you as the defendant. However, keep in mind that even if your statements are *true,* if one other person hears your remarks and malice on your part can be proven, the courts will probably rule in favor of the plaintiff. Your best defense is to make specific statements about former or present employees only in response to specific questions and to indicate orally that the information is privileged.

Foresee possible results of derogatory statements made about former or present employees.

Your Rights to Privacy

Business communicators of the present and the future need to develop an awareness and an understanding of the federal and state laws that cover the individual's right to privacy, the consumer's right to the truth about credit-buying terms and loan terms, and the individual's right to be informed when his or her words are being recorded.

The federal Privacy Act of 1974 "sets forth an individual's right with regard to the information accumulated and prohibits federal agencies from misusing the information acquired. Violating any individual's rights under this Act may be subject to civil suit for damages."[11]

Tomorrow's actions will be subject to the federal Privacy Act.

State laws governing an individual's right to privacy differ somewhat from state to state. However, most state laws provide that the right to privacy is a civil right and that "public disclosure of private facts"[12] is considered an invasion of the right of privacy. Certain *exceptions* to these laws are:

Avoid publicly disclosing private facts.

1. Publication of anything that is of public or general interest.

2. The communication of anything, even if it is private in nature, when the communication (oral or written) is considered a privileged communication according to the laws of slander or libel.

3. Publication of facts that the individual or legal entity has either consented to or has publicized previously.[13]

---

[11]J Marshall Hanna, Estelle L. Popham, and Rita Sloan Tilton, *Secretarial Procedures and Administration,* 7th ed. (Cincinnati: South-Western, 1978), p. 436.

[12]Fisher, p. 357.
[13]Ibid., p. 359.

The Consumer Credit Protection Act, popularly known as the "truth-in-lending act," was signed into law in 1968. The Act provides for:

1. "the disclosure of credit terms in almost every type of consumer credit transaction, including the disclosure of credit terms in advertisements,"
2. criminal penalties for "extortion-type credit transactions,"
3. a limitation on "the garnishment of an individual's wages,"
4. the creation of "a commission to study consumer credit."[14]

> Tomorrow's actions will be subject to the Consumer Credit Protection Act.

Louisiana Criminal Law 14–322 provides that you cannot record a telephone conversation without the consent of the *owner* of the phone to which the recording device is attached. Under certain conditions, *federal* law dealing with criminal offenses allows the taping of telephone conversations with the consent of only one party, the owner of the telephone on which the recording device is placed.

In case 360 F.2d 318 (U.S. Court of Appeals, 5th Circuit, 1966) the court allowed evidence gathered through a taped telephone conversation. The legal representative of the defendant in the case asked that the court not admit the evidence produced by the prosecution because the evidence was gathered from a taped conversation. But the court held that since a criminal charge was involved and since the owner of the telephone on which the recording device was placed consented to its use, the evidence was admissible. Another factor considered in this case was that a *federal* agency authorized the installation of the taping device on the owner's telephone (with the owner's consent).

> Tomorrow's actions will be subject to federal and state laws regarding taped telephone conversations.

South Central Bell Telephone Company has a company policy that does not permit the use of a recording device on a telephone unless a "beep" sound occurs when a conversation is recorded. Therefore, if you are served by a Bell System company, telephone conversations cannot be recorded without the consent of *both* parties. If you hear a "beep" on a Bell System telephone, you know that your words *are* being recorded. If you do not wish to have your words recorded, simply ask the other party to turn off the recorder. When the "beep" stops, you know the recording has stopped.

In summary, if *criminal* charges are involved, state and federal laws allow recording of telephone conversations if only the owner is aware of the recording. However, the Bell telephone system does not allow such a procedure unless a "beep" occurs during the recorded conversation. Civil laws and company policies usually do not permit recording telephone conversations unless both parties

---

[14]Helm, p. 317.

agree to such action; criminal laws usually allow the recording under specific conditions.

Truthful statements (written or oral), the absence of intended malice, careful planning of written and oral communications, and up-to-date knowledge of federal and state laws will safeguard the business communicator against the civil charges of slander and libel and against the criminal charges of unauthorized wire tapping.

Ethics

Ethics is "the discipline dealing with what is good and bad and with moral duty and obligation." A person's sense of right and wrong is most often a result of his or her environment, educational level, social status, religion, age, and sex. A company's ethical standards are a result of the ethical beliefs of the members of the company's management team. Therefore, ethical standards differ from company to company.

Your future business ethics depends on your past experiences.

Walter F. Beran, in an article entitled "Business Ethics," states that "ethics is the glue that maintains the individual and the greater society in an orderly relationship with each other."[15] He illustrates contemporary ethics as:

1. High office holders indicted and imprisoned
2. Businessmen engaged in clandestine corporate payments
3. Lawyers violating the laws and going to jail
4. Accountants making unreal business transactions look real
5. Doctors dishonoring their Hippocratic oath by experiments with dangerous drugs on unsuspecting patients
6. Politicians putting mistresses on their payrolls
7. Politicians and their wives accepting payments from foreign governments
8. The president's [President Carter] closest advisor exercising unwarranted privilege over other people's money
9. The movie industry making a shambles out of the time-honored custom of perquisites
10. The financial community accused of redlining.[16]

Because of these ethical maladies that exist in today's society, the general public tends to be somewhat dubious about ethics in life in general and in business and politics in particular. Your task as a business communicator will be to maintain high ethical standards: honesty, integrity, loyalty, impartiality, and industriousness. You

To eliminate today's ethical maladies, set high ethical standards for future business relations.

[15]"Business Ethics," *The Secretary*,   [16]Ibid.
April 1979, p. 6.

should avoid doing anything in secret that would be embarrassing or harmful if it were done in public. Your task, also, will be to continually monitor the ethical behavior of those who work with you as well as those who work under your supervision.

Most professions have *written* codes of ethics; and every business has some standard of ethics, either written or unwritten. The codes of ethics of the National Secretaries Association (International) and the International Association of Chief's of Police are illustrated in Figures 15–1 and 15–2.

Economic and moral issues that involve business communicators and test their ethics are often raised in two business situations:

1. The writing of persuasive communications (sales letters, advertising messages, request letters).

2. The setting of profit-seeking goals and the standards on which these goals are based.

Are these business actions ethical or unethical? As a business executive, what should you do in each case?

1. You write a sales letter to enable your company to get rid of 150 toasters that do not have the "pop-up" feature. You never mention the manual toast extraction required; instead you tell the people receiving the sales letter that you are selling the toasters at such a low price because you are having a special anniversary sale.

2. You receive a letter from a company in another city asking for a job recommendation for a former employee. The employee was dismissed from your company because of excessive absenteeism and sloppy work. You write a letter telling the company that you would prefer not to make any statements about the former employee.

Take an ethical stand on economic and moral issues in your future business dealings.

THE NATIONAL SECRETARIES ASSOCIATION (INTERNATIONAL)

CODE OF ETHICS

Recognizing the secretary's position of trust, we resolve in all of our activities to be guided by the highest ideals for which THE NATIONAL SECRETARIES ASSOCIATION stands; to establish, practice, and promote professional standards; and to be ethical and understanding in all of our business associations.

We resolve to promote the interest of the business in which we are employed; to exemplify loyalty and conscientiousness at all times; and to maintain dignity and poise under all circumstances.

We further resolve to share knowledge; to encourage ambition and inspire hope; and to sustain faith, knowing that the eternal laws of God are the ultimate laws under which we may truly succeed.

Figure 15–1

The Code of Ethics of the National Secretaries Association (International).

From the National Secretaries Association (International).

3. You write an especially persuasive sales letter to residents of a low-income housing project. The letter results in the sale of home movie equipment to fifty families with annual incomes ranging from $4,000 to $7,000. The equipment is to be paid for in 104 weekly installments of $4.50. The $468 total price is fair, but have you manipulated human hopes by the words you used and enticed families to spend money on a luxury item instead of on basic food, clothing, and shelter needs?

4. You write a letter to an out-of-town business associate asking him to provide you with information about the organization of, costs of, and equipment used in their word-processing center.

5. You write a letter to your firm's Accounting Department located in another city. In the letter you itemize the travel expenses for which you wish to be reimbursed. When you compose your letter, you get out your company's policy statement on travel expenses and *copy* the daily allowable expense for food, lodging, trips, taxi fees, car rentals, and secretarial services.

6. One of your best customers calls and says she needs a rush order on six Techniqui Quiet Control electric typewriters. You have ten such machines in stock, but *yesterday* you received an order for ten machines from another company. You know that it will take four to six weeks to get more Techniqui typewriters from the factory. You quickly agree to send your good customer the six type-

LAW ENFORCEMENT CODE OF ETHICS

AS A LAW ENFORCEMENT OFFICER, my fundamental duty is to serve mankind; to safeguard lives and property; to protect the innocent against deception, the weak against oppression or intimidation, and the peaceful against violence or disorder; and to respect the Constitutional rights of all men to liberty, equality, and justice.

I WILL keep my private life unsullied as an example to all; maintain courageous calm in the face of danger, scorn, or ridicule; develop self-restraint; and be constantly mindful of the welfare of others. Honest in thought and deed in both my personal and official life, I will be exemplary in obeying the laws of the land and the regulations of my department. Whatever I see or hear of a confidential nature or that is confided to me in my official capacity will be kept ever secret unless revelation is necessary in the performance of my duty.

I WILL never act officiously or permit personal feelings, prejudices, animosities, or friendships to influence my decisions. With no compromise for crime and with relentless prosecution of criminals, I will enforce the law courteously and appropriately without fear or favor, malice or ill will, never employing unnecessary force or violence and never accepting gratuities.

I RECOGNIZE the badge of my office as a symbol of public faith, and I accept it as a public trust to be held as long as I am true to the ethics of the police service. I will constantly strive to achieve these objectives and ideals, dedicating myself before God to my chosen profession . . . law enforcement.

Figure 15—2

The Code of Ethics of the International Association of Chief's of Police.

From David A. Hansen, *Police Ethics*, 1973, p.xvii. Courtesy of Charles C Thomas, Publisher, Springfield, Illinois.

writers she needs immediately. Then you write the customer whose order you received yesterday, telling him you have only four Techniqui typewriters left and that he will have to wait four to six weeks for the other six to be sent from the factory.

Summary

Ethical, legal actions on the part of the business communicator of the future will be necessary prerequisites for success. A knowledge of state and federal laws relating to slander and libel, an individual's right to privacy, and the consumer's right to the truth about credit and loan terms is increasingly necessary for making wise business decisions. The telephone communicator's rights regarding the recording of telephone conversations plus the multitude of other legal restrictions on and rights of American business must be clearly understood by communicators. The key to ethical, legal business relations is to set high standards for yourself and to expect the same high standards of those with whom you work.

Questions for Discussion

1. Compare a business letter to a legal contract.

2. Define libel.

3. Define slander.

4. How are libel and slander different? Alike?

5. Define privileged communication.

6. You are answering an inquiry about a former employee. How can you protect yourself from being sued for libel?

7. What are five guidelines you may use to avoid legal suits resulting from your written communications?

8. What determines whether an oral statement is public or not?

9. What are the four categories into which your oral statements must fall to be classified as slander per se?

10. What are four guidelines you may use to avoid legal suits resulting from your oral communications?

11. Explain the effect of the federal Privacy Act of 1974 on business communications.

12. Explain the effect of the Consumer Credit Protection Act of 1968 on business communications.

13. What regulations do state and federal laws place on the recording of telephone conversations?

14. Define ethics.

15. What determines an individual's ethical standards? A company's ethical standards?

Chapter 16 Written and Oral Communications of the Future

"Everyone's future is, in reality, an urn full of unknown treasures from which all may draw unguessed prizes." — Lloyd Dunsany

In the future, you, as a successful executive, will communicate your ideas even more forcefully and effectively through written and spoken words. Your well-planned oral and written messages will enable you to communicate with subordinates, peers, superiors, customers, and all members of society. A knowledge of legal and ethical standards will provide you with a solid foundation for your communication.

Initially, you may be trained for a specific entry-level job that requires technical know-how. However, as you climb your career ladder, your work will probably become increasingly supervisory or administrative. Every step up this ladder will increase your need to communicate effectively. If you become an effective written and oral communicator, you will undoubtedly be promoted and achieve your occupational goals.

The Outlook for Written Communication

Because of the vast amount of paperwork, most letters and reports of the future will be written in the deductive (direct) approach. This approach will result in a more informal style of writing and will allow the busy executive to conserve time and energy. Reports will be shortened by increasing the use of visual aids and decreasing the amount of text.

Technology will expand current data-based research systems so businesses can take advantage of all published information available in a rapidly changing society. These data-based systems will diminish the time necessary for research for reports and documents from hours and days to seconds and minutes. In less than ten minutes, you will be able to research 75,000 topics through the data-

Research will be faster and more economical.

based systems located in metropolitan cities connected by tabletop terminals and telephone equipment to libraries in every town.

In order to distribute your ideas, you may use letters, memorandums, telephones, Western Union messages, teletypewriter networks, facsimile machines, and a vast array of sophisticated devices that will enable you to say, send, mail, or even "picture" a message faster, more conveniently, and at a relatively lower cost than ever before. Memorandums designed for fast replies will aid management in decision-making. Answers will be written on the original document and returned to the sender, thus saving time and money. Mailgrams, a combination of telegraph and postal services, will be effective for long messages sent to command more attention than a letter.

The use of original-document replies will become more popular.

Format Changes

Communications for the near future will largely be printed on paper similar to that which is used today. However, changes will be made in the quality of paper. Because of advances in correcting typewriters, a less expensive grade of paper can be used. Rag content of paper will be reduced to allow for quicker, more efficient corrections.

The use of interoffice memorandums will expand. As management continues to involve employees at all levels of the organization in decisions that affect them, dissemination of information will increase.

Special attention will be given to letterheads in the near future.

In the future, most offices will have typewriters with visual display of information and electronic transmission of messages. Ellis Herwig / Stock, Boston, Inc.

Firms specializing in the selection of paper will design letterheads that portray a clear image of the company. Color will be emphasized, symbolizing the features of the organization. Design will remain simple and add to the appearance of the letter, rather than detracting from the message. The psychological influences of color will be considered in letterhead design.

Creativity will be demanded in letterhead design as businesses become more and more aware of symbolic messages portrayed by logos. Letterheads will be clear and will contain all necessary information for effective communication. No longer will firms overlook addresses, telephone numbers, cable addresses, and other vital information. Attention will be given to the selection of logos for legal, as well as commercial, acceptance.

Logos are portraits of businesses.

Increased Data

The need for written communications will increase in the near future. Employees will demand more information from superiors; specialized training will necessitate dissemination of essential information. Government agencies will require detailed product, resource, and labor information. Greater emphasis will be placed on the written word.

Data will be stored on microforms or other devices that eliminate bulky, heavy filing cabinets. Communication will be written but transmitted through machines linked by telephone wires or radio. Emphasis on correctness will increase as technology increases. Correctness will become essential because understanding the information being conveyed will be imperative.

Advanced technology will demand skill and competence.

Data Dissemination and Storage

Information will be disseminated through computers shared in much the same way that computers are now shared for data processing. Many companies can use the system at one time, each user having its own input-output terminal. Systems designed to send photographs, drawings, and maps over regular telephone lines will transmit the data. Electronic impulses will transmit information at high speeds and relatively low cost.

Equipment to display information on a visual screen (CRT units) will enable communicators to correct errors before messages are sent and will also enable communicators to receive data for reading. Teletypewriters transmitting electric impulses over telephone systems will reproduce typewritten messages simultaneously on machines in neighboring or distant offices. The use of punched tape will increase the use of teletypewriters as terminal equipment for sending and receiving messages from computers.

Satellite Business Systems plans to establish private-line networks for large businesses and government agencies by using satellites and rooftop antennas. The equipment would enable widely separated computers to communicate with each other and allow the transmission of facsimile pictures two to twenty times faster than is now possible.

Computers will maintain the majority of business records.

In the future, you may see offices where all but the most valuable documents are stored in microform equipment and in computer banks. Mailing systems will have changed to the point that postal services will become primarily delivery services for special documents. Computer-based information systems for research purposes and computer-linked typewriting and relay systems will perform the tasks in the future office.

Primarily, information will be transferred by telephone, telegraph, and computers over telephone wires or by radio—called telecommunications. With telecommunications in full operation, dictating, sending, and receiving messages and pictures will be done faster and more conveniently, at a lower cost, reflecting the advanced state of communication.

Office telephones will become computer-input devices and even the minicomputers of the future. Microwave radio transmissions will transfer to tomorrow's offices not only voices, but computer linkups, letters, reports, face-to-face conversations over long distances, and a wide variety of communicated information.

Businesses will begin to move closer to paperless society.

During this period of expanding office technology, written communications will move toward electronic delivery rather than paper and postal-service delivery. Paper will play a less important role in the offices of the future. Typewriters with visual display (CRT units) will become standard. These machines will permit visual display of information, correction proofing, and electronic transmission over telephone lines to similar equipment in the office of the recipient of the communication.

When this stage of advanced technology is reached, computer-search systems will be "old hat." The drudgery of research in past years will be gone, and research will be as easy and as common as consulting the dictionary. National information centers will be available for tie-in to homes, offices, and schools. As an added extra, individuals will be able to read their favorite magazines, newspapers, or novels on the screen of their home or office computer.

Communications will appear on the screens of the CRT units

when the "writer" dictates into the audio feature of the communication computer. This communication computer will reproduce, on the CRT units, all messages, letters, and reports needed by business. After seeing the message in completed form, the communicator will be able to send the communication by microwave transmission to the communication computer of the recipient.

Business letters and reports will begin to be read from machines, not just paper.

The Paperless Society

Paper, pens, and ink could become things of the past. These objects may rarely be seen in business offices and homes in the future. Postal services will have moved out of public sight as a daily necessity to a position of performing special administrative services.

In this future paperless society, legal information will still need to be kept in a physical and tangible form. Communication computers may have a special method to record any necessary information required for legal purposes on paper-thin, durable plastic surfaces. These legal records will be smaller than today's 8 ½ x 11 inch typing paper but large enough to be read without special equipment.

With changes in office technology, communication skills will be as important as ever. You will still have to be able to write a sentence, spell, compose messages and letters, and produce informative, concise reports. Technology in the future will offer methods that are seen as "fantastic magic" today. Future technology will move communication to a level beyond anything imaginable today.

The Outlook for Oral Communication

You as a successful executive in business, industry, or government will work with laws and policies that will necessitate more efficient oral communication. For example, employer-employee relations are changing. Governmental regulations concerning employment of the handicapped, minorities, and women will demand effective oral communication. Because of laws such as the Privacy Act of 1974, the oral interview will become more important as a communication device. Your ability to lead or participate in group discussions, conferences, and oral presentations will enable you to develop your corporate and public image. Your excellent listening skills and awareness of the importance of nonverbal clues are also a part of the communication world of tomorrow.

Listening Skills

Especially in oral communication, *listening* skills will become more essential. For example, either in a conversation or as a member of an audience, you will learn to listen carefully with full concentration. The audience, conference, telephone, and conversational activities in which you will engage as a business person will require discerning listening techniques. As communication becomes more complex in the future, you will become actively involved as a listener.

For example, in employer-employee relationships, group discussions, conferences, and oral presentations, you will use empathetic listening in order to further the goals of your business. Your skills of perception, organization, interpretation, and feedback will help you to appreciate other persons' feelings as you react to improve your public image and to work with others persuasively and effectively.

Practice empathetic listening skills.

Awareness of Nonverbal Skills

Whether you are speaking or listening, nonverbal behavior reinforces verbal messages, provides additional information, or negates a verbal message. You as an oral communicator will learn to rely less on spoken words.

Through nonverbal communication, you and your listener gain from 65 to 90 percent of the implied meaning. Therefore, in the future you will be sensitive to the nonverbal messages you are sending or receiving. Through this awareness, unproductive arguments between employers and employees or customers and business may be avoided; and your personal actions will be directed toward communicating the most effective meanings.[1]

As people become more familiar with nonverbal communication, they will study you through your actions. You will also decode messages other people are sending you through their behavior—how they act, how they sound, and how they speak. You need to study body movements that may substitute or accompany verbal messages. Then, in the future, you will try to encourage in others, through nonverbal patterns, self-confidence and feelings of goodwill. Through feedback and nonverbal messages, you will become more aware of how your oral communication is received. The sci-

Use nonverbal communication techniques to create and maintain goodwill.

[1] Jill Y. Smith, "Speaking Out: Nonverbal and Verbal Communication Training Modules," *American Business Communication Bulletin*, 42, No. 1 (March 1979), pp. 29–31.

ence of nonverbal symbols or language is developing as a part of your future as a business communicator.

The Application Package

Because of present and impending laws and regulations, the application package of the future—the application letter, the data sheet or application blank, and the interview—will become more essential to you whether you are applying for a job or seeking an employee. The application package of the future will project the image of the applicant to the best advantage to be competitive with others who are also being considered for employment.

Because of the Privacy Act of 1974, however, you as an applicant or an employer will find the oral interview an increasingly significant tool in hiring. In fact, in the survey conducted by Lahiff and Hatfield, the employment interview most strongly influenced selection decisions in 84 percent of business organizations—an increase of approximately 11 percent in the past five years. Coupled with the Privacy Act is the government's basic distaste for the use of testing in the selection process.[2] Both of these factors will lead to the increased importance of the oral interview to you as an applicant or to you as a representative who hires for your firm.

Recognize the effects of the Privacy Act of 1974 on employment practices.

Laws and Regulations Concerning Special Groups

Local, state, and federal laws and regulations mandate that you as an effective communicator be able to use oral skills of persuasion, interpretation, and negotiation while working with various groups. New laws affecting hiring, promoting, and terminating employees are extremely specific and are carefully monitored.

For example, the Vocational Rehabilitation Act, Public Law #9312, of 1973, requires that all federal contracts exceeding $2,500 include an affirmative-action clause requiring that handicapped persons be given appropriate consideration—free of any discrimination because of any handicap that does not affect performance of the specific job. This law applies to the hiring, promoting, training, transfer, termination, and accessibility and working conditions of handicapped employees. Furthermore, equal-employment-opportunity statues, rulings, or policies prohibit discrimination on

Business capabilities of the handicapped and minorities will be recognized in the office of the future.

[2] James M. Lahiff and John D. Hatfield, "The Winds of Change and Managerial Communication Practices," *Journal of* *Business Communications,* 15, No. 4 (Summer 1978), pp. 25—26.

the basis of race, color, religion, national origin, sex, age, marital status, personal appearance, sexual orientation, family responsibilities, matriculation, and political affiliation.[3]

Employer-Employee Relationships

You will use your oral skills in employer-employee relationships for job satisfaction and productivity. The mastery of oral techniques will help you to understand, to resolve differences, and to persuade others.

Employees now and in the future will demand even more challenging work, a greater voice in decision-making, and more flexibility. You as an employee or employer may enrich your work through effective oral persuasion, through discussing matters face to face.

Although your organization may use oral communication skills wisely, employees tend to be skeptical of downward communications. Even though most businesses are placing a higher priority on downward communications, employees are still generally inclined to question the content of management's communications. In fact, according to Lahiff and Hatfield's survey, approximately 25 percent fewer respondents questioned were willing to accept downward communication than were willing five years ago.[4]

However, in the same study, 53 percent of the employees reported that their organizations placed a high priority on actively seeking new ideas from subordinates—an increase of more than 17 percent over the last five years. Most employees sense a dramatic shift in the amount of freedom they believe they have to speak their minds. Such a change is seemingly indicative of increasingly healthy upward internal communications within business organizations.[5] The attitudes of employees revealed by this study of upward and downward communication will affect your future as an oral business communicator.

Group Discussion for Decision-Making

Another trend in oral communications is the increase in decision-making through group discussion. In the past, executives have made policies that affected many persons. Today and in the future,

Use your oral communication skills for decision-making.

Encourage feedback from subordinates.

[3] B. Lewis Keeling, Norman F. Kallaus, and John J. W. Neuner, *Administrative Office Management* (Cincinnati: South-Western, 1978), pp. 310—311.

[4] Lahiff and Hatfield, p. 24—25.
[5] Ibid., p. 25.

many more employees want to become a part of the team that decides and implements policies. Employers should utilize the varied knowledge, skills, and ideas of more employees.

Laws and regulations, together with the change in employer-employee relations, make oral communication on all levels more important. Therefore, you as an employee or an employer should polish your oral communication skills for participation in group discussions and for use in effective human relations in conducting business efficiently.

Use your oral communication skills in group discussions.

Conferences

Often conferences grow from group discussions. You may serve as a participant or as a conference leader who guides the activities of a group, perhaps a large one. In this case, you should ensure that all facilities are available and that the equipment and materials needed are supplied.

As a conference leader, you will need increased ability in oral communications and planning. Because group participation in problem-solving conferences has been increasingly successful during the last decade, oral communication in conferences will be more important to you in the future.

Oral Presentations, Reports, and Speeches

Today, many businesses, industries, and governmental agencies have reviewed or retrained their executives in communicating more effectively with the public and the press. This emphasis on effective oral communication is partially intended to prepare business people to meet the increased amount of anti-business and governmental criticism.

Many organizations are attempting to improve their public image through oral communication, especially by advertising on radio and television and by speaking to groups to convey the idea of business as a necessary service to the consumer and the community. Your skills in oral communication will continue to become more vital because of this increased interest in the public image of your organization.

Enhance your company's public image through your oral communication.

In fact, the *business of communication* has been emphasized as being as important as the *business!* Opening the lines of communication can improve your public image; you as an effective oral communicator will assist in this endeavor.

For many years, the importance of public image has been known.

However, the study by Lahiff and Hatfield indicates that public image has become 20 percent more important to business relationships during the last five years. One of the primary methods that has been developed for improving this public image is the increased frequency of communication to the public through informative and persuasive speeches by executives.[6]

Your oral communication, therefore, may become the antidote for the impersonality of the corporate image and the distrust of business, industry, and government that many people feel. Your skill in public speaking and communicating with groups will require technical skills, ethics, and truthfulness.

The economic situation will change and the consumer will become more discriminating. Business speakers will need to be more aware of audiences and the messages received and sent through verbal and nonverbal communication. Competition for sales and services will increase; business communicators will realize the necessity for including the consumer as a partner in the organization. Opening communication lines and sharing ideas will become not only necessary but also vital.

When do you as a communicator become a public speaker? Actually, all your skills of conversation developed in employer-employee, individual, and group relations, and your leadership techniques developed in discussions and conferences will need to be used when you make a formal oral presentation. The number of people involved are of little importance in deciding when you will be considered a public speaker. The primary difference is that your audience will listen more passively and usually respond less verbally than in a conference or a discussion.

Although communication media have been used in various forms for many years, modern technology enables you to use these devices more easily, efficiently, and frequently in the future. In fact, you as tomorrow's communicator must use visual and audio equipment in oral presentations—reporting or speaking—to be most effective.

The expanded use of media software—cassette tapes, recordings, filmstrips, projection visuals, etc.—combined with modern audio-visual hardware—tape recorders, record and cassette players, projectors, etc.—will improve the communication processes of the future. However, you must be able to choose software of the highest quality, prepare and edit material, and use the best psychological and physical approach to properly communicate your ideas.

In fact, your use of visual words, phrases, and images conveyed *concisely and quickly* is more effective than the use of large masses

Use perception and feedback to relate to your audience.

[6] Lahiff and Hatfield, p. 21.

of material poorly organized and presented. The expanded audio-visual media for the future must add, not detract, from your oral presentation. The added features such as the use of video and audio recording equipment and closed-circuit television will help you as a speaker to preview, edit, and improve your oral presentation. This part of your training for future oral communications will help you present yourself in the best manner.

According to Dr. Elmer H. Wagner, an experimental holographic system that uses laser beams to present three-dimensional images will become more easily available, less expensive, and more useful in oral presentations. You as an oral communication expert will be able to use holography through a relatively small communication-media device to project a three-dimensional image to a group of consumers or business associates. For example, you may project a three-dimensional image of a product such as a new model of an automobile, a tractor, a sample of office equipment, a computer, etc., in an impressive, practical exhibit. Your audience will be able to realistically *see* in three dimensions a piece of large, bulky equipment that you could not possibly transport for actual presentation to a group.[7]

Further research and media technology will make this new visual material available to you. Instructions and training to aid you in communication and oral presentation will be accessible. However, your imagination, improved training, and advanced techniques will be necessary to motivate the listener of the future to take the action you desire. In return, taking this action will translate into profits for your organization.

Telecommunications in the Future

Today, the telephone is one of the most important communication devices..The telephone will become even more useful in securing and giving information, receiving and making appointments, solving problems, and maintaining the public image of your organization. The telephone is speedy and direct. Most persons will interrupt any face-to-face conversation to answer a ringing telephone. Because your placing and receiving telephone calls are extremely important, you will plan your oral message and think carefully when you are conversing by telephone.

Use the telephone for speed and directness.

[7] Our thanks to Dr. Elmer H. Wagner, Head of the Department of Educational Technology, McNeese State University, for his cooperation in providing this information on holography.

The specialized telecommunications of the future hold phenomenal promise. The innovations in telecommunications, which include the combination of media such as the telegraph, telephone, and computing devices, will make communications easier for you, although some changes may be difficult to comprehend or to accept.[8]

Change is a paradox! Mark Twain, struggling with a relatively simple, new office invention—the typewriter—said "I am trying to get the hang of this new-fangled machine, but I'm not making a shining success of it."[9] However, accept the typewriter and use it; he did—successfully!

In the future, you may want to use some of Twain's willingness to experiment and to take advantage of the technology that will revolutionize the art of communication in the business and industrial world. Many basic links to communication distribution in future word-processing systems—internally and externally—will be provided by today's specialized telecommunications equipment. This equipment plus the equipment that will be developed in the future will merge into the total information system of the business office

According to R. M. Flanagan, chairman of the board and president of the Western Union Corporation, "the technology of the future will offer products and services that will quickly make today's most modern word processing equipment and techniques in telecommunication as outmoded" as the early typewriter that Mark Twain used. "In the not-so-distant future," predicts Mr. Flanagan, "even such revolutionary equipment as we now have may well be replaced by devices that combine communicating ability, memory storage, and cathode ray tube display—a personal word processing center. . . ."[10]

Already, modern computerized switching services can provide telephone features including a tone alert to let you know that another call is waiting, automatic callback when one extension is busy, and automatic arrangement of conference calls. Your telephone can be programmed to forward calls to another telephone when you leave your office briefly or take a coffee break.

Programming also allows your incoming messages to be recorded for later delivery and your dictation to be recorded on magnetic media for later transcription. Toll-charge accounting and traffic analysis information to minimize expenditures and optimize equip-

---

[8] Much of the material concerning telecommunications systems was obtained through consultation with sales representatives of the Southern Bell Telephone Company, Lake Charles, Louisiana. We appreciate their cooperation in providing information and photographs for this chapter.
[9] *Getting the Word Around,* 2nd ed. (Upper Saddle River, N.J.: Western Union, 1979), p. iii.
[10] Ibid., p. ii.

ment usage in oral communications will also help you in your use of telecommunications.[11]

Automatic dialing equipment, by storing numbers that are frequently called, will ensure accuracy, save switchboard-operator time, and eliminate regular dialing. As an oral communicator, you will need to be acquainted with these systems:

1. The Card Dialer has an automatic dialing unit that accepts up to forty small, plastic dialing cards. When a large volume of calls are placed, this telephone ensures accurate dialing of frequently called numbers and saves time.

2. The Call-a-Matic dialer contains an automatic directory of up to 500 telephone numbers that are recorded either by writing or typing on a motorized directory tape. You find the number of the person to be called by rotating the rolling wheel of the Call-a-Matic, which scans the entire list within seven seconds.

3. The Magicall dialer uses magnetic tape. Up to 1,000 numbers may be stored and indexed to permit fast number selection for automatic dialing.

4. The One-Number dialing system affords automatic dialing of preselected numbers for faster, convenient, and even emergency service. At the touch of a single button (or, in some models, when the handset is picked up), up to fourteen numbers can be dialed automatically. These numbers include access codes and a stop code for securing a second dial tone. This one-number dialing system can be combined with the last-number-dialed feature of the Touch-A-Matic telephone (discussed later) to afford you more convenience, time saving, security, and economy.

Use auxiliary telephone devices to save valuable working time.

Switchboard Systems

Switchboard (PBX or private branch exchange) systems such as the Dimension PBX, manufactured by Western Electric for the Bell System companies, can handle inward and outward WATS lines,[12] automatic identification of outward dialing (AIOD), external dialing, station-hunting dialing, operator signaling, transfer calling, provision for leased or tie-lines, and conference calling (Figure 16–1).

New switchboards can take after-business-hours calls.

[11]Joan Zaffarano, "The New Telephones . . . and All Their Smart Switchboards," *Administrative Management,* November 1975, p. 38; cited in *Word Processing—A Systems Approach to the Office,* Helen M. McCabe and Estelle L. Popham (New York: Harcourt Brace Jovanovich, 1977), p. 129.

[12]WATS lines (Wide Area Telephone Service) are leased telephone lines permitting unlimited long-distance calls to be made for a flat monthly fee.

Figure 16—1
The Dimension PBX, the Bell System's newest private branch exchange, has a capacity of up to 120 extensions. The attendant's console, specially designed for the Dimension PBX, is engineered for maximum use and efficiency of operation. AT&T photo.

The Dimension PBX permits you to select stations for service after business hours. If there is a power failure, the system automatically connects to central office trunks and continues to operate. This equipment provides many extras that will help you in your oral communications with your customers, clients, peers, subordinates, and superiors during and after office hours.

Touch-A-Matic Telephones

Touch-A-Matic telephones provide an automatic dialing system that you activate with a fingertip (Figure 16—2). This system stores up to thirty-one numbers electronically and dials any one of them at the touch of a single button. No index cards need be inserted.

Furthermore, the Touch-A-Matic memory telephone records the last number you dialed manually. If the number was busy or if you want to call it again, you simply press the last-number dialed button, and the number is instantly redialed. You are ready to communicate immediately with the person desired.

Transaction Telephones

Transaction telephones are being used increasingly by sales people for entering orders. There are slots behind the telephone dial for

Figure 16—2
The Touch-A-Matic telephone provides an automatic dialing system activated with a fingertip. It automatically dials any of thirty-one numbers accurately and quickly. AT&T photo.

inserting a card to dial the desired number, or a customer's card can be inserted to receive an order (Figure 16–3). This phone permits rapid data entry of orders by punching the keys on the telephone dial.

Touch-Tone Service

The newest Touch-Tone telephone provides many important benefits to save you time (Figure 16–4). Not only can you use it for regular telephone communication but you can also communicate directly with your computer, wherever it may be located, retrieving stored information for updating or other use. The information can be reproduced as actual typewritten copy on a teletypewriter or other auxiliary business machine. Updating and corrections can also be made by voice.

You can communicate directly with other data-processing equipment, transmitting data over regular telephone lines to business machines used in a variety of systems. This telephone also permits conference calls with your superiors and subordinates and can provide access to paging equipment and a speakerphone, if this equipment is included in your system.

Conference Calls

Telephone conferences between executives, executives and employees, as well as between executives and community and governmental agencies, will become more prevalent in the future. Advanced telephone technology has provided for equipment with automatic conference-call capability. New switching systems have made conference calling easier.

For example, you are now able to arrange conference calls through which you and several others at different locations may talk at the same time. Decision-making today requires group discussion in changing policies and procedures and formulating plans. These conference calls are often less costly and more convenient than a meeting. If used correctly, they can be a form of oral communication that makes management more efficient. Recent innovations in equipment make conference calling relatively easy and inexpensive because conference calls can be completed without operator assistance by using the modern communication systems.

Figure 16–3
The Transaction phone is being used increasingly by sales people for order entry.
Illinois Bell photo.

Figure 16–4
Touch-Tone telephone service provides direct communication with computers or other business systems.
AT&T photo.

Data-Transmission Systems

As an executive of the future, you will need to have not only an understanding of the functions of voice communication but also that of data-transmission systems. As innovations provide sophisticated communications equipment and services such as teletypewriters, computers, and specialized equipment designed to transmit information efficiently and economically, you will want to use these systems. Technological improvements are of little value when misused by employees who continue to run up overtime costs and miss deadlines by clinging to the older, more familiar methods of telecommunications when more efficient ones are available. As an executive, you will need to communicate and explain the advantages of the newer systems and be sure all employees understand how to use these systems efficiently.

Microwave Transmission

Another innovation which you will use in the future is microwave transmission. This method transmits voice or data by using radio beams of ultrashort wavelengths. You as an executive will need to understand and determine the usefulness of this transmission method in your organization.

Satellite Transmission

Satellite Business Systems—developed by IBM in cooperation with Aetna Life & Casualty company and Comsat General Corporation—is arranging private-line networks for large businesses and government agencies by using satellites to transmit data to distant points. This equipment will not only enable widely separated computers to exchange information but will also allow the transmission of facsimile pictures. This system could enable executives scattered across the country or even around the world to hold audio and video conferences quickly and relatively inexpensively. Satellite Business Systems hopes to begin providing service by late 1981.

The Satellite Business System will allow speedy communication over great distances.

Mobile Telephone Service

Another oral communication service is the mobile telephone that lets you take a telephone with you (Figure 16–5). From your car or truck, you can call to or be called from another telephone. You can place and receive local and long-distance calls as well as car-to-car calls. Your conversation actually travels partially by radio and partially by telephone wire.

Use mobile telephone service for on-the-spot communicating.

Figure 16-5
A Mobile Telephone in your automobile or truck enables you to stay in touch with your office or clients.
Illinois Bell photo.

Some of the advantages of the mobile telephone are:

1. You have a listed number as a part of the nationwide dial network.

2. You dial your calls just as you would an ordinary telephone.

3. You need not worry about missing important calls when you are away from your office.

4. You can keep a competitive edge by receiving calls and making decisions on the spot.

5. You can call ahead to finalize arrangements and coordinate activities.

6. You can change your plans or handle emergency situations quickly.

7. You can be more productive as you can make one appointment and arrange for the next one as soon as the first appointment is concluded.

The mobile telephone unit can be mounted in any convenient location in your car or truck. Special signaling devices are available to alert you to a call; for example, your horn may sound or your headlights may come on when your mobile telephone rings.

Picturephones

Picturephones combine the television screen with the telephone (Figure 16–6). Picturephones were first demonstrated as early as 1964 in calls between New York and California, but this service was first installed commercially in Pittsburgh in July, 1970.

The picturephone is extremely adaptable to conferences and sales presentations in that you can *see* as well as *talk* with all persons. Through the picturephone, you not only can hear the comments made by everyone, but you can also see their expressions and gestures—their nonverbal communication. You can study documents and reports and discuss them. At present, a speakerphone is usually used in connection with the picturephone. However, regular telephones will probably be used as the process develops.

Although picturephones are presently available in only a few large cities, their use will undoubtedly be expanded in the future, depending on their price and customer demand. As their use increases, picturephones will influence out-of-town travel, conference schedules, sales and advertising techniques, and communications within and between organizations.

Use picturephones for combined verbal, nonverbal, and visual communication.

Speakerphones

The speakerphone is a regular telephone plus a microphone and a loudspeaker. When the telephone handset is lifted, you may use your speakerphone as a regular telephone. To activate the speakerphone, you merely press the control (on the left in Figure 16–7). The built-in transmitter and volume control allow both sides of the

Figure 16–6
The Picturephone permits executives in several locations to study documents and reports and discuss problems and policies. The left screen in this picture shows other conferees in different locations.
AT&T photo.

424

Figure 16—7
The Speakerphone permits
hands-free telephoning. With
the speakerphone in the "on"
position, you can dial without
lifting the handset.
AT&T photo.

conversation to be amplified. The microphone is sensitive enough
to pick up voices clearly; a dial on the speakerphone control adjusts
the loudspeaker volume.

As Figure 16–7 shows, you can dial another telephone without
lifting the handset when the speakerphone is on. You can turn the
speakerphone off at any time by lifting the handset or by using the
"quiet feature" on the control. The hands-free feature allows you to
hold meetings and to talk to other executives, using speakerphones
at multiple locations. You will be able to get work done faster with
additional flexibility. Furthermore, using the speakerphone permits
electronic conferences that can also save substantially on time and
travel expenses when oral communication is necessary.

Use the hands-free speakerphone in lieu of a meeting.

Selecting Your Telecommunications Equipment

In the past, your telephone system was generally installed,
operated, and charged on a monthly basis by some division of the
American Telephone & Telegraph Company, the Bell System.
However, in 1968, the Federal Communications Commission made
the historic Carterfone decision that non–Bell System equipment
could be connected to Bell System lines. Since that time, customers
can purchase telephone equipment from other sources. You are no
longer required to rent a telephone system. Now, you may purchase
or lease your own telephone system, have it custom-tailored to your
special requirements, and plug it into the nationwide transmission
network operated by the telephone companies through a system
called *Interconnect*.

The attack on the Bell telephone system has been waged by hundreds of firms who are competing with AT&T by offering innovative services and equipment at lower prices. Interconnect equipment varies from private switchboards or PBX systems to a large number of telephone attachments for both home and business such as answering machines for recording calls, call diverters for rerouting incoming calls, loudspeaker telephones for no-hands conversations, and electronic dialers for automatic dialing of often-used numbers.

Larger systems may include additional features such as transferring calls to other extensions, conferences set up by the user (rather than by the switchboard operator), and automatic forwarding of calls to outside numbers.[13]

Welcome innovative tele-communications.

However, all of these new systems, services, equipment, and controlling devices are only as effective as you, the user, make them. By studying the innovations as they are made and learning about those developed in the future, you will add to your effectiveness as an oral communicator. The future in telecommunications promises great change. You as an effective oral communicator will use and study these changes as well as the legislation that affects them.

Use communication consultants when selecting telephone equipment.

Before you select new telephone equipment for your office or add to or revise your present equipment, a communication consultant should be contacted to help you select the services that will serve you best. These consultants give free, expert advice on the equipment and additional features that will meet your oral communication needs.

An array of additional features are now available from Bell System and many independent telephone companies. Some of the equipment that could have valuable applications for your company includes paging, music-on-hold, background music, message-waiting signals, privacy switches to prevent listening to a conversation on an extension phone, restricted stations, supplementary ringing devices, power-failure ringing, and headset operation. Appendix H discusses some of these features further.

Competitive electronic, computerized switching systems can also be used to give you and your organization flexibility and cost savings by allowing you to own and use your own communications systems in the future.

[13]Shirley S. England, ed., "Hooking Up to Interconnect," *The Secretary,* 34, No. 6 (February 1974), pp. 14—15.

Summary

Oral and written communications in the future will continue to be innovative because of the changes in employer-employee relationships and the increasing emphasis on the social responsibilities of business. The public image necessary to achieve those two objectives requires ethical, legal behavior on the part of all business communicators, as well as a willingness to accept the challenge of change.

You will use your oral and written communications skills effectively as you prepare a more efficient application package. The oral interview of the future will be basic in the job-seeking, promotion, and even the termination sequence because of governmental rules and procedures that exclude much basic information from the application letter and the data sheet or application blank. However, you will still need to be able to present an effective image through your written employment communications.

You will rely more often on your oral skills in communications as you participate in or lead group discussions and conferences and make oral presentations. Your effectiveness will be enhanced by your use of visual aids, listening skills, and awareness of nonverbal symbols or language.

Telecommunicating in the future, written and oral, will require that the business person develop an awareness of cost control, available equipment, and efficient usage of the telecommunication systems. Experimental equipment will aid you in refining your communication skills.

Questions for Discussion

1. What projected changes in written communications can you foresee in the future?

2. If a paperless society actually develops, why would you still have a need for writing skills?

3. What changes in the format of written communications are anticipated in the near future.

4. Discuss and explain the importance of employer-employee relationships in the future.

5. Discuss and explain the application package of the future. Why will the oral interview be more important?

6. What laws and regulations govern the hiring and advancement of members of special groups? How will these affect you as an employer or employee?

7. Discuss the difference in employees' perception of upward and downward communication in an organization. How do their preceptions affect you as an effective business communicator?

8. Explain the usefulness of group discussions of company policies as an aid in employer-employee decision-making. Why are group discussions becoming more important?

9. Explain the similarities and differences in conferences and group meetings. How can you as a participant or leader of a group meeting help to accomplish the purposes of oral communication in such meetings?

10. When do group meetings become oral presentations? Explain the value of public speaking and reporting in improving the public's image of your company.

11. Write a paragraph explaining why listening skills will be increasingly necessary for oral communication. How do you accomplish empathetic listening?

12. List and explain several nonverbal skills that will become more important to you as an oral communicator in the future.

13. What is telecommunication? How will it affect you as an employee or employer? List and explain at least five innovations of today and the future and their effect on business communication.

14. What was the Carterfone decision? How will this affect telecommunications of the future? How does this affect Interconnect?

Part Eight   Your Reference Section

Appendix A   Commonly Used Business Abbreviations

Term	Abbreviation
account	acct., a/c
accounts payable	a/p
accounts receivable	a/r
advertisement	ad
agent	agt.
amount	amt.
association	assn.
assistant	asst.
attention	attn.
attorney	atty.
audiovisual	AV
avenue	ave.
balance	bal.
brothers	bros.
capital	cap.
carbon copy	cc, CC
care of	c/o
Celsius	C
charge	chg.
collect on delivery	c.o.d., COD
company	co.
corporation	corp.
department	dept.
discount	disc.
division	div.
dozen	doz.
enclosure	enc., encl.
esquire	esq.
et cetera (and so forth)	etc.
extension	ext.

Term	Abbreviation
Fahrenheit	F
free on board	FOB, f.o.b.
gross	gr.
gross national product	GNP
identification data	ID
incorporated	inc.
interest	int.
invoice	inv.
manager	mgr.
memorandum	memo
merchandise	mdse.
miscellaneous	misc.
month	mo.
number	no.
ounce	oz.
overdraft	o.d., OD
page, pages	p., pp.
paid	pd.
parcel post	p.p., PP
post office	P.O.
postscript	PS
pound	lb.
profit and loss	P & L
public relations	PR
ream, reams	rm.
received	recd.
respond, if you please	RSVP
rural free delivery	RFD
television	TV
treasurer	treas.
very important person	V.I.P.
vice-president	V.P.
week	wk.
weight	wt.
yard	yd.
year	yr.

Appendix B   Abbreviations Used in Documentation

ca (circa)	about; approximately
cf.	compare
comp.	compiler
ed.	editor; edition
e.g.	for example
et al.	and others; and elsewhere
ibid.	in the same place; refers to the preceding footnote (recommended for use only when footnote appears on the same page or follows closely)
i.e.	that is
loc. cit.	in the place cited; refers to the preceding footnote and the same page (this usage is no longer recommended)
n.a.	not applicable; not available
n.d.	no date
n.p.	no page; no place of publication
op. cit.	in the work cited; refers to a previous footnote, but not the one immediately preceding (this usage is no longer recommended)
p., pp.	page; pages
passim	here and there throughout a publication (should be used sparingly)
sic	used in brackets showing that a word or phrase taken from a quotation contains an error but has been quoted verbatim
trans.	translator
vol.	volume

Appendix C Guides for Effective Number Usage

Using the correct form in writing numbers has caused problems for many business persons. Do you write the number in figures, or do you spell it out in words? The following guides will help you determine the proper form.

Use Words

1. Numbers one through ninety-nine (in nonscientific material).

At the national convention, twenty women served as officers.

2. Numbers that begin a sentence (avoid if possible).

Twenty desks were ordered for the new building.

3. Indefinite numbers.

millions of dollars; several thousand books

4. The smaller number when two numbers are used together.

Your order for thirteen 26-inch plates came in today.

5. Numbers that represent time when the word *o'clock* is used.

The conference starts at nine o'clock.

6. Numbers that express approximate age.

Richard is about thirty years old.

Use Figures

7. Numbers 100 and above.

He has 146 accounts.

8. Amounts of money.

The balance in my account is $455.98.

9. Percentages.

The interest rate on the loan will be 9 percent.

10. Dates.

The banks will be closed on July 4, 1981.

11. Dimensions.

You will need 8½ × 14 inch paper for that project.

12. Page numbers.

You will find the accounts receivable schedule on page 10.

13. Numbers that are compared or contrasted should be in the same form, generally depending on the largest number in the group.

Rosemary services 116 accounts; John has 99 accounts; Eleanor has 45, but they are the largest accounts we handle.

Appendix D Guides for Word Division

In preparing your letters, memos, or reports, you may occasionally have to divide words at the end of a typed line. The basic rule is to avoid dividing a word if at all possible. However, to have an attractive letter, you will find that some words must be divided. A good dictionary should be consulted for exceptions to the following general rules.

Divide

1. Only between syllables.

com·mu·ni·ca·tion; man·age·ment; pro·cess·ing

2. Hyphenated words only at the hyphen and compound words at the natural break.

daughter-in-law; up-to-date folder; two-thirds; master·piece; clearing·house

3. Between the root word and the suffix.

control·ling; *ship*·ping; *win*·ning; *stress*·ing; *fall*·ing; *bless*·ing; *sell*·ing

4. Parts of a date, if necessary, between the day of the month and the year.

May 16,·1929

5. After a single-letter syllable within a word.

busi·ness; congratu·late; partici·pation

6. Before the single-letter syllable *a* or *i* if the syllable is followed by the ending syllable *-ble, -bly, -cle* or *-cal.*

cler·ical; divis·ible; defin·able; remark·ably

Do Not Divide

7. Words of only one syllable.

through; shipped; banked

8. Words containing six or fewer letters.

only; office; report

9. One letter syllables either at the beginning or the end of a word.

a•cous•tics; i•dol•ize; stead•y

Two letter syllables at the end of a word.

cer•tain•ty; strick•en; mon•ey

10. Proper nouns, numerals, abbreviations, or contractions.

Louisiana; 1,233,682; wouldn't

11. A syllable that does not contain a vowel.
12. The last word in more than two consecutive lines.
13. The last word in a paragraph or the last word on the page.

Appendix E Guides for Addressing Envelopes

To process the large quantity of mail accurately and quickly, the U.S. Postal Service has made recommendations for addressing envelopes to permit use of high-speed sorting equipment.

Envelopes must be larger than $3 \times 5\frac{1}{2}$ inches. Mail in envelopes larger than $6\frac{1}{8} \times 11\frac{1}{4}$ inches weighing less than one ounce for first-class mail or two ounces for third-class mail will be subject to a surcharge. First-class mail weighing over one ounce or third-class mail weighing over two ounces is not subject to this surcharge. Thus, business mail sent in large manila envelopes requires regular first-class or third-class postage as in the past.

The address on the envelope should be at least one inch from both the left and right edges of the envelope, and the last line should be more than one-half inch from the bottom edge (as shown in Figure 5–10). Any directions to the post office for special service or for special handling on arrival should be positioned at least three typewriter lines above the first line of the address.

A complete address is essential. In order to be read easily by individuals or the automatic sorting equipment, the address must be arranged in an orderly manner. The basic requirement for any address is that it be complete to the point of delivery. The Postal Service recommends a block format using capital letters without punctuation. Four lines is the maximum length that can be scanned by the high-speed equipment.

The major elements of a good address in the order in which they are placed on the envelope are:

1. *Name.* The recipient's name or the name of the company should appear on the first line.

HUNTLEY ENTERPRISES
618 W MAIN ST
OMAHA NE 68132

If the letter is being sent to the attention of a person, the company name should be typed first, followed by the name of the person.

SOUTHERN BUILDING CORP
ATTN MR SAM PETERS
1725 E BEAUREGARD AVE
NEW ORLEANS LA 70126

2. *Street address or box number.* The number and name of the street should appear on the second line. Mail addressed to a multiunit building should include the number of the suite, room, apartment, or other unit on the same line as the street address.

MR ARTHUR L SMITH
1187 E BROAD ST RM 213
COLUMBUS OH 43205

If this line becomes too long, the unit should be placed above the street address.

INTERNATIONAL SUPPLY CO
ROOM 1612
1768 W WASHINGTON DR
DENVER CO 80209

If the company or individual has a post office box number, that appears on the second line instead of the address.

LBMS CORP
PO BOX 1706
EAST LANSING MI 48801

3. *City, state, and ZIP Code.* The last line should include the city, state (using the two-letter abbreviations shown in Table 5–2), and the five-number ZIP Code. No punctuation should be used in this line, but at least one space should separate the city, state, and ZIP Code. There should be no more than twenty-two letters and spaces in this line. City names containing more than thirteen letters and spaces should be abbreviated as shown on pp. xiv-xvi of the *National ZIP Code Directory.*

If both a post office box number and a street address are used, you must indicate where delivery is to be made by putting that address on the next-to-the-bottom line and underlining it. If a package is to be delivered to the street address and the invoice to the box number, the addresses would be typed in a different order. The ZIP Codes must be correct for both the box number and the street address, if they are not the same. This form is used for delivery to the street address.

CBSP TRANSPORTATION
PO BOX 6187
105 WESTBROOK DR

LANCASTER PA 17603

This form is used for delivery to the post office box.

CBSP TRANSPORTATION
105 WESTBROOK DR
PO BOX 6187

LANCASTER PA 17601

Street addresses with directional designations may use some punctuation. Note that the Postal Service recommends a comma after *ST* or *AVE,* and periods in the directional designation.

BASS REAL ESTATE CO
1200 MASSACHUSETTS AVE, N.W.
WASHINGTON DC 20002

RHOADES TEACHING MACHINES
450 SCOTT ST, N.E.
WARREN OH 44483

Numerical street names may use either numbers or words.

MISS KAY JONES
1725 E 53RD ST APT 410
CHICAGO IL 60615

MR WILLIAM BELLER
FIRST SAVINGS & LOAN BANK
700 W 1ST ST
SAGINAW MI 48603

GLOBE DENTAL SUPPLY CO
201 FIRST AVE
VANCOUVER WA 98601

Some well-known buildings do not require a street address.

THOMPSON AND THAYER
ROOM 1956
CAREW TOWER
CINCINNATI OH 45202

Rural routes with box numbers are shown:

MRS F S MUSS
RR 4 BOX 150-A
SPARKS NV 89431

Some addresses use a community name as part of the address. This may distinguish similar addresses within a post office area.

DR JAMES R VOORHEES
30 ELTON RD
HILLANDALE
SILVER SPRING MD 20903

Further information about mail handling for efficient post office processing can be obtained from your postmaster.

Appendix F What Makes a Letter Mailable?

1. Correct spelling of all words, especially names.
2. Words at the ends of lines divided correctly.
3. The letter attractively arranged on the page—approximately equal top and bottom margins and approximately equal left and right margins.
4. The right margin as even as possible—not more than six spaces between the longest and the shortest lines.
5. Neat, unnoticeable corrections.
6. Free of typographical errors.
7. Dictation transcribed without omissions or changes that would alter the intent of the message.
8. Correct punctuation for the salutation and complimentary close.
9. Correct punctuation in the body of the letter.
10. Grammatically correct sentences.
11. Correctly constructed paragraphs that contain topic sentences and supporting or explanatory information.
12. Inclusion of the date line.
13. Inclusion of the addressees' title (Dr., Mr., Ms.) in the inside address.
14. Inclusion of reference initials.
15. Inclusion of enclosure and carbon copy notations when needed.

Appendix G   What Is Word Processing?

Word processing, the phrase originally coined by International Business Machines Corp., describes the functions that transform ideas into written communications through the interaction of people, procedures, and equipment. Word processing may be used in a narrow sense to refer to automatic typewriters that speed typed-document output. In a much broader sense, however, the phrase is frequently used to include all aspects of written communication, from the input of words or symbols through their output to the ultimate distribution of the completed letter, memo, or report.

Dartnell's Glossary of Word Processing Terms defines word processing as "the automatic production of typed documents or the automation of secretarial work."[1] Word processing combines "dictating, typing, correcting, revising, copying, and duplicating correspondence and reports"[2] using sophisticated machines and the systems approach of modern business management.

Word processing allows a document to be typed in final form, then filed for later use. When needed, the document can be recalled, corrected or modified, and printed for distribution. If corrections are necessary, only those words, phrases, or sentences that are in error need to be changed.

Word processing generally includes three distinct phases of document creation: input, output, and distribution.

[1] *Dartnell's Glossary of Word Processing Terms* (Chicago: Dartnell Corp., 1975), p. 47.
[2] Helen M. McCabe and Estelle L. Popham, *Word Processing: A Systems Approach to the Office* (New York: Harcourt Brace Jovanovich, 1977), p. 2.

The *input phase* includes changing ideas or thoughts into verbal or written communications. In the office, input may be accomplished by:
1. direct verbal communications
2. handwritten communications, such as memos, letters, or reports
3. face-to-face shorthand dictation
4. machine dictation using recording equipment, the method most often associated with word processing.

The *output phase* includes creating and reproducing communications using equipment such as:
1. standard manual or electric typewriters
2. the new electronic or computer-controlled typewriters
3. automatic typewriters and text editors
4. office copying machines and duplicators
5. microform or other reprographic equipment
6. photocomposition equipment.

The *distribution phase* may be assisted by:
1. combining parts of standing text to form a new product
2. physical delivery, such as interoffice mail, U.S. Postal Service, or messenger
3. intercommunication and paging equipment or telephone systems
4. telecommunications equipment or automatic typewriter/text-editing equipment
5. time-shared services, such as Western Union's Mailgram
6. facsimile (FAX) document transmission.

History

Word processing actually began with the patent of the mechanical typewriter in 1868. Before that date, all office correspondence was done by hand with pen and ink.

In the 1930s, automatic typewriters were invented. These machines stored the typewritten material on a punched-paper roller, similar to those found on player pianos of the same era. Thus, repetitive material for form letters and contracts was typed only once, and the stored material was used again and again without retyping.

The automatic typewriter was improved in the 1950s. Instead of a roller, the typed material was stored on a punched-paper tape. The capacity of an automatic typewriter to switch from one tape to another through electromechanical programming was also developed. Using these inventions, the equip-

ment could not only perform repetitive tasks, but its increased capacity allowed it to retrieve data from a larger volume of stored text to perform a greater variety of tasks.

Electronic technology developed rapidly in the late 1950s and early 1960s. Computers became more popular as electronic components became less expensive and more compact. At the same time, new methods of storing and recording words were developed.

IBM used the new technology to produce the first modern equipment for word processing. In 1964, the Magnetic Tape Selectric Typewriter (MT/ST) was introduced. The MT/ST's important advantage was the use of a magnetic-tape cartridge for storage. Magnetic tape can be erased and reused, punched-paper tape cannot. In addition, magnetic tape can accept twice as many characters per inch, can be handled and stored more efficiently, and allows faster text retrieval.

Again in 1969, IBM led the way by introducing the Mag Card Selectric Typewriter (MC/ST). Magnetic cards were used for storage instead of magnetic tape to provide greater flexibility. This typewriter also could record on a page-by-page basis, rather than in one long strip of text. Page recording made text easier to manipulate and retrieve and became an important feature of word-processing equipment.

Other manufacturers soon began producing new models to compete with the popular MC/ST. Redactron Corporation introduced a line of mag-card typewriters in 1971. In the same year, Ty-Data produced models that used magnetic-tape cassettes as a recording medium. A new industry with many technological developments has grown since then. In 1972, Lexitron and Linolex introduced the first video-display system; and ICS and LCS announced the first shared-logic, multikeyboard computer systems for word-processing tasks. In 1973, Vydec manufactured the first word processor to use diskettes. Many other firms entered the word-processing market in the 1970s: Olivetti in 1972; Savin Business Machines in 1973; Royal and Xerox in 1974; A. B. Dick, Lanier, Digital Equipment, and Norelco in 1976; and Addressograph-Multigraph in 1977.

Word-Processing Systems

Word-processing equipment can be divided into two

main systems: standalone word processors and shared-logic word processors.

Standalone word processors.   A *standalone word processor* is a single machine that contains a microcomputer. This microcomputer controls the recording, editing, retrieval, and all other functions built into the equipment. The machine does not share its processing with a central computer. There are four types of standalone processors:

1. The *standalone mechanical system*—The keyboard printer is usually a modified Selectric typewriter that permits editing and control, has an internal memory, and records on some kind of magnetic medium. The printer produces text for editing as well as producing the final document.

2. *The standalone display system*—The keyboard activates a CRT or video display terminal and a separate printer is added to the system. Text is entered and edited, using the display screen, before the final communication is printed. This system may be programmed to perform a greater variety of tasks and may also have arithmetic or data-processing capabilities.

3. *The standalone "thin-window" display system*—In addition to displaying the text being entered or edited, the video display system permits additional display of one line or a partial line of material entered before that shown on the video screen. This system allows the operator to retrieve or check a wide variety of information (number of lines or pages entered, use of capital letters or hyphens, and other types of material) during the entry or editing process. Visual cues are provided during text entry and editing to make the operator's job easier.

4. *The electronic-typewriter system*—An upgraded electric typewriter is fitted with an internal-memory microcomputer. Text storage capability is small (about 1,000 characters—half a page of double-spaced pica type or one-fifth of this book page). Text editing capability is also very limited.

Shared-logic word processors.   A *shared-logic word-processing system* shares its processing capabilities among a number of keyboard-editing stations through a central computer. The central minicomputer typically supports about twelve keyboard-editing stations, but some new systems on the market can support thirty-five or more. Text entry and editing can be done on Selectric typewriters, CRT or video-

display terminals, or a combination of both. Final copy can be produced on a standard printer or on high-speed, computer-driven printers. In addition, many devices can be attached to the system, such as multiple storage mediums, communication devices, optical character reading for entry, and so on.

General Equipment Features

Keyboards.   The typical word processor uses a standard typewriter keyboard. More than a dozen special function keys can be added to the keyboard. Sometimes the basic typewriter keys carry additional symbols that can be activated by the special function keys.

Display screens.   CRT or video-display screens have many advantages. By allowing the printer to be separated from the keyboard, entry, editing, and printing functions can be done at the same time. Display screens offer a wide range of viewing and editing functions:

1. displaying from 21 to 102 characters in one line, and showing 1 to 66 lines vertically
2. vertical scrolling—displaying sections of a document, searching both forward and backward
3. horizontal scrolling—moving horizontally along a line of text to display more characters than are shown on the screen at one time normally
4. display highlighting—intensifying or blinking certain portions of the screen to emphasize the text shown in that portion.

Storage media and capacity.   The storage medium for a system may be paper tape, magnetic cards, magnetic tape, magnetic disks, and/or internal memory. The storage capacity can range from 1 thousand characters stored in an internal-memory microcomputer to 50 million characters on a disk (about 10,000 pages like this text).

Printers.   A variety of printers are used to create the final document in word processing. The most commonly used printers are the Selectric typewriter and the Qume or Diablo "daisy-wheel" printer. Speeds of printing range from 2.5 to 92 characters per second. Other variable features for printing equipment include:

1. a printing line, carriage, and paper width greater than normal
2. variable pitch for changing type size

3. variable line spacing for changing the space between lines
4. additional printing commands, such as changing or adjusting margins
5. bi-directional printout that permits the system to print the first line from left to right and the second line from right to left, saving time by avoiding unnecessary movement of the carriage
6. justified printout that permits the printer to create a document with an even right-hand margin
7. simultaneous printout that allows the system to print one document while editing or entering another document at the same time.

The Advantages of Word Processing
The main advantages of word processing are:
1. increased office efficiency and higher quality typewritten output
2. greater utilization of office machines
3. improved utilization of personnel with better control and supervision
4. greater career opportunities for secretaries and clerical personnel.

Improved productivity is obtained by:
1. reducing retyping time for error-free documents
2. making revisions or changes in documents easier to do
3. increasing speed of typewritten output
4. reducing the amount of proofreading required
5. equalizing the workload when dictation equipment is used.

The amount of paperwork in a business office is unbelievable and increasing. Management is constantly seeking new ways to improve production, increase speed, and reduce cost. Word processing has helped office personnel accomplish all three.

Word-processing systems will continue to be improved and refined. Technological improvements will increase flexibility, and simplify complex jobs. Higher output speeds will make the systems more productive. Other special features now in the development stage will become commonplace in business offices.

Appendix H   Additional Telecommunications Equipment Available

A considerable variety of telecommunications equipment is available for specialized purposes, in addition to that discussed in the text. Sales representatives from your telephone company or other equipment manufacturers can advise you of the equipment available to meet your special needs.

Base-free and desk-free telephones.   Desk-free telephones increase the working space available at your desk. These instruments are attached to the wall or the side of the desk leaving your entire desk top available for work. Sometimes, these phones are concealed in a drawer. A desk-free telephone may be especially useful to you when several people are working together around your desk.

Cordless telephones.   Two wireless telephones, Fracom's Rovaphone and the NoCord Phone from Allied Telephone Communications, look just like a telephone with an antenna but are completely portable. A box is installed where the phone usually sits. The telephone handset is really a battery-powered FM transceiver. You can carry the handset as you move from room to room, office to office, or to another location, but the telephone cannot be used over 300 feet from the box.

   These cordless phones are not radio telephones like those in boats and cars. Although they are not yet fully developed, you may soon see cordless phones used in your office as companies introduce a more powerful model for industrial use. When your call comes in, the phone beeps. You as an oral communicator can carry out your business wherever you are.

Signaling devices.   The ring of the telephone bell is the most common signaling device inviting oral communication. However, other devices include a gong that can be heard over a wide area and above a loud noise level. Similarly, an extra loud signal produced by a buzzer unit can be used in industry around loud machinery. You can also secure auxiliary ringing devices away from the telephone, such as ringers, bells, lights, or chimes. Other signaling devices are being developed for manufacture and will be available to you in the future.

Dialing equipment to assist the handicapped.
Dialing equipment to assist the handicapped is also available. *Touchables,* extra large push buttons on a plate that covers the Touch-Tone key pad, can assist those persons who have a handicap that makes the standard Touch-Tone buttons difficult for them to use. Persons with sight, muscular, or arthritic problems, and even those with especially large fingers, may find touchables extremely helpful.

Other devices for the handicapped.   As an effective oral communicator, you may be interested in telecommunication devices that are provided for the handicapped. Devices such as tone ringers, signal lamps, and volume controls are available for use by handicapped people with hearing or visual problems. In fact, many of these devices will be purchased by vocational rehabilitation agencies to help the handicapped in the working situation.

The tone ringer concentrates the sounds in a frequency range that is audible to the majority of people with defective hearing. Telephones with hearing amplifiers to increase the volume of sound are also available. The person whose hearing is impaired may also find the signal lamp helpful. A call may be signaled by a flashing desk or wall lamp. For both the blind and deaf, a signal light can also control a reading lamp, a flashing strobe lamp, an electronic fan, or some other appliance that can signal the ring of the telephone. Most of these telephone accessories are used in the home, however.

The signal lamp may also be used for a person who must work in absolute silence and cannot be interrupted by the ringing of the telephone. In this case, the signal lamp is generally used in addition to the regular telephone bell so the telephone can be attended by both persons who hear the ring and also those who only "see" the ring.

For persons with low voices or impaired speech, telephones with voice amplifiers that adjust the volume of the outgoing voice are available. The electronic artificial larnyx may be used by persons whose vocal cords have been surgically removed. This prosthetic device enables them to converse in a nearly normal manner.

All of these devices give the handicapped person the ability to communicate by the telephone and to handle oral communications effectively.

Privacy control.   You may desire a privacy switch by which you may deny access to the line in use to other stations or extensions. This ensures privacy for your conversation. You may also use the switch to enable your assistant or others to listen to a conversation and make notes or to participate in the conversation from another station or extension.

Several companies have available a light that goes on when someone is listening in on an extension. Phonealert's Eavesdropper Stopper from Phone City is one example.

Paging.   In order to locate personnel quickly from any telephone station, a paging system may be installed. Using wall-mounted loudspeakers, all or selected stations can initiate paging. The paging system is often used with background music, but the music is suppressed during the paging.

Musical features.   Often used with a paging system, background music can provide a pleasant environment throughout your offices. The same system can give music-on-hold to assure callers that they have not been disconnected by providing music while they are waiting on a held call.

Experimental and innovative devices.   Bell Laboratories are perfecting for future use and have in limited operation:

1. A telephone that interrupts you during a conversation to signal that a special call is waiting.

2. A telephone that gives a busy signal to a caller to whom you don't want to talk.

3. A computer voice, instead of an operator, that will answer directory-assistance calls.

Another device that is in operation to a limited extent, although not available to the general public, is a *calling-number display* connected to your telephone. This unit shows the number of the telephone calling you. At present, only law-enforcement agencies make use of this device.

Proposed for the future and already under development is a *voice analyzer* that can be attached to any telephone to give a direct readout of the stress in the speaker's voice. This device may also be used on tape, radio, and television recordings. It is being developed to determine the truthfulness as measured by the stress in the voice of the person talking.[1] However, there is still much controversy over the usefulness of a voice analyzer in most business applications.

These are but a few of the many innovations—some of which are in experimental operation—that are being developed by various electronic laboratories. Actually, the changes in equipment and facilities are really just beginning. New legislation, rising telephone rates, and microprocessor technology will produce a flood of new equipment, devices, accessories, and features in the near future for ease, convenience, speed, and cost reduction in oral telecommunications.

Your understanding of these specialized systems, services, and equipment will assist you in using, evaluating, and reducing oral telecommunications costs. Innovations in telecommunications systems, services, and equipment along with automatic and lower-cost communication devices will enable you to send your oral messages more quickly and at lower, efficient rates in the future. Modern technology will give you flexibility in the choice of media used for oral telecommunications.

[1] Dave Sagarin, "Superphone: New Ways to Make Your Phone Do More, Better," *Popular Mechanics,* 149, No. 4 (April 1978), p. 230.

Appendix I Glossary

In order to make this glossary of maximum help to you, associated entries are given after many of the definitions. Use of this glossary should help to ensure clear, accurate communication.

A's of application   Persuasive tools used in the application package that ensure attracting attention, assuring awareness, analyzing achievements, and anticipating action.

Acculturation   The process of learning and adopting new cultural or subcultural social patterns or characteristics. *See* Enculturation.

Addendum   An addition, as an appendix.

Adjustment request   A written or oral request to remedy a deficiency in a product, service, or financial record.

Administrative assistant   A job classification for an office worker whose primary responsibility is to assist an administrator or supervisor with his or her duties.

Air express   A method used for sending packages when next day delivery is needed.

AMS   Administrative Management Society.

Anecdote   A story told for the purpose of illustrating an idea or a principle; often amusing.

Antecedent   The word, phrase, or clause that acts as the reference for a pronoun.

Antiquated   Outdated, old, trite, stereotyped; refers to words or phrases used in written communications.

Appended parts An addition at the end of a report or other communication, such as a bibliography or postscript.

Appendix Supplementary material included after the report body, such as a sample questionnaire or working papers generally providing additional information not crucial to the conclusion or recommendations.

Application letter A covering letter, sent with a data sheet or résumé, for the purpose of obtaining an interview.

Application package The résumé, application letter, interview, and any follow-up letters that build a detailed description of the applicant.

Automatic dialing equipment Communication devices that store frequently called numbers, eliminate regular dialing, ensure accuracy, and save switchboard time.

Base- and desk-free telephones Telephones attached to a wall, the side of a desk, or in a drawer; used to free the entire desk top for work.

Behavioral theory A study of the accuracy of transmitting symbols from one person to another by the use of words. *See* Mathematical theory.

Bibliography A list of published works used as sources of information for a communication or report.

Body language Nonverbal messages communicated through facial expressions, gestures, posture, or appearance; also called kinesics.

Breach of contract The violation of the terms of a legal agreement.

Business communication The art and science of transmitting information in connection with an occupation or the conduct of business so the messages cannot be misunderstood.

"C of Clarity" Communication devices used to ensure understanding by emphasizing precise writing.

"C of Completeness" Communication devices used to ensure that nothing is left undone or omitted that would necessitate additional correspondence.

"C of Conciseness" Communication devices used to ensure that all words used in a communication are needed to ensure complete understanding of your message.

"C of Concreteness" Communication devices that make words, phrases, and sentences easy to understand because the ideas are expressed in a vivid and specific manner.

"C of Consideration" "People-oriented" communication devices that put your reader first in writing your message.

"C of Correctness" Communication devices that ensure accuracy in form and content.

"C of Courtesy" "Situation-oriented" communication devices conveying your inward attitude of consideration through the use of words and actions that express friendliness and goodwill.

California Test of Personality A widely used personality inventory and assessment test.

Call for the question A parliamentary procedure by a member requesting that the group stop the discussion of and vote on the motion. *See* Put the question.

Calling-number display A screen that shows the telephone number of the person calling; now available only to special groups, such as law-enforcement agencies.

Card holder A typewriter accessory that acts as a container for index cards inserted into the typewriter; usually located on the paper table behind the platen.

Carterfone decision A ruling by the Federal Communications Commission that non-Bell equipment could be connected to Bell Systems; still under court consideration. *See* Interconnect.

Cartridge-ribbon mechanism A typewriter ribbon encased in a container allowing easy installation by the typist.

Central dictation system This system has a number of dictation recorders in one location made accessible to originators (dictators) by telephone or private wires. The transcription of this dictation is also centralized.

Central selling point The aspect of a product or service that is most likely to attract a buyer; usually differentiates a product or service from competitive products or services.

Coherence The choice of words, sentences, paragraphs, and thoughts that link or tie your message together in a logical and understandable way.

Commendation letter A communication of recommendation for noteworthy service.

Communication The two-way *sharing* of a message or an idea that results in *understanding* between the sender and the receiver of the message.

Communication partner The receiver of your communication, whether written or oral; a necessary part of the process since communication can occur only when a two-way flow exists.

Computer search The use of computers to find sources of information, bibliographies, and abstracts of articles from selected files or data banks.

Computer-based information systems Computer-linked typewriting and relay systems; used for research purposes.

Conference calls The use of advanced telephone technology to allow three or more people to participate in a telephone conversation although in different locations; newer equipment provides this capacity automatically without attendant assistance.

Connotations Implications in communications.

Copy processes Ditto, mimeograph, multigraph, thermograph, photocopying (Xerox, IBM, Savin), offset printing, etc.

Cordless telephones Completely portable telephones with antennas. Handsets are battery-powered FM transceivers and can be carried to other locations less than 300 feet from the master station.

CRT (cathode ray tube) units Equipment with a visual screen that enables communicators to correct errors and to receive data for reading; used in some word-processing equipment.

Cultures Total behavior patterns and ways of living established by a group of people.

Decoding The process by which the receiver interprets the message. *See* Encoding.

Deductive order A discussion that begins with a generalization followed by details and specific information to support the generalization. *See* Inductive order.

Defendant The accused person or entity in a court action. *See* Plaintiff.

Delimitations Conscious, intentional controls on restrictions set up by the researcher to ensure accuracy. *See* Limitations.

Dewey Decimal System A number system used in classifying books and documents in libraries. *See* Library of Congress system.

Dictation Speaking for the purpose of having your words recorded for ultimate printing and transmittal to the recipient, a team effort. *See* Face-to-face dictation, Machine dictation, Telephone dictation, Typewriter dictation.

Dictionary of Occupational Titles A major occupational classification system that groups the broad fields of work. *See U.S. Census Classification System.*

Doublets Two words, joined by *and*, that express almost exactly the same idea, for example, "each and every," "fair and just," and "right and proper." *See* Redundancies.

Dual Pitch A typewriter mechanism that allows the typist to change the horizontal spacing from ten spaces to an inch to twelve spaces to an inch and vice versa.

Edwards Personal Profile A personality inventory and assessment test.

Electronic artificial larynx A special prosthetic device for use by persons whose vocal cords have been removed enabling them to converse more easily.

Empathy The ability to project yourself into another's situation.

Emphasis The use of effective word order, climactic words and sentences, comparisons and contrasts, and simple sentence structure and subordination to give your message power and achieve effective communication.

Empirical world   The real world; reality. *See* Real world, Symbolic world.

Enclosure   An addition attached to or included with a letter.

Encoding   The process by which the sender selects and organizes information into a message. *See* Decoding.

Enculturation   The process of learning one's own culture; also called socialization. *See* Acculturation.

Epitome   A summary or condensation of a report or any other communication.

Ethics   A system of beliefs about what is right and wrong.

Experimental research   A method of working with several variables, manipulating one of these factors while keeping the others constant. *See* Primary research, Secondary research.

Extemporaneous speaking   Presenting a speech that has been prepared in advance but not memorized. *See* Impromptu speaking.

Face-to-face dictation   Dictation to a shorthand-writing secretary, word processor, or stenographer in a face-to-face situation. *See* Machine dictation, Telephone dictation, Typewriter dictation.

Facsimile   A true rendering or copy, generally applied to a copy sent by leased telephone lines.

Feedback   Response to oral or written communication.

Flashing strobe lamp   A special device that indicates a telephone ring to handicapped or deaf persons; a reading lamp may also be used.

Form books   Books containing form letters and form paragraphs for use in writing routine business communications. The letters and paragraphs are written by communication experts and may be adapted to meet the objectives of a communication.

General Aptitude Test Battery   A test used by the United States Employment Office to analyze a person's aptitude for various occupations.

Gerund phrase   The *-ing* form of a verb plus an object, used as a noun; a verbal. *See* Infinitive phrase, Participial phrase.

Gestures   Movements of parts of the body to help you to express an idea.

Goodwill   The friendly, honest, courteous, and kind feeling that a business may project and a customer should expect; includes good reputation, generosity, and the "you–attitude."

Graphics   Illustrations (drawings or photographs), tables, or charts.

Gunning Fog Index   A formula used to determine the difficulty of reading matter.

Hands-free telephones   Generally applied to speakerphones that allow meetings and electronic conferences to be conducted easily among people in several locations; also useful in checking files or doing other tasks requiring both hands.

Human relations   The relationship between people.

Humanize   The ability to relate to the common goals and needs of human beings; for example, to feel successful, to be healthy, to overcome hunger and thirst, to be sheltered from the wind, rain, heat, and extreme cold.

Idioms   A language or style of speaking used by a group of people.

Idiosyncrasies   Habits or mannerisms that usually differ from those generally considered as "normal."

Impromptu speaking   Presenting a speech without advance notice and without specific preparation. *See* Extemporaneous speaking.

Inductive order   A discussion that begins with the details and specific information and ends with a generalization drawn from the material presented. *See* Deductive order.

Inference   The process of reasoning or drawing conclusions.

Infinitive phrase   The word *to* plus a verb, used as a noun; a verbal. *See* Gerund phrase.

Intellectual curiosity   A strong mental need to understand what is heard and read.

Interconnect   A nationwide transmission network permitting auxiliary equipment not manufactured by the Bell System to be attached to the Bell System network; varies from home telephone attachments to complex office and switchboard systems.

Interpretation   The analysis or synthesis of the meaning of a communication.

Jargon   The language used by a particular group, such as the language or vocabulary peculiar to engineers, investment brokers, insurance agents, etc.

Kinesics   The study of body motion and posture as related to nonverbal communication. *See* Body language.

Kuder Occupational Interest Survey   A test used to distinguish a person's interests from which inferences can be made regarding vocational choices. *See* Strong–Campbell Interest Inventory.

Letterhead   Stationery containing pertinent printed information about its user; for example, company name, address, telephone numbers, motto, logo, branch offices, and addresses.

Libel   Basically a written statement that is unjustly defamatory to a person or business. *See* Slander.

Library of Congress system   A classification system for books and documents, initially developed for the Library of Congress, employing an alphabetical series with a numbering arrangement that provides for extensive expansion. *See* Dewey Decimal System.

Limitations   Those research conditions inherent in the situation over which the researcher has little control. *See* Delimitations.

Linking words   Words that help to ensure coherence, such as *furthermore*, *however*, *moreover*, and *therefore;* also called transitional words.

Listening skills   The use of skills of perception, organization, interpretation, and follow up to develop an appreciation of other persons' feelings and reactions.

Logo   The trademark of a company.

"MLT" degree   The Master of Little Things; a degree of accuracy that you can only award to yourself.

Machine dictation   Dictation directly to a dictating machine for subsequent transcription. *See* Face-to-face dictation, Telephone dictation, Typewriter dictation.

Mailable copy   Copy ready to be mailed or distributed; copy free from typing, grammar, and composition errors.

Mailgram   A combination of telegraph and postal services.

Market   The prospective employers' locations, job opportunities, and needs as studied by the applicant in relation to job applications.

Market evaluation   The evaluation of a desired position by using research tools, analyzing positions available, and determining the sources of job leads.

Mathematical theory   A study of the accuracy of transmitting symbols from one piece of equipment to another by the use of symbols. *See* Behavioral theory.

Memorandum   An informal written communication between members of the same company or corporation.

Methodology   The manner in which one conducts research in order to collect data.

Microforms   Any form or type of film or paper containing microphotographic images.

Microwave transmission   The use of voice or data transmission through radio beams of ultrashort wave lengths that enable fast and efficient communications.

Miscommunication   The failure of the receiver of the message to understand exactly what the sender intended to convey.

Mixed punctuation   The use of a colon following the salutation and a comma following a complimentary close in a business letter. *See* Open punctuation.

Mobile telephone service   Through telephone equipment installed in a car or truck, calls may be placed or received when you are away from your office; the conversation travels by radio and telephone wire.

Musical telephonic features   Devices to make waiting more comfortable such as music-on-hold or background music used in offices for motivational purposes.

Neural transmission rate The rate at which the neurological reflexes and systems are transmitting signals to the brain.

Noise The cause of distortion in a message during transmission. *See* Semantic noise.

Nonverbal communication The messages transmitted through gestures, facial expressions, and body movements, as a wink, raised eyebrows, etc. *See* Body language, Kinesics.

Observational research A research method of carefully watching a physical occurrence and then recording what has been observed in an organized manner.

Occupational evaluation The process of studying occupations that meet your needs and interests in the job markets available.

Onionskin A thin, lightweight paper used for copies or for international mail.

Open punctuation The use of no punctuation after the salutation and the complimentary close in the business letter. *See* Mixed punctuation.

Originator The dictator in the dictation-transcription process.

Otis Quick Score of Mental Ability An IQ test used to measure a person's mental ability.

Palm tabulator A typewriter part that allows the typist to use the palm of the hand to activate the tabulator; a mechanism that aids the typist in typing columns of data.

Paper injector Generally called the paper release lever.

Paper release lever A lever, usually located on the paper table, that allows the typist to insert paper into the typewriter without using the cylinder knob or the return mechanism; also permits easy removal of the paper.

Paraphrase The restatement in one's own words of the text of a letter, report, or communication; rewording. *See* Verbatim.

Participative management A management process that emphasizes the participation of subordinates in decision-making about those policies that directly affect them in their work.

Participial phrase The *-ing* form of a verb plus an object, used as an adjective; a verbal. *See* Gerund phrase.

Perception Using the sensory processes to gain understanding of the real and symbolic worlds.

Perceptual skills The use of sensory, observational, and interpretive skills to enable you to make assumptions, evolve attitudes, and establish beliefs and values.

Perquisites A fringe benefit for persons engaged in particular types of work or for members of certain organizations.

Personal evaluation An assessment of personal qualifications, characteristics, attitudes, abilities, personality, skills, and confidences as they relate to a person's job decision.

Phonealert's Eavesdropper Stopper A device that provides a light to show that someone is listening on another extension.

Picturephone A telephonic device through which images from another location are projected on a screen; generally used with speakerphones so everyone can be heard and can participate in any discussion. Participants, products, documents, and reports can be shown on the screen.

Plaintiff The complainant in a court action; the person or entity that initiates a lawsuit. *See* Defendant.

Platen The hard, black, rubberlike cylinder on a typewriter that acts as a cushion for the typing medium (letterheads, paper, cards, envelopes) while typed impressions are being made.

Point of contact A statement in the application letter that indicates how the applicant learned about the position.

Position evaluation An analysis of information about the particular requirements, benefits, levels of difficulty, and other factors regarding your relationship as a prospective employee to the occupation or special position which you are considering or for which you are applying.

Positive tone The use of timeliness, empathy, and the "you–attitude" in your communications.

Postage-paid envelope   An envelope on which postage has been affixed; sent to your communication partner when use of the envelope will benefit *you*. Also called a postpaid envelope.

Postscript   A thought added to a letter, usually after the letter has been signed by the writer.

Prefatory parts   The parts of a report preceding the body, such as the table of contents, preface, etc.

Primary research   The gathering of information from an original source. *See* Experimental research, Secondary research.

Privacy control   A telephone switch that ensures privacy by excluding extensions and denying access to other stations except when desired.

Problem statement   A definition of the reason for the report or research.

Promotional letter   A letter written to describe a product or service so the reader will develop a positive, favorable attitude toward the product or service.

"Pseudo-goodwiller"   A person who is well intended but somewhat deceptive; one who talks about what can be done but rarely provides the assistance promised.

Put the question   A parliamentary procedure by the chairman or presiding officer requesting that the group stop the discussion of and vote on the motion. *See* Call for the question.

Questionnaire   A list of questions to be answered to obtain data for a report or other research.

Readability index   A formula for measuring reading difficulty that uses average sentence length and size of words.

"Real world"   Reality; the world gained through observation and experimentation; the empirical world. *See* Symbolic world.

Ream   A package of paper containing 500 sheets.

Redundancies   The repetitious use of two words when one would do as well, such as "up above," true facts," and "red color." *See* Doublets.

Research   The collecting and reporting of data in an objective and systematic manner.

Respondent   A person who answers the questions posed in a primary research project; a person who answers a questionnaire.

Rough draft   The first, unpolished draft of a letter or report.

Sample   A group of people used for research chosen to fairly represent the whole group (the universe).

Satellite transmission   The use of private-line networks to provide businesses and government agencies with a communication system to transmit data between widely separated computers and to transmit facsimile pictures by reflecting radio waves from permanently positioned satellites, to permit audio and video conferences in worldwide locations.

Secondary research   Research through the use of published material. *See* Primary research.

Semantic noise   The unplanned misunderstanding of words by either the sender or receiver of a communication.

Semantics   The science of word meanings or how we use words.

Sensory perception   Understanding through stimuli received by the senses.

Sign   Something that indicates the existence of a thing, event, or condition. *See* Symbol.

Signaling devices   Various methods to indicate that a telephone should be answered; may include normal ring, gongs, chimes, buzzers, lights, and special devices for the handicapped.

Slander   An untrue oral statement that results in damage to the reputation of a person or a company. Slander requires proof of damage. *See* Libel.

Socially oriented person   One who is interested in, likes to be with, talk to, and listen to people.

Solicited application   A job application written in response to announcements of openings, such as classified advertisements. *See* Unsolicited application.

Speakerphone   A regular telephone, plus a microphone and loud speaker, that enables several people to listen to and participate in a telephone conversation, or that permits full use of both hands and free movement in the office while conversing.

Stereotyped expressions Stock phrases or trite, overused words, such as "at your earliest convenience."

Stimulus Something that excites or stimulates the senses; the impetus for an action.

Stock phrases Trite, overused, or stereotyped expressions, such as "begging to remain, I am, yours truly" or "taking this opportunity to thank you in advance."

Strong-Campbell Interest Inventory A test that matches your responses to questions to those given by happily employed persons in the various occupational categories. *See* Kuder Occupational Interest Survey.

Subcultures The smaller parts of a larger culture, each having its own particular characteristics.

Subliminal advertising Advertising employing stimuli that operate below the consciousness level.

Superscript A raised numeral referring to a footnote.

Survey research The method of research in which questions are asked and the answers to the questions are recorded for analysis.

Symbol An instrument of thought. *See* Sign.

Symbolic world The world that comes from a perception of reality; not necessarily real. *See* "Real world."

Synopsis A brief, general overview of a report; a summary.

"Talk words" The vocabulary of the person to whom you are writing; differ between those of entry-level clerical help and engineers.

Telecommunications Communications by telephone, telegraph, and computers over telephone lines or by radio.

Telephone dictation Dictation by telephone to be recorded by a shorthand-writing secretary or by a recording machine. *See* Face-to-face dictation, Machine dictation, Typewriter dictation.

Touch-A-Matic telephones Specialized telephones providing an automatic dialing system for thirty-one numbers activated by pushing a single button. Also can redial the last number called manually.

Touchables Specialized extra-large push buttons on the Touch-Tone pad for persons with visual, muscular, or arthritic problems, or even especially large fingers.

Transcriber recorder A dual-purpose machine that records and plays back enabling the dictator to record dictation and to listen to the recorded dictation.

Transitional words Words that help to ensure coherence, such as *furthermore, however,* and *therefore;* also called linking words.

Transmission systems Modern oral, written, and data-communication devices that transmit information more efficiently and economically.

Trite phrases Words, expressions, and phrases that have been stereotyped and overused and lack freshness and effectiveness.

Typewriter dictation Oral dictation to a typist at the typewriter. *See* Face-to-face dictation, Machine dictation, Telephone dictation.

Typing element A spherical typewriter part that contains letters of the alphabet, numbers, and punctuation marks. By changing the typing element, different typefaces can be used.

U.S. Census Classification System A major occupational classification system that groups the broad fields of work. *See Dictionary of Occupational Titles.*

Unity The expression of only one main idea in words, sentences, or paragraphs; necessary for clear, complete messages.

Universe The entire group of people around whom a research problem is centered. *See* Sample.

Unsolicited application A job application written by a person who is unaware of an opening; usually sent to large companies that have frequent turnover in personnel. *See* Solicited application.

Verbal   A verb form that functions as a noun or an adjective; also refers to the spoken or written word. *See* Gerund phrase, Infinitive phrase, Participial phrase.

Verbatim   Repetition of an original communication word for word; a direct quotation. *See* Paraphrase.

Visuals   The supports for written or verbal messages, ranging from simple bar graphs to charts, maps, diagrams, or complex overlays and transparency presentations.

Voice analyzer   An experimental device that can be attached to a telephone to give a direct readout of stress in a person's voice; may determine the validity of the message.

Watermark   A translucent design or trademark appearing in the paper or stationery used by a company.

WATS (Wide Area Telephone Service) lines   Leased telephone lines that permit long-distance calls to be made for a flat monthly fee.

Word-processing center   The location containing dictating machines and special typewriters. Dictators use telephones or private-wire connections to the dictating machines. This system permits storage of form letters and reports and retrieval of stored material. Corrections or modifications can be made without changing other information.

Word processors   Those who transcribe dictation to the word-processing center on special computer-based typewriters that permit corrections to be made before final copy is typed.

Wordy   The use of more words than necessary to convey information, understanding, and goodwill. *See* "C of Conciseness."

Written communication   Oral conversation polished for accuracy in structure, grammar, and form in its written form.

"You-attitude"   A point of view ensuring consideration, empathy, and "thinking of your reader first."

Appendix J Bibliography

Accrocco, Anne. "Handicapped Secretaries on the Road to Independence." *Today's Secretary*, May 1979, pp. 18–19.

Anastasi, Thomas E., Jr. *Communicating for Results*. Menlo Park, Cal.: Cummings, 1972.

Auger, B. Y. *How to Run Better Business Meetings*. St. Paul, Minn.: Visual Products Division, Minnesota Mining & Manufacturing Co., 1972.

Aurner, Robert R. "Communications Impact: Power Source for Decision Makers." *Journal of Business Communication*, 5, No. 2 (Winter 1967), pp. 26–29.

Barnhart, Clarence L., Sol Steinmetz, and Robert K. Barnhart, eds. *The Barnhart Dictionary of New English Since 1963*. Bronxville, N.Y.: Barnhart/Harper & Row, 1973.

Barzun, Jacques. *Simple and Direct: A Rhetoric for Writers*. New York: Harper & Row, 1976.

Bassett, Glenn A. *The New Face of Communication*. New York: American Management Assn., 1968.

Beran, Walter F. "Business Ethics." *The Secretary*, April 1979, pp. 6–8.

Berlo, David K. *The Process of Communication*. New York: Holt, Rinehart & Winston, 1960.

Bernstein, Theodore M. *Bernstein's Reverse Dictionary*. New York: Quadrangle/New York Times, 1975.

Berry, Graham. "The Lore of Language." *Modern Maturity*, February-March 1978, pp. 61–65.

Birdwhistell, Ray L. *Introduction to Kinesics*. Louisville, Ky.: University of Louisville, 1952.

Boe, Eugene, comp. *The Wit and Wisdom of Archie Bunker*. New York: Popular Library, 1972.

Bowman, Joel P., and Bernadine P. Branshaw. *Understanding and Using Communication in Business*. San Francisco: Canfield Press, 1977.

Brown, James W., Richard B. Lewis, and Fred F. Harcleroad. *AV Instruction: Technology, Media, and Methods*. 4th ed. New York: McGraw-Hill, 1973.

Brusaw, Charles T., Gerald J. Alred, and Walter E. Oliu. *The Business Writer's Handbook*. New York: St. Martin's Press, 1976.

Butera, M. C., R. Krause, and W. A. Sabin. *College English: Grammar and Style*. New York: McGraw-Hill, 1967.

Campbell, William G., and Stephen V. Ballou. *Form and Style: Theses, Reports, Term Papers*. Boston: Houghton Mifflin, 1974.

College Placement Annual. Bethlehem, Penna.: College Placement Council, yearly.

The Concise Heritage Dictionary. Boston: Houghton Mifflin, 1976.

Dale, Edgar, and Jeanne S. Chall. "A Formula for Predicting Readability." *Educational Research Bulletin*, 21 January 1948, pp. 11–20.

Demare, George. *Communicating for Leadership, A Guide for Executives*. New York: Ronald Press, 1968.

Ehrlich, Eugene, and Daniel Murphy. *Basic Grammar for Writing: A Step-by-Step Course in All the Essentials of Clear Writing*. New York: McGraw-Hill, 1971.

————. *Writing and Researching Term Papers and Reports: A New Guide for Students*. New York: Bantam, 1968.

England, Shirley S., ed. "Hooking Up to Interconnect." *The Secretary*, 34, No. 6 (February 1974), pp. 14–16, 27.

Engle, James F., David T. Kollat, and Roger D. Blackwell. *Consumer Behavior*. 2nd ed. Hinsdale, Ill.: Dryden, 1973.

Firschein, Oscar. "On-Line Reference Searching." *IEEE Spectrum*, 12 (October 1975), p. 68.

Fisher, Bruce D. *Introduction to the Legal System*. 2nd ed. St. Paul, Minn.: West, 1977.

Flesch, Rudolf. *The Art of Readable Writing*. New York: Harper & Bros., 1949.

————. *Look It Up*. New York: Harper & Row, 1977.

Ford's Insider, A Continuing Series of College Newspaper Supplements. Knoxville, Tenn.: 13–30 Corporation, yearly.

Fowler, H. W. *A Dictionary of Modern English Usage*. 2nd ed. Rev. and ed. by Sir Ernest Gowers. New York: Oxford University Press, 1965.

Fry, Edward. "A Readability Formula that Saves Time." *Journal of Reading*, 11 (April 1968), pp. 513–516, 575–578.

Gavin, Ruth E., and William A. Sabin. *Reference Manual for Stenographers and Typists*. 4th ed. Dallas: Gregg Division/McGraw-Hill, 1970.

"Get Personal." *Ford's Insider*. Knoxville, Tenn.: 13–30 Corporation, 1978, pp. 7–8.

Getting the Word Around, A Guide for Communicating in Business. 2nd ed. Upper Saddle River, N.J.: Western Union, 1979.

Gove, Philip B., ed. *Webster's Third New International Dictionary*. (Unabridged) Springfield, Mass.: G. & C. Merriam Co., 1966.

Gunning, Robert. "The Fog Index After Twenty Years." *Journal of Business Communication*, 6, No. 2 (Winter 1968), pp. 3–13.

————. *The Technique of Clear Writing*. Rev. ed. New York: McGraw-Hill, 1968.

Guralnik, David B., et al., eds. *Webster's New World Dictionary of the American Language*. 2nd college ed. Cleveland: Collins & World Pub. Co., 1976.

Haber, Audrey, and Richard P. Runyon. *Fundamentals of Psychology*. Reading, Mass.: Addison-Wesley, 1974.

Haines, Virginia, and Catharine Ryan. *Dictionary for Secretaries*. Los Angeles: Parker & Son, 1971.

Haney, William V. *Communication and Organizational Behavior*. 3rd ed. Homewood, Ill.: Irwin, 1973.

Hanna, J Marshall, Estelle L. Popham, and Rita Sloan Tilton. *Secretarial Procedures and Administration*. 7th ed. Cincinnati: South-Western, 1978.

Hansen, David A. *Police Ethics*. Springfield, Ill.: Charles C Thomas, 1973.

Helm, Alice K., ed. *The Family Legal Advisor*. 2nd ed. New York: Greystone Press, 1978.

Hennington, Jo Ann. "Memorandums—An Effective Communication Tool for Management." *ABCA Bulletin*, 31, No. 3 (September 1978), pp. 10–14.

Hodges, John C., and Mary E. Whitten. *Harbrace College Handbook*. 8th ed. New York: Harcourt Brace Jovanovich, 1977.

Jackson, Tom. *Guerrilla Tactics in the Job Market*. New York: Bantam, 1978.

Jackson, Tom, and Davidyne Mayles. *The Hidden Job Market*. New York: Quadrangle/New York Times, 1976.

Jay, Antony. *The New Oratory*. New York: American Management Assn., 1970.

Jordan, Lewis. The New York Times *Manual of Style and Usage*. New York: Quadrangle/New York Times, 1976.

Keeling, B. Lewis, Norman F. Kallaus, and John J. W. Neuner. *Administrative Office Management*. Cincinnati: South-Western, 1978.

Kirby, Joe Kent. *Consumer Behavior*. New York: Donnelley Publishing, 1975.

Kleinschrod, Walter A. *Management's Guide to Word Processing*. Chicago: Dartnell Corp., 1977.

Kohler, Eric Louis. *A Dictionary for Accountants*. 5th ed. Englewood Cliffs, N.J.: Prentice-Hall, 1975.

Lahiff, James M., and John D. Hatfield. "The Winds of Change and Managerial Communication Practices." *Journal of Business Communication*, 15, No. 4 (Summer 1978), pp. 19–28.

Lamb, Marion. *Word Studies*. 6th ed. Cincinnati: South-Western, 1971.

Langer, Susanne K. *Philosophy in a New Key*. New York: New American Library, 1951.

Lesikar, Raymond V. *Report Writing for Business*. 5th ed. Homewood, Ill.: Irwin, 1977.

Linton, Marigold. *A Simplified Style Manual: For the Preparation of Journal Articles in Psychology, Social Sciences, Education and Literature*. New York: Appleton-Century-Crofts, 1972.

McBurney, James H., and Ernest J. Wrage. *Guide to Good Speech*. 3rd ed. Englewood Cliffs, N.J.: Prentice-Hall, 1965.

McCabe, Helen M., and Estelle L. Popham. *Word Processing—A Systems Approach to the Office*. New York: Harcourt Brace Jovanovich, 1977.

Making the Most of Your Job Interview. New York: New York Life Insurance Co., n.d.

Menning, J. H., C. W. Wilkinson, and Peter B. Clarke. *Communicating Through Letters and Reports*. 6th ed. Homewood, Ill.: Irwin, 1976.

Merleau-Ponty, Maurice. "The Primacy of Perception and Its Philosophical Consequences." In *The Primacy of Perception*. Ed. and trans. James M. Edie. *Northwestern University Studies in Phenomenology and Existential Philosophy*. Ed. John Wild. Evanston: Northwestern University Press, 1964. Pp. 12–42.

Modern Language Association. *MLA Handbook for Writers of Research Papers, Theses, and Dissertations*. New York: MLA, 1977.

Moffett, Phillip W., ed. *The Graduate, A Handbook for Leaving School*. Knoxville, Tenn.: 13–30 Corporation, 1978.

Moore, Norman D. *Dictionary of Business, Finance, and Investment*. Dayton, Ohio: Investor's Systems 1975.

Morris, William, ed. *The American Heritage Dictionary of the English Language*. New York: American Heritage, 1969.

"The Most Important Piece of Paper Is Your Resume." *Ford's Insider*. Knoxville, Tenn.: 13–30 Corporation, 1978.

Mouly, George J. *The Science of Educational Research*. 2nd ed. New York: Van Nostrand Reinhold, 1970.

Myers, Gail E., and Michele T. Meyers. *Communicating When We Speak*. New York: McGraw-Hill, 1975.

Nurnberg, Maxwell W. *Fun With Words*. Englewood Cliffs, N.J.: Prentice-Hall, 1970.

Nurnberg, Maxwell W., and Morris Rosenblum. *All About Words*. Englewood Cliffs, N.J.: Prentice-Hall, 1966.

———. *How to Build a Better Vocabulary*. New York: Popular Library, 1977.

Parten, Mildred Bernice. *Surveys, Polls, and Samples*. New York: Harper & Row, 1950.

Pasewark, William R., and Mary Ellen Oliverio. *Clerical Office Procedures*. 6th ed. Cincinnati: South-Western, 1978.

Perry, Devern J., and J. E. Silverthorn. *College Vocabulary Building*. Cincinnati: South-Western, 1977.

Phillips, David C. *Oral Communication in Business*. New York: McGraw-Hill, 1955.

Plano, Jack C., and Milton Greenberg. *The American Political Dictionary*. 4th ed. New York: Dryden/Holt, Rinehart & Winston, 1976.

Robert, Henry M. *Rules of Order*. Rev. ed. Chicago: Scott, Foresman, 1970.

Rosen, Arnold, and Rosemary Fielden. *Word Processing*. Englewood Cliffs, N.J.: Prentice-Hall, 1977.

Ruesch, Jurgen. "Psychiatry and the Challenge of Communication." *Psychiatry,* 17 (February 1954), pp. 1–18.

———. "Synopsis of the Theory of Human Communication." *Psychiatry,* 16 (August 1953), pp. 215–243.

Ruesch, Jurgen, and Gregory Bateson. *Communication, The Social Matrix of Psychiatry.* New York: Norton, 1951.

Sagarin, Dave. "Superphone: New Ways to Make Your Phone Do More, Better." *Popular Mechanics,* 149, No. 4 (April 1978), pp. 116–117, 224, 226, 228, 230.

Schneider, Arnold E., William C. Donaghy, and Pamela Jane Newman. *Organizational Communication.* New York: McGraw-Hill, 1975.

Shannon, Claude E., and Warren Weaver. *The Mathematical Theory of Communication.* Urbana, Ill.: University of Illinois Press, 1949.

Sigband, Norman B. *Communicating for Management and Business.* 2nd ed. Glenview, Ill.: Scott, Foresman, 1976.

Sippi, Charles J., and Charles P. Sippi. *Computer Dictionary and Handbook.* 2nd ed. Indianapolis, Ind.: Howard W. Sams & Co., 1972.

Smith, Alfred G., ed. *Communication and Culture.* New York: Holt, Rinehart & Winston, 1966.

Smith, Jill Y. "Speaking Out: Nonverbal and Verbal Communication Training Modules." *American Business Communication Bulletin,* 42, No. 1 (March 1979), pp. 29–31.

Spurrier, William A. *Ethics and Business.* New York: Scribner's, 1962.

Standard and Poor's Register of Corporations, Directors, and Executives. New York: Standard & Poor's Corp., yearly.

Stein, Jess, ed. *The Random House Dictionary of the English Language.* Unabridged ed. New York: Random House, 1966.

Stewart, Marie M., Frank W. Lanham, Kenneth Zimmer, and Lyn Clark. *Business English and Communication.* 4th ed. New York: McGraw-Hill, 1972.

Strunk, William, Jr., and E. B. White. *The Elements of Style.* 2nd ed. New York: Macmillan, 1972.

Thayer, Lee, ed. *Communication Theory and Research Proceedings of the First International Symposium.* Springfield, Ill.: Charles C Thomas, 1967.

Toffler, Alvin. *Future Shock.* New York: Bantam, 1971.

Transcription Skills for Word Processing. Student's Guide. Franklin Lakes, N.J.: International Business Machines Corp., 1969.

Transcription Skills for Word Processing. Teacher's Guide. Franklin Lakes, N.J.: International Business Machines Corp., 1969.

Turabian, Kate L. *A Manual for Writers of Term Papers, Theses and Dissertations.* 4th ed. Chicago: University of Chicago Press, 1973.

———. *Student's Guide for Writing College Papers.* 3rd ed. Chicago: University of Chicago Press, 1976.

Turner, Rufus P. *Technical Writer's and Editor's Stylebook.* Indianapolis, Ind.: Howard W. Sams & Co., 1964.

U.S. Department of Labor. *The Occupational Outlook for College Graduates.* Washington, D.C.: Government Printing Office, 1978–79.

———. *Occupational Outlook Handbook.* Washington, D.C.: Government Printing Office, 1978-79.

U.S. Employment and Training Administration, Department of Labor. *Occupations in Demand at Job Service Offices.* Washington, D.C.: Government Printing Office, monthly.

University of Chicago Press. *A Manual of Style.* 12th ed. Chicago: University of Chicago Press, 1969.

van Leunen, Mary-Claire. *A Handbook for Scholars.* New York: Knopf, 1978.

Webster's New Collegiate Dictionary. 8th ed. Springfield, Mass.: G. & C. Merriam Co., 1975.

West, Judy F., and Daniel R. Boyd. "Mail Processing Updated." *The Secretary,* February 1978, pp. 16–17, 26–27, 30.

Zaffarono, Joan. "The New Telephones . . . and All Their Smart Switchboards." *Administrative Management,* November 1975, pp. 34–36, 38.

Zelko, Harold P. *The Business Conference: Leadership and Participation.* New York: McGraw-Hill, 1969.

Zinsser, William. *On Writing Well: An Informal Guide to Writing Nonfiction.* New York: Harper & Row, 1976.

Index

Printed in U.S.A.

Rules in Brief

1. Grammar

Pronouns

A pronoun is used in place of a noun, and its antecedent must be clearly understood.

A pronoun must agree with its antecedent in number.

The proper pronoun form depends on how it is used in the sentence.

The nominative-case pronoun is used as the subject *(I, he, she, it, we, they, you, who)*.

The objective-case pronoun is used as the direct or indirect object of a verb or preposition *(me, him, her, it, us, them, you, whom)*.

The possessive-case pronoun indicates possession *(my, mine, his, her, hers, its, our, ours, their, theirs, your, yours, whose)*.

Subject-verb agreement

The subject and the verb must agree in number.

Use a singular verb with a collective noun regarded as a unit; use a plural verb with a collective noun regarded as a group of separate units.

Use a singular verb with nouns ending in *s* or *es* that are singular in meaning.

The verb may be singular or plural when a relative pronoun is used depending on the antecedent of the pronoun.

In sentences containing predicate nouns, the verb still agrees with the subject.

Use a singular verb with *each, either, neither, anyone, anybody, someone, somebody, everyone, one, no one,* and *nobody*.

Use a singular verb with compound singular subjects connected with *or* or *nor*.

Use a plural verb with a compound subject connected with *or* or *nor* when the subject closer to the verb is plural.

Use a plural verb when a sentence has two or more subjects connected with *and* or arranged in a series.

Verb tense

Use a verb in the past tense when the action took place in the past.

Use a verb in the present tense when the action is taking place now.

Use a verb in the future tense when the action will take place in the future.

Avoid confusion and unnecessary changes in the tense of verbs.

2. Numbers

Write out

numbers from one through ninety-nine (in nonscientific material).

numbers that begin a sentence.

indefinite numbers.

the smaller number when two series are used together.

numbers for time when *o'clock* is used.

numbers expressing approximate age.

Use figures for

numbers over 100.

amounts of money.

percentages.

dates.

dimensions.

page numbers.

Numbers compared or contrasted should be in the same form, generally that of the largest number in the series.